CAMB

J. A. CROOK, E. J ƆDGRASS

HOMER, HESIOD AND THE HYMNS

HOMER, HESIOD AND THE HYMNS

Diachronic development in epic diction

RICHARD JANKO

Fellow of Trinity College, Cambridge

CAMBRIDGE UNIVERSITY PRESS
CAMBRIDGE
LONDON NEW YORK NEW ROCHELLE
MELBOURNE SYDNEY

CAMBRIDGE UNIVERSITY PRESS
Cambridge, New York, Melbourne, Madrid, Cape Town, Singapore, São Paulo

Cambridge University Press
The Edinburgh Building, Cambridge CB2 2RU, UK

Published in the United States of America by Cambridge University Press, New York

www.cambridge.org
Information on this title: www.cambridge.org/9780521238694

First published 1982
This digitally printed first paperback version 2007

A catalogue record for this publication is available from the British Library

Library of Congress Catalogue Card Number: 81-7666

ISBN-13 978-0-521-23869-4 hardback
ISBN-10 0-521-23869-2 hardback

ISBN-13 978-0-521-03565-1 paperback
ISBN-10 0-521-03565-1 paperback

CONTENTS

TABLES AND FIGURES

Tables

Figures

TO MY PARENTS

δυσκαταμάθητα, ἀλλὰ θρεπτήρια

PREFACE

The Cambridge doctoral thesis of which this book is the final outcome began as a linguistic investigation into the manner of composition, dates and origins of the major 'Homeric' Hymns, but it was soon apparent that these questions ought only to be essayed in the broader context of the entire corpus of early Greek hexameter poetry. Whether the *Hymns* are oral poems is examined in Chapter 2; then the linguistic methodology is established and elaborated in the context of the whole epic tradition, and finally the results are tested against the other evidence, literary, historical and archaeological, for the dates and origins of the individual major hymns (I have limited the treatment of the Hymn to Demeter in view of Richardson's recent opus; regrettably, the recent Utrecht dissertation of J. van Eck on the *Hymn to Aphrodite* became known to me too late to be taken into account). But although the Hymns are both the seed and bole of this work, the reader will discover ramifications in topics as varied as the relative and absolute dates of Homer and Hesiod; the 'Contest of Homer and Hesiod'; the mutual relations of Hesiodic poems and Hymns, especially the two Hymns to Apollo; poetry as a political weapon in the sixth century; the homogeneity of the Homeric epics; how and why the poets used archaisms and formular modifications; the prehistory of the epic, its relation to vernacular dialects, and the impact of writing on what was in origin an oral tradition: that is to say, the 'Homeric Question' in general. To save this book from obesity, I have limited the discussion of some of these, such as epic prehistory and the homogeneity of Homer, to indications of what the method offers. The method and conclusions in which they are rooted is given in Chapters 3 and 4; its *a priori* assumptions are set out in Chapter 1 and reviewed in Chapter 10; individual discussions may be located by means of the indices.

The method to which I refer accords with many contemporary developments, some good, others deleterious, in its quantitative basis. Lest the traditionalist be repelled, I must mention my surprise that it was not evolved in Germany a century ago, such is the love of statistics evident in Homeric studies at that time; furthermore, I did test its principles and coherence by marathons of manual counting before resorting to the computer to preserve my mind from distraction and my eyes from dittoblepsy. The figures given here are twy-born of man and machine: the computer produced a list, in sequence of occurrence with one line's context, of all instances of a given set of characters from an accurate but unlemmatised standard text (OCT); all irrelevant cases were then eliminated by inspection, and the results for the feature in question were then calculated. If, as often, I had already counted the feature by hand, the computer's list was matched against my own, usually to the detriment of the latter; the same is true of figures supplied by others too.

My examiners cannily inquired whether I had checked other features beyond the dozen enumerated below. *Vita brevis*: but looking again at the half-dozen I rejected as too infrequent, it is clear that for this reason none cast much light on poems shorter than the Homeric epics, although no doubt more which do will appear in due course. I have consigned *γαῖα / γῆ*, *κεῖνος / ἐκεῖνος* and *ξύν / σύν* to an Appendix, to illustrate the difficulties and potential gains which such counts offer. Similar is the pair *ἱρός / ἱερός*; the Lesbian and Chian form *ἱρός* falls from 30/83 cases (36.1%) in the *Iliad* to 17/77 (22.1%) in the *Odyssey* and 0/56 in the rest of the epic corpus. Here, although the statistics may tell a tale of decline in frequency of one of the Aeolic elements in Homer, they tell little of the *Hymns* or Hesiod, and thus remain peripheral. In other criteria it is not infrequency but lack of philological clarity that is the vitiating factor, e.g. in vowel contraction, where different combinations and environments entail excessive complications.

Although numbers are rampant in this book, the use of statistical tests has been kept to a minimum, to propitiate those unfamiliar with these techniques. While not needed to show that the clusters of results in Chapter 4 are not fortuitous, as this is plain even without applying such methods, they are indispensable when one wishes to test the hypothesis that any particular result is unlikely to be due to random variation from any given value. The tests used are all standard: I refer here to *Principles of Statistics* by M. G. Bulmer, and *Statistics Made Simple* by H. T. Hayslett.

The criteria tested in this study are all binomial (I have avoided testing the distribution of n-mobile here, as it conforms to the Poisson distribution). Binomial distributions, involving a choice between alternatives as in tossing a coin, can be tested directly when small numbers of trials are involved (Bulmer 81–90, Hayslett 62–71); when more instances are counted, we can use the *normal approximation to the binomial* (Bulmer 139–45; Hayslett 91–8), the results of which will be found expressed in terms of z and π_0, e.g. '$z = 1.68$ if π_0 is set at 0.476'; π_0 denotes the expected or hypothetical frequency of the phenomenon (i.e. what I usually express as a percentage, recast as a decimal), and z denotes the value of the *standard normal variable*, which can be looked up in tables (e.g. Hayslett 230–1) to establish the area under the curve for this value, i.e. the probability of the event occurring by chance (the 'level of significance'). Thus if $z > 1.64$, the result is significant at the 5% level (i.e. the chance of random occurrence is under 0.05, or 1 in 20). These tests will be one-tailed unless stated; i.e. they determine the likelihood that extreme results at one end only of the bell-shaped graph will occur. Statisticians regard 5% significance as a reasonable basis for judgement, but the greater the level of significance the better.

Another means of comparing results is the χ^2 test, which tests two sets of observed values against one another, or observed values against those predicted (expected) on a given hypothesis, taking into account different sample-sizes (Bulmer 124–9, 154–61; Hayslett 169–76, and the table on p. 223). This cannot be used for samples where less than 5 cases in one or other alternative are expected. The higher the value of χ^2, which expresses the difference between observed and expected values, the more significant the result. A test of one feature in two works will have one *degree of freedom* (ν), but if more poems are compared, or features included, this parameter and the significant value of χ^2 increase accordingly, as will appear from Hayslett 223.

All decimals in this study are rounded up to the next significant figure: thus 70.08% becomes 70.1%, and $\pi_0 = 0.7008$ becomes $\pi_0 = 0.701$.

In this study I use the term 'sample' to denote the population tested. Quite frequently this is a slight misnomer, since the limitations of the material compel one to use the evidence of whole poems and not merely that of samples drawn from them. In such instances it would be more correct technically to speak of target populations; I hope to be forgiven my licence, committed for the sake of that neglected goddess, Brevity, and Simplicity her sister.

In conclusion I would like to stress the importance of the size of the population tested. A sample more divergent from the expected result than another of greater size may sometimes turn out to be less significant, i.e. more probably the outcome of mere random variation from the average. It all depends on the amount of divergence relative to the size of the sample. Sample-size must not be disregarded in what follows, and I am not sanguine that I have always managed to avoid this error myself.

Wherever much is owed to many predecessors, originality is a difficult concept; this is as true of this study as of the early Greek poetry which concerns it. The approach adopted here owes most to G. P. Edwards, and to the perceptive remarks he made about the directions future research might take (*The Language of Hesiod* 206ff.), but many other streams here find their confluence. In compiling and checking the statistics, the programming skills of Dr J. L. Dawson (of the Literary and Linguistic Computing Centre, Cambridge) were the *sine qua non*: responsibility for the choice of features and their analysis remains my own. I am grateful for advice, useful discussion and correspondence to many, especially the late Professor D. L. Page, Dr J. B. Hainsworth, Professor G. S. Kirk and Professor A. B. Lord. I would like to thank Professor Dr W. Burkert, Dr N. J. Richardson and Professor M. L. West for discussion of the *Hymn to Apollo*. I must apologise for differing from the latter so frequently; without the stimulation of his ideas this field would have been much the poorer, and, as he will know, my views have often diverged from his only after much agonising. Special thanks go to Dr C. Carey and my examiners Dr Richardson and Dr Edwards for detailed and valuable comments and criticisms, and above all to Dr J. Chadwick, who has guided this work throughout with much swift assistance and encouragement. In sombre times I must express thanks to the free society which has permitted and indeed funded this esoteric quest for truth, and to the Classical Faculty and University Press for its publication. Finally, if *The Language of Hesiod* prompted my approach, for introducing me to the singers of tales I shall always be indebted to Mr Andrew Wilson, *ὅς τέ με τὰ πρώτιστα καλὴν ἐδίδαξεν ἀοιδήν*.

Trinity College, Cambridge Richard Janko
November 1980

Postscript: delays in publication permit me to add that Karl Förstel's excellent work on the *Hymns to Apollo* came into my hands too late for inclusion in my text, and its relegation to the notes implies no disrespect. The publication of parts of over 100 lines of the *Eboiai* in *P. Leiden* inv. 502–9 (*Papyri, Greek and Egyptian, in honour of E. G. Turner*, ed. P. J. Parsons, P. J. Sijpesteijn and K. A. Worp, London 1981, 1–20) offers a disappointing harvest statistically, and no help to the solution of the problems discussed in Appendix C.

Vathy, Ithaca R. J.
September 1981

ABBREVIATIONS

I have in general attempted to use the standard scholarly abbreviations: those for ancient authors are as used by LSJ; for periodicals I have endeavoured to follow *L'Année Philologique*; those for books are indicated in the bibliography. As the longer Hymns and the other poems of the epic corpus are referred to so frequently, I have adopted the following conventions to refer to them:

Il Iliad (individual books are designated A, B, Γ etc.)
Od Odyssey (individual books are designated α, β, γ etc.)
Th Theogony
Erga Works and Days
Aspis Shield of Heracles (lines 1–56 excepted: these are cited as [*Aspis*] and counted with *Cat*)
Cat Ehoiai or Catalogue of Women (Hesiod, fragments 1–245 M–W)
Dem Hymn to Demeter
Ap Hymn to Apollo, which is usually subdivided into:
  DAp Hymn to Delian Apollo (*Ap* 1–181), and
  PAp Hymn to Pythian Apollo (*Ap* 182–546)
Herm Hymn 4 to Hermes
Aphr Hymn 5 to Aphrodite
Hy 6 Homeric Hymn 6, etc.

The following symbols are used in the discussion of formulaic parallels: *M 303 means 'also at M 303, at the same place in the line' (this can always be distinguished from the asterisk marking reconstructed or hypothetical forms); ~ denotes the omission of identical material; / denotes the beginning or end of a line. Note also (+) V for (before) vowel, C for consonant, and $^0/_{00}$ for 'per thousand'.

Finally, a note on accents. If we are to use iota adscript, we ought to be consistent in accenting the second element of the diphthongs in which it appears, as in all other diphthongs (cf. West *Th* p. vi). As this book concerns early Greek almost entirely, I have ventured to be consistent in this way. In retrospect, I am not sure whether it was right to do this, but the reader can judge the result of the experiment for himself.

οὔπω δὲ δύο ἢ τρεῖς ἡμέραι διεληλύθεσαν, καὶ προσελθὼν ἐγὼ Ὁμήρωι τωῖ ποιητηῖ, σχολῆς οὔσης ἀμφοῖν, τά τε ἄλλα ἐπυνθανόμην καὶ ὅθεν εἴη· τοῦτο γὰρ μάλιστα παρ' ἡμῖν εἰσέτι νῦν ζητεῖσθαι . . . καὶ μὴν κἀκεῖνο ἐπεθύμουν εἰδέναι, εἰ προτέραν ἔγραψεν τὴν Ὀδύσσειαν τῆς Ἰλιάδος, ὡς οἱ πολλοί φασιν · ὁ δὲ ἠρνεῖτο.

Lucian

Oral poetry, traditional and indeed archaistic though it is, cannot avoid the continuous process of slight and unconscious modernization.

G. S. Kirk

CHAPTER 1

INTRODUCTION AND METHODOLOGY

Apart from Hesiod and the poems attributed to his 'school', the Homeric Hymns are our sole fully extant source of information about how the rich tradition of Greek epic poetry that culminated in Homer developed in time and space. It is not our purpose here to discuss the definition of the genre;[1] technically the beginning of the *Theogony* (1–105) and *Erga* 1–10 are hymns, but we are concerned with the corpus of *Hymns* that have been transmitted to us by manuscript tradition, independently of any poems they may have introduced. Of these there are twenty-eight shorter specimens (excluding *Hy* 8, which is incontestably out of place and probably the work of the late writer Proclus),[2] none more than sixty lines long, and five of greater length, counting the *Hymn to Apollo* as two; the fragmentary *Hy* 1 to Dionysus was probably long too.

Although previous scholarship has sometimes done so, it is dangerous to treat the *Hymns* as a single corpus for linguistic purposes, as they may differ considerably in their dates and places of origin. The use of the short hymns is particularly hazardous, as they offer so little evidence: on these grounds it seems best to exclude them from the inquiry, although it may eventually be practicable to offer a few conclusions about *Hymns* 7 and 19, each about fifty lines long. Thus we are left with five Hymns as follows: *Dem*, 495 lines; *Ap*, divided into *DAp*, 181 lines, and *PAp*, 365 lines (including 325a); *Herm*, 580 lines; and *Aphr*, 293 lines, giving a total corpus of 1914 lines: the abbreviations used in referring to the various hymns are given on p. xiv. The shorter hymns amount to 395 lines.

The text of the *Hymns* is preserved in twenty-nine late Byzantine manuscripts; as Allen and Sikes[3] remarked, this indicates how little they were read compared with other early hexameter verse. Discoveries of papyri suggest that this was also true of earlier times; only three scraps relating to the *Hymns* have been found,[4] in contrast to many fragments of Homer and Hesiod, including the *Eboiai* (*Cat*). The rarity of citations and allusions in classical literature confirms the diagnosis, although there is some imitation in the learned Hellenistic poets,[5] especially of course by Callimachus. In general, Alexandrian and later scholarship appears to have paid scant attention to the *Hymns*, and excluded them from the Homeric canon:[6] nonetheless there are two occasions when the text of the *Hymns* influenced that of Homer – a second-century B.C. text of A 484ff., and Strabo's text at *o* 295[7] – and a reciprocal influence seems an inevitable supposition. The absence of scholia and the general neglect appear to have led to considerable corruption, greatest of course in the difficult *Herm*. Furthermore, there is evidence for substantial fluctuations in the text's early history. Apart from the vexed problem of duplicate lines,[8] a quotation in Thucydides (III 104) presents a number of variants that amount to far more than straightforward corruptions or failures of memory.[9] These become particularly significant when it is noticed that these variants are just what we might expect to find in a recasting of the song by an oral singer or reciter. Note particularly the following:

DAp 146 ἐπιτέρπεαι ἦτορ / *ξ 228 ἐπιτέρπεται, *PAp* 204 / οἱ δ' ἐπιτέρπονται θυμόν

Thuc. θυμὸν ἐτέρφθης / I 189 θ. ἔτερπεν, ~ -ον *α 107, ~ ἔτερφθεν **Hy* 19.45

DAp 148 / αὐτοῖς σὺν παίδεσσι ≅ γ 381 αὐτῳῖ καὶ παίδεσσι καὶ αἰδοίῃι παρακοίτι

Thuc. / σὺν σφοῖσιν τεκέεσσι ≅ Δ 162 σὺν σφῇσιν κεφαλῇσι, γυναιξί τε καὶ τεκέεσσιν, **Th* 398 σὺν σφοῖσιν παίδεσσι

DAp 148 καὶ αἰδοίῃς ἀλόχοισιν / *α. ἀ. Ζ 250, Φ 460 κτλ. (σὺν παισὶ καὶ ~, cf. σὺν παίδεσσι sup.)

Thuc. γυναιξί τε σὴν ἐς ἄγυιαν / *γ. τ. Δ 162 sup., μέσην ἐς ἄγυιαν Υ 254

DAp 149 ὀρχηθμῳῖ καὶ ἀοιδῇ / **Aspis* 282, *Theognis 791

Thuc. ὀρχηστυῖ καὶ ἀοιδῇ / *θ 253, *ρ 605

DAp 150 *στήσωνται ἀγῶνα* / cf. *φυλόπιδα στήσειν* λ 314, *ἔριν* ~π 292

Thuc. *καθέσωσιν ἀγῶνα* / cf. Ψ 258 *ἵζανεν εὐρὺν ἀγῶνα* / (but in sense of 'assembly': 'contest' first *Th* 435 (?), *Hy* 6.19)

DAp 168 *ξεῖνος ταλαπείριος ἐλθών* / *ξ. τ.* η 24, nom. pl. τ 379, acc. sing. ρ 84.

Thuc. *ταλαπείριος ἄλλος ἐπελθών* / **ἀ. ἐ.* Δ 334, **τ.* η 24 *κτλ.*

Thucydides' text of line 148 is close to Δ 162, despite the interesting *σὴν ἐς ἄγυιαν*, while ours resembles γ 381. It is difficult to say which is better. These fluctuations strongly suggest oral transmission and recomposition: the manuscript text offers only the illusion of solidity, at least here: but it is all we possess, and we must make the best of it. Further examples of independently transmitted variants due to similar causes are found in two versions of the *Hymn to Hermes*, *Hy* 4.1–9 and *Hy* 18.1–9, where we can explain the variants:

Hy 4.1–2 Ἑρμῆν ὕμνει Μοῦσα Διὸς καὶ Μαίαδος υἱόν
Κυλλήνης *μεδέοντα* . . .

Hy 18.1–2 Ἑρμῆν *ἀείδω* Κυλλήνιον Ἀργειφόντην /~ . . .

Depending on which is earlier, the alterations are due to the desire to avoid mentioning Cyllene twice, or by an accidental anticipation of the name; thus *Hy* 4 is better here.

Hy 4.3–4 Μαῖα / *νύμφη ἐυπλόκαμος* . . .

Hy 18.3–4 Μαῖα / Ἄτλαντος *θυγάτηρ* . . .

The alteration here has an identical cause: *νύμφηι ἐυπλοκάμωι* (the more frequently attested case-form) occurs three lines below in both versions. So here *Hy* 18 is better.[10] Cf. η 245–7.

These cases show that versions of what is essentially the same poem could undergo substantial change, apparently by oral transmission involving some recomposition: these versions appear to be different recordings of the same underlying *Gestalt*. But there is also good evidence that similar 'oral' variants were recorded in some branches of the manuscript tradition of the *Hymns*. In *Herm* we have the benefit of the marginalia termed *y*: thus at 212 *y* (and also M) gives *μῦθον ἀκούσας* for Φοῖβος Ἀπόλλων (the name is soon to be repeated, but this does not suffice to condemn the reading, cf. *Herm* 4); at 288 *y* has ἄντηις βουκολίοισι καὶ εἰροπόκοις ὀίεσσιν for ἀντήσηις ἀγέληισι βοῶν καὶ πώεσι μήλων. For the first cf. εἰροπόκοις ὀίεσσι *E 137, for the second ἀγέλην τε βοῶν καὶ πῶυ μέγ' οἰῶν Λ 696, πώεσι μήλων *δ 413. Other examples, usually with good formular parallels for both readings, are found at 322, 326, 366 and 563. Elsewhere (where extant) the celebrated Mosquensis sometimes affords lections of a similar type, e.g. (here with *y*) *Aphr* 214 ἶσα θεοῖσι for ἤματα πάντα. Compare its readings at *Aphr* 18, 67, *Hy* 10.4f. and *Hy* 15.5–6.[11]

This evidence for the oral transmission of *DAp*, *Herm*, *Aphr* and some shorter pieces does not of course solve the problem of whether they were orally composed. Pieces composed in writing can undergo oral transmission, like many English ballads.[12] The question of oral composition (as distinct from transmission) will be examined in the next chapter.

Although we know nothing of when or where the *Hymns* were committed to writing, it may be possible to make some conjectures about the orthography that was used. All epichoric Greek scripts except Ionic had no separate signs for inherited *ē* and *ō*, and most, including Attic and Boeotian, did not mark *ē* and *ō* caused by compensatory lengthening. Many early inscriptions wrote out elided vowels, and still more did not mark geminated sounds: it is impossible on the present evidence to establish any regional or chronological tendencies. For texts transmitted in manuscripts two sources of evidence exist: ancient errors in transcription and manuscript variations. The former is of course rare: a good example is the variant reading ἔπλετο, ἔνθεν for ἔπλητ', ἔνθεν at *Th* 193; the original text may have read ΕΠΛΕΤΟΕΝΘΕΝ – or again *Th* 74 διέταξεν ὁμῶς corrected by van Lennep to διέταξε νόμους from ΔΙΕΤΑΞΕΝΟΜΟΣ.[13] In the *Hymns* note the following:

DAp 54 εὔβων (εὔβουν *p*) from ΕΥΒΟΝ, cf. βῶν H 238.[14]

PAp 487 (cf. 503) λύσαντε βοείας. Apollonius Rhodius read this, as at III 206 he has the certain echo[15] κατειλύσαντε βοείαις, where βοεῖα is used in the usual sense of 'oxhide'; here it means 'thongs, halyards', for which the Homeric word is βοεύς, β 426 = ο 291, *PAp* 407. The inconsistency is intolerable in the same poem, so we must accept Buttmann's *βοῆας* from ΒΟΕΑΣ. *βοεύς* is not found elsewhere in Greek, which might account for the false transcription.

Here there is the reinforcing factor that the sense of the mistaken form is incorrect. Other examples are less clear; e.g. is *ἠαρινο-* in the sole ms. M at *Dem* 401 a genuine form or an etacistic error of the later tradition? It is fluctuations of this sort that Herzog uses as his second type of evidence for metagrammatism in the *Hymns*: he is easily criticised. Errors over gemination, and the confusions *ει/η/ηι* and *ο/ω* (but not *scriptio plena*, false elision or the confusions *ε/η* (ε̄), *ο/ου* (ō) or *ου/ω*) could well be attributed to the effects of later Greek pronunciation. Moreover the number of errors will increase as the manuscripts become more numerous: hence Herzog is able to produce far more 'evidence' for Hesiod than for the *Hymns*. The *Hymns* of Callimachus seem a sound yardstick, as they must have been in Ionic script from the start, and also share seven mss. with our *Hymns*. In Cahen's apparatus to I–IV (803 vv.) I counted ten mistakes over gemination, and seven confusions attributable to later pronunciation. But he gives at least one confusion of *η/ε* (IV 266), and two of *ου/ω* (III 154, IV 271). Thus we should reject cases of these types in the *Hymns*; even so there is a residue, almost all from *Ap*:

(a) Elision: *scriptio plena*, *DAp* 163 / *μιμεῖσθαι ἴσασιν*; false elision, *Dem* 122 / Δωσ(ὼ?) *ἐμοί* M, 332 *ἐπιβήσεσθ'* (*αι*) M.
(b) E-confusions: *DAp* 93 Ῥέη codd. = Ῥείη.
(c) O-confusions: *DAp* 120 λοῦον unmetrical for λόον, unless for λο̊ῦν.

DAp therefore passed through manuscripts without signs for H or Ω and without elision: likewise *PAp* and perhaps *Dem*. The case of *DAp* is especially interesting in view of its Ionic origins: although the epichoric script involved could be Euboean or Boeotian, both traditional and internal evidence for Homer's text suggests that Attic is most likely. However, this cannot have been the original form of the text, but only an intervening phase; and it would be hazardous to argue *e silentio* that *Herm* and *Aphr* were never thus transmitted, although one explanation for the beautifully preserved text of the latter might be that it was always transmitted in Ionic script.[16] Nor does evidence for metagrammatism prove that any two texts had a similar history. Thus knowledge of the early history of our texts is scant, nor do we know when the corpus of *Hymns* was assembled.

The story of Renaissance and subsequent study of the *Hymns*, particularly of the establishment of their texts, is well told elsewhere.[17] The nineteenth-century editors made many perceptive comments about the language and metre of the *Hymns*, but it was not until the 1860s that systematic studies of these aspects appeared – A. Koehn on grammar and metre, Fietkau on non-homeric vocabulary, and E. Windisch on parallel phrases in Homer and Hesiod. Each of these had enviably industrious followers: to name only the most important, E. Eberhard, Rzach and La Roche on metre and prosody; various studies on individual *Hymns* cover vocabulary and non-Homeric forms and usages – on *Dem*, Francke and Dittmar; on *DAp*, note Priem; on *Aphr*, Suhle. A number of scholars have followed Windisch in compiling Homeric and Hesiodic parallels, e.g. Sterrett, Teske and also Richardson's edition for *Dem*, Boettcher for *Herm*, Preziosi for *Aphr*.

From our viewpoint the most important editions of the *Hymns* are those of Gemoll and Allen and Sikes. The second edition by Allen and Halliday is often far less useful, and the contribution of Humbert's Budé edition is mainly literary. Most recent is Càssola's edition, which is good in some respects, but contributes little on diction. Three hymns have editions of their own – Radermacher's of *Herm*, Forderer's of *DAp* (mainly useful for its full apparatus), and Richardson's of *Dem*, containing a thorough treatment of the diction. More detailed views on the diction, dates and origins of individual hymns will be examined in later chapters.

Some useful aids to scholarship deserve mention. The *Hymns* are included in Gehring, in Ebeling and in Dunbar's Concordance, revised by Marzullo; their vocabulary is treated in the still incomplete *Lexikon des frühgriechischen Epos* of

Snell and others: for the *Hymns* must be studied in the context of Homer, but Hesiod and the other remnants of early Greek hexameter poetry must also be taken into account. To this end, using machine-readable texts of Homer, Hesiod and the *Hymns* based on the Oxford Classical Texts, to which I have added the Cyclic and Hesiodic fragments from Allen, Kinkel, and Merkelbach and West, I have compiled a concordance to early Greek epic. This differs from those of Dunbar and Prendergast in that all examples of the same cases or inflectional forms are together, and the forms are entered according to the word following, so that all formulae appear together: there is more context, and even the most common words are listed (this is also true of Minton's concordance to Hesiod). I have found this Key-Word-in-context concordance a valuable tool for the study of the epic tradition.[18]

Most of the problems to be tackled in this work have already been recognised by modern scholarship. The relationship of the poems to Homer and Hesiod was scrutinised long before the work of Milman Parry, who gave it a new dimension, that of oral poetry. If the question of the extent to which the *Iliad* and *Odyssey* are the product of a long tradition of oral poetry cannot be answered conclusively on the basis of twenty-eight thousand lines of verse, it is hardly likely to be soluble in a shorter and more heterogeneous corpus. Perhaps the best we can do is to determine whether the *Hymns* or some of them differ from Homer (and Hesiod) in any vital respect; we will examine this further in the next chapter. But there are other dimensions to the comparison with Homer and Hesiod – their dates relative to each other, their geographical relationship, and the positions they occupy in the development of the tradition. How much truth is there in the ancient claims for 'Homeric' and 'Hesiodic' schools of poetry outside Homer and Hesiod themselves? Where do individual hymns belong? How do they relate to the dialects spoken in the areas of their origins, as far as these can be established? A coherent history of the Greek epic tradition is still lacking.

Several methods have been tried in attempts to resolve the

extensive chronological uncertainties that persist. In the discussion that follows, we will consider the use made of them by their various exponents.

(i) *Historical*. The only case where external evidence exists is *DAp*, about which the scholiast on Pindar's Second *Nemean* 1 gives plenty of information; but most scholars have wished to alter the date. Allusions and quotations provide a *terminus ante quem* within the fifth century for *DAp* and perhaps *PAp*, both of which are certainly imitated in Alexandrian poetry, and *Herm* is referred to then.[19] Although the first reference to *Dem* is in Philodemus, Richardson thinks that its influence is possible as early as Ibycus and Pindar, and certain in Apollonius Rhodius.[20] *Aphr* is never mentioned or quoted: the clearest imitation of it appears to be Vergil *Aeneid* I 314–35, 402ff.

(ii) *Internal* evidence is more plentiful and more controversial. There are several types – alleged reference to known events (or lack of such reference), topographical and archaeological arguments about the foundation dates of temples which might be the one referred to by the poet, the continuity of festivals, use of myth for political purposes, etc. These must be assessed individually on their merits: among the weakest are those based on the spread of religious ideas, and supported only by our ignorance; such an idea is first in Hesiod, therefore it must have been borrowed from him. Unless we are sure on other grounds that Hesiod is earlier, this is a risky argument.[21]

In some cases it is possible to obtain accurate dating in this way: the best example is the historical work of Guillon on the *Aspis* and *PAp*, which he associates with the First Sacred War. We may also be told or be able to guess the origins of the poet and the occasion of the poem: the poet of *DAp* says he was a Chian composing for a festival on Delos: Guillon shows that the author of *PAp* was probably Boeotian but not Theban: *Dem* was probably composed at Eleusis, *Aphr* in the Troad.[22]

(iii) Another form of internal evidence is literary imitation and influence. Until Parry, a great deal of scholarly effort was devoted to determining the interrelationships of early epic on these grounds, with inevitable dangers of subjective judgements which mar most of the work on the *Hymns*; and even since then similar efforts have continued, for example by Schröder on the *Hymn to Delian Apollo*. Parry's work should make us very cautious of the principles of *exemplum* and *imitatio* when little more than single formulae are involved. Should we regard passages several lines in length repeated almost verbatim as better or worse evidence than a more remote verbal association? Even if we feel that coincidence is remote, and think we know which is the *exemplum*, how can the existence of a third passage from which both are derived be excluded?

Consider how much epic poetry has been lost of which we have a record: from notices of the Trojan Cycle[23] alone, excluding the lost works outside it and those ascribed to Hesiod, we learn of at least twenty-nine books. Assuming that each book contained 500 lines on average as in the *Odyssey* (the *Iliad* has c. 650), the total is 14,500 lines, of which about 120 survive – less than one in a hundred! However we know that the *Oedipodia*, *Thebais* and *Epigoni* contained 20,600 verses in all, of which but 23 survive, about one in 900! At least as much epic poetry has been lost as has survived, leaving aside oral poetry there may have been which was never recorded.[24]

Despite these losses this approach is still useful if used with due caution.[25] There is certainly no denying the relationships between *DAp* and *PAp* or between *Dem* and *Aphr*, although which is the prior in each pair is not securely determined. Hoekstra[26] has detected an imitation of an Iliadic passage in *Aphr* which owing to an alteration may be an important indicator of the poem's date.

(iv) Determination of priority in such cases may be eased by considering the exact language as well as the thought. A passage may display not merely *etwas unorganisches* but a more developed linguistic form or usage. Leumann's application of the principles of *imitatio* to the traditional language itself is worthwhile, but his conclusions cannot be used to support Analytic hypotheses or other chronological investigations (as Heitsch claimed), for the simple reason that the *exemplum* may survive in use long after it had given rise to the secondary usage through misunderstanding.[27]

(v) Linguistic studies now fall into two categories: the first, a continuation of the nineteenth-century philology, is represented by Zumbach. Zumbach studied isolated forms and usages in the *Hymns*, commenting on phonology, morphology and word-formation, but avoiding the discussion of frequent forms and its statistical implications. Chronology is taken for granted; Homer is earlier, and anything not in Homer is an innovation. Thus the archaism *χρυσάορα* (*DAp* 123) is borrowed from Hesiod, while *κατάκειαι* (*Herm* 254) is emended away: yet the 'Atticism' *θᾶττον* (*Herm* 255) is kept despite *θᾶσσον* elsewhere in the same hymn (212). Zumbach does not seem to have realised that he was dealing with a *Kunstsprache* composed of forms of diverse age and origin rather than a homogeneous prose treatise.

There is a frequent tendency to derive chronological arguments from a few isolated forms or usages, when scholars are attempting to date a particular hymn, or eject a passage from the text. Considering the paucity of our evidence for the Greek tongue until the late fifth century in Attica and even later in most regions, we should not be surprised to find a certain number of forms, usages and lexemes otherwise unattested until later: some of the usages noted as *Neuerungen* in last-century dissertations have since appeared in discoveries of Archaic poetry, and some non-Homeric lexemes (e.g. *ἄκτιτος*, *Aphr* 123) are Mycenaean. Another hazard is that if the forms are not in some way guaranteed, e.g. by metre, they are liable to have been altered in transmission. There is also the risk that a particular line might conceivably have been added after the composition of the bulk of the work, although most scholars now agree that with the doubtful exception of *Ap* none of the hymns contain substantial interpolations. Despite these dangers, this approach can produce interesting results, if used cautiously and alongside other methods.

(vi) During the past decades scholars have realised that Parry's proper-name–epithet systems are the most formalised area of epic diction; poets had more flexibility in the formation of phrases by modifications and analogies than was thought. After Severyns,[28] Hainsworth studied some frequent types of common-noun–epithet systems in Homer and demonstrated that modification of them is widespread. Postlethwaite has extended Hainsworth's principles in his work on formular diction in the *Hymns.*[29] He examines the frequency of the various types of mobility of common-noun–epithet systems (defining the original position as that most frequently attested), their separation and expansion, comparing samples of 434 lines from the *Iliad* and *Odyssey*; it is a pity that he did not compare Hesiod's practice as well. It emerges that in Homer there is less mobility and less separation than in the *Hymns* (except mobility in *Dem*), but the figures for expansion are too small to be usable. This increase in flexibility is complemented by the study of the proportion of common-noun–epithet expressions accounted for by formulae and formular expressions: as the frequency of common-noun–epithet expressions increases, so the proportion of formulae falls and that of formular expressions rises. There is the problem that formulae and formular expressions are defined only by the giving of a few examples; it is not clear how to distinguish a formular expression found only once from an underrepresented formula built on a common pattern,[30] especially in a limited body of material like the *Hymns*. Hence although this quantification of modification is important, and may help in the dating of the *Hymns* relative to Homer, it is but one criterion, and not always self-consistent enough to place the hymns relative to each other in the evolution of the tradition. Before we turn to other methods, it should be added that Postlethwaite also studied the extension and economy of proper-name–epithet systems, which will be discussed in the next chapter.

Since they were examining all modifications, Hainsworth and Postlethwaite defined the 'original' formula by its frequency, a disadvantage, as we have seen. A solution to this was indicated by Severyns[31] and pursued by Hoekstra, although it is unfortunately not applicable to all formulae by any means.

Hoekstra has demonstrated that formular modification and linguistic innovation proceed together both in Homer and in the *Hymns* (and also in Hesiod, although he has not treated this at length).[32] He shows that the study of modification in the light of known linguistic developments can illuminate not only the pre-Homeric stages of the epic tradition[33] but also the subsequent evolution. In *The Sub-Epic Stage of the Oral Tradition* he examines the major hymns (except *Herm*) for archaisms and innovations, and succeeds in proving by the accumulation of examples that the *Hymns* represent a more evolved phase of the tradition than does Homer, from which he concludes that they are chronologically later also: he supports this by adducing other types of evidence, such as word-formation, 'literary' imitation and historical evidence, but with admirable caution and awareness of the pitfalls and limitations. Examples of the way in which formular modification is associated with the introduction of more advanced diction will be given when we come to study that diction.

In general Hoekstra avoided statistical techniques, and gives a detailed account of his reasons in one case, to which we will return.[34] Consequently his studies do not permit a more exact placing of the hymns within the post-Homeric tradition, or in relation to Hesiod.

(vii) Previous advances have been combined and applied to the whole of early epic by Pavese, but with a shift of emphasis. He rightly rejects Hoekstra's view that the increased frequency of modification found in later poetry such as the *Hymns* necessarily represents a decline from Homer's standards into decadence, and believes that the oral tradition flourished into the fifth century. The increase in modification and advanced diction can be seen as an aid to greater flexibility and not a sign of decline.[35] But Pavese is more concerned with the problem of the relationship between Ionian epic and other 'schools' of poetry. His belief that a tradition of oral epic survived on the mainland (manifested in the epichoric verse inscriptions) has led him to resurrect Fick's view that the Ionic appearance of poems such as Hesiod's is due to the later transmission of the text under the influence of Homer: they are, he says, independent of and parallel with Ionia, with a shared nucleus of formulae but a considerable number unique to the mainland tradition.[36] The possibility that these 'mainland' formulae are in fact characteristic of a later stage of a more unified tradition is not raised. Pavese avoids the objection that the two branches of the tradition should be far less similar if developed in isolation from each other for three centuries by stressing that they are parallel. Nonetheless we would expect there to be some distinguishing features of mainland diction, and Pavese claims that there was such a mainland poetic *koinē*, but its distinctive features are very meagre: apart from short accusative plurals and the loss of post-consonantal /*w*/ without compensatory lengthening, they are mostly isolated forms from the poems of Hesiod.[37] But it is impossible to accept that mainland poets would admit the neglect of initial prevocalic digamma without influence from Ionia or at least Attica, and we shall see that the inflection Ζηνός etc. certainly originated in Ionia: this granted, the door is opened to other Ionic features. In fact the rift between Hesiod and the Ionian tradition is not as deep as Pavese's overemphasis on geographical factors (at the expense of chronology) has led him to suppose.

Pavese has also pointed out that Hesiod and the *Hymns* use a number of archaisms unattested in Homer.[38] Though these may have been acquired through the Ionic tradition or vernacular dialects, influence from a mainland tradition that subsisted at local levels to affect epichoric verse-inscriptions cannot be excluded.

(viii) Pavese also makes use of statistical methods in an attempt to show that the advanced diction is a mainland phenomenon: but we must look at this attempt in the context of previous scholars' use of such methods. The first problem that was tackled in this way is old and familiar – digamma. Hartel in 1864 was first to calculate the ratio of the observance of initial prevocalic digamma to neglect in Homer: inevitably at that date his list of digammated words was rather inaccurate, and he did not provide figures for separate books, nor even for the *Iliad* and *Odyssey* as wholes. The count has never been redone, doubtless owing to the tedious labour required. Several scholars worked on Hesiod and the *Hymns*: we may conveniently refer to Allen and Sikes,[39] who offered the digamma ratio as the sole and sufficient linguistic criterion for the relative dating of the hymns. As this was plainly inadequate, later scholarship has usually rejected the entire principle: West,[40] for example, follows Devantier in remarking that by this criterion the *Aspis* would be earlier than the *Theogony*, and suggests that other factors may be involved.

The method was also applied to the Homeric question. Bechtel[41] tried to use vowel-contraction to support an analysis of Homer, with little success. In reaction unitarians such as Shewan and Scott applied these methods, the former in defence of the *Doloneia*,[42] the latter to refute the *chorizontes*.[43] Both made the important step of using several criteria, such as the frequency of the definite article and of abstracts; Scott also compared Hesiod and the *Hymns* (as a corpus) to provide a contrast with Homer. Diligent and patient work of this sort fell into abeyance during the excitement of the discoveries first by Parry, and then of Mycenaean Greek. It was resumed by Webster and Garbrah, the latter with the old aim of testing analytic views of the *Odyssey*. He chose four linguistic criteria on the grounds of unambiguity and reasonable frequency: vowel-contraction, digamma, the genitive singular of o-stems, and the dative plural of o- and a-stems; this last did not turn out to be frequent enough for his purposes. He was very cautious indeed in the delimitation of what was to be counted, and grouped his results in books or parts of books; he did not cover more than ten, γ to μ and ψ 297–ω 548. He expressed the results as a proportion, using both less and more developed forms, which is advantageous: but the positive results he claimed are unconvincing, and not significant when subjected to statistical tests.

Webster's work[44] has a wider scope, as he appears to have examined samples from the whole of Homer and other early hexameter poetry. He took a number of 'late' linguistic criteria (contracted genitives in -ου, -εω, -έων, synizesis, neglect of digamma and singular -φι) and calculated their frequency per hundred lines in the epic corpus and also in elegy. Regrettably he does not state on how large a sample his figures are based, nor give the results for each of the criteria separately; thus his results will turn out to be misleading in some cases. Nonetheless, the idea of using several criteria for the dating of different poems was important, and it is still of interest to restate his results (the figures represent 'late' features as defined above per hundred lines): *Il* 11 (range in individual books 7.9–14.1), *Od* 13 (range 9.8–17.3), *Aphr* 16.4, *Ap* 19.5, *Dem* 21.8, *Aspis* 22, *Th* 23, *Herm* 24.5, *Erga* 30.4; Tyrtaeus 30. Webster concluded that his results could not be directly equated with a chronological sequence without taking other facts into account. In fact some distortion has been caused by the method of counting innovations but not archaisms, to which I will return.

Troxler, in his work on Hesiod's language, pays little attention to formular modification, but does examine Hesiod's usage of such frequent alternative morphs as *-ου* and *-οιο* in the o-stem genitive singular. Edwards discerned the relationship of the innovative phenomena to the modification of the traditional diction, but concentrated on less frequent aspects of Hesiod's language, the genitive singulars and plurals of the a-stem declension, and on the a- and o-stem accusative plurals, a complicated problem. He also demonstrated that neglected digamma often occurs in contexts likely to owe much to Hesiod's own creativity, but did not quantify this. His conclusion that the diction of Hesiod is more advanced than Homer's will be solidly reinforced by this study.

Pavese has taken the further step of studying the frequency of such alternatives throughout the early epic corpus, but the figures he uses are seriously incomplete. Even so an increase in advanced diction from Homer to Hesiod and the Hymns can be detected, which he attributes to factors of genre – war-narrative, peace-narrative, theological description and gnomic and rustic poetry each being less conservative than the preceding.[45] Although such factors may have a part to play, they will not explain why the *Aspis* is more advanced than the *Odyssey* in all the criteria he uses, nor why *Dem* is more advanced than the *Erga*. Moreover in the *Erga* lines 1–200 do not substantially differ in diction from the rest of the poem to which they belong, despite the different subject-matter.

Before further work of a statistical type can proceed, two objections by Hoekstra, when he refuses to use digamma for dating purposes, must be met.[46] Firstly, the value of the statistics is severely limited by the size of the hymns: and no adequate data from Homer are available for comparison, because of advances in philology since Hartel and the fact that he counted repeated verses (but not formulae!) only once. There is but one reply to the second objection – new figures must be compiled. Regarding the first, more criteria would provide a check; and if necessary simple mathematical methods do exist to calculate how likely it is that a difference exists between two proportions based on samples of differing sizes. Edwards[47] makes the same point in a commonsense way when he says that we need to know the range of variation in such proportions within a 'monolith' like the *Iliad* for single books or even shorter segments. And as he remarks, the difficulty of compiling accurate statistics from texts is being mitigated by the computer.

In the work that follows I will be extending the method of studying the alternatives in the traditional diction which may have chronological or regional implications, such as digamma. In a tradition that consists of oral improvisation rather than accurate memorisation, it is inevitable that, in those fields where the tradition hands down no ready-made diction, the improviser will draw on the only other diction he knows, that of his vernacular. The pre-Homeric stages of the tradition must have been of this nature, and the findings of Shipp[48] that advanced forms of various sorts are concentrated in Homer's similes and other digressions (without which the monumental epics would lack so much) suggest that this was true of Homer also: we will examine the problem of the extent of oral composition in the next chapter. As the oral tradition admitted change and new creation to supplement what was lost as it was handed down through the generations, the amount of archaism having its origin at any specific date will fall as innovations increase – innovations that will in their turn eventually become archaisms if the tradition persists. The rate of innovation might be altered by factors such as dialect or methods of training bards, but short of memorisation some would be inevitable. The danger of being misled by 'false' archaism in oral poetry is thus negligible: a poet might decide to dignify his verse by greater use of a more archaic morph, e.g. *-οιο*, but he will not be able to archaise consistently in several criteria; nor will most literary poets, e.g. Apollonius of Rhodes, whom we will detect using *-οιο* more than Homer did.[49]

Thus before we can place the various hymns in the development of the epic traditional diction, we must quantify the innovative elements and the traditional elements within it, just as Postlethwaite has quantified the modification to which innovative diction is closely linked; as Hoekstra realised, the complexity and scarcity of cases where the two can be proved to have arisen together makes a statistical treatment more difficult. This study goes beyond its predecessors in two ways: firstly, we will scrutinise as many criteria as possible, being deterred by rarity rather than by frequency of occurrence; and secondly, from the correlation of the results we will attempt to draw a quantified statement of the development of the whole tradition, rather than adopt the impressionistic approach that has prevailed hitherto; we will also attempt the precise delimitation of regional variation in the diction, and the establishment of relative and absolute approximate dates and origins for the various poems of the extant epic corpus, as far as is possible from a combination of the linguistic and all other types of evidence available.

But first to the question of oral composition. The next chapter will argue that here too techniques with a more numerical basis may have something new to offer.

CHAPTER 2

THE PROBLEM OF ORAL COMPOSITION

Milman Parry's most fruitful research was carried out on the two monumental epics, and he avoided other early epic poetry, partly on the grounds of its meagreness, and partly because 'these poems and hymns belong to different periods and clearly do not all follow the tradition with equal fidelity'.[1] But he did envisage the idea of a general study of early poetry outside Homer, regarding the traditional technique of verse-making: 'one will then learn, I believe, a great deal about the nature of the epic diction, of its use for different subjects, and by different poets or schools of poets, and of its decline'.[2] Some of Parry's followers, notably Notopoulos and Pavese, have concluded from such study that the hymns cannot be distinguished from Homer, and that they are therefore oral poems.

We must firstly clarify what is meant here by orality. Finnegan, in her recent book on the topic,[3] adopts a very broad definition of oral poetry, including even literature of written origin that undergoes oral transmission; hence she is unable to draw any firm line between oral and written literature. Whatever the definition of oral literature in general, I still agree with Lord that one can define a type of oral formular literature, and only diverge when he extends this term to cover all oral literature. By oral formular literature I mean poetry in which formular systems characterised by economy and extension have been developed to meet the demands of simultaneous composition and performance. Modern representatives of this type of poetry appear to be the Uzbek and Kara-Kirghiz oral epics, which can reach great lengths,[4] and also the Balkan traditions. In order to compose in this style a long training, whether formal or informal, and a semi-professional devotion to the craft are required. The formular systems discovered by Parry are indispensable to such oral composition, but of course literate poets could compose in the same formular style,[5] as scholars still can. Thus there is no easy 'litmus test of the oral style', although we can say that the Homeric poems behave very much as we expect of oral poems, and are composed in an oral style. The marks of this style are as follows:

(a) complex formular systems displaying extension and economy;
(b) a low frequency of necessary enjambement;
(c) metrical irregularities due to the '*jeux des formules*' in rapid composition.

A further feature may be inconsistencies of logic in the inappropriate use of formular epithets, and in the events of the story. Any or all of these could be imitated by literate poets, although it is difficult to believe that they would tolerate such inconsistencies as the Embassy in I with and without Phoenix. That oral composers of this type would be able to manage such literary characteristics as frequent necessary enjambement is also doubtful. Notopoulos[6] and Pavese[7] have argued that the oral tradition was widespread in Greece through the Archaic period. However, their methods cannot prove this with certainty, any more than Edwards[8] has proved Hesiod an oral poet: this remains no more than the most probable inference from the oral formular style.

We will now examine some of the features that have been claimed typical of this style, and hence diagnostic of oral poems. That we can deal briefly with many is owed largely to the work of Edwards.

The most widely used test of orality is the density of formular repetitions. This is employed by Notopoulos and Pavese[9] with varying degrees of precision. Pavese notes[10] that Notopoulos counts as formular expressions what are better excluded as structural formulae, and limits his own counts to formular expressions based on analogy, and also avoids very short phrases.[11] Even so, he supplies no precise definition of the formula or formular expression. Nevertheless it is of interest to restate his results, which were at least checked if not counted by the same person throughout the corpus, and accord with one's intuitive expectations. The percentage of verses containing formulae or formular expressions falls in the range 77–83% in *Th*, *Erga*, *Dem* and *Herm*, but elsewhere from 87% upwards. Pavese does not usually state on how many verses his figures are based, but did survey over a hundred lines in each of *DAp*, *PAp* and *Herm*. It would be hazardous to argue from this evidence that the poems that are slightly less formular are thereby any less oral; it could be a feature of poems close to Hesiod, where a greater proportion of formulae might be attested only once and therefore escape recognition.

Simple formularity does not prove orality; the formulae must be examined in terms of the qualities Parry named extension and economy. This is harder to do in the smaller and somewhat heterogeneous *Hymns* than in Homer; but it is still possible to observe that they use the same noun–epithet systems as Homer, and sometimes fill them out. Whether this extra coverage is a further and useful extension achieved by the post-Homeric tradition, or whether it is fortuitously unrepresented in Homer, is problematic.

The noun–epithet system for Apollo, an important character in Homer, illustrates the point that the Hymns use much the same systems. In the nominative, excluding a few separated and mid-line phrases, we find the system shown in table 1 (the poems in which the formula occurs are given, then the number of occurrences in each in the same sequence, and then the total).

The system seems fairly homogeneous throughout: the doublets found in Homer persist in the hymns. Most can be explained as arising from the loss of digamma, when phrases beginning with that sound became equivalent to those beginning with vowels, and new phrases with initial consonants began to be created to avoid the apparent metrical anomalies: thus *Διὸς καὶ Λητοῦς υἱός* / *ἄναξ* ∪ ∪ – ∪ *Ἀπόλλων* and *Διὸς υἱὸς Ἀπόλλων* / *ἑκάεργος* ~ / *κλυτότοξος* ~. Phrases beginning with vowels are noticeably absent. The few non-Homeric

Table 1. *The nominative epithet-system for Apollo*

/ –⏕–⏕–	C+	Φοῖβος ἀκερσεκόμης	*Il*, *Cat*, *PAp* (1+1+1=3)
/ –⏕–⏕–◡	C+	Λητοῦς καὶ Διὸς υἱός	*Il* (1)
⏕–⏕–⏕–– /	+C	Λητοῦς ἐρικυδέος υἱός	*Il*, *PAp*, *Herm* (1+1+2=4)
,, /	+CC(‘ϝ)	ἑκατηβόλος αὐτὸς Ἀπόλλων	*Herm* (1)
◡–⏕–⏕–– /	+C(ϝ)	ἄναξ ἑκάεργος Ἀπόλλων	*Il*, *Od*, *PAp*, *Herm* (2+1+4+2=9)
,,	+C(ϝ)	ἄναξ Διὸς υἱὸς Ἀπόλλων	*Il*, *Od*, *Cat*, *PAp*, *Herm* (4+1+1+2+2=10)
,,	+C(ϝ)	ἐκηβόλος αὐτὸς Ἀπόλλων	*Aphr* (1)
,,	+C	Διὸς καὶ Λητοῦς υἱός	*Aspis*, *Herm* (1+2=3)
–⏕–⏕–– /	+V	ἀργυρότοξος Ἀπόλλων	*Il*, *Od*, *Cat*, *Herm*, *Hy* 7, 9 (6+3+1+1+1+1=13)
,,	+C	Λητοῦς ἀγλαὸς υἱός	*Herm* (2)
⏕–⏕–– /	+C	Διὸς υἱὸς Ἀπόλλων	*Il*, *PAp* (3+2=5)
,,	+CC(‘ϝ)	ἑκάεργος Ἀπόλλων	*Il*, *PAp*, *Herm* (7+1+1=9)
,,	+CC	κλυτότοξος Ἀπόλλων	*Od* (1)
–⏕–– /	+C	Φοῖβος Ἀπόλλων	*Il*, *Od*, *Cat*, *Aspis*, *DAp*, *PAp*, *Herm* (very frequent)

phrases are easily explained. The doublet ἐκηβόλος αὐτὸς Ἀπόλλων (*Aphr* 151) has an analogy in ἑκατηβόλος ~ (*Herm* 234),[12] Λητοῦς ἀγλαὸς υἱός (*Herm*) is a member of the extensive substitution-system of Νέστορος ἀγλαὸς υἱός (K 196 etc.). There is thus no evident major departure from the Homeric system here.

Since *Herm* gives the impression of being least traditional among the *Hymns*, the system for Hermes (a deity less prominent in Homer) might provide an interesting contrast. The epithets listed in table 2 are in *Herm* unless stated.

It is not difficult to account for many of these doublets, which nonetheless suggest that the system for Hermes was less rigid and so less well developed than his half-brother's. Indeed Apollo's system has provided the model in two instances: Μαίης ἐρικυδέος υἱος is based on the more frequent Λητοῦς ~ , for which Κυλλήνιος Ἀργειφόντης is the proper

Table 2. *The nominative epithet-system for Hermes*

/ –⏕–⏕–	C+	Ἑρμῆς χαρμόφρων	(1)
,,	C+	Ἑρμῆς (τ') οἰοπόλος	(1)
/ –⏕–⏕–⏑	V+	Ἑρμείας ἀκάκητα *Il*, *Od*	(1+1=2)
⏕–⏕–⏕–– /	+C	Μαίης ἐρικυδέος υἱός	(1)
,,	+C	Κυλλήνιος Ἀργειφόντης	(1)
,,	+C	σῶκος ἐριούνιος Ἑρμῆς *Il*	(1)
,,	+CC	χρυσόρραπις Ἀργειφόντης *Od*, *Aphr*	(1+2=3)
⏑–⏕–⏕–– /	+C	διάκτορος Ἀργειφόντης *Il*, *Od*, *Erga*, *Aphr*	(6+6+1+1=14)
,,	+C	Διὸς καὶ Μαιάδος υἱός	(1)
,,	+C	Διὸς (δ') ἐριούνιος υἱός	(1)
,,	+C	Διὸς (δ') ἐριούνιος Ἑρμῆς	(1)
,,	+V	ἐύσκοπος Ἀργειφόντης *PAp*, *Herm*, *Aphr*	(1+1+1=3)
–⏕–⏕–– /	+C	κύδιμος Ἀργειφόντης	(1)
,,	+V	Ἑρμάων ἀκάκητα *Cat*	(1)
⏕–⏕–– /	+C	Κυλλήνιος Ἑρμῆς	(1)
,,	+C	Διὸς ἀγλαὸς υἱός	(1)
,,	+C	Διὸς ἄλκιμος υἱός (*Cat* 2, *Aspis* 1x of Heracles)	(1)
,,	+V	ἐριούνιος Ἑρμῆς *Il*	(1)
,,	+CC	κρατὺς Ἀργειφόντης *Il*, *Od*, *Dem*, *Herm*, *Aphr*	(2+2+2+2+1=9)
,,	+CC	χρυσόρραπις Ἑρμῆς *Hy* 29	(1)
–⏕–– /	+C	κύδιμος Ἑρμῆς	(4)
,,	+C	Μαιάδος υἱός	(1)
,,	+V	ἀγλαὸς Ἑρμῆς	(1)
,,	+V	Ἀργειφόντης *Il*, *Od*	(1+1=2)

phrase (it is also found in the oblique cases), while *Διὸς καὶ Μαιάδος υἱός*, though frequent in *Herm* in other cases, may be based on *Διὸς καὶ Λητοῦς υἱός*. The form *Μαιάδος* avoids a spondee ending with the fifth foot, and if dependent on the Apolline formula must have arisen before **Λητόος* was contracted. Perhaps it is better to suppose that the two systems were in close parallel for a long time, and the antiquity of Hermes' may be supported by the obscurity of some of his epithets. *Διὸς καὶ Μαιάδος υἱός* is altered to *Διὸς δ' ἐριούνιος υἱός* to admit the particle, and the latter phrase is conflated with *ἐριούνιος* Ἑρμῆς at *Herm* 145; a similar alteration to admit a particle is seen in Ἑρμῆς χαρμόφρων and Ἑρμῆς τ' οἰοπόλος, which are therefore not strict equivalents.

There is little in Hermes' system that cannot be explained by the effects of analogy from other formulae, and Richardson has come to similar conclusions about the systems in *Dem.*[13] The pattern may be described as one of sporadic creation to fill less usual spaces in the line, occasional generation of analogical doublets, but in general the same system as in Homer. The systems for common nouns too are congruent with this development, which accords with Postlethwaite's observation of the increased frequency of modification in the hymns.

The epithet system for 'earth' shows little more evolution than the filling of some gaps, and so will not be tabulated in detail here: but that for 'men' does show some development in the dative case. This is tabulated in table 3, omitting a few mid-line phrases; the total number of occurrences is given in brackets.

It is noticeable that there are hardly any formulae in the first part of the line in Homer, while these are common in Hesiod and the *Hymns*. Economy is violated in the pair ἀνδράσιν ἀλφήστῃσιν and θνητοῖς ἀνθρώποισι(ν) (both in *Th*), presumably because in their original use at line-ends they exercised different functions. The latter is itself a modification from the genitive θνητῶν ἀνθρώπων /, often in Homer; declension to the dative at verse-end was hindered by the need to use the morph -οις, only introduced in the late modifications at *Cat* 43.8, *Dem* 403, *Aphr* 52, which also possessed the advantage of admitting elided τε and δέ. Thus this is not quite equivalent to (κατα-)θνητοῖσι βροτοῖσιν. Thus the system continued to evolve towards greater coverage by means of modification, with no more than a slight loss of economy. This accords with Postlethwaite's discovery of an increase in modification in the *Hymns*: mobility, once every 33 lines in *Il* and 25 lines in *Od* on average, occurs about every 20 lines in *Ap* and *Herm*, and every eleven lines in *Aphr*; and separation, every twelve lines in Homer, happens roughly twice as often in the hymns. Were this applied to Hesiod I suspect that

Table 3. *The dative epithet-system for 'men'*

/ –⏕–⏕–	+C	θνητοῖς ἀνθρώποις *Th Erga Cat Melampodia Dem*	(6)
/ –⏕–⏕–⏑	+C	ἀνδράσιν ἀλφήστῃσιν *Th Erga* [*Aspis*] (τ')	(3)
,,	+C	θνητοῖς ἀνθρώποισιν *Th Hy* 30 *Cypria*	(3)
,,	+V	θνητοῖς ἀνθρώποισι *Th Erga Herm*	(3)
,, (sep.)	+V	ἀνδράσι (τε) θνητοῖσι *Il*	(4)
⏑–⏕–⏕–– /	C+	καταθνητοῖς ἀνθρώποις *Aphr*	(1)
,,	C+	καταθνητοῖσι βροτοῖσι *Th*	(1)
,,	V+	ὀιζυροῖσι βροτοῖσι *Il Od*	(2)
,,	V+	ἐπιχθονίοισι βροτοῖσι *Hom. Epigram* 10	(1)
–⏕–⏕–– /	V+	ἀνδράσιν ἀλφήστῃσιν *Th Erga*	(2)
⏕–⏕–– /	(C)C+	μερόπεσσι βροτοῖσιν *Il*	(1)
,,	(C)C+	δειλοῖσι βροτοῖσιν *Il Od Erga*	(7)
,,	CC+	θνητοῖσι βροτοῖσιν *Od Th DAp Hy* 7	(7)
,,	CC+	θνητοῖς (τ') ἀνθρώποις *Cat Dem Aphr*	(3)

he would resemble the hymns, judging by his developed diction, which is intimately linked with modification.

At the same time Postlethwaite calculated that the percentage of gaps in proper-name–epithet systems is very close to that in Homer, and so is the frequency of doublets: he argues for an identity of technique. Edwards reached similar conclusions about Hesiod, regarding both extension[14] and economy.[15] However, the suggestion that flexibility and thence coverage increased will explain another observation of Postlethwaite's, that the more poets used common nouns and epithets (there is an increase from one per 6 lines *Il*, to 4.6 *Od*, to 3–3.5 *Hymns*: a rough count of *Th* 1–100 and *Erga* 1–100 reveals 3–3.5 there too), the less they used formulae, and the more they used formular expressions.

The tendency to economy is only properly applied within the poetry of the same composer, and even there, as Edwards has shown, it was less strict than has been thought.[16] A few examples of how it may come to be disregarded have already been given; some more may be of interest. In *Aphr* some pairs are already found in Homer, e.g. Διὸς θυγάτηρ Ἀφροδίτη thrice beside φιλομμειδὴς Ἀφροδίτη (4x, and once with δ').

The former is concentrated in the second half of the poem, suggesting that the poet temporarily forgot that it was available.[17] / *αἰδοίην ἄλοχον* (44) beside / *κουριδίην* ~ (127, cf. T 298) arose through mobility: at line-end in the genitive singular and dative plural these phrases fulfilled different requirements. Note that this example shows greater flexibility combined with a loss of economy. A more complex case is *χαμαιγενέων ἀνθρώπων* (108) beside *καταθνητῶν*~ (5x): this might be due to the clash of two 'regional formulae'. This is Lord's term for different phrases of the same metrical value used by different poets or schools of poets to express the same 'essential idea'.[18]

Apart from *Aphr* 108, *χαμαιγενέων* appears only at *Th* 879 and *Dem* 352, while the alternative is also in *Il*, *Od*, *Cat* and *PAp*. Can we argue that *Aphr*, while preferring the Homeric, has adopted a 'Hesiodic' phrase here? Richardson[19] suggests that the phrases are not equivalent in meaning. Both propositions are rendered doubtful by the related *χαμαὶ ἐρχομένων τ' ἀνθρώπων*, found at E 442 as well as *Th* 272 (nominative) and *Hy* 29.2. But it is striking that there is another doublet in *Aphr* where a phrase peculiar to Hesiod is involved. This is *ὄρος μέγα τε ζάθεόν τε* / (*Th* 2, *Aphr* 258), versus *ὄρος καταειμένον ὕλῃι* (ν 351, τ 431 sep., *PAp* 225 *ἕδος* ~ , *Herm* 228, *Aphr* 285). Again works of the 'Hesiodic school' (*Cat*, *PAp*, *Herm*) follow Homer! Parallels between *Th* 7–8 and *Aphr* 261 suggest that the hymn has been influenced by the proem of *Th*:

Th 7–8 (Μοῦσαι) *χοροὺς ἐνεποιήσαντο* /
καλούς . . . ἐπερρώσαντο δὲ ποσσίν. /
Aphr 261 (*νύμφαι*) *καλὸν χορὸν ἐρρώσαντο.* /

Certainly the transitive use of *ἐρρώσαντο* is more developed, cf. Ω 616.

This is an appropriate point at which to discuss the problem of 'regional formulae' in Greek epic. In our context the name begs the question. Pavese,[20] in discussing the valuable list he has compiled of repeated phrases absent from Homer, does not consider the possibility that some at least of them may be due to chronological rather than regional factors. *Διὸς κούρης* Ἀφροδίτης (Υ 105) is equivalent to *πολυχρύσου* Ἀ. (*Th*, *Erga*, 3x *Cat*, *Meg. Eboiai*, *Aphr*). Homer appears not to have known the phrase, but *πολυχρύσοιο* Μυκήνης (Η 180, Λ 46, γ 305) could have provided the model for it. Even if we could find poems characterised by mutually exclusive formular 'isoglosses' it would still not be certain that the 'schools' were geographically, not temporally, separate, as obscure or 'unmetrical' formulae tend to be replaced.[21] However it is exceedingly difficult to find more than a handful of phrases which are clearly equivalent as well as widely found. A pair such as *ἀγλαὸν υἱόν / ἄλκιμον ~* are not clearly equivalent in *Il* and *Cat*, as different fathers' names precede: only in *Herm* is there duplication. It is hard to evaluate the significance of the fact that, of the Homeric alternatives *χθόνα πουλυβότειραν* and *ζείδωρον ἄρουραν* (which arose by analogy from the nominative, where the former would be metrically undesirable),[22] the former is found in *Dem* and *Herm*, the latter in *DAp*. In *ἀληθέα γηρύσασθαι* (*Th* 28), *ἀληθέα μυθήσασθαι* (*Il*, *Od*, *Dem* 121) and *ἐτήτυμα μυθήσασθαι* (*Dem* 44, cf. *Erga* 10) both Hesiod and *Dem* behave inconsistently. Two other phrases are more interesting: *στιβαροῖσι μέλεσσιν /* (*Th* 152, 673, *Erga* 149, *Aspis* 76) versus *γναμπτοῖσι μέλεσσιν /* (*Il*, *Od*, *Aphr* 238) does look like a 'Hesiodic' formula;[23] however, *θεμιστοπόλων βασιλήων /* (*Dem* 103, 215, dat. 473, nom. *Cat* 10.1) beside *διοτρεφέων βασιλήων /* (*Il*, *Od*, *Th*, *Hy* 7, nom. *Il*, *Od*, acc. *Od*, gen. sing. *Il*, *Od*, *Th*) does not partition the epic corpus as expected. Despite sustained research further examples elude me, and I conclude that if there were schools of poets they cannot be distinguished by more than a few regional formulae: the unity of the tradition is impressive.

Pavese's list of non-Homeric formulae suggests another approach. Can we discover poems' affinities by the number of phrases they share? Content is of course an imponderable, yet works of very different tenor turn out to be closer than we expect. The figures in table 4 are compiled from Pavese's list of shared formulae:[24] his definitions are loose, and a whole line is counted as a single phrase: phrases not found modified in Homer are included, but so are modifications of non-Homeric phrases. At least the list was compiled by one man, which is why I have not extended it to cover interrelationships among the *Hymns* (for *Aspis*, totals exclude 1–56).

Table 4. *Non-Homeric phrases shared between poems*

	Erga	*Aspis*	*Cat*	*DAp*	*PAp*	*Herm*	*Aphr*	*Dem*
Th	32	8	19	1	6	15	7	7
Erga	-	11	4	1	2	3	4	6
Aspis	8	-	6	1	3	4	2	5
Cat	4	6	-	0	2	2	1	1

To ensure that we are not misled by the differing lengths of the poems, the figures will each be divided by the number of lines in the shorter work of each pair (for convenience the result will be multiplied by 1000; table 4a thus represents the number of lines with shared phraseology per 1000 in the shorter work).

Table 4a.

	Erga	*Aspis*	*Cat*	*DAp*	*PAp*	*Herm*	*Aphr*	*Dem*
Th	38.6	18.9	25.3	5.5	16.4	25.9	23.9	14.2
Erga	-	25.9	5.3	5.5	5.5	5.2	13.6	12.1
Aspis	25.9	-	14.1	5.5	8.2	9.4	6.8	11.8
*Cat**	5.3	14.1	-	0	5.5	3.4	3.4	2.0

* Counting fragments 1–245 M–W as 750 lines, a conservative estimate.

Although the number of phrases is not large, we can draw some interesting conclusions. The closest relation is between the two poems of Hesiod, as we might expect: the *Aspis* is also close, but *Cat* is not, and has few affinities: the *Aspis* has some affinity with *Dem*, but less than does *Erga* with *Dem* and *Aphr*. Most interesting are the wide affinities of *Th* with all the poems except *DAp*, a very isolated poem. The position of *Aspis* may justify talk of it belonging to a Hesiodic 'school', but this is not a very useful concept, as *Cat* is about as close as four of the Hymns. If we are to think of these poems as later than Hesiod, then the evidence suggests that *DAp* alone had no knowledge of him, which accords with the Ionic origins of the poem: *Cat*, *PAp* and *Herm* (a grouping we will encounter again) resemble only *Th*, while *Dem* and *Aphr* knew both his works. The position of *Aphr* is interesting, as it has been called ὁμηρικώτατος! Apart from *DAp*, it will emerge that all the major Hymns are as late as Hesiod, or later still: only if *DAp* is later also will it be at all useful to say that all the poems we are investigating, except for *DAp*, belong, to varying degrees, to the Hesiodic 'school'.

Another method of approaching the problem of oral composition, proposed by Edwards,[25] is what he terms 'parallels of sound', the subconscious effect of the sound and rhythm of the traditional diction on the poet's craft. There is a good example at *DAp* 21:

DAp 21 ἠμὲν ἀν' ἤπειρον πορτιτρόφον ἠδ' ἀνὰ νήσους
cf. *Aphr* 4–5 . . . θηρία πάντα,
ἠμὲν ὅσ' ἤπειρος πολλὰ τρέφει ἠδ' ὅσα πόντος
Hy 30.3 ἠμὲν ὅσα χθόνα δῖαν ἐπέρχεται ἠδ' ὅσα πόντον
Th 582 κνώδαλ' ὅσ' ἤπειρος πολλὰ τρέφει ἠδὲ θάλασσα[26]
Cypria 7. 12 θηρί' ὅσ' ἤπειρος αἰνὰ τρέφει, (ὄφρα φύγοι νιν)

πορτιτρόφον is found elsewhere only at Bacchylides XI 30; its use here has puzzled commentators. In fact we may well be seeing the moment of its creation. The underlying idea of the formular line on which ours is based is 'beasts, as dreadful (many) as the land and sea nurtures', but the beasts are dropped and the sea altered to islands. The version is closest to the version of *Aphr*, as both have ἠμέν and ἠδέ, and the adjective following ἤπειρος begins with πο-. Did the Chian poet know this very line, and hastily change it as he sang? The influence of the traditional line was such that, instead of πολυβώλακα, used of ἤπειρον at **Cypria* 7.11 (he would need to alter the last two feet to καὶ κατὰ νήσους), he invented this slightly implausible compound.

There is a similar example at *PAp* 410:

πὰρ δὲ Λακωνίδα γαῖαν ἁλιστέφανον πτολίεθρον

ἁλιστέφανον is not found elsewhere in early epic. Matthiae wished to emend to Ἕλος τ' ἔφαλον ~, from B 584, but as Allen and Sikes remark,[27] such a poetic phrase would hardly be invented by a copyist; the epithet is eminently appropriate. The Laconian context has influenced the poet into using this instead of the nondescript *ἐυκτίμενον* ~.

Another adjective thus explicable is at *Dem* 113:

τίς πόθεν ἐσσὶ γρηῦ παλαιγενέων ἀνθρώπων;

This line is a conflation of three formulae: *τίς πόθεν εἰς ἀνδρῶν;* (8x Homer), *γρηῦ παλαιγενές* (*χ 395, *Dem* 101 dat., sep. Γ 386) and *χαμαιγενέων ἀνθρώπων.*[28] After *παλαιγενές* there would have been the difficult gap –⏑⏑–– / to be filled with 'men' in the genitive: the creation of this compound might be an oral poet's improvised solution to an impasse, while adhering to traditional patterns.

In *Aphr* compare 112:

. . . *Φρυγίης εὐτειχήτοιο ἀνάσσει*

This novel formation is for *εὐτείχεον* (6x *Il*), always of Troy, *πόλιν εὐτείχεα* Π 57. A good parallel is *DAp* 181:

. . . *Δήλοιο περικλύστου μέγ' ἀνάσσεις*

(*περικλύστοιο* ms. Γ). Compare also *εὐποιήτοιο* (**Aphr* 173 etc.) and *τεῖχος ἐυδμήτοιο πόληος* / *Φ 516, **Cat* 235.4.

These 'parallels of sound' could be multiplied from the major hymns, and some are striking, but I am doubtful whether they are as significant as Edwards has suggested. The importance of the voice and ear in selecting words applies to all poets concerned with the aural properties of poetry. Most, probably all, ancient verse was intended for oral performance, and it is possible to find such parallels in literary poets. Compare:

Herm 263 *οὐκ ἴδον, οὐ πυθόμην, οὐκ ἄλλου μῦθον ἄκουσα* (≅ ψ 40)

Theoc. II 82 *χὠς ἴδον, ὡς ἐμάνην, ὥς μοι περὶ θυμὸς ἰάφθη*

Note the parallel *μῦθον* – *θῦμός*. Given Edwards' necessarily loose definition of parallels of sound, how can this from Theocritus be distinguished? Similar cases may be found in such poems as *Id*. XXII. They are thus no proof on their own of oral composition, but only one witness to be considered.

We now turn from the study of formulae themselves to other features of the formular style which have been advanced as evidence for orality.

Parry[29] was the first to suggest that oral and literary poetry differ in their use of enjambement, which he classified into three types:

I No enjambement, i.e. the line ends with a complete sentence.

II Unperiodic enjambement, by the addition of a free verbal idea, using a dependent clause, participial clause or genitive absolute, or an adjective describing a noun in the previous line, or an adverbial phrase, or an addition by a coordinate conjunction.

III Necessary enjambement, where the sense is incomplete at line-end.

On the basis of 600-line samples Parry concluded that sophisticated literary poets such as Apollonius and Vergil use less type I and more type III enjambement than does Homer, by a very substantial margin. The difference is to be ascribed to the pressures of oral composition-in-performance.

Since then Kirk[30] has elaborated the terminology in a detailed study of Π, Edwards[31] has shown that Hesiod's use of enjambement on Parry's criteria is close to Homer's, and Richardson[32] was first to extend the enquiry to the *Hymns*. His work has been repeated unwittingly by Clayman and van Nortwick[33] in a computerised study of a broad range of poems, Hellenistic included, and again by Barnes[34] in reaction to this. The repetition of the count is worthwhile, since it demonstrates the extent to which the classification of enjambements is subjective; thus exact agreement is not to be expected, but approximate consensus suffices.

There is much variation in the proportions of types I and II relative to each other; but in any case it is now widely perceived that this is a side-issue. Literate poets are perfectly capable of writing verses without much enjambement. The *Batrachomyomachia* is known to be a literate composition from the reference at 2f. to writing it down on tablets. Using the OCT, with all numbered verses but no plus-verses (total 303), I found 43.2% type I, 33.7% type II and only 22.7% type III enjambement: in other words, this poem has a lower frequency of necessary enjambement than any piece of poetry studied by any of the scholars mentioned above. Again, the mock-heroic *Idyll* XXII of Theocritus is indistinguishable from real epic in terms of enjambement, with average percentages of 34.8 type I, 26.9 type II and 31.3 type II enjambement.[35] Barnes produces very similar figures based on a different text, and finds that this pattern is characteristic of the epyllia as a whole.[36] These results reveal two important points: first, that enjambement is a negative test only, i.e. that the 'oral style' of enjambement can be used by literate poets; secondly, the practice of Theocritus shows that there will be borderline cases where the amount of necessary enjambement is on the high side, but does not reach such levels as in Apollonius or Vergil.

Thus we should be suspicious, if Parry is right, of any early hexameter poems with very high levels of necessary enjambement. However, even this modest gain has been put in question by Clayman and van Nortwick, who find very high average levels of type III enjambement in the *Iliad* itself. Their percentage of necessary enjambement (37.7%) was not even approached in a four-book sample examined by Barnes, who obtained figures of 19.6% for Γ, 28.3% for Λ, 26.6% for Ξ and 32.3% for T with the average at 26.7%.[37] Finally, Barnes draws attention to the work of E. Lyding,[38] who compiled figures based on the whole *Iliad* and *Odyssey* and found levels close to Parry's for necessary enjambement (26.7% *Il*, 27.5% *Od*).

If we tabulate the frequency of necessary enjambement found by these scholars, and discount the aberrant results for Homer found by Clayman and van Nortwick, most of the poems behave consistently. In table 5 their figures are juxtaposed with Barnes' and those calculated by Parry (P), Edwards (E) and Richardson (R). Richardson's figures for *Aphr* are misleading, as the first hundred lines which he counted are

Table 5. *The frequency of necessary enjambement in the epos (%)*

	Clayman and van Nortwick	Barnes (and Lyding)	Parry, Edwards and Richardson
Il	37.7 (1562)	26.7 (L)	26.6 (P:600)
Od	32.0 (1296)	27.5 (L)	28.5 (P:600)
Th	27.8	26.4	27.9 (E)
Erga	31.2	29.1	29.7 (E)
Aspis	34.8	33.6	36.2 (E)
Dem	40.4	37.2	42.9 (R)
DAp	} 32.2	} 26.9	31 (R)
PAp			33 (R)
Herm	27.9	22.8	28 (R)
Aphr	27.9	28.3	27.6
Ap. Rhod.	48.6 (1002)	45.4	49.1 (P:600)
Aratus	43.9	43.7	-
Callim. *Hy*	36.0	35.5	34.6 (M)
Theoc. varia	29.5	31.2	-

abnormal: a count of the whole found 38.6% type I, 33.4% type II and 27.6% type III. The figures above are based on complete works, unless the sample-size is stated in brackets after the percentage. The editions used can be ascertained from the works of the scholars as cited: but experience suggests that the results are affected far more by divergent rules for counting than by the choice of editions. Lyding's results are marked 'L': the figure for Callimachus' *Hymns* marked 'M' is from G. R. McLennan.[39]

It is noticeable that Barnes' figures are consistently lower than the others', but if account is taken of the different scales *Dem* is always conspicuously high. However, Clayman and van Nortwick demonstrated that the result for *Dem* is largely due to its author's trick of placing a verb in first position of the line following the rest of the clause;[40] as Richardson hoped,[41] there is no need to invoke literate composition to save this phenomenon, yet it remains conceivable. Parry's distinction, valid for the extreme cases on which he based it, is less useful as a negative test for oral origins in poems of a predominantly oral style.[42]

Another of Parry's insights was that some metrical irregularities in Homer may be attributed to the juxtaposition and adaptation of formulae in oral composition, and might well have been avoided by a literary poet. Cases in the _Hymns_ of hiatus between short vowels and light syllables irregularly scanned as heavy were collected by Eberhard,[43] and some may now be attributed to these factors.

Apart from cases already in Homer, e.g. _πότνια_ Ἥρη or _τε ἰδέ_ (_Dem_ 190, *7x _Il_ etc.), there are several examples of hiatus caused by formular juxtapositions; I append three:

Dem 286 _παῖδ' ἀνὰ χερσὶν ἑλοῦσα ἑῶι ἐγκάτθετο κόλπωι_ cf. _ἀνὰ χερσὶν ἑλοῦσα_ *_PAp_ 318, _χερσὶν ἑλών_ frequent in Homer: _ἑῶι_ ~ *Ξ 223, interestingly with hiatus.

Dem 156 _πρὸς δὲ τόδε μέγα θαῦμα‿ὅου κλέος οὔποτ' ὀλεῖται_ _ὅου κλέος_ ~ *Β 325, _μέγα θαῦμα_ *4x _Il_, 1x _Od_, 1x _Herm_ in the line / –⏑⏑ _ἦ μέγα θαῦμα τόδ' ὀφθαλμοῖσιν ὁρῶμαι_ from which this is modified by transposition of _τόδε_. _μέγα θαῦμα_ is not found otherwise except at _Aspis_ 218 (_θαῦμα μέγα_), _PAp_ *415, _Herm_ *270, _Dem_ *403 (cf. 240), suggesting that its use alone is a modification, to which _Aspis_ 218 and _PAp_ 415 are transitional.

PAp 199 "Αρτεμις ἰοχέαιρα‿ὁμότροφος Ἀπόλλωνι . . .
cf. Υ 71 "Αρτεμις ἰοχέαιρα, κασιγνήτη Ἑκάτοιο . . ., and
_Hy_ 9 1–2 "Αρτεμιν ὕμνει, Μοῦσα, κασιγνήτην Ἑκάτοιο
παρθένον ἰοχέαιραν ὁμότροφον Ἀπόλλωνος . . .

As the poet did not know or recall the correct phrase beginning with a consonant, he was reduced to using _ὁμότροφος_ with hiatus.

Here are three examples caused by modification:

Dem 54 _ὡρηφόρε‿ἀγλαόδωρε_ / is due to the declension of the nominative at 192 (also 268 ap. _P. Berol_ 13044). At 492 another whole-line vocative has a similar hiatus: / _πότνια_ *ἀγλαόδωρ' ὡρηφόρε* . . ., showing that Demeter's vocative system was still not stereotyped, but also that the poet thought that hiatus before *ἀγλαο-* permissible, although it is not encountered elsewhere.

Dem 199 *οὐδέ τιν' οὔτ' ἔπεϊ προσπτύσσετο οὔτε τι ἔργωι* cf. E 879 *ταύτην οὔτ' ἔπεϊ προτιβάλλεαι οὔτε τι ἔργωι*. This hiatus is caused by conjugation, cf. *προσπτύξομαι* *θ 478, *ρ 509, *-εται* *λ 451. Compare the neglect of digamma due to the reverse conjugation at *Dem* 351 *μήδεται ἔργον*, cf. *μήδετο* ~ *5x *Il.*

PAp 488 *νῆα δ' ἔπειτα θοὴν ἐπὶ ἠπείρου ἐρύσασθε* (sic mss.) Agar's correction *ἀν' ἐπ'* (printed by Allen) is totally unparalleled and surely wrong; compare too *ἐπὶ Ἕκτορι* X 206. The line is a misremembering of A 485:

νῆα μὲν οἵ γε μέλαιναν ἐπ' ἠπείροιο ἔρυσσαν,

cf. / *νῆα δ' ἐπ' ἠπείρου ἐρύσαι* (*Erga* 624). This illustrates the risks of emending on such grounds.

Of cases of light syllables irregularly scanned heavy some are already Homeric, e.g. *PAp* 449 *εἰδόμενος αἰζηῷ* cf. *εἰσάμενος αἰζηῷ* *Π 716, or *DAp* 37 (Λέσβος) Μάκαρος ἕδος cf. Ω 544 *ὅσσον Λέσβος ἄνω Μάκαρος ἕδος ἐντὸς ἐέργει*. Allen and Sikes[44] suggest imitation of this passage, cf. *DAp* 30 / *ὅσσους Κρήτη τ' ἐντὸς ἔχει*, and Ω 753 with *DAp* 36. Others are caused by juxtaposition, e.g. *PAp* 209

ὅππως μνωόμενος ἔκιες Ἀζαντίδα κούρην . . .

cf. *ο 147 *ἔκιε ξ-*, and *ἔκιες, ἑκατηβόλ' Ἄπολλον* (**PAp* 229 etc.).[45]

Modification offers more examples:

Herm 23 *οὐδὸν ὑπερβαίνων ὑψηρεφέος ἄντροιο* . . . cf. I 582 *οὐδοῦ ἐπεμβεβαὼς ὑψηρεφέος θαλάμοιο*. Technically a cave does not have an *ὄροφος*.

Herm 310 *ὑμετέρας ἔκλεψα βόας, οὐδ'* . . . cf. 379 *ἔλασσα βόας, ὥς* . . . While these cases may be connected with the light a-stem accusative plural in the hymn (106), there are similar ones in Homer (B 165=181, Z 366, Σ 260, 589); there however *βόας* as an iamb is found solely in the formula *βόας καὶ ἴφια μῆλα* (7x), which may have affected the scansion here.

Herm 345 *κόνις ἀνέφαινε μέλαινα*, cf. *140 *κόνιν δ' ἀμάθυνε μέλαιναν* (note however *κόνῑς* Aesch. *Suppl.* 180, 783): similarly 371 *ἠελίοιο νέον ἐπιτελλομένοιο*, cf. *197 ~ *νέον καταδυομένοιο*.

Aphr 198–9 *οὕνεκά μ' αἰνὸν / ἔσχεν ἄχος, ἕνεκα* . . . The common formula *αἰνὸν ἄχος* is found separated at X 43, π 87 (*ἄχος* –⏑⏑ *αἰνόν* /), but never split between lines (compare *Aphr* 147–8 for a similar drastic modification with violent enjambement). For the prosody compare Π 55, / *αἰνὸν ἄχος τό* . . .

These two metrical irregularities have the same causes, and to them could be added a third – the hiatus formed when a long vowel or diphthong remains long before a word starting with a vowel. This too is less frequent in Hellenistic and later hexameter verse.

We may use a quantitative check to confirm that the hymns do behave in the same way as Homer and Hesiod in the admission of both prosodic irregularities here studied (table 6). Figures for Homer were compiled by Knøs,[46] for Hesiod by Hartel[47] for irregular 'lengthening', and by Athanassakis for short-vowel hiatus: figures for the hymns are my own. There is no doubt some inaccuracy involved in using different sources, but anomalies caused by digamma are of course excluded. The first pair of columns relates to hiatus, the second to 'lengthening': in each case the absolute number of occurrences is followed by the number of cases per thousand lines (‰).

We must beware of making too much of the figures for very uncommon phenomena, but some results are conspicuous: *Dem* has more hiatus, but less 'lengthening', hiatus is rare in *Herm* and *Aphr*, both faults are exceedingly common in *PAp*.

In general these results, if not purely random, must be due to the degree of competence in handling the traditional diction possessed by different poets, but the behaviour of *Herm* (and perhaps the shorter *Aphr*) accords with the preferences of Callimachus and Theocritus, while the converse in *Dem* resembles the practice of the *Batrachomyomachia*, where there is only one case of 'lengthening' but five of hiatus in

Table 6. *The frequency of hiatus and irregular 'lengthening'*

Work	Verses	Hiatus	‰	'Lengthening'	‰
Il	15693	123	7.8	214	13.6
Od	12110	116	9.6	140	11.6
*Th**	1020	16	15.7	7	6.9
Erga	828	10	12.1	5	6.0
Cat†	c. 750	14	18.7	10	13.3
Aspis	424	4	10.4	4	9.4
Dem	495	11	22.3	1	2.0
DAp	181	2	11.0	2	11.0
PAp	365	9	24.7	8	21.9
Herm	580	3	5.2	9	15.5
Aphr	293	1	3.4	3	10.2

* Cf. West *Th* pp. 95f.
† Cf. p. 27 n. to Table 4a.

270 verses.[48] This might suggest literary influence or interference in these poems.

Porter, in his work on the 'inner metric' or use of caesurae in the hexameter, has made important chronological claims about the Hymns. Despite a number of drawbacks in his methods, elements of them may be applied to the problem of oral composition. Porter's theory of a quadripartite hexameter has been refuted by Kirk[49] and Beekes,[50] who argues persuasively that the 'rules' for the hexameter are due to the desire to avoid the pattern –⏑⏑–⏓, with a premature closing cadence. He states that the following 'rules' govern the hexameter:

1. Word-end is obligatory after the arsis or trochee of the third foot (masculine and trochaic caesurae).
2. Word-end is desired at the end of the fourth foot (bucolic diaeresis).
3. Word-end is forbidden after the trochee of the fourth foot to avoid a closing cadence (Hermann's Bridge).
4. Word-end is avoided after the trochee or spondee of the second foot, if the word starts in the first, for the same reason (Meyer's First Law).

5. Word-end is forbidden after the fifth spondee, and avoided after the fourth, for the same reason.
6. Word-end is avoided after the arsis of the sixth foot.

Eschewing Porter's approach, these features will be examined separately. As can readily be ascertained from his Table I (type 10), omission of the third-foot caesura is very rare. It is rarer than in Homer (11–13 cases per thousand lines) in *Dem* (8‰), *DAp* (5‰), *Herm* (2‰) and *Aphr* (4‰). Contrast Hesiod (21–27‰), *Aspis* (15‰) and *PAp* (20‰). *Cat* has 14 cases in 816 usable verses (17‰), by my count. Such a rare feature could easily give a false impression in any particular poem, but *Herm* and the short *Aphr* are again prominent in the direction of Alexandrian practice.

The frequency of the bucolic diaeresis is also easily gleaned from Porter's Table V, and can be checked against O'Neill, who adds figures for some Hellenistic poets. In no case do the hymns differ substantially from Homer; nor do Apollonius or Aratus.

Hermann's Bridge is violated very rarely indeed, and it would be unwise to draw conclusions from it; there are breaches in *Dem*, and at *DAp* 36.[51]

Meyer's First Law is more promising. There are three types of violation, when words beginning within the first foot end after the trochee, dactyl or spondee of the second, e.g. *Dem* 16 / καλὸν ἄθυρμα λαβεῖν, or 441 / ταῖς δὲ μετάγγελον ἧκε. It is important that no exceptions be made for prepositions and postpositives.[52] Thus examples like *DAp* 115 / εὖτ' ἐπὶ Δήλου ἔβαινε are violations, but e.g. *Th* 764 / τοῦ δὲ σιδηρέη μέν is not.[53] Violations may be caused by enclitics or similar particles, e.g. *PAp* 190 / ὑμνεῦσίν ῥα θεῶν, but not unless they end before the third foot (e.g. δ 141). Occasionally textual uncertainty has led me to reject cases. Because it is not clear how Porter and O'Neill treated these matters, new figures are given in table 7, based on the OCT series, excepting Callimachus (Budé). After giving the work and its length, ordinary violations are listed, followed by the frequency per thousand verses (‰), and then the cases due to enclitics, and their ‰.

Table 7. *The frequency of breaches of Meyer's First Law*

Work	Verses	Ord.	‰	Encl.	‰
Il N	837	29	34.6	47	56.1
Il Π	867	30	34.6	45	51.9
Od δ	847	34	40.1	44	51.9
Od ν	440	17	38.6	21	47.7
Od π	481	18	37.4	32	66.5
Th	1020	33	32.3	51	50.0
Erga	828	29	35.0	39	47.1
*Cat**	704	19	27.0	38	54.0
Aspis	424	15	35.4	12	28.3
Dem	495	12	24.3	19	38.5
DAp	181	8	44.2	6	33.1
PAp	365	15	41.1	14	38.3
Herm	580	10	*17.2*	21	36.2
Aphr	293	14	47.8	15	51.2
*Batrach.**	270	4	*14.8*	16	59.2
Ap. Rhod. I	1-1000	30	30.0	9	*9.0*
Call. *Hy*†	941	3	*3.2*	5	*5.3*

* In *Cat* all usable verses, even when restored, are counted: in *Batrach.* those rejected by Allen are not.

† *Hy* I–IV, VI.

This gives a more complicated picture than expected. The lower figure for enclitics in all the hymns except *Aphr* is curious, but less striking than the rarity of ordinary cases in *Herm* (nearly significant, when tested against even *Dem*). Could literary interference account for the greater perfection of its verse in this respect?

The avoidance of long final syllables before the bucolic diaeresis has been more widely studied, by K. Meister[54] and Felix Solmsen,[55] as well as O'Neill and Porter. The latter do not exclude cases of enclitics and proclitics,[56] but Felix Solmsen appears to have done so, and his figures are included in the first pair of columns in table 8, giving the number of instances per thousand lines (‰): the third column gives the total frequency per thousand lines when enclitics are taken into account, followed by the source of the figure:

Table 8. *The frequency of spondees before the bucolic diaeresis*

Work	Verses	Ord.	‰	+ Encl. ‰
Il A*	611	41	67.1	118.0 Porter (*Il*)
Z*	529	47	88.8	123.0 O'Neill (*Il*)
N*	837	43	51.4	
Ω*	804	46	57.2	
*Od α**	444	30	67.6	125.0 Porter (*Od*)
*ι**	566	27	47.7	96.0 O'Neill (*Od*)
ν	440	20	45.4	
π	481	34	70.1	
*υ**	394	28	71.1	
Th	1020	35	34.3	108.0 Porter
Erga	828	38	45.9	112.0 Porter
Aspis	424	15	35.4	66.0 Porter
Cat†	872	56	64.2	97.5
Dem	495	33	66.6	110.0 Porter
DAp	181	8	44.2	71.8
PAp	365	17	46.6	79.4
Herm	580	26	44.8	86.0 Porter
Aphr	293	7	23.9	52.0 Porter
Batrach.†	270	21	77.8	96.3
Ap. Rhod. I	1362	15	11.0	20.0 O'Neill

* The results for ordinary violations here are from Solmsen; cf. n. 55.

† In *Cat* all usable verses, even when restored, are counted; in *Batrach.* those rejected by Allen are not.

In this criterion also *Aphr* has a conspicuously low result, but is joined this time by *Aspis* and perhaps *Th* in tending towards Hellenistic versification (compare 11‰ including enclitics, O'Neill's figure for Callimachus). Note that many cases are 'resolvable' at a more archaic stage, e.g. *Dem* 293 *ἅμ' ἠοῖ φαινομένηφιν*, *PAp* 452 *πόθεν πλεῖθ' ὑγρὰ κέλευθα*, *Herm* 300 *καί μιν πρὸς μῦθον ἔειπε* (for *ποτί*).

For the avoidance of any of these metrical blemishes, literary interference is not the only possible explanation; they might conceivably be related to the change from sung to spoken poetry. A singer might be able to disguise them more easily than a reciter, such as Hesiod may have been (the Muses gave him a *σκῆπτρον* (= *ῥάβδος*?), not a lyre).[57] However, Lord[58] has remarked that metrical faults can be more frequent in dictated than in sung texts!

This concludes our study of the inner metric: but as the outer metric (patterns of dactyls and spondees) has been used to make chronological deductions by F. P. Jones and F. E. Gray, discussion of it is relevant here. They used the data of La Roche[59] in a study of the frequency of different hexameter patterns in early epic and two Hellenistic poets. Unfortunately they treated both Hesiod and the *Hymns* as homogeneous blocks, which disintegrate when the figures for individual hymns are unscrambled. For example, *Dem* contains far more spondaic fifth feet than any other early poem.[60] The commonest type with five dactyls is demoted to second in *Erga*, *DAp* and *Aphr*, as in Callimachus; it is very difficult to establish any general trends in these patterns. However, a simpler test tells us more. It is well known that the use of spondees tends to diminish in Hellenistic poetry. Ludwich[61] has calculated the spondaic content for all Greek hexameter poems; although based on obsolete texts, his totals are largely correct and would not be much altered if recounted.[62] The percentage of spondees in the first five feet in the first dozen books of the *Iliad* ranges from 24 to 28, in a similar sample from the *Odyssey* from 25 to 27, and in Hesiod and the various hymns from 25 to 29 – with one remarkable exception, *Herm* at 21%. This compares with Callimachus (20–3%) and Apollonius (23%); could an oral poet possibly avoid spondees to this extent?

It is time to summarise our discussion of the problem of oral composition. The most important point to remember is that it is easier to disprove oral composition than to prove it. All the tests that can be applied are negative; if the poetry is in a formular style, with systems displaying extension and economy, then this is no more than compatible with orality. The same is true of the avoidance of prosodic and metrical blemishes.

It is revealing that the strictly formular tests of density, extension and economy could not discriminate between Homer and *Herm*, where the infrequency of hiatus, respect of Meyer's First Law and low incidence of spondees lend mutual reinforcement to the suspicion of some degree of literary interference;[63] but this does not prove that it is a literary composition, as intermediate stages can be imagined; for example, an oral poet might have worked through his poem read back by his amanuensis and made piecemeal improvements to it. *Dem* has aroused similar suspicions, but the only evidence is enjambement. Another doubtful case is *Aphr*, regarding the rarity of hiatus and especially of spondees before the bucolic diaeresis; in view of the poem's brevity I would think that the question remains unresolved. But both hymns to Apollo, as well as Homer and the poems ascribed to Hesiod, display none or hardly any of these traits, and there is no evidence against their being oral compositions in the fullest sense of the term.[64]

CHAPTER 3

DIGAMMA, ALTERNATIVE MORPHS AND OTHER CRITERIA

The role played by the statistical analysis of common features of the poetic diction has been touched on already in Chapter 1, especially regarding digamma. It is a pity that this is where it was first applied, as in fact the case is among the more complicated. It is now usually accepted that the phoneme /u̯/ disappeared in initial prevocalic position from the epic diction of the Ionian poets at the same time as it was lost in their vernacular.[1] However, in poetry of other than Ionian origin, difficulties arise. As we shall see, in no extant specimen of extended verse is there any example of the complete retention of this phoneme (written ϝ and termed digamma), even from areas such as Boeotia where word-initial digamma survived. We must conclude with Edwards[2] that the influence of Ionic diction was such that digamma was not pronounced, even where it was possible to do so. Traces of it persist because of the conservative nature of the traditional diction; however, if the tradition is at all open to innovation, then we expect these traces to become less frequent in less conservative or later poetry, and we are not disappointed.

Edwards[3] has remarked that in Hesiod digamma is often neglected in connexion with features that are peculiarly 'Hesiodic', such as 'indirect names' (*kenningar*) or such unhomeric features as the a-stem accusative plural in -ᾰς or forms like *κᾰλόν*. By 'neglected' it is meant that there is elision, epic correption of a long vowel or diphthong, or the maintenance of a light closed syllable before a word which we know from epigraphical and/or comparative evidence to have begun with prevocalic /u̯-/. Each of these types of neglect proves that the phoneme could not have been pronounced there, whereas the observances do not prove the contrary. Observances are of two kinds: where hiatus (whether of a short vowel, long vowel or diphthong) occurs before once-digammated words, and where an initial consonant or double consonant seems to be needed to make a naturally light syllable heavy (occasionally both are combined, e.g. *πατέρᾱ ὅν*). These two types correspond to the two types of metrical blemishes which sometimes occur without the agency of digamma, and were studied in the previous chapter:[4] but these account for a very small proportion of the cases.[5] For our present purposes it is as irrelevant to distinguish between the different types of observances as between the neglects.

Edwards' innovatory contexts include modifications, which are already beginning to appear in Homer, e.g. the declension *μελιηδέος οἴνου* / Σ 545, γ 46, *Dem* 206 (accusative 2x *Il*, 5x *Od*, *Hy* 29.6), which also involves a contracted genitive singular in -*ου*; or the alternation *καί μιν φωνήσας ἔπεα πτερόεντα προσηύδα* with ~ *φωνήσασ'*, cf. *ὣς ἄρα φωνήσασ' ἀπέβη*. . . : *ἔργα τέτυκτο* or ~ *τέτυκται* is frequent at line-end – 3x *Il*, 2x *Od*, *Dem* 140, *Herm* 12; digamma is observed at λ 610 and *Herm* 12 only. This is modification in the sense that the environment in which the formula is used is altered; note that in this instance mere frequency is not the best guide to discerning the original usage. Moreover study of the cases of modification involving neglects of digamma would not yield statistically satisfactory results for any particular hymn without including neglects where they cannot be conclusively proved. Hence we should look at the problem from the other direction: do a higher proportion of observances than of neglects occur in traditional phrases?

This question is complicated by the problem of defining traditional phrases or formulae.[6] Here the best that can be done is to make arbitrary definitions and apply them consistently:

Class A: Forms found in the same phrase as in Homer, even if only once there; this is to guard against underrepresented formulae. The phrase is defined as occupying five or more syllables or two or more feet, and consisting of two words as printed in the OCT. Shorter phrases are assigned to Class C.

Class B: This consists of Homeric phrases found in slightly modified form, i.e. by declension or conjugation that does not affect the syllables either side of the *u̯-.

Class C: Forms exactly attested in Homer, but not in phrases as defined above; n-mobile is ignored for these purposes.

Class D: Forms not found in Homer, including cases of neglect where Homer always observes digamma.

The criteria for observations and neglects have been stated above; internal digamma, and initial **dw-*, **wr-* etc., are of course excluded, but **sw-* is not. A further difficulty is whether certain lexemes began with digamma or not. Chantraine[7] succinctly lists most of the evidence, and I have in general followed his lead. In detail the following arbitrary decisions are applied consistently:

(a) No words in *ὀ-* or *ὠ-* are counted, excepting those in *οἰ-*.[8] This entails the omission, not only of words like *ὀφείλω*, where Mycenaean has overthrown weak inscriptional evidence for digamma, but also *ὄχος*, where it has reinforced it, and made the total neglect of digamma in epic still more curious, and *ὄπα*, which Homer treats in the same way as other digammated words.

(b) The following are not counted: *ἀρνειός*, *ἑᾱνός* adj., *ἑλέλιξεν*, *εἱλίποδας*, *ἐπέεσσι*, *ἔρυμαι* 'save' (despite Myc. */wruntoi/?*), *εἰδυῖα/ἰδυῖα* (due to the activities of editors), *ἴφθιμος*,[9] *ἑός* as from **sewos* > *suus*.

(c) The following are counted, despite misgivings in some cases: *εἴλη*, *εἶρος*, *ἐμέω*, *ἔργμα*, *ἔρση*, *ἐρύκω*, *ἧλος*, *ἴαχε*, *ἴδιος*, *ἱδρώς*, *ἰλαδόν*, *ἴρηξ*, *ἱστίη* and the proper names *Ἑκάτη*, *Ἑλένη*, *Ἑλίκη*, *Ἑλικών*, *Ἔργινος*, *Ἑσπερίδες*, *Ἰλήιος*, *Ἰλιονεύς*, *Ἴλιος*, *Ἰόλαος*, *Ἶρις*, *Ἶρος*, *Ἱστίαια*, *Ἰφιμέδεια*.[10]

(d) Enclitics are not counted (*ἑ*, *οἱ*, *ἕο*, *ἕθεν*), as the digamma may in fact be internal, as West has argued.[11] The special status of enclitics is reflected in our manuscripts of Homer: as Chantraine noted,[12] n-mobile and paragogic *κ/χ* are not added to a preceding vowel in cases like *δαΐέ οἱ* E 4, *οὔ οἱ* B 392 etc. Digamma persists here in the Lesbian of Sappho and Alcaeus while lost elsewhere:[13] but I have counted possessive *ὅς* despite their usage.

(e) All compounds as printed in the OCT are excluded. While I am reluctant to exclude such forms as *ἀποεῖπεν*, it is then difficult to know where to draw the line.

(f) A number of environments were excluded by Garbrah from his count of digamma. The length of the vowel in *πρίν* is ambiguous and so cases following it are discounted. Garbrah excludes cases of hiatus after *τί*, *τι*, *νῶι*, *περί*, *ὁ*, *τό*, *τά*, *πρό*, *ἀντί*, *ὅτι*, but in fact very few cases exist where words with initial vowels follow these. Nor do I follow him in his exclusion of the following morphological categories: a-stem plurals in *-αι*, aorist active endings in *-αι*, aorist infinitives in *-σαι*, athematic infinitives in *-ναι*, and words with final *-υ*. Although none of these are elided, there seems no reason to suppose that poets tolerated hiatus with them to any extent: e.g. *ὀξύ* is never followed by a vowel not once digammated, and there are only 13 cases of *εὖ/ἐΰ* in hiatus with vowels beside 53 cases involving digamma in the early epic corpus. But Garbrah is certainly right to exclude cases involving n-mobile and paragogic *κ/χ* as proving nothing.

(g) Instances of contracted genitive singulars standing in arsis before words beginning with digamma are counted, although these could conceivably stand for *-οι'*.[14] Figures for these are given later in this chapter, and are not sizable.

Before presenting comprehensive statistics for initial digamma, we will first examine its use in more limited samples to test whether a higher proportion of observances than of neglect occurs in traditional phrases. Cases in *Dem* and *Aphr* are classified according to the scheme detailed above, regarding their occurrence in Homeric phrases. The results are shown in table 9.

In *Dem* there are sixteen cases of observances involving enclitics, but no neglects, in *Aphr* ten observances and one neglect; this accords with the situation in Homer, where of about 780 examples there are about twenty-five neglects, or about 3%.[15] The sharp contrast with the general rate of neglects shows that we are right in excluding enclitics. The hypothesis that observances of digamma are less frequently introduced in non-Homeric (and therefore often innovative) contexts than

Table 9. *Classification of the instances of digamma in* Dem *and* Aphr

Class	*Dem* Observances	Neglects	*Aphr* Observances	Neglects
A	16	5	16	2
B	4	2	4	0
C	10	10	14	4
D	3	11	3	1

are neglects is confirmed by the test: 45.7% of observances but only 20.0% of neglects occur in Class A phrases.

This demonstrates the validity of the digamma criterion as a yardstick for the evolution of the early epic diction, but not of course a yardstick that is sufficient by itself: others will be offered shortly. In the past its use has been vitiated by the failure to do this, and by the failure to compile statistics on the same basis throughout early epic. Although there may be some disagreement over the somewhat arbitrary choices that have had to be taken in our selection of lexemes and environments in which we see traces of digamma, it will not be disputed that these choices must be applied consistently everywhere. The results are shown in table 10.

The range of variation in individual books of the *Iliad* is 7.0–27.7% neglects, in the *Odyssey* 5.7–31.0%, due to the smaller book sizes. The important observation to be made is that *Od* is slightly more advanced than *Il*, but much less than Hesiod and most hymns: and the *Erga* is more advanced than *Th*. We will come across this pattern again.

We must now discuss two methodological problems: how reliable are these results? and why examine the proportion of neglects and observations rather than the frequency of neglects per thousand lines?

If we use the proportion of neglects as the criterion, the statistical tests for calculating the limits within which the result may reasonably be expected to lie (the confidence limits) are straightforward, as we are dealing with a series of

Table 10. *The criterion of digamma*

Work	Observances	Neglects	Total	% Neglects
Il	1498	312	1810	17.2
Od	1391	303	1694	17.9
Th	59	30	89	33.7
Erga	90	55	145	37.9
*Cat**	75	34	109	31.2
Aspis	47	18	65	27.7
Dem	33	28	61	45.9
DAp	17	9	26	34.6
PAp	38	11	49	22.4
Herm	26	30	56	53.6
Aphr	37	7	44	15.9

* All restored forms are used. The compilation was done from my Concordance to Early Epic; v. sup. p. 7.

binominal populations (in each case, digamma is observed or it is not). It is also straightforward to calculate the probability that a result could lie at any level other than the one obtained. But if we used the absolute frequency of neglects, we would encounter the more difficult Poisson distribution. For the purposes of this treatise mathematics will be minimised by the introduction of other criteria, which will have the effect of reducing the element of chance.

As for the second problem, I have already suggested that the observances do matter: each time the poets wish to use a word beginning with digamma, they must choose whether to observe it (probably, for them, to admit a metrical or prosodic irregularity) or not, often forfeiting the convenience of a ready-made formula (the process was not of course as conscious as this, at least for oral poets). The absolute frequency of neglects was one factor that led Webster[16] to rate the *Erga* the most advanced poem in early Greek hexameter verse, despite the fact that observances of digamma are also more frequent there, presumably due to a greater use of such words as *οἶκος*. Thus his method is too prone to be influenced by the vagaries of content. The same goes for the *Aspis*, which has a higher absolute frequency of neglects than *Th*, yet also more observances, and thus a lower proportion of neglects. But detailed discussion of the results must wait until we have assembled more criteria as a basis for comparison.

We will now examine some alternative morphs in nominal declension, which for Ionian bards originated in the interplay between the conservative diction handed down by the tradition and innovations derived from their vernacular. The alternatives selected are as follows:

(a) the genitive singular of masculine a-stems;
(b) the genitive plural of a-stems;
(c) the genitive singular of o-stems;
(d) the dative plurals of a- and o-stems;
(e) the accusative plurals of a- and o-stems.

(a) The genitive singular of masculine a-stems

This topic has been treated for Hesiod by Edwards,[17] who compares the practice of Homer. The history of these morphs is uncomplicated. The 'Aeolic' *-ᾱο*, already attested in Mycenaean, was replaced in Ionic by *-εω͡* (*-ω* after vowels) as a result of quantitative metathesis after the fronting of *ᾱ*. Where this ending precedes a vowel, as in Πηληϊάδεω Ἀχιλῆος (A 1), the older *-ᾱο* may be substituted, with elision of the final *-ο*. It is however guaranteed before consonants and at the ends of lines. Among the dialects, Attic replaced it with the o-stem ending in *-ου*, which is only found in the *Hymns* at *Herm* 158 Λητοΐδου, *Hy* 16.3 Φλεγύου v.l., cf. *Cat* 70.39 Κομή[το]ụ. The other dialects preserve either the old ending or its reflex, contracted *-ᾱ* in Lesbian and some forms of Doric.[18] In Hesiod, Edwards concluded that *-ᾱο* is usually found in traditional contexts, and thus it will not be necessary to demonstrate as in the case of digamma its association with traditional phraseology. The statistics for early epic in table 11 were compiled in the same way as those preceding; the figures for Homer are similar to Chantraine's,[19] and those for Hesiod tallied with

Table 11. *The criterion of masculine a-stem genitive singulars*

Work	-*āo*	% -*āo*	-ε͜ω/-ω +V	~+C	Total	Grand total
Il	173	77.9	28	21	49	222
Od	80	72.7	25	5	30	110
Th	5	41.7	0	7	7	12
Erga	5	55.5	0	4	4	9
Cat	27	90.0	0	3	3	30
Aspis	3		0	0	0	3
Dem	3		0	1	1	4
DAp	2		0	0	0	2
PAp	0		0	0	0	0
Herm	1		0	1	1	2
Aphr	0		1	2	3	3

Edwards'.[20] In the first column are the results for -*āo*, followed by the percentage of the total they account for; then the number of cases of -ε͜ω/ -ω before vowels; then the frequency of the same endings before consonants or at line-end, where they are guaranteed, followed by the total of these two columns and the grand total. The two cases of -ου are not counted.

Clearly little can be learnt about the hymns from a morpheme as rare as this. It is interesting to discover that *Cat* is more conservative than Hesiod here, and that as with digamma the latter shows little sign of being influenced by his old-fashioned vernacular speech, but excels Homer in *Ionismus.*

(b) *The genitive plural of a-stems*

This has also been handled by Edwards,[21] who finds its behaviour in Hesiod similar to the preceding case. In early epic we find five different endings: -*άων*, closest to inherited *-*āsōm*; -*έων*, with the Ionic quantitative metathesis of -*ᾱ́ων* via -*ήων* to -*έων*, which is very rarely disyllabic but usually scanned with synizesis; the contracted *-ῶν*, normally postvocalic but exceptionally found even in Homer in pronouns, adjectives and nouns; and *-ᾶν*, a non-Ionic contracted form used twice by Hesiod. In table 12 these are tabulated from left to right in the same order, except that the percentage comprised by *-άων* is given in the second column, and at the end the total of more advanced morphs is followed by the grand total. Details of compilation are as for the preceding tables; *ἑάων* is omitted.

This is more informative. The increase in the use of the developed forms of the morph proceeds in roughly the same ratios between the works of Homer and Hesiod as in the two previous cases studied. Their use exceeds the Homeric frequency in *PAp* and *Herm*; the result for *DAp* is unusably small; *Dem* and *Aphr* have a lower frequency. As we shall see, there is reason to suspect 'false archaism' over *-οιο* in *Dem*, but in this case, of thirteen examples of *-άων*, eight are in Class A phrases as defined above,[22] four in Class C, and the only non-Homeric form is *ἀρουράων ἐριβώλων* at 471, paralleled in the accusative singular at Φ 232, which suggests that it may be an old traditional phrase.

(c) The genitive singular of o-stems

The old o-stem genitive singular in *-οιο*, apparently attested in Mycenaean *-o-jo*, is essential to many old formulae of the epic language, but disappeared from all the inscriptional dialects (surviving only as *-οι* in East Thessalian) to be replaced by the contracted product of **-οο*, which appears as *-ου* in epic. Troxler[23] has demonstrated that instances where this cannot be resolved into **-οο* in thesis before a consonant, or **-οι'* or **-ο'* before vowels, in arsis and thesis respectively, are more common in Hesiod than in Homer. Thus there are three categories of forms: *-οιο*, the resolvable cases, and *-ου* that cannot easily be removed. There are also some lines in Homer where an underlying *-οο* is certified by metrical irregularities,[24] e.g. *κ* 60 *Αἰόλου κλυτὰ δώματα*. These are included under **-οο* in the results that follow, where care has been taken to

Table 12. *The criterion of a-stem genitive plurals*

Work	-άων	% -άων	-έων	-έ͜ων	-ῶν	-ᾶν	Total	Grand total
Il	188	83.9	2	22	12	0	36	224
Od	130	80.2	1	21	10	0	32	162
Th	24	61.5	0	10	4	1	15	39
Erga	6	54.5	0	4	0	1	5	11
Cat	16	66.7	0	8	0	0	8	24
Aspis	4	30.8	1	4	4	0	9	13
Dem	13	81.2	0	1	2	0	3	16
DAp	1	50.0	0	1	0	0	1	2
PAp	3	50.0	0	1	2	0	3	6
Herm	4	57.1	1	2	0	0	3	7
Aphr	6	85.7	0	0	1	0	1	7

exclude adverbs like ὑψοῦ (but not of course *αὐτοῦ*). But we must first establish that *-ου* is commoner than *-οιο* in innovative contexts, and vice versa. Classifying the instances in *Dem* and *Aphr* according to the system defined above,[25] listing for this purpose all the resolvable cases as 'dub.' and omitting those where digamma is involved, we obtain the results shown in table 13.

Table 13. *Classification of the o-stem genitive singulars in* Dem *and* Aphr

	Dem			*Aphr*		
Class	*-οιο*	dub.	*-ου*	*-οιο*	dub.	*-ου*
A	8	3	2	7	4	5
B	1	1	0	0	0	1
C	12	6	8	7	2	2
D	16	3	15	2	5	6

Dem does not behave quite as anticipated. Of its sixteen instances of *-οιο* in Class D, less than half can be accounted for as unhomeric proper names in Homeric substitution-systems. However, the figures from both hymns confirm the innovatory nature of *-ου*, and we can see sometimes how it is introduced by modification, e.g. at *Aphr* 36:

. . . *Ζηνὸς νόον ἤγαγε τερπικεραύνου* /

This is modified by declension and separation from the frequent nominative, accusative and dative formulae *Ζεὺς τερπικέραυνος* / etc. (nom. 3x *Il*, 2x *Od*, acc. 2x *Od*, 1x *Erga*, fr. 280.13 M-W, dat. 4x *Il*, 4x *Od*, *Cat* 7.1, *Dem* 485, *DAp* 5, *Hy* 1.4, 12.5), blended with the formula *Ζηνὸς/Διὸς νόον αἰγιόχοιο* / (*Cat* 43.52, 76, fr. 303.2, *Herm* 396). The neologism would have been avoided by saying *ἤγαγεν αἰγιόχοιο* or using *μητιόεντος* (*Erga* 51, 769, *PAp* 344, other cases elsewhere). This example shows the force of analogy leading to violations of economy and the completion of paradigms by using this monosyllabic ending in place of the old disyllabic one; the situation will turn out to be similar in the o- and a-stem dative plurals.

From the following statistics, compiled as before, we may gather the general situation in early epic. The first table is concerned with the frequency of *-οιο*, which is followed by its percentage, the total of other o-stem genitive singulars and the grand total (table 14). Cases involving digamma are not included in the figures, but will be enumerated in table 15.

There are in fact two criteria here; the frequency with which, when an o-stem genitive singular was needed, poets used the traditional *-οιο*, and, when they did not, the proportion of forms in *-ου* that are certain. Troxler has not perceived this, but it is confirmed by the practice of Apollonius Rhodius. In Book I he has 131 examples of *-οιο* (63.6%), 33 of *-ου* and 42 doubtful cases. His use of *-οιο* is greater than the *Iliad*'s, but the proportion of resolvable *-ου* is not. He clearly felt *-οιο* to be a desirable archaic element in his style. Thus we should keep *-οιο* and *-ου* apart, as any contamination of them would distort the results. Table 15 therefore ignores *-οιο*; the first three columns display the frequencies of the

Table 14. *The criterion of genitive singulars in -οιο*

Work	-οιο	% -οιο	Others	Grand total
Il	1094	51.9	1012	2106
Od	715	46.6	819	1534
Th	78	38.8	123	201
Erga	36	28.8	89	125
Cat	64	39.3	99	163
Aspis	36	42.3	49	85
Dem	37	49.3	38	75
DAp	11	34.4	21	32
PAp	21	45.6	25	46
Herm	41	55.4	33	74
Aphr	16	39.0	25	41

resolvable cases of *-ου* according to the forms into which they may be resolved, followed by cases where digamma might have stood (these are bracketed and not included in the totals) and the total number of resolvable cases; next the number of irresolvable cases of *-ου*, and cases involving digamma (again bracketed and not counted in the totals); lastly the grand total, and the percentage of irresolvable cases (headed *-ου*).

The percentage ranges in the books of the *Iliad* are 43.6–61.5% *-οιο*, and 25.7–54.2% certain *-ου*; the corresponding figures in *Od* are 32.2–62.2% and 26.7–75%, showing how dangerous it is to rely on single criteria. Nonetheless both criteria present the same pattern of change that we have observed already between *Il* and *Od*, *Th* and *Erga*, with a very big shift between *Od* and *Th*. Elsewhere the pattern is less consistent: while *-ου* is commoner everywhere except in *DAp* (where the sample is smallest), there are high totals for *-οιο* in *Dem*, *PAp* and *Herm*. This is false archaism, which was not practised in the use of *-ου*, which was more convenient for the declension of formulae, as well as an innovation that poets would not be aware of as such. But we must await the correlation of a wider range of criteria before we can establish the full extent of such 'false archaism'.

Table 15. *The criterion of genitive singulars in -ου*

Work	*-οι'	*-οο	*-ο'	+ϝ	Total	-ου	+ϝ	Grand total	% -ου
Il	111	289	237	(7)	637	375	(13)	1012	37.0
Od	87	211	173	(4)	471	348	(8)	819	42.5
Th	4	6	47		57	66		123	53.6
Erga	11	4	15		30	59	(1)	89	66.3
Cat	9	13	26		48	51	(1)	99	51.5
Aspis	4	2	9		15	34	(1)	49	69.4
Dem	5	2	6	(1)	13	25	(1)	38	65.8
DAp	0	3	12		15	6		21	28.6
PAp	0	3	9	(1)	12	13	(2)	25	52.0
Herm	2	7	9		18	15		33	45.4
Aphr	2	0	9		11	14		25	56.0

(d) The dative plurals of o- and a-stems

There are six endings in early epic: *-οισι(ν)*, *-οις*: *-ηισι(ν)*, *-ηις*, and rarely *-αισι(ν)*, *-αις*. The first of each pair will be termed 'long' endings, the second 'short'. The situation is not in fact so simple: the short endings are found more frequently before vowels than before consonants in Homer, which has led to the suggestion that in prevocalic environment they are (or were originally) elided long endings. Thus, as in the o-stem genitive singulars, we have three categories – long forms, doubtful cases before vowels, and short forms before consonants and at the ends of lines which are thereby guaranteed. But the history of the morphs is more controversial. Ruijgh[26] has argued that the short endings in Homer go back to 'Achaean' and appear in Mycenaean as *-o-i*, *-a-i*. Both he and Shipp[27] reject the argument that they are more frequent in the *Odyssey*. By my figures there are 48 cases of certain short forms in *Il* and 70 in *Od*. Shipp suggests that this is hardly of significance when ἐρετμοῖς (1x *Il*, 9x *Od*) and μεγάροις (2x *Il*, 13x *Od*) are deducted. This gives 45x *Il*, 48x *Od*, which I still find suggestive in view of the difference in length between the epics, and confirmed by the usage of other poets.

Ruijgh supports his theory by arguing that the endings are formular in character, and conserved because convenient for the declension of formulae. This is the reverse of the truth, as Shipp has shown. To his list of short endings in Homer introduced by modification I add the following:

Ω 25	/ ἔνθ' ἄλλοις μὲν πᾶσιν	*nom. 2x *Il* 5x *Od*, acc. 2x *Od*
E 465	λαὸν Ἀχαιοῖς /	λαὸς Ἀχαιῶν 4x *Il*, λαὸν ~ 20x *Il*.
Γ 274	Ἀχαιῶν νεῖμαν ἀρίστοις /	*ω 38 Ἀ. υἷες ἄριστοι, *λ 179 κτλ. Ἀ. ὅστις ἄριστος

Ruijgh's interpretation of Mycenaean *-o-i*, *-a-i* is often rejected in favour of /*-oihi*, *-āhi*/,[28] while the distinct instrumental in *-o* is identified with the IE instrumental in **-ōis* (Sanskrit *-aiḥ*) and thought ancestral to -οις, whence short a-stem forms were developed by analogy. The short endings were generalised in all mainland dialects, including Arcadian; Argive (and Cretan) and Attic are but partial exceptions. Long endings survive in Pamphylian, and alongside short forms in Ionic and Lesbian, particularly in the article, for which reason Kretschmer suggested that the latter arose by haplology in cases of homoeoteleuton; but elision seems as good a cause. This situation is true of both literature and inscriptions.[29]

The distribution of these morphs in early epic has already been charted by Reichelt in Homer and Hesiod, and by Troxler[30] in the latter: Richardson[31] has added the *Hymns*, but rejects this as a dating criterion due to the peculiar behaviour of *Herm*. As usual, we will first test the extent to which these forms are introduced in innovative contexts on the smaller sample of verse comprised by *Dem* and *Aphr*, classifying the instances according to the system devised above[32] (cases before digamma are not included in the totals, nor are those involving δεπάεσσι, ἐπέεσσι and ὀχέεσσι, where long endings may easily be restored – another pointer for the direction of change: for the purposes of table 16 no distinction will be made between a-stems and o-stems, and short endings before vowels will be denoted 'dub.').

The preponderance of long forms in Class A Homeric phrases and short forms in Class D proves beyond doubt that short

Table 16. *Classification of the o- and a-stem dative plurals in* Dem *and* Aphr

	Dem			*Aphr*		
Class	long	dub.	short	long	dub.	short
A	21	5	0	17	0	0
B	11	1	0	8	0	0
C	22	3	5	19	5	0
D	12	1	20	9	4	4

endings tend to occur in innovative contexts, and the reverse for long endings.[33] We have already seen some examples of their introduction by modification.[34] This increase in the use of short forms is confirmed by the figures for the use in all early epic. As with the genitive singulars, there are in fact two criteria here – the frequency with which long endings are used, and when they are not the proportion of short endings that are guaranteed by initial consonants following or the line-end. Table 17 gives the numbers of the various long endings, their total, the percentage they comprise and the grand total of all o- and a-stem dative plurals.

The decline in the usage of long endings outside Homer is similar to that in the other criteria we have examined, excepting only *PAp* and *Herm*, which as we shall see are cases of false archaism. As with the o-stem genitive singulars, short endings are less amenable to this. In table 18, which shows short and doubtful endings, the three types of doubtful ending are given in the order *-οις'/-ηις'/-αις'*, then the total number of these prevocalic cases, the number of cases before digamma (bracketed, and not included in the totals), then the three short endings in the same order *-οις/-ηις/-αις*, followed by the total number of guaranteed short endings, the percentage they represent, and the grand total of short and doubtful cases. *τοῖσδε* and *τοισδεσσι* are not counted, and cases involving *δεπάεσσι*, *ἐπέεσσι* and *ὀχέεσσι* (26x *Il*, 20x *Od*) are excluded.

Again the developed forms are found least often in the

Table 17. *The criterion of 'long' o- and a-stem dative plurals*

Work	-οισι	-ηισι	-αισι	long	% long	Grand total
Il	1118	410		1528	85.4	1788
Od	1030	250		1280	85.2	1502
Th	100	43		143	71.8	199
Erga	67	28		95	66.9	142
Cat	76	31		107	78.1	137
Aspis	29	13		42	68.8	61
Dem	46	19	1	66	65.3	101
DAp	14	2		16	72.7	22
PAp	48	12		60	88.2	68
Herm	56	24		80	88.9	90
Aphr	36	17		53	80.3	66

Iliad, despite small samples in some of the Hymns. This is the seventh criterion where we have seen the same pattern of change in the direction of innovation in the Homeric epics and two works of Hesiod.

Table 18. *The criterion of 'short' o- and a-stem dative plurals*

Work	dub. (+V)	Total	+ϝ	short (+C)	Total	% short	Grand total
Il	143/69/0	212	(6)	38/9/1	48	18.5	260
Od	125/26/1	152	(6)	57/12/1	70	31.5	222
Th	22/2/2	26	(2)	20/8/2	30	53.6	56
Erga	11/7/0	18	(3)	23/6/0	29	61.7	47
Cat	7/2/0	9	(1)	16/1/4	21	70.0	30
Aspis	7/3/0	10	(3)	4/2/3	9	47.4	19
Dem	10/0/0	10	(0)	17/3/5	25	71.4	35
DAp	1/1/0	2	(0)	3/1/0	4	66.7	6
PAp	4/0/0	4	(1)	4/0/0	4	50.0	8
Herm	5/2/0	7	(2)	1/0/2	3	30.0	10
Aphr	6/2/1	9	(0)	3/0/1	4	30.8	13

(e) The accusative plurals of o- and a-stems

This criterion is more complicated and controversial than those preceding. Edwards[35] has demonstrated that by Hesiod (as distinct from the poet of *Aspis*) these accusative plurals were regarded as light syllables, and consequently were placed far more often before consonants than vowels. Occasionally he actually used the ending -ᾰς, also found at *Cat* 150.15 ἰδὲ Σκύθας ἱππημολγούς / and *Herm* 106 ἀθρόας οὔσας / (the case of λαγός, *Aspis* 302, is isolated and possibly corrupt).[36]

These endings originated in Common Greek *-*ans* and *-*ons*. Compare Argive and Cretan, where the *n* was lost before consonants but retained before vowels, e.g. τὸς καδεστάνς but τὸνς ἐλεύθερονς. Elsewhere, after the loss of the nasal, syllabic weight was maintained either by lengthening the preceding vowel, or by combination with a consonant beginning the next word. In East Thessalian, Arcadian and some West Greek dialects the preconsonantal form -ος was generalised, and presumably so too was -ᾰς; but evidence for the length of the a-stem forms is not available from inscriptions, and the orthography does not always reveal the quantity of the o-stem morph. Elsewhere the prevocalic form prevailed, in Lesbian (and Elean)[37] diphthongised to -αις, -οις; in Ionic and Attic the change occurred after the shift of ā to η was completed. No short forms are found in Homer (a few apparent instances are dismissed by Edwards).[38] Edwards also demonstrated that many cases of heavy accusative plurals in Hesiod are dependent on traditional phraseology,[39] as we might expect.

Edwards' study of the problem in Hesiod did not include the examination of the wider range of poetry found in the hymns: the following statistics repair this deficiency, and are compiled on the same basis as those preceding. Cases at the ends of lines are excluded, as they provide no evidence (although Hesiod's derivation of Πήγᾰσος from πηγάς / (*Th* 281–2) suggests that he pronounced them short): so too τούσδε, τάσδε. Cases before digamma are listed separately, and not included in the totals. In table 19 are given the numbers of cases of -ους before vowels and consonants, then the

Table 19. *The criterion of o-stem accusative plurals*

Work	-ους +V	-ους +C	+ ϝ	% +V	Total
Il	260	367	(13)	41.5	627
Od	161	261	(8)	38.1	422
Th	12	39	(0)	23.5	51
Erga	6	26	(1)	18.7	32
Cat	5	26	(1)	16.1	31
Aspis	7	7	(0)	50.0	14
Dem	2	3	(0)	40.0	5
DAp	1	4	(0)	20.0	5
PAp	1	8	(2)	11.1	9
Herm	9	16	(3)	36.0	25
Aphr	7	7	(0)	50.0	14

number before digamma, the percentage represented by cases before vowels, and the grand total.

Again we see a shift from *Iliad* to *Odyssey*, and thence a big drop to Hesiod. The evidence that Hesiod used short accusative plurals is reinforced by the attested forms in -ᾰς, although one is tempted to ask why no similar endings occur in the o-stems. The reason may have been hit upon by von Blumenthal, when he suggested that the analogy of the consonant-stem endings in -ᾰς led to the short endings, which stand in the third column in the table of a-stem accusative plurals (table 20), otherwise identical to table 19.

Even excluding the short endings from the totals (as in table 20), Edwards' discovery that Hesiod avoided putting these accusatives before vowels, where they had to be scanned heavy, is upheld: the result in *Dem* is a signal vindication of his approach, and the short endings are associated with low results in *Cat* and *Herm*, although the a- and o-stem results respectively are higher than might be expected. *PAp* displays the same inconsistency as *Cat*, while *Dem* follows *Herm*, if its o-stem result can be trusted. *Aspis* and *Aphr* have clear-cut

Table 20. *The criterion of a-stem accusative plurals*

Work	-ᾱς +V	-ας +C	-ᾰς	+ϝ	% +V	Total
Il	180	203		(2)	47.0	383
Od	112	154		(3)	42.1	266
Th	7	35	(6)		16.7	42
Erga	2	15	(3)		11.8	17
Cat	6	13	(1)	(1)	31.6	19
Aspis	5	7			41.7	12
Dem	1	15			6.3	16
DAp	1	2			33.3	3
PAp	5	4			55.6	9
Herm	5	16	(1)	(1)	23.8	21
Aphr	6	8			42.9	14

high results like Homer's. The application of statistical tests to see which results are random[40] leads to the following conclusions. In *Herm* the o-stem results are considerably more advanced than those of the a-stems. In *Cat* however there is no significant divergence, and both endings may in reality stand at levels slightly anterior to Hesiod's *Theogony* (as in other criteria).[41] It is at least clear that the o-stem result is not a random divergence from a Homeric value, as found for instance in the *Aspis*; a peculiar divagation as is possible in *PAp* cannot be excluded entirely. If these two poets did treat the o-stems as short and the a-stems as long, I cannot explain why. In contrast, results like those of *Herm* can be accounted for quite straightforwardly by supposing that the poets thought that the a-stem accusative plural was in poetry the same as the consonant-stem ending, but had no hesitations about the o-stem morph as offered by their vernacular. Such behaviour will belong to a self-conscious stage of the tradition, when it was more artificial than before: we shall see below that *Dem* to some extent, and *Herm* with *PAp* to a greater degree, did originate in such a stage of the epic tradition.

Pavese[42] and others have suggested that short accusative plurals may be a mainland phenomenon, and it is true that cases of -ᾰς are limited to 'Hesiodic' poems; the old theory of West Greek or Thessalian influence[43] and Edwards' suggestions about the difficulties of non-Ionic bards in converting ᾱ to η everywhere in the a-stem declension except the accusative plural will together suffice to explain the facts. But there is one fact they cannot explain: the behaviour of the *Odyssey*. In each criterion there is a drop between *Iliad* and *Odyssey* in the number of cases before vowels, of 3.4% in o-stems and 4.9% in a-stems - a small decrease, but exactly of the sort to which we became accustomed in the first seven criteria, a shift in the direction of Hesiod's practice.

There is only one possible interpretation of this movement - that even in the Ionic branch of the tradition these accusative plurals came to be regarded as short. An absolute choice must have been taken one way or the other, and we can explain the *Odyssey*'s position by the large number of older formulae with long endings that it retained. The irrefutable objection will be made that there is no evidence whatsoever for short accusatives in the Ionic dialect. But the paucity of our evidence for the speech of a sufficiently early date (the late eighth century) may well conceal some area where a generalisation of the preconsonantal forms was overwhelmed by convergence with neighbouring regions. There is the parallel case of the preposition ἐνς, where Attic generalised the (prevocalic) εἰς and Ionic tended to prefer (preconsonantal) ἐς, although in some places the original distinction was maintained to the fourth century.[44] In the *Odyssey*, of 271 cases of the preposition before vowels there are 62 of ἐς (22.9%), showing that the preconsonantal form was generalised for poetic purposes, if not in the vernacular.[45] Why was this not done in the accusative plurals? It is not enough to reply that the case of κᾰλόν/κᾱλόν shows that Homer was more conservative in the maintenance of syllabic weight than Hesiod. The difference is in part due to the fact that in the early stages of the epic tradition ἐν with the accusative was still found.[46] Thus, as Edwards remarks,[47] some phrases of great antiquity may have ἐς standing for ἐν: this is supported by the fact that the *Iliad*, which we have usually found to be more archaic than the *Odyssey* in diction, in 230 prevocalic occurrences of the preposition 65 are of ἐς, a higher proportion (28.3%) than in the *Odyssey* (in these figures cases before digamma are disregarded). Moreover, although the phonetic environment is very similar,[48] it is not quite the same – a proclitic preposition bearing no independent accent – and might be treated differently to some extent.

If the conclusion that the Ionic tradition came to consider these accusative plurals to be light is correct, then we would expect to see a decline in prevocalic position in later Ionian verse. Within the epic only *DAp* belongs to this category, and its results are ill-grounded on only eight cases *in toto*; of these two precede vowels. The chance that this represents an Iliadic level is about one in seven.[49]

We will now turn to two criteria that have regional features. The first is the *alternations within the paradigm of* Ζεύς. In Indo-European we can reconstruct the declension of the name of the sky-god **Dyēus* as accusative **Dyēm*, genitive **Diwós*, which appear in Greek as Ζῆν, Διός (the locative Διί replaced the old dative */Diwei/*, attested in Mycenaean). Analogical pressure led to a new accusative Δία in most dialects:[50] however, in some areas Ζῆν was altered to Ζῆνα, whence Ζηνός and Ζηνί were created. These forms had a wide currency in extant Greek poetry, but in inscriptions they are limited to East Ionia[51] and the Dorian isles of the southern Aegean, including Rhodes and Crete: the same innovation happened independently in Elis. The distribution of these forms in early epic is very interesting. In table 21 are given the totals of the three analogical forms in Z-, then those in Δ- except the accusative, then the totals of the two types, the percentage of those in Z-, and the grand total (the figures are compiled on the same basis as those preceding).

Omitted are cases of Ζῆν standing at line-end and before vowels; this archaism is very rare (7x *Il*, 1x *Od* and 2x *Th*). Also, for simplicity's sake, I have omitted the innovation Δία,

Table 21. *The criterion of* Ζηνός/Διός *etc.*

Work	Ζῆνα	Ζηνός	Ζηνί	Διός	Διί	Total Δ-	Total Ζ-	% Ζ-	Grand total
Il	1	14	7	171	78	249	22	8.1	271
Od	1	8	3	84	16	100	12	10.7	112
Th	3	3	3	28	3	31	9	22.5	40
Erga	0	6	0	11	4	15	6	28.6	21
Cat	0	4	1	14	5	19	5	20.8	24
Aspis	0	0	1	16	0	16	1	5.9	17
Dem	0	0	1	6	1	7	1	12.5	8
DAp	0	0	0	4	1	5	0	0	5
PAp	0	0	0	12	1	13	0	0	13
Herm	0	2	1	32	0	32	3	8.6	35
Aphr	0	5	0	7	0	7	5	41.7	12

again infrequent (8x *Il*, 3x *Od*, 2x *Th*, 2x *Erga*, 1x *Cat*, 1x *Herm*).

The first important point is the preponderance of Διός, Διί everywhere; the second is that the proportion of forms in Ζ- increases from the *Iliad* by roughly the same steps that we have already seen in nine criteria. But there is an interesting variation: most of the 'mainland' poems use the form less than we expect, especially *Aspis*, *PAp* and *Herm*. This does not look coincidental, and the result for *DAp* is no evidence to the contrary, owing to the minimal size of the sample.[52] Thus although these Ionian forms spread in the tradition like the neglect of digamma, they were avoided by some mainland poets. Hesiod is an interesting exception, providing further proof of close and sustained influence from Ionia or the Ionic tradition on his poetry. Elsewhere the avoidance of Ζηνός must be attributed to its absence from the vernacular dialects of the mainland, coupled with a cessation of Ionic influence on the diction. Note however that its exceedingly frequent use in *Aphr* is consonant with a vernacular from which it was absent, e.g. Lesbian, by 'hyperionism'.

Here at last we have a criterion that does coincide rather better with what might have been predicted from the spoken dialects. Our next criterion displays a similar pattern.

The behaviour of νῦ ἐφελκυστικόν or n-mobile was first examined systematically by Fr. Isler, who provided careful and extensive statistics for its use, both to obviate hiatus and to make a naturally light syllable heavy by position before a following consonant, in the entire range of Greek hexameter poetry to Nonnus. While the use to prevent hiatus remained roughly constant, the use before consonants diminished in later poetry, suggesting that further study of this as a possible chronological indicator might bear fruit.

Hoekstra[53] has since argued a rather different point, that the frequency of this usage increased in the course of our epic tradition. As a statistical approach will be indispensable to settle these questions, it is as usual crucial to establish exactly what we are counting. New figures are required, even if we follow Isler, because of some deficiencies in his work:

(i) He does not specify that he excludes cases before clusters of consonants, especially πλ- and other groups of mute and liquid, where our manuscripts often give n-mobile. I shall exclude these.

(ii) Outside Homer, he does not exclude cases before liquids, nasals and the other continuants σ and * ϝ, where light syllables may be scanned heavy for other reasons. Although not all words beginning with these sounds have this effect, and it might be permissible to include such forms as συ or μέν, even μή produces this effect on occasion by an etymologically unjustified extension of the principle, so this type of case is best omitted altogether. In any case it would not affect our conclusions to any degree.

(iii) The results from Hesiod and the *Hymns* are based on outdated texts, and therefore I have recounted according to the OCT, and the results have been checked against computer print-outs as usual. The figures for elegy and iambus were obtained by hand from the text of M. L. West.

In counting n-mobile, Isler admitted the following cases:

(a) verbs ending in -ϵ, e.g. φέρϵ(ν); (b) the suffix -θϵ(ν) in indeclinable roots, including ἑκάτερθϵ(ν), but not (ἀ)κρῆθεν, ἔνθεν etc., where the nasal is always present; (c) κϵ(ν); (d) the suffix -φι(ν), with σφι(ν), and also ἄμμι(ν), ὔμμι(ν); (e) dative plurals in -σι, e.g. τοῖσι(ν); (f) verbal endings in -σι, e.g. τίθησι(ν); (g) (ἐ)είκοσι(ν). His last category, ἐγώ(ν), is relevant only to hiatus. Hoekstra proposes more radical exclusions, which have not been adopted for the following reasons:

(i) κϵ(ν). However obscure etymologically, I see no cause to suppose that the nasal here was regarded as in any way different from other cases of n-mobile by Homer's time.

(ii) Hoekstra wishes to discount all categories ending in -ι, because of Schwyzer's idea that a *j*-glide may have been used instead to nullify hiatus. It is impossible that this affected cases where n-mobile is guaranteed by the metre before a following consonant! Indeed the existence of such cases shows that in the surviving epic n-mobile was also employed to obviate hiatus. Consequently in the figures given in table 22, I have followed Isler rather than Hoekstra.

I exclude cases before *δϝ-, but not those before πόλις and πόλεμος, where πτ- may have stood (very few).[54] ἕκαθεν is counted, although ἕκαθϵ does not happen to be attested: so too ἕνεκεν, where the form without n-mobile is only found in inscriptions. In the first column is given the number of lines in each work, then the number of cases of n-mobile as defined above before consonants, and finally the frequency per thousand lines (‰).

Individual books of Homer range as low as Hesiod and as high as *Aphr* in this criterion, and the risk that the result in any particular poem is misleading cannot be excluded; however the results accord convincingly with what we might have predicted from our knowledge of the dialects and the areas in which, from internal evidence, the poems seem to have originated, and here at last Hesiod unwittingly reveals that he did not really come from Ionia after all. The statistics suggest that in poetry from Ionia or of the Ionic 'school' n-mobile is frequently used to make position, and that this is linked with its prevalence in the Ionic dialect; whereas in poetry of other

Table 22. *The frequency of n-mobile before consonants in the epos*

Work	Verses	N-mobile +C	Frequency ‰ verses
Il	15693	559	35.6
Od	12110	451	37.2
Th	1022	22	21.5
Erga	828	18	21.7
Cat	c. 750	23	30.7
Aspis	424	10	23.6
Dem	495	22	44.4
DAp	181	11	60.8
PAp	365	5	13.7
Herm	580	9	15.5
Aphr	293	14	47.8

origin the device is less often employed, where it was alien to the poets' vernacular dialects.

Thus the licence is common in Homer and in *DAp* (by a Chian bard). Its frequent use in *Dem* is very interesting, as in other respects *Dem* is close to Hesiod. This may support an Attic origin; as Buck and others point out,[55] inscriptions show n-mobile to have been a marked characteristic of Attic–Ionic from the earliest times, and it is not found in verbal forms in early inscriptions elsewhere. Shorter works using the licence often are *Hy* 7 (twice in 59 lines), *Hy* 19 (5x in 49 lines), and the following that are less likely to be of Ionic origin: the *Megalai Ehoiai* (thrice in 26 verses), *Cypria* (twice in about 50 lines) and *Ilias Mikra* (thrice in 34 lines). These last two works may have originated in Aeolis, and we note that *Aphr* is also prone to use n-mobile, which is well-established in Sappho and Alcaeus,[56] but not in Lesbian inscriptions.[57]

It is encouraging that Hesiod's usage is consistent. *Cat* has a maximum of 30.7 cases per thousand lines, on the conservative estimate of its length as 750 lines (including *Aspis* 1–56 as usual); on a more generous estimate of 900 complete lines this yields 25.5 cases per thousand lines, not much different from the genuine Hesiod. This sort of figure may be more accurate, as several cases are restored. The *Aspis* is similar, while *PAp* and *Herm* use the licence even less, but do not jettison it completely. That all these poems have such results strengthens the view that they are not in general misleading.

We may derive further support from the practice of the elegiac poets of the archaic period (table 23). West's text was used, and for Theognis only the verses recognised as genuine by him.

In the case of Archilochus the sample is unreliably small: otherwise the Ionian poets use n-mobile freely. The Spartan Tyrtaeus hardly employs the device at all, but Theognis of Megara is fairly free with it, more so in fact than Solon. Solon's iambic and trochaic poems have three cases in sixty lines, or 50‰, which is comparable to Semonides (ten cases in 184 lines, or 54.3‰): the different metre means that these figures are not strictly comparable with those for elegiacs. According to Isler, later epic poets such as Aratus and Callimachus used it less often, except for Apollonius. The *Batrachomyomachia* has nine cases in 303 verses, or 29.7‰, by my figures.

As we have seen, poets like Hesiod appear to disfavour this usage rather than drop it entirely; or perhaps we should say that when confronted with a metrical problem they did not think of it as readily as Ionian poets did. For we cannot attribute many of the instances of it to traditional phraseology. Classifying them according to the system devised above,[58] only 4 out of 22 cases in *Th* occur in Class A or B phrases:

Class A: *Th* 173 = *Z 212, 323 = *Z 181.

Class B: *Th* 412 *πόρεν δέ οἱ ἀγλαὰ δῶρα* / ≅ Π 185* ∼ *ἀγλαὸν υἱόν*, cf. **π* 230 *ἔπορον* ∼; = *Herm* 470* (*ἔπορεν δέ τοι* ∼).

Th 871 *ἐκ θεόφιν γενεή*, cf. Ψ 347 ∼ *γένος ἦεν*/.

In the *Erga* not one of the eighteen cases is in such a phrase; in *Dem* and *Aphr*, which use n-mobile more often, proportions of no more than 3/22 and 2/14 respectively. This is because the use of n-mobile to make position was often a makeshift

Table 23. *The frequency of n-mobile before consonants in elegy and iambus*

Poet	Verses	N-mobile +C	Frequency ‰ verses
Archilochus	37	0	–
Mimnermus	83	4	48.2
Solon	219	4	18.3
Theognis	304	11	36.2
Tyrtaeus	154+	1	6.5
Xenophanes	72	3	41.7

device of composition, a means of escape from impasses when the tradition was otherwise deficient. *Th* 412 shows it in use to permit a convenient conjugation of a formula. There does not appear to be any difference in the number of verbal forms found in Hesiod, which suggests that its rarity in these mainland poets is not connected with the practice of the Locrian and Thessalian dialects, where only the dative plurals have n-mobile.[59]

Thus the situation has turned out to be more complex than envisaged by Hoekstra, but there is a sense in which he was correct: within the Ionic tradition itself there is an increase in the frequency of n-mobile making position not only from *Iliad* to *Odyssey*, but also a marked increase to *DAp*, where the result is for once quite certain: the increase is of the same order of magnitude as we have seen in other criteria. Hence it may be true that cases of enjambement with a run-over word in n-mobile do indicate 'evolutionary' trends, but this is part of a larger development, and one absent from the poetry of Hesiod and other mainland poets.

Here at last we have found two manifestations of regionalism in the Greek epic tradition which are both sufficiently frequent and unobvious enough to avoid the dangers inherent in more isolated peculiarities. That such manifestations are so arcane is an impressive testimony to the fundamental unity of the tradition.

In the next chapter we shall see how the evidence presented here for diachronic and regional developments may be correlated and interpreted, and some implications it has for the history of the Greek oral epic tradition as a whole.

CHAPTER 4

DIACHRONIC AND REGIONAL DEVELOPMENTS

In the preceding chapter we have scrutinised various linguistic criteria that appear to have undergone development in the course of the epic tradition: we will now turn to the conclusions to be drawn from their synthesis.

In all the criteria tested (except the frequency of n-mobile used to make position, where Hesiod diverges), we have seen almost invariably a change in the percentages of the same order of magnitude between the *Iliad* and the *Odyssey*, then a large shift in the same direction to the *Theogony*, and a smaller one to the *Erga*: the two poems of Hesiod stand in the same relation to each other as do the two monumental epics, but at a more advanced stage. Other criteria may be found which reflect the same pattern.[1] The next step is to answer the question, exactly how much more advanced is Hesiod and why, and where do the various hymns fit in?

There are two possible ways of quantifying the amount of development in the diction. The problem is that we must in effect devise means of equating the different scales for the ten criteria. At this stage the results for the use of n-mobile to make position will not be considered, as they are calculated on a different basis from the rest – frequency per thousand lines instead of the percentage of innovative versus traditional forms. In the other criteria we must discover how the facts that e.g. *Il* and *Th* have 17.2% and 33.7% neglects of digamma, but 51.9% and 38.8% of o-stem genitive singulars in *-οιο* respectively, can be fitted into a common framework along with a hundred or so other results for the eleven poems studied.

The first method is to plot each of the ten criteria onto a graph and adjust the scales to obtain the best possible fit, whether between all the poems or only between the four works of Homer and Hesiod. In the second method two fixed points are taken as standard, and the other works marked accordingly. This maximises the fit between the two works chosen as standard and reduces it elsewhere. It has the advantage that the other poems can be placed exactly in terms of the development of diction between the two poems. The other method is basically the same, and has been used to check that the two works that I have chosen as standard – *Il* and *Th* – have no aberrant results. I have selected these two works on the grounds that they are large and have closely grouped results with no apparent abnormalities.

The operation of this technique is displayed in figure 1. The horizontal axes present the percentage changes between *Il* and *Th* in the various criteria, while the common scale places the level of the *Iliad* at 0 and the *Theogony* at 3; thus all the results for these two poems are at the points on the graph corresponding to 0 and 3 respectively, while those for other works, plotted in terms of the various scales, may be read off on the common scale in terms of units of the development of the diction between the *Iliad* and *Theogony*. Next we must present the results solely in terms of the common scale mentioned above with one line for each poem.

This procedure is shown in figure 2; the results for *Il* and *Th* are again at 0 and 3 respectively. In all these charts the following symbols are used to mark the various criteria:

- *ϝ* Percentage of neglected digamma (pp. 42–8).
- *αο* Percentage of masculine a-stem genitive singulars in -*ᾱο* (pp. 48–9); the results from *Aspis* and the hymns are omitted, as based on five or fewer cases.
- *άων* Percentage of a-stem genitive plurals in -*άων* (pp. 49–50): *DAp* omitted (small sample).
- *οιο* Percentage of o-stem genitive singulars in -*οιο* (pp. 50–3).
- *ου* Percentage of o-stem genitive singulars in -*ου* that cannot be resolved (pp. 50–4).
- *οισι* Percentage of o- and a-stem dative plurals ending in -*σι* (pp. 54–7).
- *οις* Percentage of o- and a-stem dative plurals ending in -*ς* that do not stand (elided?) before vowels (pp. 54–7).

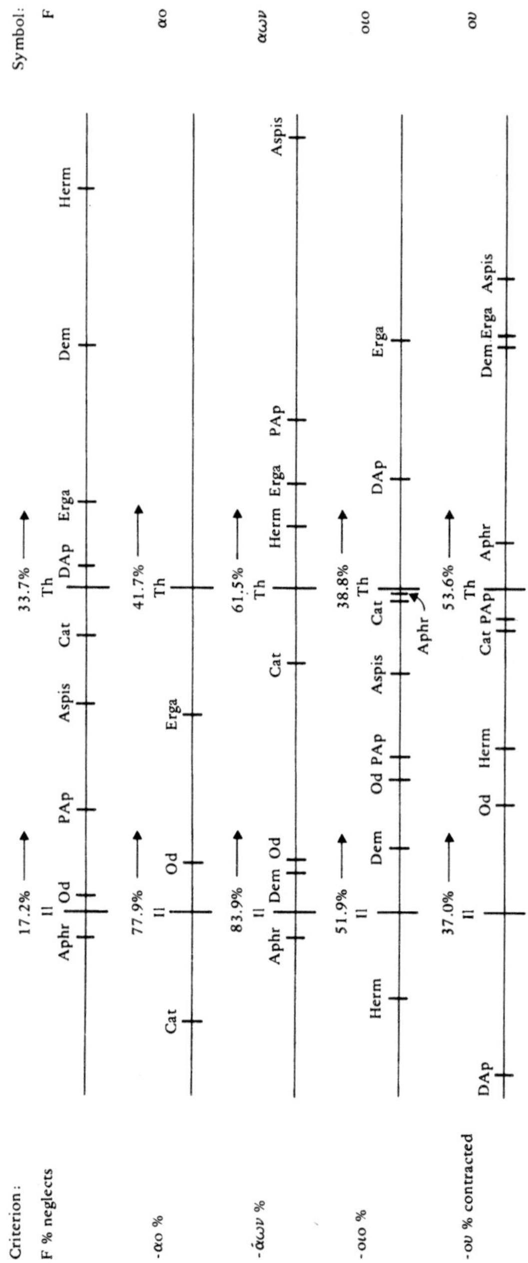

Figure 1: The correlation of the criteria

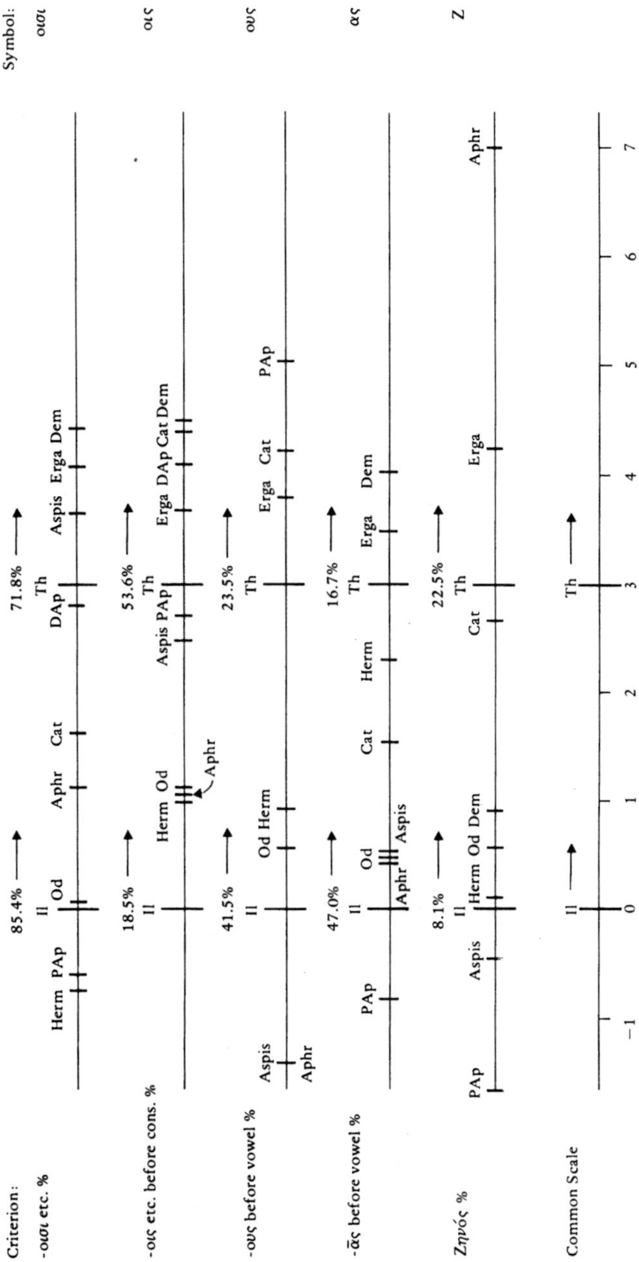

Figure 1: The correlation of the criteria, contd.

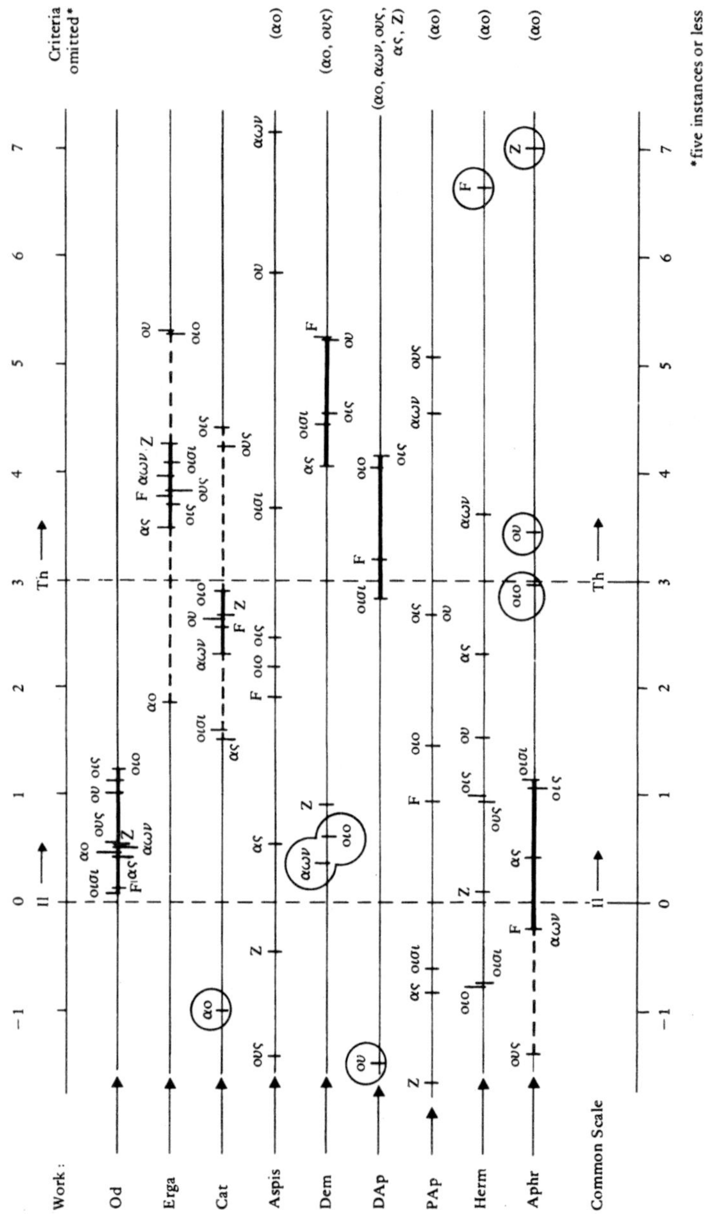

Figure 2: The criteria in the different poems compared

ους Percentage of o-stem accusative plurals standing before vowels (pp. 58–9): *Dem* and *DAp* omitted.

ας Percentage of a-stem accusative plurals in -ᾱς standing before vowels (pp. 58–60): *DAp* omitted.

Z Percentage of oblique cases of Ζεύς in Ζηνός etc. (pp. 62–3): *DAp* omitted.

It at once appears from figure 2 that most of the poems with which we are concerned have concentrations or clusters of results. The *Odyssey* is close to but always after the *Iliad*; the *Erga* in the same relation to the *Theogony*, although its results for the o-stem genitive singulars are more advanced. Groups may also be defined for *Cat* at c. 2.7 units on the common scale, for *DAp* (at c. 3.5 units) and *Dem* (c. 4.68). *Aphr* tends to cluster at about the Iliadic level, but exhibits advanced usage in the use of Ζηνός and in both of the o-stem genitive singulars (like the *Erga*). Three poems have wildly scattered results, *Aspis*, *PAp* and *Herm*.

These results may be grouped into three types:

(i) Archaic grouped: *Il*, *Od*, *Aphr*.

(ii) Advanced grouped: *Th*, *Erga*, *Cat*, *Dem*, *DAp*.

(iii) Inconsistent: *Aspis*, *PAp*, *Herm*.

What then do these results mean? Why do some poems have clusters of results, but others have a wide scatter? When the results are, in the main, clustered, why do some of them diverge? The answer to these questions demands careful consideration of the basic principles involved. Firstly, we must take account of random error. Some of the results divergent from the clusters may be unreliable and attributable to mere hazard. Such results must be discarded after statistical tests: this is true, for instance, of the *-αο* result for *Erga.*[2] Results which do not diverge merely at random are circled on figure 2: even when a result has been shown by statistical testing to be most unlikely to occur at random, the unlikely still remains possible! In compiling figure 2 I have circled those results with less than a 5% probability of occurring if the true frequency was at the level of the cluster of results. One-in-twenty cases is not itself a very satisfying level of probability to work with, and to derive methodological principles I shall use examples much less likely to be random than this.

One such case is the use of *-οιο* in *Dem*. Here the sample-size is a comfortable 75, and the odds are much better.[3] The chance that this is a random result is under 1 in 100. Here we can isolate the cause of the divergence with confidence, and it affords another basic principle. *Dem* has proportionately more cases of *-οιο* than does the *Odyssey*, but is more advanced than Hesiod's *Erga* by most other criteria. Now one can think of three dimensions to the evolution of the poetic diction – time, space and the poet's own stylistic choice. The overuse of *-οιο* here is clearly not chronological in cause (we know from other linguistic evidence that the poem does not date from Homer's time): nor can it be due to the influence of the poet's local dialect, as *-οιο* was not retained in the inscriptional dialects, and seems unlikely to have been current in the seventh century (except in East Thessalian perhaps: but the Hymn is more probably of Attic or Boeotian provenance).[4] Thus some sort of deliberate choice on the part of the poet or a predecessor is responsible. What sort of choice?

The reply is not far to seek. If we study the diction of Apollonius of Rhodes, for instance (any other Hellenistic or later hexameter poet would serve the purpose), we find him using *-οιο* more than Homer did,[5] but naturally enough rarely admitting the effects of digamma.[6] He clearly deemed *-οιο* a desirable archaic garnish for his style, and used it abundantly, indeed with exuberance, but was either unwilling or less probably unable to copy the archaic style in all its features, as his failure to observe digamma demonstrates. The discrepancy in the language of *Dem* is more limited, but does seem to be due to stylistic choice on the author's part. As he is repeatedly using an archaic morph not current in his own era's vernacular, I shall call such overuse of an archaic morph 'false archaism'. This is a slightly different use of the term from its normal denotation of an archaism *incorrectly formed or used*, such as the false interposition of digamma intervocalically in some Corcyrean and Corinthian verse-inscriptions by c. 600 (Friedländer 11a,b *Ποτειδάϝōνι*; id. 26.1 Τλ*ασίαϝο*).

Our type of false archaism results from conscious choice at some point in the tradition, but any oral singers who learnt from a poet who practised this style would take it for granted as part of the inherited tradition. Thus strictly, in any particular case, we have only a *terminus ante quem* for false archaism, as we cannot prove that the poet did not derive his usage from elsewhere. (For a further refinement in the typology of false archaism, see overleaf.) This type of archaism can be distinguished from the proportion of naturally current archaisms in an oral tradition because of the inconsistency when compared with other criteria, as in Apollonius' case.

Certain morphs are particularly favoured as spices to confer upon the poets' style a more archaic and exotic savour. Genitive singulars in *-οιο* and 'long' dative plurals in *-οισι* and *-ηισι* both contain an extra syllable of metrical utility, and possess the added virtue of being alien to most spoken dialects.[7] In *Herm*, for instance, we find archaic usage in both types of ending - more archaic than in the *Iliad* in fact, while other criteria are more advanced, digamma prodigiously so. Likewise *PAp* exhibits archaic treatment of the dative plurals, and *-οιο* occurs with suspicious frequency. Nobody believes for a moment that either Hymn is as old or older than Homer, so chronology is not the cause: nor is geography, as both morphs are foreign to the local speech of the poets.[8] *PAp* can in fact be dated reliably to the early sixth century,[9] and *Herm* is probably later still,[10] so again we are sampling mutton done up as lamb. However, in these poems the false archaism is not confined to criteria where one would expect conscious stylistic choice.

To illustrate: the *Pythian Hymn* postdates Hesiod - yet why is its frequency of, for example, contraction in *-ου* less than Hesiod's? Surely the poet did not deliberately set out to avoid placing this morph in metrical positions where it is guaranteed as contracted? How could he have had any inkling that *-ου* was contracted from **-οο* anyway? Some other factor is at work: close study of this Hymn indicates that the poet is ingesting a good deal of his diction, not from his immediate elders steeped in oral tradition (whose diction ought by now to be highly evolved), but from texts fixed at a much earlier stage of diction, in particular Homer's *Catalogue of Ships* in B and his *Odyssey.*[11] Profound influence of the *Shield of Achilles* in Σ on the *Aspis* has already been noted by several scholars:[12] this poem is similar in provenance and date to *PAp*, and similarly has several criteria less advanced than Hesiod's *Theogony*.

We may consequently distinguish two sub-types of false archaism: false archaism limited in scope as in *Dem*, where a poet deliberately peppers his verse with a limited number of archaic morphs to obtain an archaic effect; and more extensive false archaism, when poets derive much of their language and phraseology from texts fixed at an epoch long past, as in *Aspis*, *PAp* and *Herm*. This is probably, but not necessarily, linked to the spread of literacy, depending on whether we think that the text of Homer was fixed by written texts, careful memorisation, or a combination of the two. I see no obstacle to the existence of dictated texts, certainly none in c. 600. However, these poets may not have picked up Homeric diction from reading texts of Homer themselves, but only from hearing others recite; the orality of each poem must be assessed on its merits (in Chapter 2, for example, I concluded that the composition of *PAp* was not affected by writing, any more than the poems of Homer and Hesiod were affected by it). Cf. Lord's remarks on the use and effect of the song-books in Jugoslavia (*ST* 23, 137). I shall use the term 'false archaism' to mean false archaism of limited scope and not the more extensive kind, unless stated: the latter is discussed at 126 f. and 173 below. For false archaism as false formation, cf. sup. 77. As the scope of false archaism is determined by the number of features displaying it, the term may be used of individual features (as in what follows) without any specification as to scope.

False archaism may be identified in the following criteria:

1. Digamma: *Aspis*, *PAp*. If these results are not merely due to loans from Homer, both poets, seemingly from Boeotia or thereabouts, would have no difficulty in maintaining the effects of a phoneme still pronounced in their vernacular.

2. -αο: *Cat* (significant at 0.5% when tested against the cluster at 2.8 units on the common scale).[13]

3. -άων: *Dem* (significant at 1%).[14]

4. -οιο: *Dem*, *Aspis*, *PAp*, *Herm*.

5. -ου: *DAp* (significant at 1%).[15] There seems no reason why a poet should archaise falsely in this criterion and no other. I cannot explain this result, unless it is sheer chance.

6. 'Long' dative plurals: *PAp*, *Herm*.

7. Both o- and a-stem accusative plurals are treated as in Homer by *Aspis*: *PAp* has a high a-stem result, but is advanced in the o-stems, *Herm* the converse. This complicated matter needs discussion elsewhere.[16]

8. *Aspis*, *Dem*, *PAp* and *Herm* all use Ζηνός much less than expected. In *Dem*, the small sample-size means that the result is not statistically significant when tested against the cluster at 4.7 units on the common scale;[17] the other poems have no clusters, and so cannot be tested. However, the fact that they all ignore this Ionic innovation is remarkable, and characteristic of what post-Hesiodic mainland verse we can analyse. This is not, as explained above,[18] due to false archaism: no poet would avoid Ζηνός on chronological grounds, as indeed the form would seem poetic to those who did not know this Aegean innovation in their own speech. Instead, it must have dropped out of the tradition after Hesiod, as it was alien to the spoken dialects of the mainland and so not readily thought of during composition (the two occurrences in *Aspis* and *Dem* are in Hesiodic and Homeric phrases, but this is not true of *Herm*). The same applies to the use of n-mobile to make position.

A few results are more advanced:

1. Digamma in *Herm*. This might be due to hyperionism, or to a desire to avoid what were felt as metrical anomalies (this poet's versification is more careful than that of most, as we saw in Chapter 2).
2. Advanced results for both criteria in the o-stem genitive singulars are paired in *Erga* and *Aphr*. This is certainly not random in the case of *Aphr*,[19] but may be in *Erga*.[20]

3. *Aphr* has an indisputably high use of Ζηνός; the best explanation seems to be that the hymnodist is trying hard to compose in Ionic, and succeeding only too well in this particular. As Ζηνός is not an archaism, this is not false archaism but hyperionism.[21]

Having seen which of the results falling outside the clusters are unlikely to be due to chance, and how most of them are accounted for, we must inquire into the meaning of the clusters themselves. These are shown in table 24. The point on the common scale at which the average or mean of the cluster lies is followed by the number of criteria included in the cluster, and then the spread of the cluster about its mean. On the right are listed errant results; those more advanced than the cluster are marked with a +. Cases of false archaism where there is no cluster are bracketed; poems with a low use of n-mobile are shown.

Above I listed three factors that might affect a poet's diction: time, place and style. The neglect of Ζηνός and n-mobile are caused by a combination of time and place, and false archaism is a function of archaic models and stylistic choice. There remains for evaluation the chronological factor. Was Pavese right to attribute the linguistic differences he noticed between Homer and Hesiod solely to region and style, assuming a 'mainland tradition' not inherited via Ionia, and different styles for different types of poem, war-narrative, peace-narrative, theological and rustic poetry each being less conservative than the preceding? These hypotheses are easily refuted,[22] but it is valuable to see the alternative to a chronological explanation of the divergences clearly set out.

The approach in this study is based on the *a priori* hypothesis that, in an oral or largely oral tradition, we expect the frequency of archaisms to decline and innovations to increase as old formulae are gradually forgotten and new phraseology is brought in. To test this, one must quantify archaisms and innovations and ascertain whether there is any consistent pattern of development. Chapter 3 presented the evidence

Table 24. *Clusters of criteria and the errant results*

Work	Cluster at	Criteria	Spread	Errant results
Il	(0)	(10)	(0)	nil
Od	0.6	10	1.2	nil
Th	(3)	(10)	(0)	n-mobile
Erga	3.85/3.94	7/10	0.8/3.4	n-mob., *αο*?, *οιο*+?, *ου*+?
Cat	2.61/2.76	5/9	0.6/2.9	n-mob., *αο*, *οισι*?, *ας*?, *οις*+?, *ους*+?
Aspis	no cluster defined			n-mob., (*ους*, *ας*, Z, ϝ?, *οιο*??)
Dem	4.68	5	1.2	*αων*, *οιο*, Z?
DAp	3.54	4	1.3	*ου*
PAp	no cluster defined			n-mob. (ϝ, *οιο*, *οισι*, *ας*, Z)
Herm	no cluster defined			n-mob. (ϝ+, *οιο*, *οισι*, Z)
Aphr	0.1	6	2.5	*οιο*+, *ου*+, Z+

that there is such a pattern; that in nearly all criteria there is a consistent change, not only in the direction of the shift but also in its magnitude, from Homer to Hesiod. Even the percentages of the raw data shift by the same amount in many cases.[23] How could this come about? How could poets manage to sprinkle their verses with just the right amount of archaism and innovation in so many disparate criteria of such high incidence? Can we suppose that they could deliberately weigh out the proper quantities of ingredients again and again? Surely this is unacceptable. The epic poet may use artificial diction, but the purposeful concoction of consistent and imperceptible shifts of language is far from his spirit. Such shifts must be unconscious.

It follows that, when we find a cluster of results, this implies that the poet concerned is using the traditional diction 'naturally', at more or less the stage at which he found it. Thus, for example, Homer and Hesiod must have found the tradition at linguistically discrete stages, Hesiod's stage being more advanced than Homer's.

But does 'more advanced' necessarily equal 'later'? Causes of uncertainty can be imagined easily. Firstly, the circumstances of individual poets. One might learn his diction in his youth, and preserve it substantially unaltered to his dotage:

any pupils he taught would acquire more archaic diction than their peers. However, for this to happen the bard would have to be rather an uninspired reproducer of the tradition, or geographically isolated, or both. At the other extreme, a great poet would probably make great innovations and elaborations in retelling the songs of others, and spearhead the advance of the tradition. From the start we must admit a certain indefinable latitude of individual variation.

Next we must consider the content of the poems: by this I mean not Pavese's broad categories of genre, but the more subtle factor of how developed the tradition was for coping with the poet's wishes, and how much of the material transmitted to him he used without substantial alteration. One might argue, for example, that more was contributed to the *Iliad* than to the *Odyssey* by the tradition, and less by the monumental poet. In the absence of the *Ur-Ilias* and *Ur-Odyssee* proof either way is unobtainable; I suspect that the greater the poet, the more he makes his sources his own. This is certainly true of such Jugoslav *guslari* as Avdo Međedović:[24] and it is also true in the one place where we have two versions of similar material by the same poet, namely Hesiod's two versions of the tale of Prometheus and the creation of the first woman. It is notable that the diction of *Erga* 1–200 is on the whole more advanced than that of the *Theogony*, although the mythological portion of *Erga* is less advanced than the remainder in language.[25] Hesiod's diction did advance; and *nothing contradicts the hypothesis that the* Iliad *and* Odyssey *are also the work of one man whose diction advanced with his age.*

What about regional factors? Forms that are old-fashioned or forgotten in one area may be standard in another: thus ϝ-, *-ᾱο* and *-ᾱ́ων* are the norm in Boeotia long after their modification in Ionia, but the reverse applies to *-οισι*. This factor would not apply to all criteria, however; we would expect it to affect only a few scattered results, and it does not explain the clusters. Nor can the other extreme of hyperionism do so. There is no reason to doubt that sometimes poets, trying hard to compose in an alien dialect, might go too far in being Ionic;

but reflection shows that this is unlikely to have affected more than a few criteria: there is nothing particularly Ionic about contracted o-stem genitive singulars, let alone 'short' dative plurals where elision is out of the question, yet in general these do not behave at all differently from the other criteria.

Another factor to be considered is training and organisation.[26] In Ionia, according to ancient testimony, at least some of the bards were organised and trained in a guild; it would not be surprising if, sooner or later, they were taught to avoid modifications and neologisms as the idea of a fixed text gained ground. Nonetheless, *DAp*, certainly the creation of an Ionian poet, shows considerable evolution in its diction, proving that the Ionic tradition continued to evolve, at least to this point.

Before contemplating the vexed matter of the development of the tradition elsewhere, a brief review of Ionia itself is needed. The *Iliad* reveals knowledge of such localities as the Cayster (Β 459ff.) and the lachrymose Niobe on Mount Sipylus (Ω 614ff.); in the *Odyssey* the incidental reference to the palm-tree on Delos (ζ 162ff.) looks significant.[27] Nobody seriously doubts that both epics originated in Ionia, and the linguistic evidence is in accord: nor can there be any doubt about the Ionian provenance of *DAp*. These poems are the nucleus of the Ionian tradition.

Within this tradition linguistic development is far from negligible. In all ten criteria, and also in n-mobile (not to mention others like γῆ),[28] there is a consistent progression from *Iliad* to *Odyssey*, and there are only three criteria where the progression does not continue to *DAp* according to the available evidence. Moreover in all but one of the criteria where the sample is of a reasonable size, there is a consistently large gap between *DAp* and *Od*, just as there is a small but consistent difference between the two monumental epics. In terms of the diction, about five times the interval between the Homeric poems elapses before *DAp* is reached.[29] That *Od* is later than *Il* is not in doubt; the design of the former as a sequel, and its advance in ideas about the responsibility of the individual, compel this sequence. But we cannot of course equate these intervals directly with years, because of the idiosyncratic variations discussed above, which may have caused the rate of change to have varied unpredictably. Nevertheless, it is difficult to avoid the conclusion that this development correlates approximately with the passage of time.

As we have seen, several mainland poems possess clusters of results too, representing something other than the efforts of bards struggling to pepper their verses with a suitable admixture of Ionic forms. As in Ionia, the language of Hesiod and the other mainland poets with clusters of results must approximate to that of the tradition as they knew it. But did they know the same tradition as their Ionian contemporaries? This in fact constitutes two separate problems:

(i) Did the diction of mainland poetry develop in the same way as in Ionia?

(ii) Was it in advance of, at the same stage as, or behind the Ionic tradition?

The first question is easy. In nine of the ten criteria on which figure 2 is based, *Th* stands to *Erga* as does *Il* to *Od*: it is always less advanced. That *Th* is prior is established from a comparison of *Th* 225 with *Erga* 11ff. (the doctrine of the two Erides).[30] We have already seen that content has not affected this; yes, there was the same development.

This answer has an inescapable implication: the mainland tradition was under Ionian influence. Traces of local traditions which were not may survive in a few scraps such as the Attic formula λαμπράν τε σελήνην,[31] *Ilias Parva* fr. 12,[32] and a few hexameters by Alcman on Homeric topics,[33] as well as some of the epichoric verse-inscriptions: but no extended poem still extant is uninfluenced by the Ionic diction, as Pavese would have us believe.[34]

Why was this influence so dominant? Edwards[35] offers the sole plausible explanation: 'only an exceptional flowering of the Ionian epic, such as Homer represents, can account for the pre-eminence of Ionic as the language of hexameter poetry in Hesiod's time'.

The second question is more difficult, and the best that

can be done is a weighing of probabilities. I have already shown that the conservatism of Boeotian and other mainland dialects, and the possibility of hyperionism, can in Hesiod's case be disregarded, because of the clustering of his results. It is equally problematic to suppose that Hesiod could have learnt his diction at the same stage as Homer, and then introduced all these Ionian modifications, when on his own showing he was not an Ionian and never lived there. The mere fact that his diction is Ionic cannot disprove that he is Homer's contemporary; but the vast amount of advanced diction in all criteria is a great obstacle.[36] Hesiod composed in the same tradition as Homer: he learnt his diction at a more advanced stage of that same tradition: and, in the same tradition, more advanced must in general mean later, in both relative and absolute terms.

There is one major complication in *Cat*, where the cluster of results is on average *less* advanced by a small margin than *Th*. This is unexpected, because, of course, *Cat* is the *sequel* to the *Theogony*. The difference is not very large, smaller in fact than the gap between *Th* and *Erga*, and could well be dismissed as due to random statistical variation, assuming that *Cat* is really contemporary with *Th* or not much later. But this option is in fact closed, I think. The difference between *Th* and *Cat* is somewhat accentuated if we transfer the disputed passage at the end of the *Theogony* (lines 901–1022) to *Cat*, and re-calculate all the statistics. The effect of doing so is presented in Appendix C. The diction of this passage is consistently less advanced than the rest of *Th*. If it is transferred, *Th* moves slightly forward in relation to the other poems, but not enough to alter their relative positions: however this does emphasise that the cluster of results at a level slightly anterior to *Th* is a reality.

This is quite contrary to what we expect, but my proviso that we must be prepared for a certain degree of idiosyncratic variation between poets should be kept in mind. We can quantify this variation only by analogies with that observed within single poems, as in Appendix B, where the divergence between

Erga 1–200 and the remainder of the poem is very reminiscent of that between *Th* and *Cat* as wholes. Linguistic tools are inevitably somewhat blunt, and if it seems arbitrary to suggest that a poet contemporary with Hesiod may show up as a third of a unit prior to him, or that Hesiod himself may vary by this amount (as is in fact proven), this seems to me less arbitrary than to reject the well-documented linguistic evolution as an approximate chronological indicator.

Before examining historical evidence for dating some parts of the poem, I must deal with the question of interpolation. The loose structure of *Cat* would seem to invite interpolations, whether brief or longer, by interested parties who might feel that their pretended ancestors had been unjustly slighted or omitted. It is generally assumed that this did happen, although it must at once be added that there is not a single case where interpolation into this poem has been reliably demonstrated, except that of the *Aspis*. If substantial interpolations have occurred, the diction is likely to be mixed and misleading to our inquiry. Stylistically, I find the fragments homogeneous, but this subjective finding can scarcely be confirmed by science, given the fragmentary state of the whole.

Let us, with these important caveats, treat the poem as a unit. The historical evidence for its date is meagre, and not as decisive as might seem at first glance.[37] The *locus classicus* for dating *Cat* is frr. 215ff.,[38] but on present evidence we cannot be at all sure that this passage is related to the foundation of Cyrene in Libya c. 631. Nor does the apparent knowledge of a passage in the *Iliad* assist us.[39]

If this is so, nothing contradicts the apparent linguistic date of *Cat*, provided we are prepared to admit a certain latitude of individual variation in the pace of linguistic change. The style of *Cat* is that of a composer with less range but some fluency in the diction, and otherwise very like Hesiod. The *communis opinio* that the continuation of *Th* and *Cat* itself is not his has been unquestioned of late; it rests on the obvious stylistic differences between the two works, and on the dating of the passages just mentioned. Otherwise the poem's diction is close to Hesiod's. It is inconceivable that *Cat* ever stood alone without a *Theogony* preceding it; if the dating *can* be trusted in detail (and I advance this with no great confidence), it would seem that our *Theogony* has replaced an earlier one, whether by someone else or by Hesiod himself.[40] But a better explanation for the discrepancy is surely the inevitable bluntness of our linguistic implements, which cannot be expected to be accurate within a decade. The amount of innovation by particular poets, and what they learnt from predecessors, must be expected to vary over short periods, and even from poem to poem. But the consistency of the diction, the absence of widespread false archaism, and the presence of Ζηνός, are strong arguments against dating this poem much, if at all, after Hesiod.

There is one further direction in which these statistical techniques can be extended: to provide a sequence and relative placing for the start of the linguistic innovations during the prehistory of the epos. Noting that digamma is neglected 17% of the time in the *Iliad* but 33% in the *Theogony*, the point at which digamma would be neglected 0% of the time can be calculated, and the relative position of this point plotted in terms of the common scale of the evolution of the epic diction. The procedure is demonstrated on figure 3. Counting *Il* as 0 and *Th* as 3 units (as in the previous figures), we obtain the following sequence:

1. *-οιο* ceases to be sole o-stem genitive singular ending: -11.0.
2. Contraction in **-οο* first appears: -6.7.[41]
3. O- and a-stem dative plurals begin to admit elision: -3.2.[42]
4. Digamma is first neglected: -3.0.
5. *-αο* ceases to be sole a-stem masculine genitive singular ending: -1.8.
6. Quantitative metathesis first appears in *-άων*: -1.7.
7. The Ionic declension Ζηνός etc. first appears: -1.6.
8. 'Short' o- and a-stem dative plurals arise which cannot be elided: -1.5.

9, 10. O- and a-stem accusative plurals being to be biassed

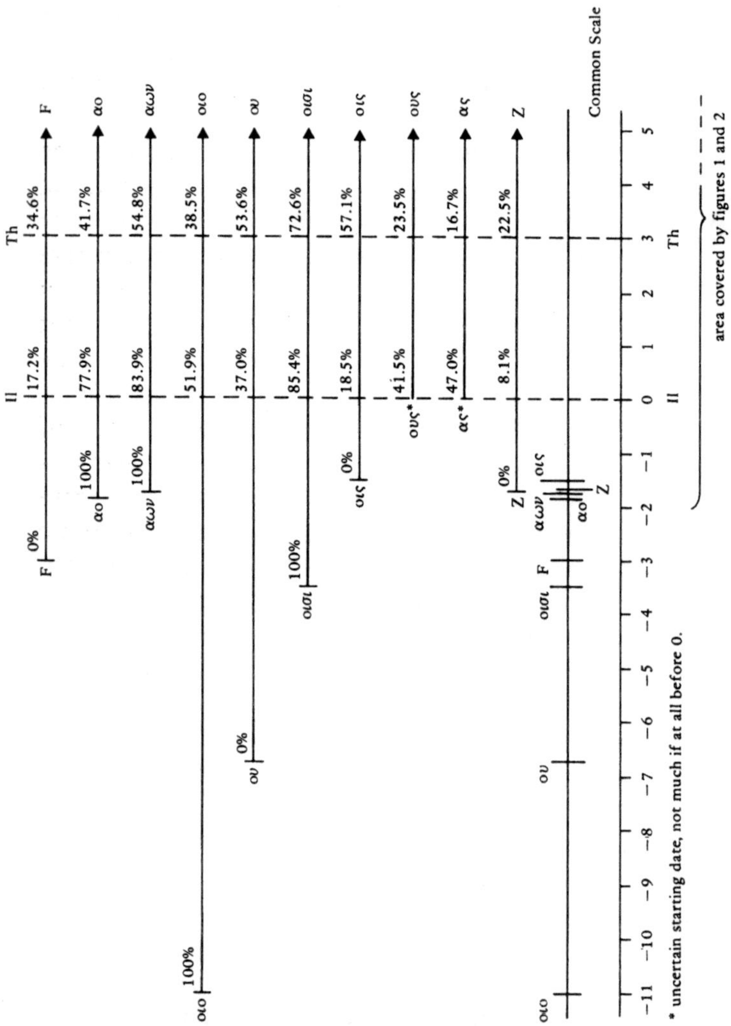

Figure 3: The relative dating of developments in pre-Homeric epic diction

towards appearing before consonants: not before -1.4 and -0.4 respectively.[43]

This sequence has interesting implications. Only by means of its internal consistency can we test the reliability of this sequence; there is nothing against it by this test. In these illiterate epochs the absolute dates for these developments are unknown and unknowable, especially if regional vagaries are taken into account. There is little evidence for Ionia, when we consider how sound-shifts often spread not by inheritance from a reconstructed ancestral dialect, but by geographical convergence among neighbours: there is less still for other areas, such as Aeolis. But the pattern of the changes as reconstructed here is internally coherent, and accords interestingly with an old theory about the prehistory of the epic. It is not Ionia with which we are concerned regarding most of the developments, but Aeolis.

It is a well-established but currently unfashionable fact of Homeric scholarship that the oral epic tradition passed at some stage through an Aeolic phase.[44] Of course our *Iliad* cannot be mutated into Aeolic, as Fick tried to prove; but there is a residue of Aeolic forms that stubbornly resist modern attempts to annihilate them, as Chantraine confesses.[45] The hostility to Aeolisms arises from a preference for the neater theory that the epos was brought straight to Ionia from Attica and the Peloponnese, thus descending directly from major southern centres of Mycenaean civilisation: the Aeolic forms are attributed to passing exchanges with a parallel epic tradition.[46]

Transient contacts with Lesbian bards will not however suffice: we are not faced merely with isolated forms borrowed for their metrical convenience. This explanation might do for such Asiatic Aeolisms as *ζα-* for *δια-* in compounds, *ὄππως* and *ὄπποτε*, or the original Aeolic *ἔμμεν* and even the (frequently used) blend of Aeolic and Ionic *ἔμμεναι*, standard in the vernacular of Lesbos and adjacent coasts. But it will not do for some other phenomena, the most important of which is the treatment of *-āo*. If the Ionians were simply borrowing metrically valuable forms from adjacent dialects, we would expect them to convert them into the currency of their own speech as far as possible: thus we expect to find genitive singulars in *-ηο* and genitive plurals in *-ήων* instead of *-āο* and *-άων*, but we do not. An identical dilemma is posed by the Aeolic preposition *ποτί*, equivalent to Ionic *πρός*: the East Greek expected form is *posi*, with assibiliation, and this has now turned up in Mycenaean. If the Ionians were drawing on an inherited Ionic tradition, we would expect them to be using the assibiliated form. Evidently the reason why they took over *ποτί* is because they no longer knew *posi*, which implies that if they inherited a Mycenaean tradition they lost some rather crucial pieces of its basic substructure. The same is true of the adoption of *-āο*, as K. Meister[47] argued long ago: if the Ionians took their genitives singular from an ancestral Ionic tradition, we would expect them to use the latest form that was metrically identical and did not disrupt old formular systems, i.e. *-ηο*, and to front long alpha just as was normal in everyday Ionic speech. Therefore Meister concluded that genitive singulars in *-āο* did not become *-ηο* because the Ionians adopted the ending when they were already using forms with quantitative metathesis, i.e. *-εω*.

Could the Ionians have taken over genitives in *-āο* and *-άων* at this time as part of the incidental borrowing that is postulated? To this we can firmly answer no. *-āο* cannot have been borrowed from without as an isolated form, as it is not only very frequent but (more important) glutinously embedded in many formular systems, and the same applies with equal force to *-άων*. Therefore the Ionians must have taken over the old formulae for a-stem genitives when they were themselves already using forms with quantitative metathesis; and the formulae for a-stem genitives are such a crucial and characteristic part of the epic diction *in toto* that it must follow that they adopted the whole of the epic diction at this stage.

This study contributes new evidence for the Aeolic phase. The point at which quantitative metathesis appeared in the traditional diction is established at -1.7 units on the common scale, according to the a-stem genitives. This should represent the stage at which the Ionians took over the Aeolic tradition.

It does not give the date of quantitative metathesis in Ionia, which must by Meister's argument have happened somewhat earlier, at least in the area which moulded the epic diction to its final shape. For as we see it the diction has undergone some evolution subsequent to metathesis of quantity: as Wathelet notes,[48] disyllabic -εω, -έων are very rare, the former indeed extinct; the prevailing species are monosyllabic with synizesis. This implies that the earlier changes, or at least those directly preceding, belong to the era of Aeolic diction. Of these the most prominent is the neglect of initial digamma before vowels. Hoekstra[49] has already suggested from his study of the epic diction that the loss of initial digamma was recent in the tradition, but metathesis of quantity more recent still.

The neglect of digamma thus began in the Aeolic phase of the epos, before its adoption in Ionia. This is important, if correct. Both branches of mainland Aeolic, in common with the vast majority of the Greek dialects, retained initial digamma until the fifth century or later. The only dialects which did not are Ionic and those adjacent to Ionic, namely Attic, island Doric and Lesbian.[50] Clearly the epic tradition was not borrowed from the Dorian isles like Thera, nor are there any organic Atticisms indicative of an Attic phase wherein digamma might have begun to be neglected; and given the other Asiatic Aeolisms about which there can be no doubt, such as ἔμμεναι, there is nowhere else but Lesbos whence the tradition could have come. Although there is no later parallel to a genre switching dialect, conditions in later centuries of literacy and improved communications were rather different from those prevailing down to the middle of the eighth century; and scattered indications persist from historical times that the dialect of hexameter poetry was not always fixed.[51] One obstacle to acceptance of the Aeolic phase has always been the obscurity of the historical circumstances of the transition from Aeolic to Ionic; but in fact archaeological, historical and onomastic material invites us to assume a northward spread of Ionians at the expense of Aeolians in precisely the area where Homer is most insistently located by tradition.[52]

Aeolis is in fact a peculiarly appropriate region for the elaboration of the legends and stories underlying the *Iliad* and *Odyssey*. Not only is Achilles from Phthia an Aeolian hero, but so too is Agamemnon, whose self-styled descendants ruled in Cyme and in Mytilene to Alcaeus' day, while those of Hector and Aeneas, their prominent opponents, held sway in parts of the Troad nearby: moreover Lesbos had designs on the Hellespontine region in historical times, and these claims may have been upheld by the existence or fabrication of a long pedigree. All the essentials for a 'national' epic on the Trojan theme were present in Aeolis, including the possibility of a sympathetic portrayal of some Trojan characters. Thus no major leap of faith is needed to believe in an Aeolian genesis of elements of the Trojan story. As Meuli[53] showed that an *Argonautica* underlies episodes in the wanderings of Odysseus, so Bethe, Murray and others have proved that incidents and characters in the *Iliad* derive from Thessalian and Boeotian sagas, including a *Thebaid*: Andromache for instance, and probably Hector too, as well as many of his opponents, originated in this way.[54] Is it sheer coincidence that these cycles of tales blend an Aeolic savour with the participation of heroes from most parts of the mainland, including the Peloponnese?

The Lesbian phase in the prehistory of the epos accounts for the curious behaviour of the o-stem dative plurals, wherein we expected the inherited instrumental morph -οις to be much commoner than in actuality. Lesbian altered original -ονς in the accusative plural to -οις after the migration to Asia Minor (in this diverging from East Thessalian). After this time, it would be natural for Lesbian bards to shun the short instrumental in -οις in favour of -οισι.[55] Sappho and Alcaeus use τοῖς and ταῖς in the article: the sequence of changes revealed here shows that these arose in elision before vowels rather than the 'haplology' advocated by Kretschmer. Like Ζηνός, 'short' dative plurals where elision is impossible do not arise until after the Ionic phase has begun, as signalled by quantitative metathesis, nor do the light accusative plurals.

Can the distances between these changes in the diction be relied upon, as well as their sequence? Parry, in a seminal discussion of the rate of change in different oral poetries, wrote that 'the language of oral poetry changes as a whole neither faster nor slower than the spoken language, but in its parts it changes readily where no loss of formulas is called for, belatedly when there must be such a loss, so that the traditional diction has in it words and forms of everyday use side by side with others that belong to earlier stages of the language'.[56] There is a suggestive piece of evidence to support his insight: in several of the linguistic criteria the percentage shifts between *Il* and *Th* are the same, *even though the innovations have different starting-points*: ϝ, οιο, ου, οισι, ους and Z all advance by 13–18% between *Il* and *Th*,[57] although αο, αων, οις and ας move, for some reason, by greater amounts.[58] The coincidence of the two o-stem genitive singular criteria with much more recent innovations suggests that the rate of change did in general remain steady over the period between the start of these post-migrational innovations and the time of Hesiod.

If the rate of development did remain steady, we are still left with only a series of relative placings and intervals: absolute dates must be derived by other means. Using two fixed points, we can offer dates that will still be approximate only, given idiosyncratic variations. In Appendix E, I give tables to display the consequences of taking various fixed points. The main conclusion is that Homer's date has to be raised unacceptably high for Hesiod to antedate c. 700. In fact *Th* is best dated to the decades before 670: the arguments are given below.[59] If the *Iliad* was fixed at c. 750 (a view which seems to be gaining ground), we obtain the following sequence: appearance of *-*oo*, c. 1050; contraction in *-*oo*, c. 930; neglect of digamma, c. 830; quantitative metathesis, c. 800; (*Il*, c. 750;) *Od* c. 735; *Cat*, c. 680; (*Th*, c. 670) *DAp*, c. 655; *Erga*, c. 650; *Dem*, c. 625. The inception of false archaism[60] and rarity of Ζηνός in *Dem* recur and mesh in neatly in *Aspis* and *PAp*, dated historically to the opening decades of the sixth century, wherein the diction is to an increasing extent drawn from fixed texts of far older works, especially Homer's. But this is only an example of how the sequence can be articulated. Many problems remain unsolved in the analysis and interpretation of the preceding statistical studies, some of which will be examined in more detail in the context of the individual Hymns. But the glottochronometric technique has at least provided a framework, and a framework which expresses in quantified form the intuitions of a solid majority of scholars who have studied these questions since the inauguration of Ptolemy's Museum at Alexandria.

Excursus: the date of Hesiod and the Lelantine War

Some evidence associates Hesiod with the Lelantine War between Eretria and Chalcis. Hesiod tells us that he took part once in the funeral games of one Amphidamas at Chalcis.[61] Plutarch adds that the latter was killed in a sea-battle during the Lelantine War,[62] a circumstantial detail which, as West remarks,[63] is unlikely to have been invented.[64] It is of course possible that the sources may have confused two men of the same name, and that Hesiod sang for a relative, grandfather or grandson of Plutarch's Amphidamas, but West's suggestion that specific references in the *Theogony* are eminently suited to such an occasion, and that our *Theogony* was therefore the poem Hesiod performed on that occasion, is extremely persuasive.[65]

However, the date of the Lelantine War is itself not settled, whether Hesiod can be linked with it or not. There is dispute over its very nature: was it a brief but severe struggle, or rather a prolonged series of wars and border raids that spanned more than one generation? If the latter, then clearly it will help us little in dating Hesiod: but against this is Strabo's remark[66] that in general the Chalcidians and Eretrians were on friendly terms. This statement is largely unsupported and has been questioned.[67] However long the war was, two main dates are offered for its climactic events: the late eighth century, or the mid-seventh.[68]

The main arguments for thinking the war occurred in the

late eighth century are these. Firstly, the synchronism with Hesiod. There seems to be a widespread unawareness of the circularity of this argument. Secondly, in 734 Eretrian colonists were ejected from Corcyra by the Corinthians. This is compatible with the systems of alliances deduced by modern scholarship for the Lelantine War.[69] But it by no means proves that the Lelantine War ensued shortly afterwards: the allies may have lined up as they did owing to traditional ties of long standing and the discovery of common interests long before. In any case, Corinth seems to have taken over some Chalcidian sites in the West as well.[70]

Thirdly, Coldstream[71] adduces several pieces of archaeological and historical evidence for trouble in Euboea in the late eighth century. The settlement at Lefkandi was abandoned c. 710, at which time the heroon at the west gate of Eretria was built for the bodies of warriors and their relatives (perhaps at first merely the burial-plot of a noble *genos*?). He connects this with reports that Corinth built ships for Samos,[72] that Rhegium was founded from Chalcis after a bad harvest, and that the Eretrians expelled from Corcyra were stoned when they tried to return home (but might they not have been exiles?). This is all circumstantial, and even if Coldstream is right there is evidence that the war may have lasted into the seventh century. Archilochus (fr. 3) says that the warrior lords of Euboea will fight not with bows or slings, but with swords, for they are skilled in this type of warfare. Forrest[73] interprets this as a reference to the supersession of more old-fashioned methods by hoplite tactics, and suggests that Archilochus refers with a shudder of fear to a threat of war in Euboea that never materialised, which would be far worse than the Lelantine War had been because of the new tactics (he thinks of the Acanthus incident of c. 655). But it is better to suppose that Archilochus refers to the gentlemanly agreement between the two sides in the Lelantine War recorded by Strabo, μὴ χρῆσθαι τηλεβόλοις.[74] This pact, inscribed in the Artemisium at Amarynthus, may have been mentioned by Ephorus: such an inscription would be unlikely in the eighth century, but its terms accord fully with the spirit of the seventh.[75] Forrest[76] deems it absurd to ban weapons which the hoplite reform was rendering obsolete anyway. Indeed: but the pact seems unlikely to be doing that. Greenhalgh[77] more plausibly suggests that the war was fought with mounted hoplites, and that missiles were banned to avoid injuries to the horses, on which the rule of the aristocracies in both cities depended. Thus there is reason to think that the war lasted until Archilochus was of an age to comment on it, i.e. well into the seventh century. Amphidamas (we believe) was killed in a sea-battle. Richardson has acutely pointed out[78] that Thucydides (I 13. 4) dated the oldest known sea-battle (fought between Corinth and Corcyra) to c. 681 or c. 664. If Thucydides is right, and Hesiod did perform at Amphidamas' funeral, then it follows that it took place no earlier than this, and that Hesiod was composing poetry at roughly the same date as Archilochus.[79]

Can these historical arguments, replete with uncertainties as they are, be reconciled with literary considerations? West has attempted to use alleged cases of *exemplum* and *imitatio* to establish a *terminus ante quem* for Hesiod of c. 650.[80] There are grave difficulties in the method,[81] as most of the parallels he lists may simply be formulae from the oral epic tradition, even ἀρετῆς . . . ἄκρον ἵκεσθαι (*Erga* 291, Tyrtaeus 12.43, where the latter is thinking not of Hesiod's road metaphor, as West claims,[82] but rather of winning a prize, cf. fr. 12. 13f., fr. 14), or *Th* 120–2 Ἔρος . . . λυσιμελὴς . . . δάμναται beside Archilochus 196 West ὁ λυσιμελὴς . . . δάμναται πόθος, where the similarity is striking but there is no decisive proof of priority or indeed means of excluding coincidence. More crucial are cases where more extensive passages from Hesiod are imitated, apparently. The parallel between Hesiod's description of high summer (*Erga* 582ff.) and Alcaeus 347 L–P is well-known, but some parallels between Hesiod and Semonides of Amorgos merit closer scrutiny than hitherto. Semonides reflects passages in *Th* more pointedly than is usually recognised. Some details in the iambus on women seem to confute Hesiod's misogynistic sentiments at *Th* 594ff. and 607–12, where women are likened to drones, and Hesiod continues that even if you do succeed in finding a good woman, your offspring will cause you grief unceasing. In contrast to this Semonides attributes excellent virtues to the busy woman *ἐκ μελίσσης*, who produces a *καλὸν κὠνομάκλυτον γένος* (fr. 7.83–93). This is the only type of woman whose offspring is referred to in the entire fragment; the coincidence is striking. Reminiscence of the *Theogony* will also explain the wording of fr. 7. 21f.:

τὴν δὲ πλάσαντες γηΐνην Ὀλύμπιοι / ἔδωκαν ἀνδρί . . .

Does this recall the myth of the creation of woman, *Th* 570f.? Note also the expression at fr. 7.115f.:

Ζεὺς γὰρ μέγιστον τοῦτ' ἐποίησεν κακόν,
καὶ δεσμὸν ἀμφέθηκεν ἄρρηκτον πέδην . . .

The imagery here is surely suggested by the binding of Prometheus, a prominent feature of the tale as told in *Th* (521ff., 615f.), but absent from the version in the *Erga*.

Thus there is evidence suggesting that Semonides knew the *Theogony*, but the distich closest to Hesiod has its analogue in the *Erga*:

γυναικὸς οὐδὲν χρῆμ' ἀνὴρ ληΐζεται
ἐσθλῆς ἄμεινον, οὐδὲ ῥίγιον κακῆς. (Semonides fr. 6)

cf. *οὐ μὲν γάρ τι γυκαικὸς ἀνὴρ ληΐζετ' ἄμεινον*
τῆς ἀγαθῆς, τῆς δ' αὖτε κακῆς οὐ ῥίγιον ἄλλο. (*Erga* 702f.)

The phrasing is identical; yet, as the context in Semonides is lost, and nothing is inorganic in either, we cannot tell on this evidence alone which is earlier or whether both are not derived independently from a third proverbial source.[83] The possibility that Hesiod is imitating Semonides should not be rejected out of hand either. His view of women here is noticeably more generous than in *Th*,[84] and the same shift is found at *Erga* 94ff., where Pandora is not the sole and sufficient cause of evil among mankind, but brings a jar of evils with her. Further, we find that the simile of the drones is no longer applied to women, but to the indolent (*Erga* 303ff.).[85] Perhaps Hesiod found a good wife after all, and modified his opinions accordingly; perhaps he mellowed with age in this respect, if in no other; but the specific alterations he makes to express his change of mind can most readily be explained if he had heard and taken note of Semonides' strictures against the earlier tirade in the *Theogony*.

The floruit of Semonides is traditionally given as 664–1,[86] which agrees with our tentative conclusion that Hesiod was roughly contemporary with Archilochus: contemporaneity of Archilochus and Semonides is reported by Clement of Alexandria.[87] Thus *Th* may best be placed after the outbreak of the Lelantine War in the closing years of the eighth century, and certainly not after c. 660, so as to allow imitation by Semonides, while *Erga* will date from later in Hesiod's career.[88] The coincidence of his active life with the period of decisive Oriental influence on Greek vase-painting surely helps to explain the undoubted Near Eastern elements in his thought.

CHAPTER 5

THE HYMN TO DELIAN APOLLO

After the examination of the general development of the epic diction in the two previous chapters, we will now review the dates and origins of each of the longer Homeric Hymns in more detail, beginning with what I have suggested is the sole extended representative that survives of the post-Homeric Ionian tradition, namely the *Hymn to Delian Apollo.*

First the partition of the *Hymn to Apollo* into two must be briefly defended. Although a few scholars still resist,[1] Ruhnken's division of the poem on formal grounds after line 178 (or rather 181, for these three lines are still in the Ionian sphere) commands general acknowledgement on two grounds - that 177f. is a normal conclusion to a complete hymn, quite in accord with other examples of the genre,[2] and that the geographical outlook and religious interests of the two sections differ profoundly: the first is concerned with the Aegean islands and adjoining coasts, whereas the second is familiar with central Greece, and pungently aetiological after the manner of Hesiod.[3]

Further arguments may be drawn from the diction. P. K. Huibregste[4] was first to undertake a systematic examination of the metre and language, and even went into aspects of statistical stylometry such as sentence-length and the frequency of particles. Such methods are still at a pioneering stage, and their application in this case open to the objection that we have no guarantee that the poets' practice in these matters did not change with time. But whether the differences Huibregste detected in some of his criteria are significant or not, subsequent work has revealed discrepancies in the use of Apollo-formulae and the frequency of repetitions;[5] moreover M. L. West has pointed to the greater neglect of digamma in *DAp* as further evidence.[6] In fact all the linguistic criteria scrutinised in Chapter 3 (where the numbers are at all large) have led to the same conclusion, and the sheer size of the gap in most cases can be seen at a glance in figure 2. It is especially striking in the frequency of n-mobile before consonants, where the two Hymns are poles apart.[7] We have seen that this criterion is a good marker of geographical origin, and here accords with the origins of the two poems as indicated by their divergent outlooks. It is to be hoped that whoever lopped them into a unity may have no more disciples.

The reason why he did so is easily discovered in the similarity between the two poems, which has induced most scholars since Ilgen to conclude that *PAp* imitates *DAp*. This conclusion has lately been capsized, and will be reexamined below.[8]

We must meanwhile assess the integrity of *DAp* itself, which is assumed to end after v. 181. Apart from isolated lines, the only passage that has been seriously questioned is the opening, lines 1–18. Kirk[9] has suggested that these verses are a later addition to the Hymn. While the linguistic methods of quantitative analysis developed in the preceding chapters are of little assistance in judging so short a passage, isolated details encourage the view that the only peculiarity about this passage is its incompetence: the poet began a description of Apollo's arrival that was so far-fetched that he had to put it into the past tense, thereby converting it to a description of Apollo's first appearance on Olympus; in the ensuing confusion he made other errors such as *πρὸς κίονα πατρὸς ἑοῖο* (v.8). There is no conceivable defence for this, and some other peculiarities Kirk cites are difficult, e.g. the construction of line 17. The prologue as a whole is certainly untraditional, in contrast to that of *Herm*:[10] but in fact the structure of the entire hymn is idiosyncratic,[11] and there are plenty of oddities elsewhere in its language. Non-Homeric vocabulary is no help, as Kirk is aware. Modifications here can be paralleled elsewhere:

15 Ἀπόλλωνά τ' ἄνακτα καὶ Ἄρτεμιν ἰοχέαιραν

The use of the accusative here is paralleled at 159, *Th* 14, 918, while the nominative Ἄρτεμις ἰοχέαιρα occurs eight times in Homer (cf. *Dem* 424). West has listed similar cases in Hesiod of non-Homeric declension of noun–epithet phrases for gods.[12] Ἀπόλλωνά τ' ἄνακτα is modified with neglect of digamma in favour of τε, cf. Ἀπόλλωνι ἄνακτι *A 36, *Th* 347. Other modifications entailing neglect of digamma are found at 22 (cf. *Aphr* 10), 46 (cf. 137), 71 (cf. *Aphr* 256). A short dative plural is introduced at 18 ὑπ' Ἰνωποῖο ῥεέθροις /, cf. -οιο ῥέεθρα / *Ξ 245, *Φ 25, *Ψ 205, *ζ 317, **Th* 695: ῥεέθροις is unique in the epos. Another short dative is found in violent enjambement at 91.[13]

Kirk's strongest objection is to ἀγχοτάτω (18): he points out that it departs from the 'traditional' ἄγχιστον in an uneconomical manner. However, ἄγχιστον is attested solely at ε 280, at a different point in the line, and Càssola[14] remarks that the formation is paralleled by ἑκαστάτω (K 113) and τηλοτάτω (η 322). Above all, Zumbach's claim that it is an Atticism is totally unfounded (cf. Hdt. II 169.4).[15]

One violation of economy has passed without comment: φαίδιμα τόξα τιταίνει / (4) is surprising in view of καμπύλα τόξα / (131), especially when we note that φαίδιμος is never found elsewhere at this place in the line, nor applied to an inanimate object (81 contrary examples). ὕδατι καλῶι / (120) for ὕδατι λευκῶι / (*Ψ 282, *ε 70, **Erga* 739) is less curious, as it can be explained as *variatio* anticipating φάρεϊ λευκῶι / (*121, *Σ 353). A more striking case is πόλιν ἱμερόεσσαν / (180) for the usual ~εὐρυάγυιαν / (4x *Il*, 1x *Od*). However, this may be a later replacement, related to ἱμερόεντα πόλιν (*Cat* 43.62 cf. Tyrt. 4.4). Thus the violation in line 4 lacks an exact parallel in the rest of the Hymn. Yet overall there are no solid grounds to exonerate the Chian bard from his bad start, much though we may wish to do so. The peculiarities of this passage are best explained by the view that the poet's creative flow was badly disrupted because of his initial blunder. As Kirk admits,[16] the dangers of the qualitative approach to the authentication of short passages lie in subjectivity, and certainty is hard to attain.

It would be inappropriate to discuss here other controversies about doublets and short insertions in this piece.[17] There are no other sizable passages that have been doubted, and what follows applies to the bulk of the poem. We are in the exceptional position of possessing copious evidence, both external and internal, for its date and occasion. The external source is the scholiast on Pindar *Nem* II 1, on the Homeridae:

> *ἐπιφανεῖς δὲ ἐγένοντο οἱ περὶ Κύναιθον, οὕς φασι πολλὰ τῶν ἐπῶν ποιήσαντας ἐμβαλεῖν εἰς τὴν Ὁμήρου ποίησιν. ἦν δὲ ὁ Κύναιθος τὸ γένος Χῖος. ὃς καὶ τῶν ἐπιγραφομένων Ὁμήρου ποιημάτων τὸν εἰς Ἀπόλλωνα γεγραφὼς ὕμνον ἀνατέθεικεν αὐτωῖ. οὗτος οὖν ὁ Κύναιθος πρῶτος ἐν Συρακούσαις ἐρραψῳίδησε τὰ Ὁμήρου ἔπη κατὰ τὴν ξθ' Ὀλυμπιάδα* [504/1], *ὡς Ἱππόστρατός φησιν.* (*FGH* 568 F 5)

West[18] has argued that the date and occasion of this performance may be historical, representing the first record of a series of rhapsodic contests at Syracuse. If Cynaethus really was the author of this hymn (as the scholiast expressly states), then its *terminus post quem* must be around 570, to accommodate his life-span. Most scholars, however, prefer to reject the scholium or raise the date, although they are happy enough to accept that it is the work of a Chian bard, and there is nothing in its language to contradict this. What light can linguistic criteria throw on the date of the Hymn?

That it is post-Homeric is beyond doubt. Hoekstra[19] has assembled some evidence, and more has been usefully compiled by Schröder.[20] I therefore exclude everything adequately discussed by Hoekstra, and must still be selective. It is difficult to sift, and set out, a heterogeneous mass of material, comprising formular modifications of various types, changes in meanings and constructions, and vocabulary which does not happen to be attested in Homer. However, the value of new words and constructions is very limited, and it is easy to compile long lists of phenomena otherwise undocumented until classical or hellenistic times, given our scanty evidence for the Greek language in earlier periods. Richardson's list[21] of such features in *Dem*, a poem unlikely to differ in date from *DAp* by more than two generations, illustrates this fact admirably. Only a few items of vocabulary implying social or cultural change constitute valid evidence, and I will therefore concentrate on the modifications involving linguistic development missed by Hoekstra, before giving a sample of the other types of evidence:

36 / Ἴμβρος τ' εὐκτιμένη. Hermann, by *petitio principii*, rejects τ'. Homer always has ἐυκτίμενος (17x *Il*, 15x *Od*, 2x *Cat*, *Aspis*, *Aphr*). There is a similar case at *Aphr* 262, τε καὶ εὔσκοπος Ἀργειφόντης; including examples of the accusative and dative, this formula is attested with ἐΰσκοπος at Ω 24, 109, α 38, η 137 (cf. λ 198), *PAp* 200 and *Herm* 73. Still closer to this is the reading of M at *Hy* 10.4, Κυθήρης εὐκτιμένης for Σαλαμῖνος ἐυκτιμένης in the other manuscripts.[22] *DAp* 36, perhaps affected by Ω 753,

ἐς Σάμον ἔς τ' Ἴμβρον καὶ Λῆμνον ἀμιχθαλόεσσαν

has broken up the usual pattern of Λέσβον (etc.)|| ἐυκτιμένην (I 129 etc.).[23]

71 πρῶτον ἴδηι φάος ἠελίοιο /: **Aphr* 256, cf. 278. Despite the post-Homeric parallels, this neglect of digamma is not necessarily post-Homeric. Cf. inf. p. 153 on *Aphr* 256.

102 ἐυκτιμένης ἀπὸ νήσου / may reflect phrases like ἐυκτιμένηι ἐνὶ Λέσβωι (*δ 342 etc.) and ἐυκτιμένην κατ' ἀλωήν (*ω 336); but such phrases are never found in the genitive, and the contracted genitive singular in -ου supports the case for modification here. Compare 138 νήσων ἠπείρου τε and **Th* 964 νῆσοί τ' ἤπειροί τε.

95, 105 λευκωλένου Ἥρης / (separated / Ἥρης φραδμοσύνηις λευκωλένου 99). This formula is usually nominative (22x *Il*, *Th*, 2x *Cat*), although the accusative (Υ 112, *Hy* 1.7, *Herm* 8 = *Hy* 18.8), dative (A 572, Friedländer no. 34) and vocative (Friedländer no. 10)[24] are also found. These genitives are unparalleled, and recall the post-Homeric proper-name–epithet declensions at 15 and 159.[25] Note that the separation with mobility at 99 entails the introduction of a short dative plural φραδμοσύνηις (Baumeister's correction). This is more advanced than the only other uses of the word in the epos, *Erga* 245 / Ζηνὸς φραδμοσύνησιν Ὀλυμπίου, cf. *Th* 626, 884, 891.

Another departure from Homeric[26] usage (I am not sure whether it can be termed a modification in the strict sense) is the use of 89

αὐτὰρ ἐπεί ῥ' ὄμοσέν τε τελεύτησέν τε τὸν ὅρκον

after the actual words of the oath have preceded in direct speech. As Schröder remarks,[27] Homer uses this verse only when the oath is not given, after the phrase *ἐπώμνυεν ὡς ἐκέλευον* vel sim. (six times, cf. *β* 378). Contrariwise *αὐτὰρ ἐπεὶ τό γ' ἄκουσε* always follows direct speech in Homer (eight times), but not at *DAp* 107 (or indeed *Dem* 334),[28] and the *indirect* speech after *ἔπεα πτερόεντα προσηύδα* (111) is unique (124 contrary examples in the epos).

151 *ἀθανάτους καὶ ἀγήρως ἔμμεναι αἰεί* /. This is modified by declension from *ἀθάνατον καὶ ἀγήραον* (*ἤματα πάντα*), *ϵ* 136, *η* 257, *ψ* 336, *Cat* 23. 12, 23. 24, nominative Θ 539, *Aphr* 214 (possibly contracted), *Th* 949 (accusative, and certainly contracted). Note that the declension here inevitably involves contraction, resulting in an unwelcome spondee before bucolic diaeresis.[29] A further indication of modification is the severance of the usual link with *ἤματα πάντα*. But these are not necessarily post-Homeric features - compare M 323, P 444 and *ϵ* 218.[30]

Of all these cases, 15, 18, 36, 87f., 89, 95, 99, 102, 105, 107 and 159 can be claimed as post-Homeric with some confidence. Hoekstra has discussed a few more, rejecting *υἱεῖ θέλοι* (46), but proving that the use of n-mobile at the trochaic caesura in 113 and 133 is post-Homeric. His conclusion, that there is almost nothing to justify the view that 1–138 is post-Homeric, errs greatly on the side of caution (isolated archaisms are not contrary evidence), although he does admit that the poet was unable to manage traditional formulae in describing the Delian panegyris towards the end of the poem.[31] In fact our investigations have shown that there are post-Homeric modifications throughout, and Hoekstra is mistaken here.

Isolated usages and vocabulary offer more scope both for speculation and for error. I offer only a selection:

42 *Μερόπων ἀνθρώπων* /. As Allen and Sikes remark,[32] the

addition of *ἀνθρώπων* to the name of a race, the Meropes, is not Homeric, but here suggested by the formula *μερόπων ἀνθρώπων*: for a parallel process cf. *Μέγαρα σκιόεντα Cat* 204.48. The model is e.g. Homer's Σίντιες ἄνδρες. The innovation is also found at *PAp* 398, 424 Πυλοιγενέας ἀνθρώπους.[33]

45 *ὠδίνουσα ἐκηβόλον* is here transitive, in Homer intransitive (Λ 269, ι 415). The transitive use is known from Sophocles onwards.[34] Can we really be sure that it was unknown to Homer?

64 *δυσηχής* 'of ill repute' from *ἠχώ*, not from *ἄχος* as in Homer, where it occurs ten times in the formulae *πολέμοιο* (*θανάτοιο*) *δυσηχέος*. The use of the nominative is itself an innovation, as well as the sense: but how can the misunderstanding be dated?[35]

68 *πρυτανευσέμεν*. This root is first at E 678 as the name of a Lycian, which betrays knowledge of its foreign origin (cf. Aeol. *πρόταvις*, Cretan *βρυτανεῖον*). It is not otherwise found until Stesichorus (fr. 49), unless at Sappho 99.7 L–P. Perhaps the history of *τύραννος* (first in Archilochus) and *τυραννεύω* (Solon onwards) is similar.

90 *γόνος* in the sense of 'birth' not 'offspring' is otherwise first at Aesch. *Supp* 173: contrast *γονήν* at 63.[36]

125 *ἐπήρξατο* is never used by Homer in the sense of 'dispense', or without *δεπάεσσιν*: for this use cf. *IG* 12(9) 192.10 (Eretria, fourth century).

163 *μιμεῖσθαι*. This root is not otherwise attested (except for Theognis 370) until Pindar and Aeschylus, and (like *πρυτανευσέμεν*) may indicate a cultural change that postdates Homer. But it too offers little hope of precise chronology.

What do such scraps teach us? More about the history of the word from the fact that it occurs here than about the date of the Hymn, given the paucity of our evidence. Moreover there are a number of non-Homeric archaisms in words and formulae to be considered: Hoekstra[37] has pointed to cases at 25, 54, 117, 123 and 127, and Pavese[38] has added *σπάρξαν* (121). As remarked already, it is difficult to gather more than a vague impression, using methods like these, that

DAp is post-Homeric: we cannot say by how much. It was to overcome such problems that the statistical methods elaborated in the two previous chapters have been advanced. In view of the brevity of this Hymn, this is an appropriate place at which to review their working. As only the *Iliad* and *Odyssey* are certainly products of Ionian bards,[39] we may recapitulate the results of these three poems in the criteria of Chapter 3: in table 25 the figures of *Il*, *Od* and *DAp* are given in sequence, followed by the sample-size in the latter (abbreviations for the criteria are as at pp. 71f.).

Of the results based on more than twenty examples, three out of four are considerably more advanced than *Od*: of the other seven, only two are less advanced, and these are based on the tiniest of samples. In other words, the diction of *DAp* is consistently more advanced, to a marked degree. Detailed study shows that roughly five times the interval between the Homeric epics elapses until *DAp* is reached.[40] We have already discussed the likely chronology of the Ionic tradition, which depends on our views about the date of Homer, the interval between the Homeric epics, and the assumption that the tradition developed at a steady rate. The problems here are soluble if we accept that Hesiod belonged to the same tradition. If so, then *DAp* is roughly contemporary with him. It is worth recalling that, from a statistical treatment of Pavese's lists of 'Hesiodic' phraseology in the Hymns, *DAp* emerged as conspicuously less 'Hesiodic' than the other Hymns, even when allowance is made for its brevity.[41] If the poem were much later than Hesiod, it would be surprising to find no trace of his influence. One possible mark of Hesiodic influence is the close literary relationship between *DAp* and *PAp*, a poem that is certainly post-Hesiodic and probably early sixth-century in date. There is certainly a bond of imitation between the two poems; the argument as to which is the model and which the copy is not definitely settled and still continued, but it is safe to say that to date the majority of scholars support the priority of *DAp*. I shall revert to this presently. In this context it should be recalled that *PAp* displays marked affinities in phraseology with Hesiod's *Theogony*, but these affinities are

Table 25. *The criteria in the* Iliad, Odyssey *and* Hymn to Delian Apollo

	Il	*Od*	*DAp*	sample-size
% neglects of digamma	17.2	17.9	34.6	26
% -*αο*	78.0	72.7	100.0	2
% -*αων*	83.9	80.2	33.3	3
% -*οιο*	51.9	46.6	34.4	32
% -*ου*	37.0	42.5	28.6	21
% long datives	85.4	85.2	72.7	22
% short datives	18.5	31.5	66.7	6
% -*ους* +V	41.5	38.1	20.0	5
% -*ᾱς* +V	47.0	42.1	33.3	3
% *Ζηνός* etc.	7.8	10.8	0	5
n–mobile +C ‰	35.6	37.2	60.8	11

notably lacking in our Hymn.[42] If the Chian was familiar with a post-Hesiodic Boeotian poem, it is still more surprising that there is no indication that he knew the work of Hesiod himself. But this is an argument from silence, and before reconsidering this matter, we must first examine the Hymn's relation to other poems.

Schröder has recently proposed the theory that *DAp* post-dates an alleged *Ur-Ilias*, but is prior to other sections of the *Iliad.*[43] His arguments are methodologically erroneous, relying as they do on subjective means of detecting *exemplum* and *imitatio* that take no account of the work of Parry. Here are some examples:

DAp 22 *πᾶσαι δὲ σκοπιαί τοι ἅδον καὶ πρώονες ἄκροι* (cf. Θ 553, Π 299)
23 *ὑψηλῶν ὀρέων . . .*
Μ 282 *ὑψηλῶν ὀρέων κορυφὰς καὶ πρώονας ἄκρους*
DAp 24 *ἀκταί τ' εἰς ἅλα κεκλιμέναι λιμένες τε θαλάσσης*
Μ 284 *καί τ' ἐφ' ἁλὸς πολιῆς κέχυται λιμέσιν τε καὶ ἀκταῖς*
cf. *ν* 234f. *ἀκτὴ / κεῖθ' ἁλὶ κεκλιμένη . . .*

Schröder[44] thinks the *Iliad* earlier here, yet its diction is more advanced: whereas *λιμέσιν τε καὶ ἀκταῖς* / has n-mobile making position as well as a short dative plural, *λιμένες τε θαλάσσης* is paralleled at ε 418 and 440, and has no peculiarities.

DAp 78 cf. *M 168 *οἰκία ποιήσονται.* Schröder[45] suggests that this phrase is less appropriate of seals than of wasps, and therefore depends on the *Iliad*!

DAp 97 *μούνη δ' οὐκ ἐπέπυστο . . .* Εἰλείθυια
N 521 *οὐδ' ἄρα πώ τι πέπυστο . . .* Ἄρης

DAp 98 *ἧστο γὰρ ἄκρωι Ὀλύμπωι ὑπὸ χρυσέοισι νέφεσσιν*
N 523f. *ἀλλ' ὁ γὰρ* ,, ,, ,, ,, ,, / *ἧστο*

It is not clear from internal evidence which way the influence goes here.[46]

DAp 114 *βὰν δὲ ποσὶ τρήρωσι πελειάσιν ἴθμαθ' ὁμοῖαι*
E 778 *αἱ δὲ βάτην* ,, ,, ,, ,,

There is no reason to think the simile less appropriate in *Il.*[47]

DAp 147 *ἑλκεχίτωνες* of the Ionians, as at N 685, where armed warriors are meant, but the epithet may be conventional and formular.[48]

In the inevitable absence of clear rules for determining priority in such parallels, the impression emerges that our poet knew *Il*, especially M, N and Ω.[49] But if we did not know that he was later on other grounds, it would be presumptuous to make any judgement on these facts one way or the other.

The poet's relation to Hesiod is equally obscure. The two share the phrase *ἁγνῶς καὶ καθαρῶς* (*DAp* 121, *Erga* 337).[50] Allen and Sikes[51] suggest that this is copied blindly from Hesiod, on account of the alleged superfluity of *ἁγνῶς*. Again this may be nothing more than a shared formula that does not happen to be attested elsewhere. Note also 99 (above, p. 103). Other alleged similarities have even less substance, such as the mention of Coeus at *DAp* 62;[52] the treatment of the diphthong as a short vowel followed by intervocalic yod in *μεγάλοιο* Κο̆ί̯οιο (or Κόοιο: *Κρόνοιο* codd.) is paralleled in *γᾰι̯ήοχον* at *Th* 15, but also in Κόω (Alcaeus 304.2 L–P), Homeric *ἔμπᾰι̯ον*, *χαμᾰι̯εῦναι*, and in other archaic poetry from Ionia and elsewhere.[53] *DAp* 81 *ἔμμεναι ἀνθρώπων χρηστήριον* has a parallel in *Cat* 240.6f. *ὅν χρηστήριον εἶναι / τίμιον ἀνθρώποις*,[54] but *PAp* 288 *ἔμμεναι ἀνθρώποις χρηστήριον* is closer. Finally Ἀπόλλωνα *χρυσάορα* is shared by *DAp* 123 and *Erga*

771. Zumbach[55] rightly states that this is an archaism, which has more advanced cogeners at E 509 and O 256 etc.:[56] but his conclusion that it is therefore borrowed from Hesiod is not necessarily correct. Indeed we have seen above,[57] in the examination of statistics based on Pavese's collection of 'Hesiodic' phrases in the Hymns, that *DAp* has less Hesiodic phraseology than any other long hymn (even when its brevity is allowed for), and that by a very wide margin.

One fact alone ruffles the serenity of our poet's Aegean solitude, namely his poem's relation to the work of a mainlander composing at about the time of the First Sacred War.[58] Does the Pythian Hymn imitate the Delian, as is usually thought, or is M. L. West correct to argue for the reverse in a recent article?[59] As we saw,[60] the opening of *DAp* is problematic: West thinks it tries to outdo that of *PAp*. Note parallels, both verbal (2 cf. 187, 11 cf. 206, 15 cf. 199) and thematic (the arrival of Apollo on Olympus occasions rejoicing, especially for Leto). The priamel line 19 (= 207) is thought awkward here: West says that the line ought to introduce a choice of topics, but none is offered, whereas the priamel at 207ff. (introduced by the same unparalleled verse) is unexceptionable. Not everyone will agree that the confession of an *embarras de choix* is unsuitable here,[61] and in any case emulation of *PAp* is not the only explanation for these oddities that can be proffered.

The catalogues of places[62] that follow share but one name, which has the same epithet: *ναυσικλειτή τ' Εὔβοια* (31, cf. *219). The epithet appears only once elsewhere (ζ 22) and is not applied to a toponym. Although we may deem it less appropriate to the reduced Euboean sea-power of the sixth century, it yields no hint as to priority.

We next face the problem of the suitability of a motif, that of a temple as recompense for a barren situation. At 526ff. the kidnapped Cretans complain about being transported to so unfruitful a spot as Delphi, but Apollo promises that they will thrive on the sheep slaughtered by his votaries – otherwise there will be trouble! This is generally and properly considered an *aition* (typical of *PAp*) for the confiscation of the Crisaean plain after the First Sacred War, c. 586 B.C.[63] Similar ideas and phrases feature in Leto's request to Delos to receive her, in return for which kindness she promises that the sacrifices to Apollo will compensate for the island's natural infertility (51–60). West thinks the motif less integral here, and therefore borrowed, but judgement is bound to be subjective, as the contrary opinion of most scholars indicates.[64] Verbal parallels offer more hope. With 50

καί μιν ἀνειρομένη ἔπεα πτερόεντα προσηύδα

cf. 525 *τὸν καὶ ἀνειρόμενος* Κρητῶν *ἀγὸς ἀντίον ηὔδα*.

Both lines are abnormal, for we expect *καί μιν φωνήσας* (very common, cf. *PAp* 451) and the feminine ~*φωνήσασ'*~ at 50 (O 35, 89, 7x *Od*, *Dem* 320). *ἀνειρόμενος* occurs elsewhere only at δ 461, 631 in the phrase *ἀνειρόμενος προσέειπε* /. *PAp* 525 is influenced by the type of 463:

τὸν καὶ ἀμειβόμενος Κρητῶν *ἀγὸς ἀντίον ηὔδα*.

The violation of economy may be sheer coincidence, but it is curious that it should happen here in the passage parallel to *DAp* 50; for in fact the latter is not a true violation of economy at all. For one thing, *καί μιν φωνήσασ'*~ is not found within *DAp* (nor indeed is the masculine ~ *φωνήσας* ~): secondly, *ἀνειρομένη ἔπεα* in 50 avoids the neglect of digamma inherent in *φωνήσασ' ἔπεα*, and therefore has every appearance of being the original phrase for the feminine, dating back to the era when digamma was still pronounced. It is no cause for concern that Homer uses a later modification: compare 123 Ἀπόλλωνα *χρυσάορα* with the Homeric modification Ἀπόλλωνα *χρυσάορον* (O 256).[65] There are strong grounds for thinking *PAp* the imitator here. Another case is *DAp* 54f.:

οὐδ' εὔβων σέ γ' ἔσεσθαι ὀίομαι οὔτ' εὔμηλον,
οὐδὲ τρύγην οἴσεις . . .[66]

cf. 529 *οὔτε τρυγηφόρος ἥδε γ' ἐπήρατος οὔτ' εὐλείμων*.

This is close to δ 606f., of Ithaca,

. . . αἰγίβοτος, καὶ μᾶλλον ἐπήρατος ἱπποβότοιο.
οὐ γάρ τις νήσων ἱππήλατος οὐδ' εὐλείμων . . .

while 54f. recalls o 406, *εὔβοτος εὔμηλος οἰνοπληθής* . . , from

Eumaeus' description of the happy isle Syrie, Ὀρτυγίης καθ-ύπερθεν (cf. *DAp* 16), which may be further reflected in the vignette of the Delian festival - note that the line-ends of ο 409f. are identical with those of *DAp* 161 and 165. δ 606f. was surely drawn upon by *PAp* partly because the passage presented a good contrast of hill and plain, and partly because Telemachus too was (politely) asking to go home.[67] But τρυγη-φόρος is isolated here and looks intrusive: reminiscence of *DAp* 54f. may have been triggered by the 'parallel of sound' εὐλείμων / εὔμηλον. Other parallels are indecisive (52 cf. 523; 57f. cf. 538f.; 59 cf. 528). Leto's request to Delos and her reply also have verbal parallels in a scene of similar theme, namely that in which Apollo, wandering in search of a site for his oracle, asks Telphusa (57f. cf. 249, 260; 80ff. cf. 247f., 258ff.). Note ἔμμεναι ἀνθρώπων χρηστήριον (81) beside 259 (= 288) ~ ἀνθρώποις ~, with the introduction of a 'short' dative plural (the genitive is found at 248: a shift to the dative seems more natural than vice versa, and suggests that *DAp* is prior).

Delos chauvinistically claims not only the first temple but also the first oracle (81). West argues from the murky obscurity of this oracle in antiquity that it is a fiction invented to rival Delphi's, and another example of our poet trying to outdo his 'model'. Evidence for the oracle is certainly shaky before Roman times, but in any case chauvinism versus Delphi does not prove that the *Pythian Hymn* is the target.[68]

Parallels between 151ff. and *PAp* 190ff. (on death and old age), 153f. and 204 (verbally very similar), adduced by Kakridis[69] as evidence for the unity of *Ap* as a whole, prove neither this nor the priority of either section. Dornseiff's argument for unity is similarly mistaken, but the parallels he bases it on are more significant.[70] He connects *Hy* 27 to Artemis with the openings of *both* parts of *Ap*. Note τόξα τιταίνει (*DAp* 4, **Hy* 27.5); ἰοχέαιραν / (*DAp* 15, **Hy* 27.2); ὑψηλῶν ὀρέων (*DAp* 23, **Hy* 27.7); κάρηνα . . . ὄρεα σκιόεντα (*DAp* 33) beside the later modification ὄρη~ (*Hy* 27.4–6, cf. **Herm* 95), as well as the thematic parallels of fear of the deity's bow, entering a god's house, unstringing the bow and hanging it up. In *PAp*, compare Apollo's arrivals at Delphi and Olympus with Artemis' at Delphi, the Graces' dance, and *PAp* 189f. *ὀπὶ καλῇ / ὑμνεῦσίν ῥα θεῶν δῶρ' ἄμβροτα* beside *Hy* 27.18f. *ἀμβροσίην ὄπ' ἱεῖσαι / ὑμνεῦσιν Λητώ*: but here there are parallels at least as good in *Th* (with *Th* 7ff. cf. *Hy* 27.15, 18f.; *Th* 44; *Th* 68f.). I am persuaded by the parallels with *DAp*, but not by those with *PAp*: the modification *ὄρη σκιόεντα* surely indicates that *Hy* 27 is imitating *DAp*. Now *Hy* 27, like *PAp*, is the product of a Delphic milieu; the few indications available suggest a late date for the Hymn, perhaps similar to that of *PAp.*[71] If another bard at Delphi knew and imitated the Delian Hymn, does this not increase the likelihood that the case of *PAp* was similar?

Like the quantitative linguistic evidence, detailed phraseological study of the parallel passages supports the priority of *DAp* against West's theory: so too does the historical evidence.

The evidence to which I refer is Thucydides' discussion (III 104) of our Hymn and the ancient Delian festival. His ascription of the poem to Homer is no proof of its antiquity: Stesichorus is said to have ascribed the *Aspis*, dating from his own early years, to Hesiod.[72] But subtler arguments remain. Thucydides contrasts the fifth-century festival, limited to *χοροί* from Athens and the islands, with the earlier one, which included an *ἀγὼν γυμνικὸς καὶ μουσικός* (cf. *DAp* 149). He conjectures (*ὡς εἰκός*) that the *ἀγῶνες* ceased due to some *ξυμφοραί*, so plainly he does not know what happened. The Ionian Revolt or Persian Wars seem too recent for such oblivion, and Pisistratus, who purified Delos c. 540–30, is unlikely to have permitted the contests to lapse. Therefore they must have lapsed some time before, perhaps by the early sixth century. The only other Delian *ἀγῶνες* in our sources are those instituted by Polycrates in 523 or 522,[73] to celebrate his dedication of Rheneia to Apollo. The *Suda*[74] records that, in a quandary over nomenclature, he enquired of Delphi, only to be told '*ταῦτά σοι καὶ Πύθια καὶ Δήλια*', which was understood, presumably *ex eventu*, to foreshadow his death soon after.[75] Now *καὶ Πύθια καὶ Δήλια* is strangely reminiscent of our Delian–Pythian cobbled hymn, so disparate in its parts.[76] How, then, did the Hymn come to be cobbled together?

One curious fragment relevant here has been disregarded.[77] It derives from that self-same well-informed scholiast (ad Pind. *Nem* II 1) who told us of Cynaethus: his source here is apparently Philochorus (*FHG* 328 F 212). These verses are attributed to Hesiod (fr. 357 M–W):

ἐν Δήλωι τότε πρῶτον ἐγὼ καὶ Ὅμηρος ἀοιδοὶ
μέλπομεν, ἐν νεαροῖς ὕμνοις ῥάψαντες ἀοιδήν,
Φοῖβον Ἀπόλλωνα χρυσάορον, ὃν τέκε Λητώ.

This blatantly contradicts Hesiod's explicit statement that he crossed the sea only as far as Chalcis (*Erga* 650f.). Yet the lines must have been composed for a reason, not as sheer nonsense.[78] Now the story of Homer and Hesiod meeting goes back to Alcidamas the disciple of Gorgias at least. Our extant *Certamen*, here drawing on Alcidamas' *Museum*, complies with the *Erga* in locating the contest at Chalcis.[79] Once the venue was envisaged as Chalcis, as 'authenticated' by Hesiod himself, who but an utter fool would wish to invent a contest on Delos, when sceptics had only to point to *Erga* 650f.? This is no doubt why the lines were so widely ignored, especially when Alcidamas' version was so successful. It seems more probable that they were finally driven out of circulation by the *Museum*, and therefore antedated it.[80] Even if these lines were the work of a fourth-century forger, we would still need to ask him: why the bizarre choice of Delos, and why Hymns to Apollo? One answer and one only can I see – that at some period hymns called 'Homeric' and 'Hesiodic' were recited together on Delos in Apollo's honour.[81] *DAp* and *PAp* may be given these titles most aptly, although neither is of course by Homer or Hesiod.[82] We cannot discover whether the author was following or initiating this tradition on Delos, but we can assign it a *terminus ad quem* of 523 or 522, when Polycrates hesitated over Πύθια καὶ Δήλια. If the author was at that time trying to legitimise the performance of *DAp* and *PAp* together on Delos, the reaction of the modern scholar who took this fragment literally indicates the success he might expect for this ploy among an unsophisticated audience.[83]

Now this is not exactly what we hear of Cynaethus, but there is a suspicious resemblance. Such a fraud could readily be misreported as what we do hear, namely that Cynaethus wrote the Hymn to Apollo and ascribed it to Homer.[84] Which hymn is meant here – the Delian by itself, or the composite poem? Both parts appear to be too early for the transmitted date of Cynaethus (504–501): *DAp* roughly contemporary with Hesiod, *PAp* c. 585 and in any case mainland in origin, judging by diction and outlook. Only the hybrid hymn can date from this time. The evidence is circumstantial but coherent, and we may conclude that Cynaethus was responsible for the epic performances at Polycrates' grand Delian and Pythian festival to celebrate the dedication of Rheneia and his own magnificence.[85] Whether he caused the loss of the opening of *PAp* in the process is hard to determine:[86] that he did much more than mere stitching at the seams I find improbable.[87]

If the Delian Hymn is the work neither of Cynaethus of Chios in the late sixth century nor of Homer in the eighth (and the linguistic evidence is perfectly sound on this point, despite the brevity of the poem), then to whom does the author's *sphragis* refer? The verses revealing his domicile in Chios (172f.) cannot be rejected as an interpolation, as the praise of Chios at 38 defends them. Nor is there any valid reason to alter Cynaethus' date, as many have tried to do.[88] Can we then believe in an otherwise unknown and nameless Chian bard of the seventh century, who in a fit of braggadocio had the nerve to contend that his poems would always be the best – poems now lost without trace? As Burkert remarks,[89] this is an extraordinary claim for an obscure and anonymous author. 'The best poet of all times, the absolute classic: this is meant to be Homer.' For Simonides (fr. 8 West), 'man of Chios' was an adequate reference to Homer, which nobody could mistake.

The views that the author means the Homeridae collectively,

or a particular member of that fraternity speaking through Homer's mouthpiece, founder on the poem's wording, and we are driven back to Homer himself.[90] Since the hymn is plainly not by the composer of the *Iliad* and *Odyssey*, at least in its present state, we seem to have uncovered another fraud, if a more pious one. But forgery is involved only as long as we apply the standards of a literate and literary society. The pious fraud is at once comprehensible, indeed familiar, in an oral tradition, where poets may claim to be singing the song of a great predecessor, while altering that predecessor's song substantially during free oral recomposition-in-performance.[91] In Chios, a close-knit guild of followers and descendants endeavoured to preserve the deeds and poems of their founder; so, in this Hymn, the honoured bard is surely Homer, and it is one of the Homeridae of Chios who bestows on him the praise which he deserved, but would surely have hesitated to utter himself.

CHAPTER 6

THE HYMN TO PYTHIAN APOLLO

The partition of the *Hymn to Apollo* into two sections has been defended in the previous chapter, and needs no repetition here. But before proceeding further we must pause to examine the integrity of 182–546 as they stand. Two passages have been challenged – the Typhon episode and the conclusion.

The episode of the birth of Typhon (305–55) is not obviously relevant to the story and has often been deemed an interpolation. Its beginning is rather forced – the dragon at Delphi adopted from Hera the dreadful Typhon, whom once Hera bore in anger at Zeus... The closing lines demand goodwill for their understanding: 354ff. (Hera) *δῶκεν ἔπειτα φέρουσα κακωῖ κακόν* (sc. Typhon), *ἡ δ'* (sc. the dragon) *ὑπέδεκτο* · / *ὅς* (sc. Typhon) *κακὰ πόλλ' ἔρδεσκε* . . . / *ὅς* (whoever) *τηῖ γ'* (sc. the dragon) *ἀντιάσειε* . . . However, although this is uncommonly clumsy, it is not incomprehensible, and does not prove that the passage was interpolated. As Van Groningen[1] remarks, it is hard to tell whether this popular episode was included by the same poet, or inserted by another. He compares the insertion of *Aspis* into *Cat*, but that was certainly by a different poet. The episode of Odysseus' boar-hunt on Parnassus (*τ* 393–466) is a better parallel; its relevance to the story is indeed greater, but its position in terms of the tension of the narrative is the same.[2] In each case something important has just happened, whose consequences cannot be foreseen: Eurycleia has recognised Odysseus' scar, and Apollo has just killed the dragon. Then follows the digression, before we are returned to the consequence – Eurycleia nearly tells Penelope, and Apollo invents the name Pytho. Of course for us the emphasis is lost: we cannot see such an *aition* as a great climax; yet this poet repeatedly indicates that aetiology is his main aim. How does the language of this section affect our view of its authenticity?

On inspection the passage appears to contain fewer oddities than does the rest of the poem. Oddities cannot by nature be quantified as such, but if we calculate the frequency of non-Iliadic forms we find that in these 52 lines there are 0.65 per line, which is the lowest figure for any fifty-line stretch in this Hymn. It is next approached by 461–510, with 0.84 cases per line, while all other sections average 1.0 or above.

The application of the linguistic criteria of Chapter 3 is hindered by lack of evidence: four observances of digamma to one neglect, no cases of *-οιο*, one doubtful o-stem genitive singular and two in *-ου*. The digamma result is normal for the Hymn, and the rarity of *-οιο* is scarcely surprising, as it is based on such an exiguous sample. There is, however, one important result in these criteria: of nineteen o- and a-stem dative plurals, seventeen are 'long', two doubtful and none short. The proportion of 'long' dative plurals is therefore 89.5%, compared to 87.8% in the rest of the Hymn (43/49). These are remarkably high figures, higher than that in the *Iliad*, and very striking for a poem of this date. That both figures are so high is a good piece of evidence in favour of the same authorship, or at least of a very similar origin.

The few peculiarities of this passage that might relate to local dialects will take us no nearer an answer, but deserve discussion in themselves.

330/*τηλόθεν οὖσα*. Unless we accept Hermann's emendation *τηλόθ(ι) ἐοῦσα* (cf. Θ 285, Φ 154), or alter to *εὖσα* or *ἐοῦσα*, *οὖσα* is certainly an Atticism; but it is one already found at *η* 94 (and possibly *τ* 230, 489). Compare also *Cat* 204.91 *παρθένον οὖσαν*, *Herm* 106 *ἀθρόας οὔσας*, *Hy* 19.32, 29.10, Parm. 8.57, Emped. 129 D–K. It seems to be found in poetry of varied origin, and thus, whether in origin an Atticism, archaism, or replacement for some other form, such as *εὖσα* (Cos, Rhodes, Hdt.) or *ἔσσα* (Lesbos, Argolid, Laconia), this occurrence is rather uninformative. See further on *Herm* 106 below.

325 *ἀθανάτοισιν οἱ οὐρανὸν εὐρὺν ἔχουσι* / departs from traditional usage, where the old formula uses *τοί* rather than n-mobile to avoid hiatus: 2x *Il*, 9x *Od*, 1x *Th*. This accords with our expectation that *τοί* is more of an archaism than n-mobile. But *οἱ* is used where metrically necessary elsewhere (4x *Od*), and we cannot conclude that the author of this episode had *οἱ* in his vernacular – indeed, he might even be over-Ionising,[3] or simply using the relative pronoun *οἵ*.
344 *Διὸς ἤλυθε μητιόεντος* / shows that the poet did not always go out of his way to use n-mobile: he could have said *ἤλυθεν αἰγιόχοιο* (although this is never preceded by n-mobile in the extant epos), or indeed *ἤλυθε τερπικεραύνου* (cf. *Aphr* 36[4]). Instead he employs a Hesiodic phrase, cf. *Th* 286, 457, *Erga* 51, 273, 769, *Hy* 24.5 (Delphic).

In general the use of n-mobile here, where it can be reliably quantified, i.e. when making position before a consonant, hardly differs from the rest of the poem: there are only two cases, neither valid as they precede nasals. This accords with the low frequency of this feature elsewhere in the Hymn.[5] Once, when the licence could have been used, it is not: at 333 the usual *φώνησέν τε* / (*Il*, *Od*, *Dem* 53, *Hy* 7.16) is replaced by *καὶ φάτο μῦθον* (cf. Ψ 491, φ 67). Compare *εἰπέ τε μῦθον* (256 with digamma observed, 286 neglected).

The Typhon episode has a few phrases reminiscent of Hesiod. Note *γαῖα φερέσβιος* (341), cf. **Th* 693, *Dem* 450f., 469, *Hy* 30.9. With 346 *αὐτωῖ ἐφεζομένη πυκινὰς φραζέσκετο βουλάς* compare *Erga* 583f. *δενδρέωι ἐφεζόμενος λιγυρὴν κατεχεύετ' ἀοιδὴν / πυκνόν* . . . , which is closer than Γ 152; but *Hy* 23.3 *ἐγκλιδὸν ἑζομένηι πυκινοὺς ὀάρους ὀαρίζει* is still closer. 352 *πῆμα βροτοῖσιν* / cf. *μ 125, *Th* 223, 592, but contrast **Th* 329 *πῆμ' ἀνθρώποις* /. 354 *δῶκεν . . . κακωῖ κακόν* . . . cf. *Th* 585 *τεῦξε καλὸν κακόν*.

Apart from parallels with the creation of Woman, there are some with Hesiod's own Typhon episode: for the motif of throwing down, with 318 cf. *Th* 868; 352 cf. *Th* 874; 334 cf. *Th* 840, both followed by a reference to Tartarus rather than the usual Styx (*Il*, *Od*, *DAp*); with 335 cf. *Th* 820f., 851 for the link with the Titans. However, we could not tell from all this which was prior, and the connexion may not have been direct. We shall see that this is in surprising contrast to the knowledge of the *Odyssey* probable elsewhere in *PAp*. However, Hesiod's story diverges, and we conjecture that *PAp* is consciously altering his version. Hesiod's Typhon is the last child of Gaea, mated with Tartarus (820–2), and unconnected with Hera. Here the tale is of Hera's revenge for the birth of Athena. Moreover, Hesiod says that Echidna marries Typhon rather than rears him.[6] Stesichorus, however, gave the same account as the Hymn, which shows that this version was current in the sixth century, although which of the two came first cannot be determined by this alone (Stesichorus fr. 62, = *PMG* 239).[7]

There are two similarities between the language of this passage and *Dem* – the use of φερέσβιος noted above, and 347f. and *Dem* 28f.:[8] 347f. ἀλλ' ἥ γ' ἐν νηοῖσι πολυλλίστοισι μένουσα / τέρπετο οἷς ἱεροῖσι . . . *Dem* 28f. ἧστο θεῶν ἀπάνευθε πολυλλίστωι ἐνὶ νηῶι / δέγμενος ἱερὰ καλά . . . This may be no more than coincidence: νηοῖσι πολυλλίστοισι is probably based on νήεσσι πολυκλήισι (Β 175 etc.), while *Dem* 28 resembles ζ 204, . . . ἀπάνευθε πολυκλύστωι ἐνὶ πόντωι. Note the equivalent at *Dem* 355f. ἀπάνευθε θυώδεος ἔνδοθι νηοῦ / ἧσται . . . , modified from 385 cf. *Aphr* 58, as the contracted genitive singular shows. But again there is probably no more than an indirect connexion between the two poems. In the main body of *PAp* the two diverge – Hyperion is the sun himself (369), as usually in Homer. Contrast μ 176, *Th* 374, 1011, *Dem* 26, 74, *Hy* 28.13, 31.4. At 532 note / νήπιοι ἄνθρωποι δυστλήμονες, cf. *P. Berol.* 13044 of *Dem* 256 ἄφρονε[ς] ἄνθ[ρω]ποι ~, closer than M's version νήιδες ἄνθρωποι καὶ ἀφράδμονες with *correptio Attica*.

Concerning the Typhon episode we may conclude that there are neither literary nor linguistic grounds for supposing that it is an interpolation by a different poet, and there is some linguistic evidence against; at the very least it comes from the same sub-tradition as the rest of the poem.[9]

Apollo's warning at 540ff. has also been doubted. Although

a short passage, it is crucial to the date and occasion of the Hymn. These lines have always been understood as a threat to the Delphic priests uttered around the time of the First Sacred War. Scholars reluctant to accept such a date for the whole poem have seen this as a later addition, but it can be defended on three grounds:

(a) Richardson[10] has pointed out that *Aphr* ends with a similar warning from a god, followed abruptly by the close of the Hymn. There is thus nothing intrinsically suspicious about this conclusion. Note too that the two poems share the otherwise unknown line

εἴρηταί τοι πάντα· σὺ δὲ φρεσὶ σῇσι ⏑– – (*PAp* 544, *Aphr* 289).

(b) The warning follows directly from what has preceded. The priests are to live on the offerings, and not covet agricultural land. A diet largely of meat was obnoxious to the Greeks,[11] and the warning might well be necessary. The struggle for the control of the Crisaean plain may have had other phases, but never a more important one than the First Sacred War. After it, the arable plain was turned over to the grazing of Apollo's flocks, and the locals were rendered totally dependent on the cult and the Amphictyons.

(c) There is no need to posit a lacuna after 539, if we accept Baumeister's conjecture[12] *ἐμὴν ἴθυντε θέμιστα* (for *μάλιστα* codd., cf. *δίκηι δ' ἴθυνε θέμιστας Erga* 9), and introduce a conditional clause in the next verse: *εἰ δέ τι τηΰσιον ἔπος ἔσσεται ἠέ τι ἔργον*, with the threat as the apodosis (542f.). *εἰ δέ*[13] may have been replaced by *ἠέ* after the analogy of *ἠέ τι ἔργον*. *εἰ* with future indicatives in both halves of the conditional and *ἔπειτα* in the apodosis is found at B 379. This slight change circumvents the objection that the text of this conclusion is lacunose, and the evidence that the conclusion belongs with what precedes is good.

These passages are appropriate to the era of the First Sacred War, traditionally dated to the decade after 595. The poem as a whole cannot be much later, as the equestrian events at the Pythian Games were instituted in 582, and Telphousa told Apollo to move to Delphi to avoid the disturbance caused by horses and mules, which would detract from his worship (262ff.). This is not an entirely unassailable argument, as the races were conducted far below in the plain. Nonetheless the *aition* for the Delphic priesthood loses point if much later than this.[14]

We shall return to this war when discussing the poet's origin: we must meanwhile survey the evidence that the Hymn is post-Homeric, even if we cannot vindicate the fairly precise date implied by the historical evidence. Most of the post-Homeric modifications in this poem have been discussed by Hoekstra,[15] and his work needs no repetition. I shall therefore give only cases he has missed of post-Homeric phonology and morphology, and then some cases from semantics and vocabulary. The few peculiarities of 305–55 have been considered above.

275 *ὣς εἰποῦσ' Ἑκάτου πέπιθε φρένας*. Note the association of neglected digamma and contracted *-ου* here. *Ἑκάτου* is unique, but *ἑκάτοιο* occurs ten times in the epos, and the sole case with neglected digamma is *PAp* 276. 275 is definitely post-Homeric: cf. *πεπιθεῖν φρένας* **Aphr* 7, 33 only. Further examples involving neglected digamma discussed by Hoekstra are at 447, 488 and 506, of which the last two are certainly post-Homeric.[16]

263 *ἐμῶν ἱερῶν ἀπὸ πηγέ͜ων* / (-*ῶν* M), cf. *φ* 312 *πηγέ͜ων*. Our phrase is modelled on e.g. *ἱερωῖ ἐνὶ δίφρωι* / P 464.

295 *αὐτὰρ ἐπ' αὐτοῖς* /, cf. ~ *αὐτῆς* *Λ 629, ~ *αὐτωῖ* **δ* 134, **μ* 422, but also ~ *αὐτοῦ* *Λ 38. Note too *αὐτοῖς* / X 513, *υ* 213.

507 / *ὑψοῦ ἐπὶ ψαμάθοις, παρὰ* . . . cf. *A 486 ~ *ὑπὸ* . . . , *Ψ 853 *ἐπὶ ψαμάθοις* + V-. Here the later form of the morph is guaranteed by the change of preposition. None of these need be post-Homeric.

Similarly shadowy impressions that the Hymn is post-Homeric may be obtained from some usages and terms it contains:

250 etc. *Πελοπόννησον*. Our earliest reference to the Peloponnese is in the *Cypria* (fr. 11.3f. A *νῆσον* . . . *Πέλοπος*), cf.

Tyrtaeus 2.15, Alcaeus 34.1L–P, still *divisim*. The compound first appears here and in *Cat* 189, if the scholiast's remark is correctly interpreted.

251 Εὐρώπην 'north and central Greece'. This is the earliest use of the term: it is first found in the modern sense in Pindar (*Nem* IV.70).

285 *τεκμήρατο*. The use of this verb with an infinitive is not Homeric;[17] there are eight contrary examples.

406 λαῖφος does not mean a sail in Homer, but a rag (twice): it is used of bedding at *Herm* 152, of a lynx' skin at *Hy* 19.23. It first denotes a sail in Alcaeus, 326.7 L–P.

As usual, neither forms nor usages of isolated occurrence convey more than vague indications of post-Homeric composition. Hoekstra argues that the modifications of most importance are the duals used as plurals at 456, 487 and 501,[18] and the oddities at 361f., 488, 506 and 538, to which I would add 275. There are however quite a number of archaisms, underestimated by Hoekstra:[19]

213 *ὁ δ' ἵπποισῡ· οὐ μὴν* . . . Pavese points out that the irregular scansion here may be a relic of an old dual, cf. *E 13 *ἵπποιν, ὁ δ'* . . .[20]

229 etc. *ἔνθεν δὲ προτέρω ἔκιε̄ς*, Ἑκατηβόλ' Ἄπολλον. Note the observation of digamma here. Gemoll[21] remarked that this refrain to mark stages in a journey may be based on the similarly used

ἔνθεν δὲ προτέρω πλέομεν, ἀκαχημένοι ἦτορ (ι 62 etc.: 5x ι and κ).

We shall see evidence below that our poet knew the *Odyssey* or something very similar, and the lack of *correptio epica* in *προτέρω ἔκιες* may suggest adaptation; yet so does the mysterious *brevis in longo* in *πλέομε̄ν ἀκαχημένοι*.

Other retentions of the effect of digamma are more normal: 471 *οὔ τι ἕκοντες* cf. δ 377, χ 351 ~ *ἑκών*; 534 *ῥηΐδιω̄ν ἔπος ὔμμ' ἐρέω* is the plural of *λ 146 *ῥηΐδιον τοι ἔπος ἐρέω* . . . (the lines are otherwise identical). Priority cannot be established here, as each phrase includes one observance and one neglect of digamma. 540, however, *ἠέ τι τηΰσιον ἔπος ἔσσεται ἠέ τι ἔργον*, is close to the lost formular prototype

* *ἠμὲν ϝέπος ἠδέ τι ϝέργον* / that must underlie / *ἢ ἔπος ἠέ τι ἔργον* (γ 99, δ 329; transposed) and the declension *ἠμὲν ἔπει ἠδὲ καὶ ἔργωι* / *Dem* 117, which is further separated to *οὔτ' ἔπεϊ* ⏑⏑ – ⏑⏑ *οὔτε τι ἔργωι* E 879, *Dem* 199, and with *καί* for *τι* at A 395; the separated phrase is found modified to the genitive plural at Λ 703.

376 *ἐξαπάφησε*, cf. *ἐξαπαφοῦσα* 379. Pavese[22] remarks that *ἀπαφεῖν* is an archaism, and indeed it is: but the weak aorist is a younger form: compare *ἐτύχησε* < *ἔτυχον* at O 581 and below on *Herm* 119.[23] Hoekstra suggests that *ἐξαπάφησε* is in fact *false* archaism for *ἐξαπάτησε* (*Erga* 48, *Dem* 404).[24]

389 *ὀργιόνας* is agreed to be a mistaken spelling for **ὀργειόνας*, the expected Homeric spelling of **ὀργηόνας*, > Attic *ὀργεών*. The same misspelling is found elsewhere (e.g. Antim. *Lyde* fr. 67 ap. cod. Phot.). If Mycenaean *wo-ro-ki-jo-ne-jo* is connected (and this is doubtful[25]), it must have a different suffix.[26] The form is certainly interesting, as later poets use forms such as *ὀργειῶνας*, which presuppose quantitative metathesis.

528 *πῶς καὶ νῦν βιόμεσθα; τό σε φράζεσθαι ἄνωγμεν.* There are two interesting verbs here. *βιόμεσθα* might be a replacement for *βεόμεσθα* after *βίος*; cf. *βίονται* in an oracle ap. Phleg. *Mir* 2 (where Emperius conjectured *βέονται*).[27] Wyatt offers the sophisticated explanation that this is a short-vowel subjunctive with ablauting root, i.e. *βέομαι*: *βιόμεσθα* like *εἴω*: *ἴομεν*.[28] However, an imitation of this line by Apollonius Rhodius proves that the text is corrupt. At I 685 and 693 Apollonius uses the two half-lines *πῶς τῆμος βώσεσθε* and *τάδε φράζεσθαι ἄνωγα*. This is no coincidence, as there are other borrowings in this part of the *Argonautica*,[29] so we have an independent early witness for the text. There has been much debate as to whether *βώσεσθε* is for *βι̯ώσεσθε* (with a harsh synizesis) or a regularly formed future of *βόσκω* (cf. *δόσκον*: *δώσω*; both roots originally ended in the *o*-coloured laryngeal $^{*}ə_3$, just as *βάσκω* and *φάσκω* with roots in the *a*-coloured $^{*}ə_2$ have futures *βᾰ́σομαι* and *φᾰ́σω*). The contexts favour *βόσκω*, and the question is settled by the parallel passage in *DAp* (53–60): whether source or copy of

PAp, here is another early witness, and at 59 all mss. have a part of *βόσκω*. We should thus, from Apollonius and *DAp*, restore as *difficilior lectio* an aorist subjunctive *βώμεσθα* here, from *ἔβων / *ἐβόμην, in conformity with the original paradigms of root-aorists like ἔβāν, ἔφāν and *ἔδων / ἐδόμην.[30] But Apollonius' ἄνωγα (I 693) is no reason to alter ἄνωγμεν (which is protected by τῶν, *PAp* 524). Hoekstra[31] hesitates to deem this an archaism, as the singular is normal in this phrase (6x *Od*, *Erga* 367): but this is a correct athematic perfect active, cf. εἰλήλουθμεν etc.[32] and perhaps ἴθυντε at 539.

538 προφύλαχθε is probably a modification for the sake of the metre of the correct athematic perfect second plural imperative πεφύλαχθε, cf. middle δέδεχθε here and πεφύλαξο *Erga* 797 etc., active ἄνωχθε χ 437. The change need not be post-Homeric,[33] but could have occurred at any date – even, of course, during transmission. Pavese[34] proposes that προφύλαχθε is an unreduplicated perfect, cf. ἐπίτευκται (Hesychius). This too seems possible. What is certain is the plethora of verbal archaisms here, especially if ἴθυντε is the right reading at *PAp* 539: compare the passive ἀπίθυνται in Hippocrates (*Fract* 7). However, on the evidence available it cannot be determined whether these and other archaisms derive from lost Ionic poetry, hypothetical mainland epos or simply mainland dialects.

This combination of post-Homeric modifications with interesting archaisms, typical of the Hymns in general, is important in this case for its implications about the sources of *PAp*'s diction. The idea was mooted above that the poet drew part at least of his diction from far older fixed texts, notably from Homer;[35] this will explain his use of most of the features studied in Chapter 3. But it is clear that the poet had access to other poetry as well, from formular archaisms like 540 as well as unhomeric phrases shared with other poets, e.g. 275, or 240 beside *Cat* 70.18. The archaisms and innovations just studied do not provide more than a vague post-Homeric date, but the poem's relation to others on a wider basis is more helpful. As usual, common features are of more value than isolated ones. Thus *PAp* accords with *Aspis*, *Dem* and *Herm* in the disuse of Ζηνός and false archaism in -οιο, with *Aspis* over digamma, and with *Herm* over false archaism in 'long' dative plurals and disuse of n-mobile (even more marked than in Hesiod and *Aspis*). *Dem* still has most of its results clustered; its poet has not yet begun to draw on Homeric diction directly. Whether his contemporaries were doing so yet cannot be known, but *Dem* is likely to be earlier rather than later in this group of mainland works. *Aspis* and *PAp* show signs of a general retreat into archaism, but this is less marked in the former, and has gone still further in *Herm* (note how not only such obvious criteria for false archaism like -οιο but also -ου and -οις fall back between *PAp* and *Herm*, as can readily be seen in Figure 2). Judging by the increase in false archaism, the sequence seems to be *Dem*, *Aspis*, *PAp* and *Herm*.

Within this group, *PAp* has an odd treatment of the accusative plurals: in a-stems, 5/9 precede a vowel; in o-stems, 1/9. This is the reverse of the peculiarity noted above in *Herm*, where o-stem results are less advanced than a-stems, and more similar to *Cat*, where o-stems are rare before a vowel (16.1%) but a-stems more common (31.6%), despite the light ending Σκύθᾰς at 150.15. *PAp*'s results are odd, and can only be ignored on the hypothesis that the average for both criteria is really about 3/9, and that they have diverged from this theoretical mean in opposite directions.[36] There are statistical obstacles to setting the theoretical mean for a-stems at 1/9 or for o-stems at 4/9.[37] Another peculiarity (but a more explicable one) is *PAp*'s use of εἰς, in the strongest possible contrast to that of *Herm*, just as in the case of digamma. The background to this phenomenon has been delineated above:[38] in Table 26 I show its incidence in those poems with more than five cases in all. The first column gives the number of instances of εἰς before vowels (excluding once-digammated words), the second those of ἐς, then the total, and lastly the percentage of cases represented by ἐς. The chance that *PAp* has a result similar even to *Od* is very small,[39] and minute if *Herm* is

Table 26. *The distribution of* εἰς *and* ἐς *before vowels in the epos*

	εἰς + V	ἐς + V	Total	% ἐς + V
Il	165	65	230	28.3
Od	209	62	271	22.9
Th	10	7	17	41.2
Erga	11	5	16	31.2
Cat	13	4	17	23.5
PAp	12	0	12	0
Herm	3	9	12	75.0

compared.[40] We conclude that the result is abnormal. The situation is very similar to that in the digamma criterion, where *PAp* has false archaism (only 22.4% neglects, total 49), but *Herm* has a very high proportion of neglects (53.6%, total 56). Here it appears that *PAp* prefers εἰς, while *Herm* prefers the innovatory ἐς. But for the parallel situation in digamma, it could be argued that these might be differing reactions to a vernacular which retained ἐν with the accusative, e.g. Boeotian: but this seems improbable, as we would then expect *PAp* to be consistent in preferring to observe digamma and use ἐς. But this is not the case. Consequently more straightforward archaism must be the cause, whether deliberate or (more likely) due to the influence of Homer; archaism which *Herm* tried to avoid in introducing more Ionic usage. ἐς must have been thought (rightly or wrongly) to be more appropriate to verse in the Ionic dialect, just as digamma was neglected in Ionian speech. We can conclude little from this about the vernacular of the poet of *Herm*. But the high observance of digamma in *PAp* strongly suggests that its composer retained it in initial position in his everyday speech, even granting that some observances, and the impetus to maintain them, originated in the poet's knowledge of Homeric epic. It is certainly true to say that at this stage and branch of the epic tradition, where the poets were composing in an Ionian dialect that differed substantially from their vernacular, the development of the poetic diction was affected more by Homeric poetry and probably by ideas of what Ionian diction should be like than by the vernacular dialects of the mainland. This contrasts with the situation during the Aeolic phase and the transition to the Ionic dialect: but we are not entitled to conclude from this that this later poetry is either less oral or less creative. We must judge these aspects by other criteria. But clearly outside Ionia the epic diction had become even more remote from everyday speech than it had been in Homer's time.

It is therefore not surprising that forms in which we can detect the influence of local dialects are lacking, both in *PAp* and, in general, elsewhere. *διέθηκε* (254) has been alleged by Schürmann[41] to be Attic, but is in Herodotus, and also *Cat* 43.40. *ἐπηύξατο* (362) is Attic[42] according to Moeris 175, and appears eleven times in Homer unaugmented, but the text could well be questioned over such a tiny detail. *οὖσα* (330) may indeed be Attic, but that does not prove the whole poem of Attic origin, but merely that there was at some date in the development of this regional tradition some Attic influence: we would no more argue from *λαμπράν τε σελήνην* (*Th* 19, 371) that Hesiod was an Attic poet. As remarked above,[43] *οὖσα* is also known in *Od*, *Cat*, *Herm* and two shorter Hymns. Moreover in *PAp* both the high observance of digamma and the great reluctance to use n-mobile to make position militate against Attic authorship. *Dem* shows a far more credible pattern than does *PAp* in this regard.

The internal evidence for the poet's origin and loyalties has been hotly discussed, especially by French scholars, as it is important for the history of central Greece at this time. P. Guillon[44] was the first to suggest in detail how various episodes in this poem and the *Aspis* can be explained as propaganda for the two sides in the First Sacred War. There is no external evidence that Thebes took part against the Amphictyons, but the pattern Guillon discerns does account for peculiar events in the poems. He explains the *Aspis* as a threat from the Theban Heracles against Thessaly, which led the Amphictyons to victory; Cycnus is portrayed as preying on the pilgrims to Delphi. As Sordi remarks,[45] one ripost to this was the myth of Heracles struggling with Apollo for the Pythian tripod. Our poet pointedly remarks that Thebes was still an uninhabited wooded hill (225–8), and was therefore younger than Delphi. This accords with the legend that Cadmus founded the city in response to a Delphic oracle.[46] Guillon also proposes that the itinerary of Apollo is related to the membership of the Amphictyony, and the Telphousa episode to Theban attempts to seize a strategic pass on the road to Delphi south of Lake Copais. I find this more convincing than Ducat's suggestion[47] that both the allusion to Thebes and this episode, along with the absence of any mention of Apollo's sanctuary at the Ptoion, refer simply to the priority of Delphi as his main shrine. Sordi[48] originated this with the view that the reference is not to Thebes itself, but to the site of the Ismenion, which is quite absurd when we read 226:

οὐ γάρ πώ τις ἔναιε βροτῶν ἱερῃῖ ἐνὶ Θήβηι.

These attempts to refute Guillon's view that the poem is for the Amphictyons and against Thebes are unsuccessful. Guillon himself argued that the poet was probably from western Boeotia, which was often under Theban pressure yet distant enough to resist. The digression on Onchestus (230–8) is evidence of interest in Boeotia and knowledge of obscure local rituals. Note, moreover, the importance of the place in *Herm.* Two minor details may confirm his specification of the area of the poet's origin or at least loyalties: the complimentary reference to Trophonius and Agamedes, builders of Apollo's temple (295–7), recalls both Lebadeia, where Trophonius had an oracular shrine, and Orchomenus, where their father Erginus was king.[49] Secondly, the impiety of the Phlegyans who lived on the eastern slopes of Parnassus (278–80) may touch on some local hostility, perhaps that of the Amphictyons to the Phocians. Compare Ephorus' description of the progress of Apollo from Athens to Delphi, including the killing of Tityus at Panopeus.[50]

The linguistic evidence concurs with an origin in Phocis,

say, or Boeotia, especially in the ignoring of Ζηνός and n-mobile, and the high observance of digamma, but cannot offer quite such an accurate localisation (or indeed dating) as the historical evidence.

We have already discussed the relationship of this poet to Hesiod,[51] and remarked that the only parallels are in the Typhon episode, and that these are not particularly close. A more striking relationship is that with the *Odyssey*. The similarity of 229 etc. to a line repeated in the wanderings has been discussed above:[52] in the latter part of the poem the amount of direct correspondence is very great, and has often been remarked.[53] However, the copying is far from slavish, and the parts copied widely separated. The *Odyssey* provided good models for nautical adventures, and it may be that both poets are simply using a shared tradition, but examination of the coincidences suggests a more direct relationship between the two poems.

Such a relationship is certainly needed to explain the phrases shared by *PAp* with the *Catalogue of Ships* in B: 422 Ἀρήνην ἵκανε καὶ Ἀργυφέην ἐρατεινήν is based on B 591, . . . καὶ Ἀρήνην ἐρατεινήν /: 423 is identical with B 592. Another parallel with this part of the *Catalogue of Ships* is 410 ἁλιστέφανον πτολίεθρον, remodelled from B 584 Ἕλος τ' ἔφαλον ~: the adaptation of a phrase describing Helos to suit Taenarum proves that *PAp* is secondary here.[54] Yet even in this passage one suspects that there may have been some conflation with the *Odyssey*, as the sacred flocks of Helios at Taenarum are unparalleled, and may recall μ 127ff., the cattle of the Sun.[55] 424 repeats 398, suggesting (if the order can be trusted) that the poet thought Pylos was on the Alpheus. 425 appeared in Strabo's text of the *Odyssey*[56] with καλλιρέεθρον or πετρήεσσαν for καὶ παρὰ Δύμην, which was too far round for the voyage of Telemachus. Thence it has entered our printed texts as ο 295. There are several similarities between the two voyages: 426 = ο 298, and 427 = ο 297, with ἀγαλλομένη for ἐπειγομένη. Although 428 (referring to Ithaca) is not closely paralleled, 429 =

α 246, *ι* 24 and *π* 123, and the mention of these western isles inclines me to think that the poet had the *Odyssey* in mind. The parallel with *ο* is resumed at 433f. = *ο* 293f. (with minor differences). Similar patchwork reappears later: 452–5 = *γ* 71–4 and *ι* 252–5; 466f. = *ω* 402f.; 467f. = *ν* 232f., but there are changes in the latter line:

PAp 468: *τίς δῆμος τίς γαῖα, τίνες βροτοὶ ἐγγεγάασιν;*

ν 233: *τίς γῆ τίς δῆμος, τίνες ἀνέρες ἐγγεγάασι;*

These alterations suggest that the copying is not mechanical, nor does it appear to be artistically motivated; the vagaries are rather those one might expect to encounter in an oral transmission. A violation of the tendency to economy suggests strongly that the poet knew not only our *Odyssey*, but also the extant ending of it. 499

αὐτὰρ ἐπὴν σίτοιο μελίφρονος ἐξ ἔρον ἧσθε

violates this tendency beside 513 *αὐτὰρ ἐπεὶ πόσιος καὶ ἐδητύος ἐξ ἔρον ἕντο* (7x *Il*, 14x *Od*).[57] 499 has a close parallel at *ω* 489, *οἱ δ' ἐπεὶ οὖν ~ ἕντο*. We can account for this line as follows: the most frequent formula (*PAp* 513 etc.) was perfectly satisfactory for the third person plural, but when the first plural was needed it had to be modified. *αὐτὰρ ἐπεί* remains in both versions: ~ *σίτοιό τ' ἐπασσάμεθ' ἠδὲ ποτῆτος* (*ι* 87, *κ* 58) and ~ *τάρπημεν ἐδητύος ἠδὲ ποτῆος* (Λ 780). That two phrases should be created is not surprising, when we consider how much more frequently the third person is used. Yet Λ 780 is modified back to the third person at *ε* 201 (~ *τάρπησαν* ~), violating the tendency to economy. This is by analogy of *αὐτὰρ ἐπεὶ τάρπησαν* (Ω 633, *δ* 47 = *κ* 181). Despite all this modification, *PAp* 499 = *ω* 489 is the only line where there is no reference to drink as well as food. The omission can be explained, if the line modifies ~ *σίτοιό τ' ἐπασσάμεθ' ἠδὲ ποτῆτος* back to the third plural. It is true that *σίτοιο μελίφρονος* might be an old phrase – compare 461 *σίτοιο γλυκεροῖο*, probably the original of *σίτου τε* ~ (Λ 89). Yet there are other parallels between this part of *ω* and *PAp*: 426 = *ω* 431, and 466f. = *ω* 402f., including *οὖλέ τε καὶ μέγα χαῖρε*, a phrase unattested elsewhere. Therefore the memory of this part of the *Odyssey* (about which there has been so much debate) may have affected our poet's choice of phrase for post-prandial satisfaction.

In sharp contrast to his knowledge of our *Odyssey*, indications of acquaintance with the *Iliad* (apart from the *Catalogue of Ships*) are scant indeed.[58] The only one worth quoting is 441f. (describing Apollo):

τοῦ δ' ἀπὸ πολλαὶ / σπινθαρίδες πωτῶντο.[59]

Compare Δ 77 (a simile, of Athena):

τοῦ δέ τε πολλοὶ ἀπὸ σπινθῆρες ἵενται /

Even here the link is probably indirect. The imbalance in the number of parallels with the monumental epics reinforces the conviction that the poet did know the *Odyssey*, much as we possess it, early in the sixth century. This is important if true. It implies that the text of the *Odyssey* had attained a certain degree of fixity before that date, and was capable of exercising considerable influence over an oral poet. For the Odyssean passages in *PAp* are no mere literary cento, but owe much to the spontaneous play of oral composition. Departures from the usual epic practice, and violations of the tendency to economy, are normally explicable by analogies of various types within the traditional diction. Here are a few more examples:

198 *εἶδος ἀγητή* is for *εἶδος ἀρίστη* (B 715, η 57, *Dem* 146; accusative Γ 124, Z 252), blended with the invariably masculine *εἶδος ἀγητός* (Ω 376, accusative X 370, ξ 177, nominative plural E 787, Θ 228).

255 *διηνεκές*, for Homer's *διαμπερές* (very common). Homer uses only *διηνεκέως* (*Od* 3x; *Th* 627 – contrast *διαμπερέως* Hes. fr. 280.3). But *διαμπερές* is read by some mss. at 295, and by all in the formula *διαμπερὲς ἤματα πάντα* (*PAp* 485, cf. δ 209, *Aphr* 209, reversed in *Cat* ap. *POxy* 2509.12).

268 *σθένος ἐστὶ μέγιστον*: contrast *κράτος ἐστὶ μέγιστον* (6x *Il*, 2x *Od*), *μέγα κράτος* 6x *Il*, *μέγα σθένος* 5x *Il*.

304 *μῆλα ταναύποδα* is the standard phrase, compare ι 464, *Herm* 232; yet at 412 we find *μῆλα βαθύτριχα* in a line resembling *Herm* 232. This is no arbitrary change, but operates by a common analogy: *καλλίτριχα μῆλα* is found at ι 336 and 469, and *καλλι-* and *βαθυ-* are often interchanged

when a different initial quantity is desired, e.g. *καλλι-* and *βαθύζωνος*. Here the poet temporarily forgot that he knew a phrase appropriate to this space, and created a new one by analogy. A similar analogy operated between *χρυσοπλόκαμος* at 205 and *καλλιπλόκαμος* at *DAp* 101, and the pairs *χρυσοπέδιλον* /-*ου* (λ 604, *Th* 454, 952, *Cat* 25.29, 229.9) and *καλλιπέδιλον* (*Herm* 57); *χρυσοστέφανον Th* 17, 136, *Hy* 6.1 (gen. *Cat* 26.13) and *καλλιστέφανος Dem* 251, 295, cf. Ischia cup line 3 (gen.).

In *PAp* we encounter something new in the development of the traditional diction, namely false archaism on an extensive scale. This seems to be a mainland feature, incipient and sporadic in *Dem*, but rampant here, and clearly due to the influence of texts like the *Odyssey*. This implies knowledge of texts somehow fixed at an earlier linguistic stage, but does not contradict our conclusion in Chapter 2 that there is no evidence in favour of literary interference in the composition of this Hymn. False archaism is fully compatible with this conclusion, and so is the dating of the poem in the second decade of the sixth century, to c. 585 to be precise, when the victorious Amphictyons declared the Crisaean plain sacred to Apollo: this is the burden of Apollo's closing threat, and there is no reason to think the passage spurious.

The poet's origin is less securely determined. Considerations of content imply that he performed at Delphi and had loyalties to western Boeotia,[60] and was presumably a Boeotian; but Boeotisms are absent from his diction. The consistency with which the seventh- and sixth-century epos of the mainland avoided local forms deserves to be reiterated; only a few Atticisms and West Greek phenomena in Hesiod and some later poets disrupt the pattern. The absence of West Greek forms from this poem does not suffice to overthrow the idea that Hesiod may have acquired them at Delphi: it is probably only coincidence, and there is plenty of other evidence to show that the poem belongs firmly in the mainland tradition, and more closely to a group including *Dem*, *Aspis* and *Herm*.

CHAPTER 7

THE HYMN TO HERMES

Despite various attempts to dissect it in the past, the integrity of the Hymn to Hermes is not nowadays seriously disputed,[1] and we can proceed at once to examine its diction on this basis. We are confronted by two problems – the text of the poem is in places very corrupt, and there is hardly any evidence, external or internal, for its date and origin. Estimates have varied to as late as the fifth century or after.[2] We must also take cognizance of the unequivocal implication of the metrical evidence examined in Chapter 2 that the poem is not a straightforward product of oral composition.

Hoekstra[3] considered the diction of *Herm* so definitely post-Homeric that he omitted it altogether from his study. Nonetheless it is worth illustrating the fact that the post-Homeric phenomena are similar to those found in the other Hymns. In fact the evidence is scarcer than might be expected, as many modifications depend on contracted o-stem genitive singulars and 'short' dative plurals of the o- and a-stems, of which we are largely deprived here by the poet's archaising preference for the genitive in *-οιο* and 'long' dative plurals.

Ἑρμῆν 1 etc. The contracted form is general in the Hymns, rare in Homer. It is contracted following quantitative metathesis from Ἑρμείᾱς, derived from *Ἑρμᾱ́hᾱς (Myc. *e-ma-a*$_2$). The intermediate form Ἑρμέᾱι +V (E 390) is counted as contracted in table 27. The uncontracted forms at *Erga* 68 and *Cat* 66.4 end in *-ην*, *-ηι* instead of the Homeric *-ᾱ*: cf. *Hy* 19.28, 36.[4] Three cases of Ἑρμάων in *Cat* are discussed elsewhere,[5] and omitted from table 27.

The complete reversal of the pattern in *Herm* from that in Homer is clear from these statistics.[6]

46 / ὣς ἅμ' ἔπος τε καὶ ἔργον, cf. 531 ἐπέων τε καὶ ἔργων.

Table 27. *Contraction in the name* Hermes *in the epos*

	Uncontracted	Contracted	Total	% Contracted
Il	14	2	16	12.5
Od	17	4	21	19.0
Th	0	2	2	
Erga	1	0	1	
Cat	1	4	5	80.0
Dem	0	2	2	
Herm	0	31	31	100.0
Aphr	0	1	1	

These are modified with neglects of digamma, from / *ἢ ἔπει ἢ ἔργωι* Α 504, *Dem* 65, separated Α 395, Λ 703, and *ἔργον τε ἔπος τε* / Ο 234, 3x *Od.*[7]

Another modification with neglect of digamma is 180f.:

. . . *χρυσόν, ἅλις τ' αἴθωνα σίδηρον / καὶ πολλὴν ἐσθῆτα* . . .

This blends ε 38 *χαλκόν τε χρυσόν τε ἅλις ἐσθῆτά τε* . . . / *πόλλ'* . . . (cf. ν 136) with *χαλκός τε χρυσός τε πολύκμητός τε σίδηρος*, Ζ 48 etc. The neglect of (internal) digamma in the enclitic *οἱ* (143) is paralleled in Homer.[8]

In the o-stem genitive singulars modification is often obscured by the archaising preference for *-οιο*. Of 41 cases of *-οιο*, eleven are unattested in Homer (Class D above, p. 44). This is still fewer than in *Dem* (16/37 in Class D), which also has false archaism.[9] Some phrases are shared with other Hymns, e.g. *θυώδεος Οὐλύμποιο* 322, *Dem* 331; *ὑπὸ πτυχὶ Παρνησοῖο* 555, *PAp* 269. Note too *Ἀρκαδίης πολυμήλου* / 2, *Cat* 23.32, *Anth Pal* XIV 73.5, perhaps modified from the dative seen in Friedländer no. 142 (Camarina, fifth century). Other modifications introducing contracted genitives in *-ου* are 41 *πολιοῖο σιδήρου* / cf. *πολιόν τε σίδηρον* / 2x *Il*, 3x *Od* (note the simultaneous introduction of *-οιο*); 198 / *ἐκ μαλακοῦ λειμῶνος* cf. *Hy* 19.25 / *ἐν μαλακῶι λειμῶνι*; 353 *ἠδὲ καὶ αὐτοῦ* / cf. ~ *αὐτοί* / 2x *Il*, 2x *Od*; 529 / *ὄλβου καὶ πλούτου δώσω* cf. / *ὄλβωι τε πλούτωι τε* Π 596, Ω 536, ξ 206. One phrase modified elsewhere is 10 *μεγάλοιο Διὸς νόος ἐξετελεῖτο* cf. *Th* 1002 *μεγάλου δὲ* ~.

69 / *αὐτοῖσίν θ' ἵπποισι καὶ ἅρμασιν* . . . The original formula appears to have been *ἵπποισι καὶ ἅρμασι κολλητοῖσι* / (Δ 366 etc.), which was modified in three ways – by simple separation (ρ 117), by loss of the adjective (Ψ 8 etc.) and by the introduction of preconsonantal n-mobile to produce *ἵπποισίν τε καὶ* ~ (*Cat* 26.36 etc., separated E 199, Ψ 286). Here they are combined: the adjective is lost and the formula moved within the line, but the influence of the type with n-mobile has contributed to *αὐτοῖσίν θ'*.

145 λελάκοντο is from λάσκω, λέληκα. The aorist (ἔ)λακον is Homeric, ἐλάκησα Aristophanic. Zumbach[10] compares λελάθοντο (Δ 127): λέληθα (Semonides). Note also the causal aorist λέλαχον (H 80 etc.) beside the perfect εἴληχα (Aeschylus etc.). However 119 *τετορήσας* is more advanced than *ἔτορον* (Λ 236). Aristophanes has *τετορήσω* (*Peace* 381); the form blends (*ἀντι-*)*τορήσας* (K 267) and *ἐτέτορεν* (Hesychius).

449 *ἔρωτα* is certainly an innovation. In the epos all other examples of the nominative *ἔρως* can be replaced by *ἔρος* without harm to the metre (so too *γέλως* / *γέλος*), while the oblique case-forms with dental suffix are not found at all (except in a verse quoted by Plato ap. Allen V p. 148). The dental suffix occurs in *χρώς* at K 575, σ 172, 179, *Erga* 556, in *ἱδρώς* at *Erga* 289. In *ἔρως* it first appears in Sappho (23.1 L–P).

569 χαροποῖσι λέουσι, cf. *Th* 321 χαροποῖο λέοντος, are both modifications from an adjective that was originally athematic, as preserved in the man's name Χάροψ (Λ 426).[11] But this is not post-Homeric, cf. *χαροποῖό τ' ἄνακτος* for *Χάροπός τε ϝάνακτος B 672. However, the formula is perhaps post-Homeric, cf. *χαροπῶν τε λεόντων Hy* 14.4, and the thematic nominative *χαροποί* ~ λ 611, *Aspis* 177, *Aphr* 70, *χαροποῦ τε λέοντος Orphica* 79 Kern.

In this Hymn vocabulary absent elsewhere in early epic is conspicuously abundant; I offer but a selection.

75 *ψαμαθώδης*. Despite Zumbach,[12] this is not a new type altogether: compare *λυσσώδης* N 53, where again there can be no question of smell.

80 *ἀνόητος* 'unthought of', a unique sense. The normal meaning 'stupid' is found from Herodotus onwards. It is arguable whether the word could have been used without this connotation after his time. Compare 125 *πολυχρόνιος* 'ancient', here only; 'long-lasting' Herodotus etc.

208 *σαφές*. Homer has *σάφα* only, while *σαφής* first appears in the fifth century: but note *σαφέως* *Dem* 149, *σαφηνέως* cj. Carey ap. *DAp* 171.

314 *οἰοπόλος* (originally 'lonely') is used of mountains and remote places five times in Homer, of deities first in Pindar (*Py* IV 28, fr. 61.16 B of Artemis): cf. Ap. Rhod. IV 1322, 1413 of the Hesperides, and here of Hermes. Whether it is here misunderstood to mean 'shepherd' is quite uncertain: compare *οἰονόμος* (*BCH* 21.599; Delphi, fourth century). The use describing a deity is post-Homeric.

361 *αὐγαί* alone meaning 'eyes' is first elsewhere in Euripides (*Andr* 1180, lyrics). Compare *Rhesus* 737, Plato *Rep* 540a.[13]

447 *μοῦσα* 'song' is also found in *Hy* 19.15, Aeschylus, Pindar etc.[13]

471 *τιμαί* plural first appears in Hesiod and *Dem*.

472 etc. *μαντεῖαι* for the usual *μαντοσύνη* (Homer, *Cat* 37.14, Pindar) is paralleled in Tyrtaeus (4.2), Herodotus and Attic.

481 *κῶμος* first occurs in Theognis and Pindar, but compare *κωμάζω* *Aspis* 281, Alcaeus 374 L–P.

The increased frequency of non-Homeric vocabulary in this poem requires no statistical demonstration.[14] Despite the dependence of vocabulary on subject-matter, the conclusion that this Hymn differs substantially from the others in this respect is unavoidable. The difference is not necessarily a function of lateness, but may be connected with the humorous tone, drawing on words from a lower register of the language. Although it would certainly be more difficult to compose orally using a greater amount of unepic vocabulary, it is doubtful whether such use constitutes disproof of oral composition. More important are the features of a metrical nature where the Hymn is distinct from the rest, as discussed in Chapter 2 above,[15] where firm support was forthcoming for the allegation of some literary interference in its composition. Although many phrases may appear to be simply gratuitous innovations, they can turn out to have respectable formular parallels elsewhere: for example, at 375 *φιλοκυδέος ἥβης* / duplicates expected *πολυηράτου* ~ (nom. **Aphr* 225, *ἥβης πολυηράτου Cat* 30.31 cf. 205.2, *ἥβην πολυήρατον ο* 366). In spite of the uniqueness of *φιλοκυδής*, this is clearly an analogical modification of *ἐρικυδέος ἥβης* **Th* 988 (cf. *ἥβης ἐρικυδέος* Λ 225), and has a parallel at *481 *φιλοκυδέα κῶμον*, which is based on *ἐρικυδέα δαῖτα* / (Ω 802 etc.).

Amid the numerous late features, the poem also contains a scatter of apparent archaisms:

80, 440 *θαυματὰ ἔργα* /. This formula, preserving digamma, is not in Homer. It recurs at *Aspis* 165, *Cat* 204.45, *Hy* 7.34. The adjective is itself unhomeric, but for the pattern compare *θέσκελα ἔργα*. Yet we cannot be sure that this is an exclusively mainland formula - *Hy* 7 may be Ionian on the grounds of tone, nautical setting and the use of n-mobile.[16] Perhaps Homer and Hesiod simply chance not to have known or used this phrase: but I think it more likely that it is not an archaism at all, but a formula, constructed on older models, that is characteristic of an advanced stage of the tradition. Indeed *Herm* has several phrases of this type where the digamma of *ἔργα* is observed - *ἀρίσημά τε* ~ 12, *ἐνδέξια* ~ 454, *ἐπαμοίβιμα* ~ 516 (cf. 16, 127).

130 *κρεᾰ̆ων* is unique in epic: compare the metrically equivalent *κρειῶν Il*, *Od*, *Herm* 64, 287 and *κρε̆ῶν* or *κρε̯ῶν ο* 98, *κρέεσσι Orac*. ap. Hdt. I 47 (Delphi, c. 550). The only similar form is the *κρεάεσσι* of late epic.[17] Our form is plausibly derived directly from **kréwə₂sōm* > Skt. *kraviṣām*, *κρεάων* > **κρηων* (*κρειων*); but it seems more probable that it is remade after the nominative singular *κρέας* and dative plural *κρέασι*. Note too that *κρειῶν ἐρατίζων* is a formula found twice in *Il* (Λ 551 = P 660) as well as *Herm* 64 and 287, whereas 130 lacks formular associations.

152 *γνυσί* from *γόνυ*, compare *δρυσί* : *δόρυ*. This is certainly an archaism. See below, p. 146.

241, 449 *ἥδυμον ὕπνον*. The misdivided form *νήδυμος* is

widely distributed (*Il*, *Od*, *Aphr* 171, *Hy* 19.16), while ἥδυμος is ascribed to Hesiod by Tzetzes.[18] The latter was also known to later poetry, cf. Simon. 79, Epich. 179, Antim. 74, and as a *varia lectio* in Homer (B 2 etc.). In any case, only where digamma is shown to be neglected by elision, correption or the precession of a light syllable can the existence of the more archaic ἥδυμος be guaranteed! If the form is characteristic of mainland poetry only, and we accept the testimony of most manuscripts that Homer already used νήδυμος, then ἥδυμος must be a relic of lost mainland hexameter poetry, or borrowed from Ionic verse before Homer's time (an unlikely contingency), or simply taken from spoken dialect.[19]

254 κατάκειαι without intervocalic sigma is phonetically correct and old, cf. Arcadian κεῖοι.[20] In Homer the sibilant is restored analogically, as in nearly all dialects. But note that the form is not metrically assured. There are no grounds for Zumbach's suggestion that later editors are responsible for the restoration of the sigma in the text of Homer.[21] Despite Pavese, neither Hermes' birth on Cyllene nor -κειαι prove the *Hymn* Arcadian.[22]

272 / βουσὶ μετ' ἀγραύλοισι, 412 ἐπ' ἀγραύλοισι βόεσσιν / (separated 492) exhibit the plural of a formula found only in the singular in Homer: βοὸς ἀγραύλοιο / K 155, P 521 etc., separated μ 253, χ 403 cf. Ω 81. Nothing shows that these long dative plurals in *Herm* are not genuine archaisms. Note however 262 / καὶ βοῦς ἀγραύλους, 567 ἀγραύλους ἕλικας βοῦς /, where the latter may stand for ειλίποδᾱς ἕλικας βοῦς (*Il Od Erga Cat*) to avoid a 'false' quantity (cf. εἰλίποδας βοῦς / 216). This suggests that the Hymn's system of epithets for cattle may not in fact be old. Many of the other 'long' o- and a-stem dative plurals are likewise not Homeric – 19/80 are in Class D as defined above.[23]

287 / οὔρεος ἐν βήσσῃς, ὁπόταν has a more advanced relative before consonants at Π 766, *Erga* 510; but it is more advanced than ~ βήσσῃισιν (Λ 87, *Th* 860), with an alternation of P_1 and T_1 formulae. However 553 ὠκείῃισιν ἀγαλλόμεναι πτερύγεσσι / is linguistically less advanced than *Th* 269 / ὠκείῃς πτερύγεσσι . . . , but modified by separation.

383 ἐπιδαίομαι is an old verb, found elsewhere only at *Th* 789 and in Mycenaean.[24]
388 ὠλένη 'forearm' is not found elsewhere in epic, and, as Pavese[25] remarks, is attested in a Mycenaean cognate and given as Cypriot by the *glōssai kata poleis*. We may add that it is quoted as Cleitorian (Arcadian) in *Anecdota Graeca* (ed. Bekker) 1096. But the meaning is latent in λευκώλενος, and the noun is common in tragedy and later prose, so this archaism is not very significant.
400 χρήματα meaning 'cattle' is unique in the epos. The sense 'thing' is already found at *Erga* 344, *Herm* 332, Archil. 122.1. Allen and Sikes[26] suggest that the form may be a gloss for κτήνεα; compare Hesychius' κτήνεα· χρήματα, βοσκήματα.
406 νεογνός is also found at *Dem* 141, and from Aeschylus onwards. In formation it is an archaism (cf. Latin *prīvignus*),[27] yet hardly very significant.
447 ἀμηχανέων, cf. φηλητέ͜ων with synizesis 175, 292. Genitive plurals feminine in -έων without synizesis are very rare in the epos (3x Homer, *Aspis* 246), and represent a less advanced stage, which is here metrically necessary. The adjective is less likely to be from ἀμηχανής, agreeing with a masculine μελεδών, but the possibility cannot be excluded entirely. But of course the morph is more advanced than -άων as at 220, 276, 430 and 537 (220 and 537 are in common formulae). ἀμηχανέων is thus an archaism dating from a transitory stage in Attic and Ionic soon after quantitative metathesis – unless of course it is a mere metrical expedient.
524 ἐπ' ἀρθμῷ καὶ φιλότητι. Pavese[28] suggests that this represents an old formula, cf. H 302 ἐν φιλότητι διέτμαγεν ἀρθμήσαντε. We may add Theognis 1312 ἄρθμιος ἠδὲ φίλος, Aesch. *Prom.* 192 εἰς ἀρθμὸν ἐμοὶ καὶ φιλότητα, cf. Call. fr. 497a Pf.

The archaisms that remain significant after this scrutiny are no more numerous than one might expect in such a long hymn. Against the weight of post-Homeric diction they avail not. Small details confirm the picture, e.g. the use of ἄδικος (316), first at *Erga* 260 etc., *Cat* 10.3, cf. *Dem* 367. A number of unusual formulae are shared with Hesiod and other closely related mainland poems: the closeness of *Cat*, *PAp* and *Herm* to *Th* (but not to the *Erga*, which shares more phrases with *Dem* and *Aphr*) has been demonstrated by statistical means above.[29] Some of the correspondences are very striking:

76 *δολίης δ' οὐ λήθετο τέχνης*, **Th* 547; 110 *θερμὸς ἀυτμή*, **Th* 696; 243 *γνῶ δ' οὐδ' ἠγνοίησε*, **Th* 551; 415 *πῦρ ἀμαρύσσων*, **Th* 827. These parallels are all with episodes that may have become popular at an early date: Prometheus, the Titans and Typhon. The parallels between similar episodes and *Dem* have been pointed out by Richardson[30] as evidence for knowledge of the *Theogony*. However it is clear that the poet was not making a mere patchwork from Homer and the *Theogony*, but had a wider knowledge of the later poetic diction as represented in the other works of 'Hesiod' and the Hymns. This is shown by shared phrases:

36 = *Erga* 365; 37 *ἐπηλυσίης πολυπήμονος*, **Dem* 230; 120 *ἔργωι δ' ἔργον* cf. *Erga* 382 *ἔργον ἐπ' ἔργωι*; 176 *Λητοῦς ἐρικυδέος υἱός*, **PAp* 182; 236 *χωόμενον περὶ βουσίν*, *[*Aspis*] 12; 322 *θυώδεος Οὐλύμποιο*, **Dem* 331. The attempts of Radermacher[31] to argue from 176 and 322 that *Herm* postdates *Dem* and *PAp* are unsatisfactory, as in the first case the shared phrase may be no more than an under-represented formula, while the argument that *θυώδης* is more frequently used in *Dem*, and 322 is therefore borrowed into *Herm*, is patently unreliable. A more interesting example is *ἑκατηβόλος αὐτὸς Ἀπόλλων* (234) beside *Aphr* 151 *ἑκηβόλος* ~, where the emphatic sense of *αὐτός* is still present: at 234 it is not. The usage has simply become stereotyped, as Allen and Sikes recognise.[32] 234 is therefore more advanced – but this does not suffice to prove that the whole poem is later; however, this is probable on other grounds.

The historical evidence that has been extracted from the text for dating purposes is insubstantial. The lyre with seven strings was reinvented by Terpander, but is taken for granted in the Hymn: this implies a *terminus post quem* somewhat after the mid-seventh century,[33] which is no surprise. The caduceus is possibly sixth-century or later.[34] Accepted evidence for any *terminus ante quem* is even slighter. Jacoby's suggestion that Hellanicus' discussion of Hermes φιλητής (*FGH* I, p. 111: cf. Schol. ad Σ 486) proves knowledge of the Hymn is not cogent. But the *terminus post quem* can perhaps be lowered. The threat of Hermes against Delphi (178ff.) may be related to the events of the First Sacred War.[35] Humbert[36] suggests that the wealth of Delphi referred to there could be due to contacts with Croesus, and favours the last third of the sixth century. His argument may be supported by the desire of the Hymnodist to defend the Pythian oracle from charges of greed and falsity manifested at 543ff. Here Apollo promises to give true oracles to those who come with favourable omens; but as for him who comes relying on birds that cry in vain,

φήμ' ἀλίην ὁδὸν εἶσιν, ἐγὼ δέ κε δῶρα δεχοίμην (549).

The first blunder we know of in the oracle's history was the failure of the Spartan attempt to conquer Tegea, but this does not seem to have damaged its credit.[37] The first major calamity was the fall of Croesus, and here there might well be cause for reproaches such as are put into Croesus' mouth by Bacchylides (III 37f.), before the king's miraculous rescue from the pyre: as in the Tegean episode, Herodotus (I) preserves the apologia of the riddling oracle, and a variant of the tale of rescue. The rapidity with which these tales appeared convicts the oracle, or at least its supporters such as the poet of *Herm*, of some embarrassment. There were of course subsequent occasions (notably during the Persian Wars) when the priests made mistakes, but never would the mention of gifts have such point.[38] This may give us a new *terminus post quem* of c. 547, but there is no certain *terminus ante*, as the fall of Sardis was topical in poetry and vase-painting for many years, although I doubt whether it would have merited an apologia after the middle of the fifth century.

Whether or not this is correct, the date should not be lowered too far, since false oracles are excused by incorrect auspices or paltry gifts (562) rather than by human misunderstanding of a riddling message, the explanation that is first heard around 500 B.C. and becomes prevalent thereafter. For the older view compare *Cat* 240.10f.:[39] contrast Heraclitus fr. 93 D–K, Aeschylus *Ag* 1255, and so forth.

Gräfe's[40] fifth-century dating of the poem rests on the idea that the cults of Apollo and Hermes are characteristic of the upper and lower classes respectively, whose conflict (reconciled in the poem's symbolism) was absent from Athens during the tyranny, and not overt until the era of Cimon and Themistocles: but even if the Hymn were Attic, and the two gods did have different classes of worshippers, there is no proof of any particular date. Eitrem's[41] attempts to find fifth-century elements are also inadequate.

Following the lead of Koster,[42] Görgemanns[43] has recently produced much the best case for a date around the beginning of the fifth century. Firstly, he points to the evolution of self-conscious oratory, and especially the use of an epilogue and the argument from probability at 265 (which was particularly associated with Corax and Tisias). Secondly, the interest in the role of improvisation in the discovery of music, the effect of music on the hearer, and the discussion of how music can be both a divine gift and a *τέχνη*, a *τέχνη* needing *τρίβος* and a certain natural aptitude (447ff., 483ff.), all this is strongly reminiscent of early sophistic theory and remarks in Pindar during the 470s and 460s. The cumulation of evidence is impressive, and Görgemanns concludes that the hymn dates from around the start of the fifth century. This is certainly compatible with the other evidence of all kinds, and convincing in itself.

N. O. Brown[44] suggested that the twelvefold division of meat at 128f. refers to the cult of the twelve gods at Athens, instituted in 522/1. Far from proving that *Herm* was composed then, this does not even yield a *terminus post quem*, for two reasons: there is no mention of Athens anywhere in the *Hymn* (and we shall see that linguistic evidence for an Attic poet is lacking), and the cult of the twelve gods is known elsewhere, especially at Olympia. Indeed Càssola plausibly suggests that this sacrifice near the mouth of the Alpheus was an *aition* for the cult *there*.[45]

As we have seen, *Herm* shares several linguistic features with *PAp*: false archaism in *-οιο* and 'long' dative plurals, and the rarity of *Ζηνός* and of n-mobile before consonants.[46] But the differences are also interesting: *PAp* archaises with digamma and uses only *εἰς*, whereas *Herm* neglects digamma to a great extent and uses mainly *ἐς*.[47] This does not entitle us to assume that the poet lacked either digamma or *εἰς* in his vernacular: it is more likely to be a feature of poetic diction. Poets aware of the Ionic tint in the diction might try to 'correct' the poetry in the direction of spoken Ionic, particularly, as we have seen in the case of *PAp*,[48] when knowledge of Homer's less advanced diction had increased the pressure for false archaism, not only in such obvious forms as the 'long' dative plurals or genitive singulars, but also (for speakers of Boeotian) in the observance of the effect of digamma. This last has been 'corrected' by our poet or his predecessors in the direction of what was known of the Ionic vernacular, but the others have been allowed to persist. If there is such a direct link between *Herm* and the sub-tradition of *PAp*, the chronology is affected: it is difficult to believe that such a tradition could have remained uncontaminated for more than, say, three generations. As we shall see, religious predilections constitute another link between these two Hymns.

In short, a date for the poem towards the close of the sixth century fits the evidence best, and so does its attribution to Boeotia. A number of forms have been alleged to point to its dialectal origins:

17 *γεγονώς* is remodelled for *γεγαώς* (Homer, Hes. fr. 280.19) after *γέγονα* etc., as in Alcaeus (72.11 L–P) and later dialects, including the *koine*. In view of other alleged Atticisms Zumbach[49] claims it as Attic. But even if the form is sound (it is not guaranteed by metre in place of the older form), this innovation is too widely distributed in time and space to be useful here.

50 *πήχεις* accusative is no more than a scribal Atticism: moreover M reads *πήχῡς*.[50]

50 *ἀμφοῖν* is not found elsewhere in epic, where there is evidence for the use of *ἄμφω* dative (*Dem* 15, Φ 162 v.l.) and genitive (Hes. fr. 338 ap. Plut. et al.: Ar. *Wasps* 725 et al., *ἀμφοῖν*). This is corroborated by Hellenistic and later epic usage.[51] If the text is sound, *ἀμφοῖν* is certainly unepic, but not necessarily Attic, as Zumbach suggests.[52] It might, for instance, be Boeotian.

76 *ἴχνη ἀποστρέψας*. Zumbach[53] argues that the emendations of Hermann (*ἴχνι'*) and Ilgen (*ἴχνε'*) are superfluous. Even if this were certain, that the Atticism is more than scribal is not: compare *τεμένη* λ 185 (-*ε͜α* Aristarchus), *τεύχη* / H 207 etc.[54] Zumbach has missed the more certain *ὄρη σκιόεντα* (95, **Hy* 27.4) which is modified from *ὄρεα σκιόεντα* / (ε 279 = η 268, *DAp* 34, *Herm* 70). The contracted forms are common in the late Hymns, at least according to our manuscripts: cf. *πίση* / *Hy* 19.2, *τεύχη* / *Hy* 28.15.

98 *ὄρθρος* is claimed as Attic by Zumbach,[55] but occurs at *Erga* 577.

106 *ἀθρόᾰς οὔσας* /. On the short accusative plural v. sup. pp. 58–62, where we have seen that there is no need to agree that these forms are West Greek, as in Hesiod they merely carry further tendencies apparently already visible in *Od*; nonetheless West Greek, Thessalian or Arcadian influence may have assisted the appearance of the short forms, although I prefer A. von Blumenthal's idea that the existence of forms in -*ᾰς* in consonant-stems was responsible.[56] We have already noted the curious fact that the percentage of a-stem accusative plurals scanned heavy before vowels is much lower (23.8%) than that of o-stems (36%). Both are rather higher than Hesiod's level. Although *Cat* is inconsistent in the opposite fashion, both poems seem more reluctant than was Hesiod to admit the light ending -*ᾰς*. Excluding line-ends, the proportion of a-stem endings that are light is as shown in table 28 in the works where they occur (verse-ends of course excluded). In support of this observation observe that both *ἀθρόᾰς* and *Σκύθᾰς* (*Cat* 150.15), as well as some examples in Tyrtaeus,[57] are impossible or very awkward in dactylic verse. As for *οὔσας*, this is certainly an Atticism, but one

Table 28. *Light a-stem accusative plurals in the epos*

	Th	*Erga*	*Cat*	*Herm*	(Empedocles)
-ᾰς	6	3	1	1	(2)
others	42	17	19	21	(10)
total	48	20	20	22	(12)
%-ᾰς	12.5	15.0	5.0	4.5	(16.6)

familiar in this branch of the tradition, as we saw in discussing *PAp* 330.[58] Moreover, its evidential value is diminished by the fact that Attic ὤν cannot be due to contraction, but corresponds to Latin *sons*, and the form might therefore be an inherited archaism in poetry.[59] The introduction of both of these peculiarities is eased by the fact that the phrase is modified from ἄθροοι ἦσαν / α 27, ~ εἶεν / *DAp* 152, just as the examples at *Th* 60 and especially *Erga* 564 and 675 are modified from phrases in the nominative, e.g. *Erga* 564 τροπὰς ἠελίοιο / after τροπαὶ ἠελίοιο / ο 404.[60]

109 ἐνέλεψε σιδήρωι mss., ἐνίαλλε M. Radermacher[61] emended to ἐν δ' ἴλλε σιδείωι (sc. ὄζωι) 'he turned it in (a bough of) σίδη', a name for the pomegranate and for a water-lily common near Orchomenus in Boeotia (Nic. *Th* 887, Thphr. *HP* IV 10.1). He was followed by Humbert[62] in assigning the poet a Boeotian origin on the strength of this conjecture. Whether or not the conjecture is correct,[63] this view is mistaken: as Càssola remarks, fire-sticks need to be made of woody material, not water-lily, and σίδειος must mean 'of pomegranate', which grew widely.

112 κᾶλα. Zumbach[64] suggests that this is borrowed from *Erga* 427, and the similar phraseology supports this – / πολλὰ δὲ κάγκανα κᾶλα beside / πόλλ' ἐπικαμπύλα κᾶλα (*Erga* 427). West[65] remarks that κᾶλα appears as a feature of the Laconian dialect (meaning 'ships') at Ar. *Lys*. 1253 and elsewhere, and concludes that its currency may have been restricted to Doric and mainland areas in historical times. However, whatever the exact derivation, there is nothing that excludes the form from Ionic, whether it is contracted from

ἄϝε like δᾶλός, or αϝα like ἄτη. Moreover it is attested not only in Cyrene (*Berl. Sitzb.* 1927, 157) and Callimachus (fr. 242 Pf.) with the meaning 'wood', but also in Ion of Chios (*TGF* 19 F 29 N) in the sense 'logs'. Evidence for a limited distribution of this word is simply inadequate, and only the developed meaning 'ships' need be distinctively Laconian.

114 φύζαν mss., φύσαν E, φῦσαν D'Orville. φύζαν is too well-established to be emended away easily, although rejected by Humbert and Càssola. Moreover Hesychius has a gloss ἐφύζα· ἐφύσα. Allen and Halliday[66] allege that the form is Cretan, where the reflex of **ty* was probably *ts* written ζ in early inscriptions (e.g. μέζατος, ὄζος = ὄσος).[67] Frisk[68] derives φῦσα from *φυτι̯α vel. sim., with subsequent simplification of the sibilant after the long vowel (cf. Skt. *phutkaroti*). It is most improbable that there should be a Cretan form in this poem, and the graph ζ for *ts* is unknown outside inscriptions: φύζα seems more likely to be derived from an alternative form of this onomatopoeic root ending in *d*, cf. perhaps Latin *pustulum* from **put-* or **pud-*, cf. *rōstrum*:: *rōdō*.

140 ἐμάρᾱνε is an Atticism of the same kind as ἀγξηράνῃ, Φ 347,[69] with ᾱ for η after ρ; it is open to the same kind of objection as θᾶττον below – that it could be no more than graphic. Compare however 75 πλᾱνοδίας with metrical lengthening: the word appears as πληνοδίαι in Hesychius, with a hyperionism. Yet even if these examples of ᾱ are genuine, they do not prove an Attic poet.

152 περ' ἰγνύσι used to be compared to περοίχεται (*Th* 733) as exhibiting a feature common to Delphian, Locrian, Lesbian, Boeotian and Doric poetry.[70] However Forssmann[71] has pointed out that this is better read περὶ γνυσί, with an archaic reduced-grade dative plural of γόνυ, cf. δρυσί: δόρυ. Moreover, the Hesiodic parallel is now discredited.

158 Λητοΐδου ὑπὸ χερσί. This Atticism is not in Zumbach, but again cannot be relied upon; it could be a surface alteration for Λητοΐδεω (so Hermann). Compare Κομή[το]υ, τόν *Cat* 70.39, Φλεγύου βασιλῆος in most mss. at *Hy* 16.3 (-ύος AtDKN, -εος HJ, -υα Schol. Pind. *Py* III 14), and

Λητοΐδου in an ancient epigram at Delphi reported by Phaenias.[72] Λητοΐδης (also at 253) is itself unhomeric, but occurs at *Aspis* 479, *Cat* 51.3, and on the chest of Cypselus (Paus. V 18.4), and is perhaps a late and/or mainland feature.[73]

208 ἔδοξα 'I thought' is paralleled in sense in the epic only at H 192 δοκέω, and *Aphr* 125 ἐδόκουν (where the contraction -ουν for -εον is a superficial Atticism). As Zumbach[74] remarks, the sole form of the aorist in homer is δόκησε (*Od* bis): ἔδοξα is first otherwise in Pindar, *Nem* IV 37, and the sense 'think' is well attested in Herodotus,[75] so there is insufficient evidence that either form or usage is Attic.

222 βῆμα is listed by Zumbach as Attic only, but occurs in Sappho and Pindar![76]

255 θᾶττον all mss. except M, which has a lacuna. At 212 θᾶσσον is transmitted by all mss. θᾶττον has often been seized upon as evidence for Attic[77] or Boeotian origins. Pavese[78] believes that it escaped during the wholesale transfer he postulates from the supposed mainland diction to the Ionicised version, on account of the identity with the Attic form. But it is rash to trust the text where it is so self-contradictory.

313 διαρρήδην and 431 πρέσβις are found only in Attic prose,[79] but are hardly very significant.

342 εὐθὺ Πύλονδ' ἐλάων, 355 εἰς Πύλον εὐθὺς ἐλῶντα. This is Attic for ἰθύς, the form attested in all major early epic poems except *Cat*, *DAp*, *PAp* and here: note however 148 ἰθύσας, and *Cat* 25. 11 (ἰθύοι restored) beside εὐθύ[ς] 43.63. In no case is either vocalism metrically guaranteed. The etymology of the two forms is obscure, but εὐθύς is not restricted to Attic in inscriptions[80] or poetry: it is common in Pindar, and both forms occur in Theognis, Tyrtaeus and Bacchylides. There is a doubtful case in Alcaeus, 130.13 L–P. This need not disprove even Boeotian origins for *Herm*, despite the Boeotian and Ionian preference for ἰθύς: the phrases may have originated elsewhere, and, as Càssola remarks,[81] εὐθύς is simply non-Homeric, but not ineluctably Attic.

400 ἠχοῦ is well restored by Fick from the variously accented mss. However, its similarity to the ἠχοῖ of an Oropian inscription (*IG* 7 235.16), combined with the supposed evidence of θᾶττον at 255, led him to propose[82] Eretria or Oropus as the poet's place of origin. Such conclusions are unjustified. ἠχοῦ is certainly unusual (it is recorded in Hesychius), but we cannot rediscover its distribution: ἦχι is found in Homer, A 607 etc.

405 ἐδύνω is thought to embody an Attic contraction by Zumbach,[83] along with several different contractions in *Dem.*[84] There is no reason to accept his views.[85]

456 οἶδας / Ψ, οἶσθα M (467 οἶδας / omnes). The textual fluctuation forbids us to regard either the retention of the inherited οἶσθα or the Ionic innovation οἶδας as significant.[86] The archaism is usual in Homer (8x *Il*, 6x *Od*, *Aspis* 355, *Herm* 382), where it is always metrically guaranteed, except at A 85: οἶδας only occurs at α 337, where it is at line-end.

473 τῶν νῦν αὐτὸς ἔγωγε † παῖδ' ἀφνειὸν † δεδάηκα. Pavese[87] plausibly suggests that an Aeolic form πεδα(ι)φνειον of the Hesychian adverb μεταίφνιον· ἐξαπίνης underlies the crux. The preposition πεδά (attested in Mycenaean) is an archaism retained by several dialects – Lesbian, Arcadian, Laconian, Argive, Cretan, Theran and Rhodian as well as Boeotian.[88] But his view that it was not altered to μετα- because not well understood in Attic is unnecessary: compounds in πεδα- occur in Aeschylus as well as Pindar.

Although several traces of Attic transmission survive this destructive criticism, only one organic Atticism escapes – οὖσας 106, also found in *Od* and *Cat*. εὐθύ 342 is a more widespread mainland form. To the argument from silence is added that from the rarity of n-mobile before consonants: contrast the practice of *Dem.*[89] In the preceding pages we have seen considerable affinities in diction as well as content with *PAp*, which is from the western part of Boeotia and has close links with Delphi.[90] Even though there are as usual in the tradition no actual Boeotisms in the language, *Herm*'s content supports this view. The role of Onchestus (88f., 186ff.) is particularly fascinating – in Apollodorus it is the men of Pylos who inform on Hermes[91] and Antoninus Liberalis locates the incident on Maenalus.[92] *PAp* too dilates upon Onchestus, which was an important religious centre for all Boeotia.[93] Both poets accord the sanctuary the outstanding honour of being implied to have existed even in the days when gods were still being born, in *PAp* even before the foundation of Delphi which is the theme of the Hymn.[94] Apollo's concluding discourse (*Herm* 533–66) displays a similar concern with Delphi,[95] and quite possibly our Hymn too was composed for performance there. I have suggested above that the defence of false oracles harmonises with Görgemann's arguments and considerations of language in indicating the closing decades of the sixth century as the era of the poem's creation. Its light-hearted tone, unepic vocabulary and penchant for unusual compounds are reminiscent of the comic and satyric genres that were beginning their literary development during this period. Such broad humour was by no means an Attic monopoly: witness, for example, scenes in Pindar's ninth and tenth Pythian Odes. Its incorporation into the traditional genre of hymnody may represent an imaginative departure from the past by its Boeotian author, and may somehow be related to our affirmation above that the Hymn is not oral in the same sense as are the poems of Homer and Hesiod, or indeed the two *Hymns to Apollo*.[96]

This is not to imply that the Hymn is without an oral foundation: I consider it probable that the poem has a long traditional ancestry, and *Hy* 18 is a collateral relative.[97] Note the preservation of the obscure phrase νυκτὸς ἀμολγῷ at line 7, which is replaced by the comprehensible νυκτὸς ἐν ὥρῃ elsewhere in *Herm* (67, 155, 400).[98] This is no surprise, since whether oral composition-in-performance or a more stereotyped epic recitation is involved, the beginning is likely to be the portion repeated most often and heard with the keenest attention. It is no surprise either that beginnings may be found to have influenced other poems, as in the case of the proem of the *Theogony* and *Aphr* 258ff.,[99] or that of

Herm and *Hy* 19.28ff.[100] But I would be surprised if this proem goes back substantially unchanged beyond the eighth century, because of the modification Ἀρκαδίης πολυμήλου, also found at *Cat* 23.32.[101] The phrase is lacking in Homer, but compare Ἀργεάδην Πολύμηλον / Π 417, and there is a noteworthy parallel to the whole proem at Π 180ff., on the birth of Eudorus, where several phrases are similar:

. . . τὸν ἔτικτε χορῷ καλὴ Πολυμήλη,
Φύλαντος θυγάτηρ· τῆς δὲ κρατὺς Ἀργειφόντης
ἠράσατ' . . . (180-2)

With / Φύλαντος θυγάτηρ compare / Ἄτλαντος ~ (*Hy* 18.4). With Π 187f. τόν γε μογοστόκος Εἰλείθυια / ἐξάγαγε πρὸ φόωσδε . . . cf. *Herm* 12 / εἴς τε φόως ἄγαγεν̄ . . . : but the same elements reappear more clearly in the narrative of Apollo's birth at *DAp* 115 (μογοστόκος Εἰλείθυια /) and 119 (/ ἐκ δ' ἔθορε πρὸ φόωσδε). This shows the antiquity of narratives of this sort, one of which was here subsumed by our Boeotian poet of the later sixth century.

CHAPTER 8

THE HYMN TO APHRODITE

The *Hymn to Aphrodite* is the most admirable of the major *Homeric Hymns*, yet one remarkably obscure in terms of date, place of origin and relation to other poetry; external evidence is entirely lacking, and the poem is hardly quoted or referred to throughout antiquity.[1] The only archaic poems extant with which it has any relationship are the *Hymn to Demeter* and, as will be demonstrated, Hesiod's and Sappho's.

Linguistic support has been sought for very diverse datings of the Hymn. Following G. Hermann,[2] Reinhardt[3] and Porter[4] have believed it to be as early as Homer. Heitsch,[5] Hoekstra[6] and Kamerbeek[7] have since argued that its diction is post-Homeric, while Freed and Bentman[8] (following Suhle[9]) have urged a fourth-century or Hellenistic date. Commentators[10] on the Hymn have usually adopted a more moderate dating, after Homer but before the sixth century. Argument has also ranged over whether our Hymn antedates the *Hymn to Demeter*, and whether it is by the same poet as the '*Aeneis*' in Υ. It is not my aim to deal with this last problem, although my conclusions will make it quite clear that *Il* and *Aphr* are not the work of the same poet. In any case the arguments of Heitsch[11] have in this respect been soundly refuted by Lenz,[12] who shows that there is no reason to believe the '*Aeneis*' later than the bulk of the *Iliad*.

At first sight the diction of the Hymn is very archaic, and at a similar stage to that of Homer. This is reflected in the criteria as displayed in Figure 2, where all but three results are at Homeric levels.[13] The exceptions are the very common use of the East Ionic innovation Ζηνός for Διός,[14] and the drop in the use of the archaic o-stem genitive singular in *-οιο* and concomitant increase in the incidence of contracted *-ου*: the same phenomenon is found in Hesiod's *Erga*.[15] Another interesting oddity is the increased use of n-mobile before a consonant, which should exclude the mainland (except Attica) as a place of origin, and suggest a post-Homeric date: but this result could merely be a random departure from Homeric practice.[16] These facts are self-contradictory at first sight, and present very real difficulties: is this a poem of Homeric date, with the more advanced features random or regional in origin? Or is it post-Homeric, with the archaic diction a regional characteristic or a deliberate choice (since it is too well-established to be random)?

We shall see that the Hymn is indeed post-Homeric, and this leaves us with a choice between explanations for the archaism of the bulk of the poem's diction. One might argue that the diction of *Aphr* was affected extensively by the influence of a fixed text from a much earlier date, namely that of the Homeric epics (but we must then account for some curious inconsistencies):[17] alternatively, I shall advance the theory that the archaic diction is caused by the influence of the original Aeolic tradition, to which the fragments of the *Cypria* also belong (in this case the inconsistencies in the amount of archaism in some features can be explained). Hence our conclusions about this poem have a wider importance, and must be weighed very carefully.

Heitsch and Kamerbeek have already remarked a number of post-Homeric forms and usages in *Aphr*, which have been multiplied and reinforced by Hoekstra's study of formular modifications.[18] The same conclusion has been reached in quantitative terms by Postlethwaite,[19] who has shown that modifications of noun–epithet formulae are at least twice as common here as in Homer. In table 29 the frequency of mobility and separation in such phrases is given for Homer and the Hymns:[20] the figures represent the average number of lines containing one such case (the Homeric figures are based on A 176–611, β 1–434: *Ap* is unfortunately undivided).

Aphr thus exhibits both types of modification more often than any other poem examined by Postlethwaite. This is a very significant discovery, and confirms the conclusion of

Table 29. *Mobility and separation in noun–epithet formulae*

	Il	*Od*	*Dem*	*Ap*	*Herm*	*Aphr*
Mobility	33.4	25.5	35.4	18.8	20.7	10.8
Separation	12.8	12.4	6.1	7.3	5.6	4.8

Hoekstra and others that the Hymn is post-Homeric. Here then is another puzzle: as we have seen, modification and the increase in advanced diction everywhere else proceed together;[21] so why not here?

Hoekstra's study of modifications involving linguistic innovation in *Aphr* is in general so well conceived and executed as to require no duplication: in the section that follows I shall do no more than refer to some crucial cases and fill some gaps, in particular in the genitive singulars and dative plurals, which he has disregarded. Despite the number of verses also found in Homer (the second largest in any of the Hymns[22]), such modifications are numerous. Some neglect digamma:

169 / *βοῦς τε καὶ ἴφια μῆλα* cf. *βόας καὶ ἴφια μῆλα* (and nom.) 3x *Il*, 6x *Od*. The suppression of *τε* would beg the question.[23]

256 *πρῶτον ἴδηι φάος ἠελίοιο* / **DAp* 71 (cf. *Aphr* 278 ~ *ἴδηις θάλος* . . .). The formula is normally used of 'living and seeing the sun's light' (3x *Il*, 5x *Od*, *Aphr* 105), or of leaving it (2x *Il*, *Od*, *Erga*, *Aphr* 272), or of the sun setting (3x *Il*, 4x *Od*). The closest parallel is *Cat* 58.12 *πρὶν ἰδέειν λαμπρὸν φάος* ~ /, cf. E 120 *ὄψεσθαι λαμπρὸν* ~ /. The neglected digamma betrays this modification in *Aphr* and *DAp*: Homer has only *πρῶτα ἴδον* Ψ 462, *πρῶτος ἴδε* X 25, *α* 113 = *ρ* 328.

There are three striking neglects of postconsonantal digamma:

29 *δῶκε κᾰλὸν γέρας ἀντὶ γάμοιο* /. As Hoekstra says,[24] this is modified by the alternation of P_2 and T_2 formulae from ‖*κᾱλὸν γέρας* λ 184, cf. ‖*ἐμὸν* ~ λ 175.[25] I was at first inclined to reject the view of Solmsen[26] and Heitsch[27] that this is borrowed from Hesiod, *Th* 585 *τεῦξε κᾰλὸν κακὸν ἀντ' ἀγαθοῖο*: on their evidence it need be no more than a

formular pattern that happens to lack other attestation. But there is another quite remarkable parallel at *Th* 602f., *πόρεν κακὸν ἀντ' ἀγαθοῖο· / ὅς κε γάμον φεύγων*... (cf. also *Th* 582 with *Aphr* 5[28]). *Aphr* uses the phrase of Hestia eschewing marriage; in view of the close similarities between *Th* 2–8 and *Aphr* 258–61 (where *Aphr* appears to be dependent, as it uses a unique Hesiodic phrase, thereby violating economy with 285[29]), the argument that *Th* influenced *Aphr* here is overwhelmingly strong. Yet it need not follow that *κᾰλόν* was alien to the latter's vernacular: cf. 261 *ἀθανάτοισι κᾰλὸν χορὸν ἐρρώσαντο* beside ‖*κᾱλὸν χορόν* **Hy* 27.15, ‖*κᾱλοὶ χοροί* **μ* 318 (again by alternation of P_2 and T_2 formulae[30]). For a similar modification cf. Friedländer 47.1 (*LSAG* no. 30) *ἄγα]λ̣μα* ‖*κᾰλό̣ν* (Delos, c. 550–530(?), a Parian (?) votary) beside *κᾱλὸν ἄγαλμα* / (ibid. 113 (*LSAG* no. 149): Spartan, c. 490) and / *καλϝὸν ἄγαλμα* (ibid. 37: Ptoion, c. 550–525(?)). I suspect that such neglects of digamma were widespread in post-Homeric epic verse, rather than an Aeolic feature, as Kamerbeek[31] suggests for this poem and Hesiod. Chantraine[32] shows that similar phenomena are creeping into Homer, where, however, *κᾰλός* is unattested beside *κᾱλός* (293x).

194 *οὐ γάρ τοί τι δέος παθέειν*. Neglects and observances of digamma in **δϝέος* etc.[33] are distributed as shown in Table 30.[34] The neglect at *Aphr* 194 may be caused by inversion of *παθέειν δέος* (*ε* 347).

Table 30. *Neglects and observances of digamma in δέος etc.*

	Il	*Od*	*Th*	*Erga*	*Aspis*	*Cat*	*PAp*	*Aphr*
Obs.	14	5	–	–	2	–	1	–
Negl.	3	2	2	2	–	1	1	1

Four times the poet introduces a contracted genitive singular[35] in *-ου* by modification:

36 *Ζηνὸς νόον ἤγαγε τερπικεραύνου* /. A unique modification.[36]

40 *κασιγνήτης ἀλόχου τε* /. Cf. (also of Hera) the accusative at Π 432, Σ 356 and *Hy* 12.3; a case of declension here.

152 / *τόξου ἀπ' ἀργυρέου προΐηι*, cf. *ἀπ' ἀργυρέοιο βιοῖο* / A 49, Ω 605; but also / *τόξου ἀπὸ κρατεροῦ* +C, Θ 279.[37]
176 / *ἐξ ὕπνου τ' ἀνέγειρεν* is modified by insertion of *τ'* from *K 138 and (at verse-end) ψ 22.

In the dative plural note the following:
52 *καταθνητοῖς ἀνθρώποις* / is declined from the genitive found at Z 123, 6x *Od*, 2x *Cat*, *PAp* 541, 5x *Aphr*. There is a further modification of this (through separation by *τ'*) at *Cat* 1.7. This is avoided at **Th* 903 *καταθνητοῖσι βροτοῖσι*.
54 *ἐν ἀκροπόλοις ὄρεσιν* +C is modified by transposition from *ἐν ἀκροπόλοισιν ὄρεσσιν* / E 523, τ 205. *ὄρεσι(ν)* occurs elsewhere in the corpus only at *Herm* 33, beside *ὄρεσσι* 9x Homer etc. The shape ⏑⏑ — in dative plurals of neuter s-stems is rare: cf. the strange expression at 126 *παραὶ λέχεσιν καλέεσθαι* (also **Cat* 22.9), which Hoekstra[38] derives from *παραὶ λεχέεσσι κλιθῆναι* (α 366, σ 213). *λέχεσιν* is not found elsewhere – contrast *λεχέεσσι* 17x Hom., *λέχεσσι* 3x Hom. But *βέλεσιν* +C is found at Λ 657, π 277.
102 / *ὥρῃσιν πάσῃσι*: for n-mobile here too cf. *Dem* 265 / *ὥρῃσιν δ' ἄρα* (*Cypria* 4.8 / *ὥραις παντοίαις*).
135 / *σοῖς τε κασιγνήτοις* is transposed from *κασιγνήτοισί τε σοῖσι* / E 474, cf. / *οἷο κασιγνήτοιο* Γ 333, / *οὓς τε κασιγνήτους* *Hy* 7.31.

Of the other criteria in Chapter 3, I pass over n-mobile in view of Hoekstra's thorough discussion,[39] but the poet's use of *Ζηνός* merits scrutiny.
36 *Ζηνὸς νόον ἤγαγε τερπικεραύνου* / has a P_2 modification of a T_2 formula, cf. *Διὸς νόον* (6x *Il*, 3x *Od*, 3x *Th*, 1x *Erga*, 1x *Cat*, 3x *Herm*). *Ζηνὸς νόον* is found only at *Erga* 483, 661, *Cat* 43.52, fr. 303.2: the only approach to it in Homer is *Ζηνός τε νόος* (Π 103). Similar is 187 *Ζηνὸς γουνάζομαι αἰγιόχοιο* /: a T_2 expression *Διὸς* ⏓⏓ — ⏓⏓ *αἰγιόχοιο* / appears at P 176.

I will now discuss the other real and alleged post-Homeric phenomena in the order of their occurrence in the text.
4 *οἰωνούς τε διιπετέας*. Homer has solely *διιπετέος ποταμοῖο* (7x). The adjective means here 'that fly through the air'

rather than 'fallen from Zeus/the sky'. Whether this is derived from the root of δίεμαι or of **dyēus* is immaterial. Both senses of **dyēus* are inherited, and frequency is hardly a reliable guide as to whether this is archaism or innovation.[40] But the use of τε might suggest a modification.

7 τρισσάς. Kamerbeek[41] alleges that this word (not in Homer, first at *Cat* 233.2) is post-Homeric; but there is no metrically equivalent synonym, and the formation is old.

19 διαπρύσιοι. This adjective (also *Herm* 336) is not in Homer, who uses only the adverb διαπρύσιον (7x).

24 / πότνιαν in the accusative is unhomeric. πότνια occupies the fifth foot 47x *Il*, 18x *Od* and often: the first modification seems to have been πότνιαν Ἥρην /[42] (*Th* 11 = Epimenides 13.3, declined from the usual nominative), cf. πότνιαν ἁγνήν / (*Dem* 203). The use at verse-beginning looks like a run-over modification, and also occurs at *Th* 926.[43]

32 θεῶν πρέσβειρα is built on πρέσβα θεά (4x *Il*, cf. Τ 91, γ 452) after the analogy of such words as σώτειρα.[44] Cf. / γαῖαν παμμήτειραν *Hy* 30.1 beside / γῆ πάντων μήτηρ (*Erga* 563), γαῖά τε παμμήτωρ (Orph. 168.27 Kern) and παμμῆτορ τε γῆ Aesch. *Prom* 90. πρέσβειρα is first otherwise in Aeschylean parody at Aristoph. *Ach* 883, cf. Eur. *IT* 963.

49 / ἡδὺ γελοιήσασα conjugates e.g. ἡδὺ γελώοντες σ 111.[45]

65 κοσμέω 'array' is also found at *Th* 573, *Hy* 6.11. In Homer it means 'marshal' (Β 554 etc.).[46]

74 / σύνδυο κοιμήσαντο 'two by two'. The coalescence of σύν with a sequent numeral appears in ξυνεείκοσι (ξ 98), and cf. Κ 224 / σύν τε δύ' ἐρχομένω.[47] I am not sure that this goes beyond Homer.[48]

92, 195 μακάρων. But for once in *Od* (κ 299, in the genitive plural), this epithet never designates the gods without θεοί explicitly stated in Homer (14x *Il*, 19x *Od*). Heitsch[49] dubs this a Hesiodic trait – cf. *Th* 33, *Erga* 136, 718, 730: add *Aspis* 328, *Dem* 303, *Hy* 12.4 (nom.), *Hy* 29.8, and with ἀθάνατοι (and oblique cases) only *Erga* 706, *Aspis* 79, *Dem* 22, *PAp* 315, 473, *Herm* 441, *Aphr* 268.[50]

98 νυμφῶν after νυμφάων 97 has led many to postulate a double recension. But νυμφῶν for νυμφέ͜ων (μ 318, *Th* 130)

may be merely a graphic atticism, and a similar alternation occurs at *Dem* 494f. (ὠϊδῆς and ἀοιδῆς).

102 *σὺ δ' εὔφρονα θυμὸν ἔχουσα*. Kamerbeek[51] notes that this means 'cheerful, cheering' in Homer (4x): the sense 'gracious' is first in Pindar (*Ol* IV 14). Our phrase recurs in the dative at *Hy* 30.14 and Panyassis fr. 12.16, but in Homer solely *θυμὸς ἐύφρων* / *ρ* 531. See below on 262 for the significance of the alternation *ἐυ-/εὐ-*.

112 *Φρυγίης εὐτειχήτοιο ἀνάσσει* /. On the formation cf. sup. p. 29. Hoekstra[52] lists it as post-Homeric, but how can this be proved?

114 *διαπρό* temporally (= *διαμπερές*) is not so used in Homer (21 contrary instances), and is first so attested in Hellenistic poetry.[53]

140 *ἀγλαὰ δέχθαι ἄποινα* (= A 23, 377) for the receipt of a dowry. Homer calls the dowry *μείλια* at I 147,[54] but difference in this usage does not prove one of date. Nor is the formula necessarily misapplied.[55]

170f. *γλυκὺν ὕπνον ἔχευε* / *νήδυμον*. Heitsch argues that the meaning of *νήδυμος* < **'ϝᾱ́δυμος* has here been forgotten, as it is conjoined with *γλυκύς*.[56] But cf. *ν* 79f. *νήδυμος ὕπνος* . . . / *νήγρετος, ἥδιστος* . . .[57]

179 *οἵην δή με τὸ πρῶτον*, cf. 185 *αὐτίκα σ' ὡς τὰ πρῶτα. τὸ πρῶτον* and its plural never begin with an iamb in Homer (18 contrary examples), but cf. *γ* 320 *ὅν τινᾰ πρῶτον*.[58] Our poet modified 185 to introduce *με*.

196f. (Aeneas) *ἐν Τρώεσσιν ἀνάξει*
καὶ παῖδες παίδεσσι διαμπερὲς ἐκγεγάονται.

ἐκγεγάονται (cf. *Anth. Pal.* XV 40.20 *ἐκγεγάοντο*) is thought a future by Chantraine,[59] modelled on the perfect: cf. *ἐρχατόωντο* < *ἔρχαται*. He suggests that the sigma was omitted, as too bold, on the analogy of such forms as *ἐλάω*. The context secures a future sense. Pavese[60] thinks the thematic ending Aeolic, but *finite* present endings in the perfect are characteristic rather of Sicilian Doric and the dialects of Rhodes, Cnidus and Carpathus.[61] Thus Chantraine's theory, implying an evolution within the epic diction itself, is superior: the form need not be post-Homeric, as *ἐρχατόωντο* is not.

Aphrodite's prophecy resembles Poseidon's in the '*Aeneis*', Υ 307f.:

. . . Αἰνείαο βίη Τρώεσσιν ἀνάξει
καὶ παίδων παῖδες τοί κεν μετόπισθε γένωνται.

Hoekstra[62] has attempted to derive a dating for *Aphr* from the divergences between the two versions. Poseidon predicts continued rule for the Aeneadae, Aphrodite merely continued descent through the generations. Hoekstra thinks the difference reflects the historically attested decline in the family's fortunes recorded by Strabo,[63] who says that the royal Aeneadae at Scepsis retained the title *βασιλεῖς*, *ἔχοντές τινας τιμάς*, even when an oligarchy was instituted and then, upon Milesian colonisation, a democracy. Milesian settlement began in the second quarter of the seventh century, but the oligarchy may have antedated this, so we have no absolute *terminus ante quem*.[64] Moreover the change may be trivial, a continued line of descent implying continued kingship for the royal *genos* (and in name they never lost the kingship, as Strabo reveals). Further, the *aition* proves knowledge of the Aeneadae, but not performance before them.[65] It is not overbold to say that *Aphr* 'bears no trace of having been written on a definite occasion, or for a particular person'.[66]

199 *ἕνεκα* 'because' was supposed by Suhle[67] to indicate a late date for our poem, but is defended if *εἵνεκ'* is restored at *PAp* 308 (for *ἥνεκ'* M, *ἥνικ'* cett.).[68] Alternatively, Kamerbeek[69] suggests the punctuation *ἔσχεν ἄχος· ἕνεκα βροτοῦ ἀνέρος ἔμπεσον εὐνῇ*. The asyndeton is no bar to this solution.[70] Hoekstra[71] claims that this is taken from Σ 85, . . . *ὅτε σε βροτοῦ ἀνέρος ἔμβαλον εὐνῇ*; but I see no reason to accept that 199 is a 'direct imitation of Homer by crude modifications' and hints at a more literary origin for *Aphr* than for *Ap* and *Dem*.

224 *γῆρας ὀλοιόν* for *ὀλοόν* is apparently extended from a legitimate feminine *ὀλοιή* (Α 342, Χ 5) by metrical lengthening.[72] Cf. on 245 infra.

229 *εὐηγενής* in Homer means 'noble' of people (Λ 427, Ψ 81) – here it describes a beard! Heitsch[73] suggests a misunderstanding of *εὐγένειος*, but the evidence is insufficient to

prove a difference in usage; nor, in this poem, should we exclude some humorous verbal play.

245 /νηλειές is by metrical lengthening for /νηλεές (Π 33 etc.); cf. *Th* 770 /νηλειής, where the lengthening is essential to avoid a cretic. Here it is not, and this usage is therefore secondary to Hesiod's.

246 καματηρός is post-Homeric in formation. The ending is extended with misdivision from the correct ἀνιη-ρός < ἀνίη, whence derived adjectives from o-stems in the same semantic range, like πονηρός (Hes. fr. 248f., 302.20, Aristeas 1.3 Kinkel) and καματηρός. Note that Hesiod's ὀμβρηρός (*Erga* 451) represents a further extension of the suffix.[74]

259 ἕπομαι 'belong to' is otherwise unattested until much later, e.g. Plato, as Kamerbeek[75] notes. But he fails to persuade me that *Th* 268 is transitional to this sense.[76]

262 Σειληνοί τε καὶ εὔσκοπος Ἀργειφόντης. Hermann deleted τε to conform to Homer's usage – ἐύσκοπος ~ (and oblique cases) is found at Ω 24, 109, α 38, η 137 (cf. λ 198), *PAp* 200 and *Herm* 73. This is *petitio principii* and parallels exist anyway at *DAp* 36 Ἴμβρος τ' εὐκτιμένη[77] and perhaps *Aphr* 102 above.

263 ἐρόεις is an adjective with a lyrical flavour, like καλυκῶπις (*Aphr* 284). It is unhomeric, and distributed as follows: *Th* 245, 251, 357; *Cat* 169.1; *Dem* 109, 425; *Herm* 31; *Aphr* 263; *Hy* 32.20; Alcaeus etc.

267 ἠλίβατος ('tall' of trees) is used by Homer only of rocks (4x, cf. *Th* 786, *Herm* 404, *Hy* 19.10), by Hesiod of a movable stone (*Th* 675) and a cave (*Th* 483); *Aspis* 421 has it describing a πεύκη in one ms. (vulgate: πέτρη). Heitsch has argued a change of usage on this weak evidence.[78]

267 τεμένη δέ ἑ κικλήσκουσιν. Hoekstra[79] thinks ἑ plural introduced by an ungrammatical modification of e.g. δ 355 Φάρον δέ ἑ ~. But there are other possibilities. With B 196f. βασιλήων . . . φιλεῖ δέ ἑ μητιέτα Ζεύς Monro[80] compares the change of number at δ 692f.: ἑ plural might result from misunderstanding such a passage. Pavese[81] thinks this an archaism, cf. Latin *se*. The same problem arises over ὅς and ἑός 'their' (*Th* 71, *Erga* 58, Zenodotus' reading at Γ 244,

and later poetry). Hoekstra[82] remarks that the use of *τεμένη* of trees alone, without reference to the owner, is unhomeric.
276 *ὄφρα ⟨κε⟩ ταῦτα μετὰ φρεσὶ πάντα διέλθω*. The sense 'recount, go over' is unknown before Pindar, *Nem* IV 72, Aesch. *Prom* 872.[83] The epos has *πάντα διίξομαι* or a conjugation thereof for this idea (I 61, T 186, *Dem* 416), and the phrasing is awkward here.[84]
284 *καλυκῶπις* is found also at *Dem* 8, 420 and Bacchylides fr. 20A 17 Snell. This duplicates *κυανῶπις* (μ 60, 5x *Cat*, *Aspis* 356) and *ἑλικῶπις* (A 98, 3x *Th*, 3x *Cat*, *Hy* 33.1). Like *ἐρόεις* (263), this is a romantic and lyrical formation, and thus post-Homeric;[85] it is surely misremembered or adapted from *κυανῶπις*.
291 *οὐρανὸν ἠνεμόεντα*. Elsewhere this epithet is reserved for lofty places or islands (21x in the epos). The usual phrase is *οὐρανὸν ἀστερόεντα* (5x Hom., 2x *Th*, *Dem* 33). Analogical substitution could have occurred at any date, and was probably influenced here by the proximity of *Ἴλιον ἠνεμόεσσαν* (280). Poets' choices between formular doublets were often affected by the memory of the previous choice;[86] something analogous has happened here. It is thus improbable that the poet avoided *ἀστερόεντα* as unsuited to the evening sky (168f.): there is nothing peculiar about the breaches of the tendency to economy in the Hymn that should make us suspect literary composition.[87]

Before summing up, I redress the balance with some non-Homeric archaisms:
10f. *πόλεμοί τε ἄδον . . . / ὑσμῖναί τε μάχαι τε . . . ἄδον* has an observance of initial digamma unparalleled in Homer: cf. **Th* 926 *κέλαδοί τε ἄδον πόλεμοί τε μάχαι τε*, **DAp* 22 *σκοπαί τοι ἄδον* (introducing a neglect). So too 92 *χαῖρε ἄνασσ'*: cf. ~ *ἄναξ*, *Hy* 15.9, 31.17, 32.17. Both of these formulae are hymnic in character, and suggest (as one would *a priori* expect) that these parts of the hymn have a long history in the tradition (and that Hesiod was not the first to divide up the spheres of divine activity).
227 *παρ' Ὠκεανοῖο ῥοῇς* is modified by separation,

introducing a contracted genitive in -ου, at *ω 11 Ὠκεανοῦ τε ῥοάς, *Th 841 ~ ῥοαί. This is not false archaism in -οιο, of which there is no trace in *Aphr*. But ῥοῇς +V is itself a modification (cf. Π 719) for the usual -οιο ῥοῇσι / (3x Hom.).
Three phrases with 'long' dative plurals are unparalleled in Homer:
142 τίμιον ἀνθρώποισι / *PAp 483, cf. *Cat* 240.7 /~ ἀνθρώποις ⟨lacuna⟩.
205 πάντεσσι τετιμένος ἀθανάτοισι / *Dem 397 (fem.), cf. Delphic oracle ap. Tzetzes *vit Hes* 30 (Μούσῃσι ~ ἀθανάτῃσι).
239 ἐν ἀθανάτοισιν ἑλοίμην / *Dem 328 (~ ἑλέσθαι ms.).
Note also the preference for a 'long' dative shown at 261 ἀθανάτοισι κᾰλόν instead of ἀθανάτοις κᾱλόν (if the text can be trusted).
At 63 oil is apparently described by the words ἀμβροσίῳι ἑανῷι (=Ξ 172, where the inexplicable ἑδανῷι is read by all but a few authorities). A. Hurst has cogently argued that in fact these words do not describe the perfumed oil at all, but straightforwardly mean 'for her immortal raiment'; Mycenaean documents record the use of perfumed oil for garments (e.g. PY Fr 1225 /*wehanoihi aloiphā*/). *Cypria* 4.2ff. presents an epic parallel, and the text should not be emended.[88]
123 ἄκτιτος is found otherwise only in Mycenaean.[89]

This concludes our survey of possible archaisms and post-Homeric elements in *Aphr*. The archaisms do not suffice to subvert the view of Kamerbeek, Heitsch and Hoekstra that the poem is rich in post-Homeric modifications, forms and usages. Crucial examples are 24 (Hesiodic), 29 (Hes.), 52, 92, 102 (*Dem*), 126 (*Cat*), 135, 148, 179, 194, 195 (Hes.), 224, 245 (Hes.), 246, 256 (*DAp*), 261, 262 (*DAp*), 263 (Hes.), 284 (*Dem*) (parallels in brackets). This conclusion concurs encouragingly with Postlethwaite's results;[90] moreover we have seen on the basis of two passages (*Aphr* 29 beside *Th* 585, 602f.: *Aphr* 258ff. beside *Th* 2–8)[91] that our poet very probably knew Hesiod's *Theogony*, even if the other similarities listed by Heitsch[92] are simply shared post-Homeric traits.[93] Before examining *Dem* to see whether it does provide another literary *terminus* in the other direction, we should turn to scrutinise the arguments that have been put forward for dating *Aphr* to the fifth century or after.

Such a dating was first advanced by Suhle[94] on the grounds that various forms and usages in the hymn are not otherwise encountered until much later. We have already seen that evidence of this sort is of minimal value by itself.[95] Freed and Bentman adduce other arguments,[96] which require a brief rebuttal here.

That the text is in good condition is no more than a function of the Hymn's uncomplicated diction, and in fact there are traces of variant lines (e.g. 136a), not to mention the doublet at 274f./276f. similar to that in *DAp* (136–8/139). The Hymn's obscurity in antiquity duplicates that of *Herm*, which, though nearly twice as long, is cited but once.[97]

Since *Aphr* contains fewer forms and lexemes unattested in Homer and Hesiod than the other major hymns, Freed and Bentman suggest that, whereas the other Hymns were composed when the language was close enough to Homer's to make its 'purification' unnecessary, our Hymn was not. This involves a misconception about the nature of Alexandrian aspirations, which were towards technical perfection rather than the close imitation of the oral formular style. Indeed *variatio* and novelty were welcomed. It is only much later that the Atticist movement in prose provides a parallel. The alleged 'poverty of vocabulary' in the poem may be caused, not by the need to use only 'vocabulary in texts', but by a limited oral repertoire. The presence of whole lines from Homer is an ambivalent criterion.[98]

Lastly, Freed and Bentman claim that the Aphrodite of the proem is a nature-goddess, a concept first found in Aeschylus fr.44 (the famous piece from the *Danaides*), where Aphrodite portrays herself as the creative principle manifested in the elements. But it is one thing for her to have power over all gods, men, animals and birds by land and sea (*Aphr* 1–6): it is quite another for her to animate the elements themselves as the principle of desire and reproduction, and thus ensure the continuance of the natural cycles of living creation. We should therefore by no means accept the *Danaides* as a *terminus post quem*.[99]

All who have examined the topic in detail agree that some of the numerous and striking similarities between *Aphr* and *Dem* suggest that *Aphr* has been imitated by *Dem*, and therefore antedates it.[100] But as usual in the matter of detecting *exemplum* and *imitatio* care and good fortune are needed to ensure that we can bar the gate against that remotely conceivable beast, a common source. The following similarities seem to me the most interesting:

(a) *Aphr* 31f.

πᾶσιν δ' ἐν νηοῖσι θεῶν τιμάοχός ἐστι,
καὶ παρὰ πᾶσι βροτοῖσι θεῶν πρέσβειρα τετυκται.

cf. *Dem* 268f.

εἰμὶ δὲ Δημήτηρ τιμάοχος, ἥ τε μέγιστον
ἀθανάτοις θνητοῖσί τ' ὄνεαρ καὶ χάρμα τέτυκται.

The prosodic and syntactic peculiarities of *Dem* 269, as well as the necessary enjambement (absent from *Aphr*), suggest that *Dem* is secondary. μέγιστον may have entered from *Aphr* 37 – ὅς τε μέγιστός τ' ἐστί, μεγίστης τ' ἔμμορε τιμῆς. Two further arguments clinch the case. First, as Podbielski remarks,[101] τιμάοχος is more in place in *Aphr*, where it is predicative and Hestia is receiving honour from Zeus, than in *Dem*, where it is no more than a decorative epithet. Secondly, τιμάοχος violates the 'law' of economy in *Dem*, where it is equivalent to Δημήτηρ ὡρηφόρος 192, cf. 268 ap. *P Berol.* 13044; but there is no breach in *Aphr*. The example of *Aphr* induced the poet of *Dem* to abandon Demeter's own epithet here. In the context of Homer one would expect τιμᾱ́οχος to be an Aeolism, due to the preservation of ᾱ, but Kamerbeek's affirmation[102] that it is Aeolic needs support from other evidence before we can safely say that it is more at home in the Aeolic *Aphr* than the Attic *Dem*. We shall see other grounds below for thinking that *Aphr* is indeed Aeolic in origin, so Kamerbeek should be right.

(b) *Aphr* 58 *θυώδεα νηόν* /, cf. *Dem* 355 *θυώδεος ἔνδοθι νηοῦ* /, 385 / *νηοῖο προπάροιθε θυώδεος*. *Dem*'s separated phrases, one embodying a contracted genitive singular, the other a form in *-οιο* (wherein *Dem* archaised and *Aphr* did not), have a secondary look.

(c) *Aphr* 82 *παρθένωι ἀδμήτηι μέγεθος καὶ εἶδος ὁμοίη*

Dem 145f. *παρθένος ἀδμής* / . . . *εἶδος ἀρίστη* /.

Here again a full line in *Aphr* relates to an enjambed line in *Dem*: on the other hand, note that *παρθένωι ἀδμήτηι* may represent a modification by mobility of the formula *παρθένος ἀδμής* / ζ 109, 228, *Cat* 59.4, *Dem* 145.

(d) *Aphr* 136 / *οὔ σφιν ἀεικελίη νυὸς ἔσσομαι*

Dem 83f. (cf. 363) *οὔ τοι ἀεικὴς* / *γαμβρός* . . .

For yet a third time the parallel in *Dem* is enjambed, indeed violently (i.e. the noun is in the line following the adjective). We saw above[103] that necessary enjambement is a feature distinctive of *Dem* from other early epic.

(e) *Aphr* 157 *ἐς λέχος εὔστρωτον*, cf. *Dem* 285 *ἀπ' εὐστρώτων λεχέων*, *Th* 798 *στρωτοῖς ἐν λεχέεσσι* for Homer's *τρητοῖς ἐν λεχέεσσι* vel. sim. (6x). The Hesiodic example suggests that we must be wary of a post-Homeric formula: but Podbielski[104] points out that *Aphr* 157 is glossed by the poet *χλαίνῃσιν* . . . *ἐστρωμένον*, showing consciousness of a neologism. Cf. also *κἀνδρὸς εὔστρωτον λέχος*, Alcaeus 283.8 L–P. This is not the only similarity between *Aphr* and Lesbian poetry; although the Tithonus episode has no apparent connexion with Sappho 58 L–P,[105] a link with Sappho 44 L–P will be unveiled below.[106]

(f) The divine epiphanies at *Aphr* 173f. and *Dem* 188f. both contain the words *μελάθρου* / *κῦρε κάρη*: but neither the asyndeton at *Aphr* 173 nor the sense 'lintel' for *μέλαθρον* in *Dem* (cf. Hsch. s.v.) settles the question of priority. Lenz[107] argues that the epiphany is unnecessary and unmotivated at *Dem* 188f., but the decision here is surely as subjective as that over the appropriateness of *κατ' ὄμματα καλὰ βαλοῦσα* at *Aphr* 156 and *Dem* 194.[108]

The opening lines of *Dem* contain two phrases also found close together in *Aphr*:

(g) *Aphr* 257 *νύμφαι . . . βαθύκολποι* / cf. *Dem* 5 *κούρῃσι . . . βαθυκόλποις* / (both of nymphs). The *Iliad* uses this epithet only of Trojan women (3x), but Zenodotus read Μοῦσαι . . . βαθύκολποι / at B 484. The short dative βαθυκόλποις / looks like a modification.

(h) *Aphr* 284 *νύμφης καλυκώπιδος*, cf. *Dem* 8 *καλυκώπιδι κούρῃ*, cf. 420 Ὠκυρόη καλυκῶπις. We have seen other examples of the influence of the opening of one poem on another, e.g. of *Th* on *Aphr* 258ff.; the assumption of such influence here runs quite counter to the other evidence. Moreover both the rape of Persephone and the vignette of the Hamadryads could be called memorable passages; and Humbert[109] has suggested that *Dem* 23f. ('neither gods nor men heard her voice, nor did the olive-trees') is inspired by *Aphr* 259, where the tree-nymphs are said to belong neither to gods nor to men.

To conclude, then, the similarities between *Aphr* and *Dem* are so extensive and detailed that a connexion between them is certain, and the likelihood of a common source seems very small. Decisive are the cases of enjambement in *Dem* (a, c, d), modifications in *Dem* (c, d), and the unnecessary use of *τιμάοχος* with a breach of economy in *Dem* (a), which prove that *Dem* is secondary, and therefore constitutes a *terminus ante quem* for the composition of *Aphr*. We already have a *terminus post quem* in *Th*: can greater precision be attained?[110]

Apart from one unique phrase where priority cannot be decided (*ὁμόθεν γεγάασιν* / *Aphr* 135, *Erga* 108), other more extensive parallels with Hesiod's *Erga* deserve review:

Aphr 1 = 9 *ἔργα πολυχρύσου Ἀφροδίτης* /,

**Erga* 521 *ἔργ' εἰδυῖα πολυχρύσου Ἀφροδίτης*.

Aphr 14 *παρθενικὰς ἁπαλόχροας*,

**Erga* 519 *παρθενικῆς ἁπαλόχροος*.

While *πολυχρύσου Ἀφροδίτης* is a common phrase,[111] and the juxtaposition of *ἔργα* easily ascribed to coincidence, *παρθενικὰς ἁπαλόχροας* is not (cf. only Theognis 1341 (Euenus?) *παιδὸς ἐρῶ ἁπαλόχροος*), and three other parallels between the two passages reinforce the link: *Aphr* 5 *πολλὰ τρέφει ἠδ' ὅσα πόντος* /, cf. *Erga* 507 *Θρηίκης ἱπποτρόφου εὐρέι πόντωι* /, where Hesiod has a deformation of the standard formula; v. sup. p. 28.

Aphr 6 / *πᾶσιν* (sc. *θήρεσσι*) *δ' ἔργα μέμηλεν*, cf. *Erga* 531 *πᾶσιν* (sc. *θήρεσσι*) *ἐνὶ φρεσὶ τοῦτο μέμηλεν* /.

Aphr 9 / *οὐ γάρ οἱ*, **Erga* 526, with an unusual neglect of digamma.[112] Note also *Aphr* 264f. beside *Erga* 509f. Moreover these passages are thematically similar: 'of all deities and creatures, only three goddesses reject the works of golden Aphrodite, Athena, who . . . taught the tender maidens at home their household tasks', and 'Boreas can blow through the coats of all animals, except the sheep's, and . . . can blow through (to) the tender maiden who stays at home with her mother, knowing nothing of the works of golden Aphrodite.' The shared ideas of a force that subdues everything with certain exceptions, of the works of golden Aphrodite, and of the virgins at home, when added to the phraseological parallels, oblige us to accept that the two passages are connected. The question is, how?

The commentators disagree: Gemoll[113] thinks that Hesiod is the lender, and this might gain some tenuous support from the modification at *Aphr* 6, where *ἔργα μέμηλεν* is moved from the line-end, giving a 'false closure' after the second trochee and n-mobile preventing hiatus at the trochaic caesura, whereas *Erga* 531 has good parallels in Homer (T 213, *α* 151, *ζ* 65; *ἔργα* (*ταῦτα* etc.) *μέμηλε* / 10x Hom., *Herm* 266, 437).[114] But the same shift in this formula is found in Hesiod (*Erga* 238, cf. *Herm* 267). West, however, is more hesitant:[115] he notes the two main parallels, but does not comment on their proximity to each other. Hesiod, he remarks, 'attaches her' (the girl) 'rather oddly to the list of creatures that Boreas does not blow through'. Below[116] he amends a proposal of Evelyn-White[117] but still to the effect of excluding these lines, at least in Hesiod's original version. In considering the maiden an intruder here he concurs with Evelyn-White, who was led by this consideration and the Ionic month-name Lenaeon at 504[118] to suspect an interpolation from *Aphr*; however, the typically Hesiodic *kenningar* such as ἀνόστεος (524) forced him to conclude that the whole passage is of composite authorship. That he and West do not agree on the analysis is a sign of the arbitrary method; yet nobody has canvassed the obvious and simple solution that Hesiod is in fact the imitator.

However, opinions can differ as to whether the Hymn exhibits greater clarity of structure and a more suitable context for Aphrodite and the maidens, as West and the writer maintain; three other considerations support the hypothesis. First, we have already seen three cases in which the beginnings of poems have influenced other poems; in a culture where the dissemination of poetry was largely by oral means this is hardly surprising. However, we have seen a contrary case in the relation of *Dem* 5–8 to *Aphr* 257, 284.[119] Secondly, compare the creation of Pandora at *Erga* 63ff.:

> . . . παρθενικῆς κἄλὸν εἶδος ἐπήρατον· αὐτὰρ Ἀθήνην
> ἔργα διδασκῆσαι, πολυδαίδαλον ἱστὸν ὑφαίνειν·
> καὶ χάριν ἀμφιχέαι κεφαλῇ χρυσέην Ἀφροδίτην . . .

cf. *Aphr* 14f. (*Athene*) παρθενικὰς ἁπαλόχροας ἐν μεγάροισιν
ἀγλαὰ ἔργ' ἐδίδαξεν . . .

The only comparable passage extant is *υ* 66–72, on the education by various goddesses of the daughters of Pandareos, where Hera purveyed beauty, Artemis height, ἔργα δ' Ἀθηναίη δέδαε κλυτὰ ἐργάζεσθαι (72). Here the phrasing is very different, and allows us to exclude this as a source.[120]

The significance of these verbal similarities only becomes clear when we compare the parallel account of Woman in the *Theogony* (570–89). The only parallels here with *Aphr* are 582 cf. *Aphr* 5, and 585 cf. *Aphr* 29, where *Aphr* is the imitator.[121] It is suggestive that, despite the many similarities between Hesiod's two versions, not only the word παρθενική but also the teaching of household tasks by Athene and the role of golden Aphrodite are completely absent from the *Theogony*, where Athene arrays Hephaestus' creation unaided. Such correction and elaboration of details accords with the way Hesiod retouches other topics, such as the doctrine of the two Erides (*Erga* 11ff., cf. *Th* 225).[122] Influence from *Aphr* would explain the changes here.

Thirdly, Hesiod's description of winter contains three Aeolisms – 510 *πίλνα*,[123] 526 *δείκνυ*, and especially 534 *ἐπὶ νῶτα ἔαγε*, which is strikingly similar to Sappho 31.9 *γλῶσσα ἔαγε*. Hiersche[124] suggested that this is a relic of old Aeolic poetry independent of Homer: he could have cited the other Aeolisms in support. It has not been remarked within how narrow a compass the Aeolic forms that have survived philological scrutiny are distributed within Hesiod's poems:[125] there are none at all in *Th*, none in the first five hundred lines of the *Erga*. Aeolisms in Hesiod occur in only two passages, the Description of Winter (504–35; cases at 510, 526, 534) and the Advice on Seafaring (618–94; cases at 635,[126] 666, 683, 693 and an outlier at 696).[127] The Asiatic Aeolic features in the latter passage are usually attributed to the influence of Hesiod's father from Cyme, who may be presumed to have discoursed on his travels to his sons in his own Aeolic dialect. Why this should affect the Description of Winter is far from obvious, and in the light of the other evidence for the influence of *Aphr* on this passage, and the Aeolic origins of the hymn, we may conclude that here it was knowledge of a body of Aeolic poetry, including at the minimum our hymn and the poem it introduced, which caused Hesiod to employ these forms. Such poetry need not have been in the Aeolic vernacular, but could have been Ionicised hexameter verse containing sporadic Aeolisms from everyday speech.

In fact it can be argued that Hesiod's Aeolic father was himself interested in poetry. Nagy (*The Best of the Achaeans* 296ff.) has recently reemphasised the suitability of Hesiod's name, which seems to be formed from *ἵημι* and **ϝοδ* – as in *αὐδή* or Skt. *vadati* (so Frisk and Chantraine *Dict. Et.* s.v.). That a poet should have a suitable name does not of course disprove his historicity, or suggest that the name is a product of the tradition; otherwise we would have to deny Stesichorus' existence as much as Homer's or Hesiod's.

Poetry, like other trades and professions, tended to run in families, and Hesiod conspicuously identifies with his father's interests. His father named one son Perses; a eulogy of Hecate, daughter of Perses in myth, is prominent in the *Theogony* (411–52), and makes sense if Hesiod is continuing a family tradition of her worship (cf. West, p. 278). His own naming is explained if his father was himself the bearer of poetic traditions from that most fecund border-region which also produced the Homeric epics, and wished that his new-born son would in his turn hand on the traditional epos – a wish which Hesiod dutifully received inspiration to fulfil.[128]

Marked influence from the Aeolic tradition on the *Erga* may also explain the (perhaps only random[129]) shifts in Hesiod's use of the o-stem genitive singular morphs, which are such a distinctive characteristic of the diction of *Aphr* and the *Cypria*. This presumes that Hesiod adopted a number of advanced genitive singular formulae from that tradition – a hypothesis which must remain no more.

Thus I argue that *Aphr* was composed not merely between *Th* and *Dem* (a view that is now deservedly acquiring the status of a *communis opinio*), but within Hesiod's own lifetime, in the interval between *Th* and *Erga*. In particular, the opening of *Aphr* exerted an influence analogous to that of the opening of *Th* on *Aphr*. But it would be wrong to claim that the proof of this is absolutely conclusive.[130]

In passing from the Hymn's date to its area of origin, it is interesting to note a number of verbal parallels between its opening and Sappho's epicising narrative of the wedding of Hector and Andromache (44 L–P):

Aphr 12ff. ἄνδρας . . . ἐδίδαξε /
ποιῆσαι σατίνας καὶ ἅρματα . . . /
/ ἡ δέ τε παρθενικὰς ἀπαλόχροας . . .

Sappho 44.13 σατίναι[ς], 15 παρθενίκαν τ' ἀ̣π̣[αλ]ο̣σφύρων,[131] 17 ἄνδρες ὔπαγον ὐπ' ἀρ̣[ματ; *Aphr* 19f. χοροί . . . πτόλις, cf. Sappho 44.12 πτ̣όλιν εὐρύχο̣ρο̣ν. The similarities here do not look accidental, especially the rare word σατίναι. This denotes a carriage, mentioned also in Anacreon (*PMG* 388.12, of Asiatic luxury) and in Euripides (*Helen* 1311, of Cybele's car). Three out of four times it is in an Idaean setting, and its etymology is certainly not Greek: from a cognate **satili̯a* derives Armenian *sayl*, Hesychian *σάτιλλα* (both designating the constellation 'the Waggon') and the root is probably **k̑at-* 'battle' (i.e. 'war-waggon'), cf. Skt. *śátrus* 'enemy', OIr. *cath*, OHG *hadu*, OE *heaðo* 'battle', in a satəm tongue like Thracian.[132] But we cannot determine the direction of borrowing, and the contact with Sappho cannot strictly be cited as evidence for the Aeolic origin of the Hymn. It is time to examine possible dialectal forms in the Hymn, in the order of their occurrence.

13 *σατίναι* is probably a (Thracian?) loan-word in Aeolis and Ionia, as we have seen.

29, 261 *κᾰλός*. At 29 this was certainly drawn from Hesiod,[133] but was not therefore necessarily alien to the poet's vernacular. Post-consonantal loss of digamma without compensatory lengthening was characteristic of Attic, island Ionic and Asiatic Aeolic,[134] but the feature may have spread more widely in post-Homeric epic diction: it is already apparent in some Homeric forms.[135]

31 *τιμάοχος* is again a possible Aeolism – but could have other origins.[136]

54 *πολυπιδάκου* Ἴδης. The thematic variant of the adjective *πολυπῖδαξ* is also found at *Cypria* 5.5, and as a *varia lectio* in Homer at Ξ 157, where Aristarchus rejected it as *τελέως ἄγροικον* (schol. A). Strabo[137] tells us that the dwellers around Ida *πολυπίδακον . . . τὴν* Ἴδην *ἰδίως οἴονται λέγεσθαι*, but little weight can be given to this, as there are numerous examples of athematic adjectives that shifted to thematic declension, regardless of dialect.[138]

71 *παρδάλιες* mss. M, *x*, ACGPQV^1; *πορδάλιες* BL^{2}L^{3}NR^{1}R^2. Shipp[139] claims the latter as an Atticism (cf. Strabo 619C), but as the reading occurs as a variant in Homer and is only supported by a minority of mss. in the *p* group nothing can be built on this (it is usually thought Aeolic).

98 *νυμφῶν* for *νυμφέ͜ων* is an Atticism that is merely graphic, and has Hesiodic and even Homeric parallels anyway.[140]

125 ἐδόκουν has an Attic contraction of -εο-, but again this is probably only graphic: the sense 'I thought' is not confined to Attic.[141]
127 τέκνα τεκεῖσθαι / is conjugated to the future from ~ τεκέσθαι / (χ 324, *Dem* 126, cf. *Cat* 31.4). ἔτεκον :: τεκεῖσθαι has an exact Homeric parallel in ἔπεσον :: πεσέεσθαι (8x *Il*), wherever these futures originate as a class.[142]
147 ἕκᾱτι M, ἕκητι mss. cett. The former is Doric and tragic, but could of course have other sources outside Attic–Ionic; its absence from Lesbian, for instance, may be mere coincidence. The same problem arises over νιν (280, where M's reading νῦν may be rejected with confidence): this is paralleled in the epos only at Hes. fr. 296.3 (the *Aegimius*: codd. of Stephanus Byzantinus – but note μιν in fr. 298 as quoted by Plutarch), *Cypria* 7.12 (codd. of Athenaeus), and cf. Theognis 364 (all mss.). μιν is not attested in the *Cypria*, but several times in *Aphr* (42, 61, 83, 91 etc.). Neither μιν nor νιν is attested in the Lesbian poets. Pavese[143] has alleged that these readings are relics of a version of the Hymn in mainland dialect, but Kamerbeek[144] is surely right to suggest that these are superficial changes in the transmission, influenced by the Callimachean Hymns and other Doric verse that was so often copied together with our Hymns.[145]
190 ὅς τε θεαῖς εὐνάζεται has an interesting parallel in a strikingly similar context in Homer, at ε 119:

οἵ τε θεαῖς ἀγάασθε παρ' ἀνδράσιν εὐνάζεσθαι

(elsewhere in Homer θεαῖς occurs only as a weak variant for θεῇς at Γ 158). The origin of these forms is unknown, and there is nothing to support Wackernagel's view[146] that they are Atticisms, certainly not in the Archaic period when Attic used -ησι or -ᾱσι.[147] At best they are late Atticisms introduced during transmission for -ῃς. However, there is statistical evidence that encourages us to trust the texts despite the lack of a metrical guarantee. According to our texts, -αις tended to oust -ῃς in the diction of post-Homeric epos. The figures in table 31 (which ignore the distinction of whether a vowel or consonant follows) speak for themselves.[148]

Table 31. *-ηις and -αις in the epos*

	Il	*Od*	*Th*	*Erga*	*Aspis*	*Cat*	*Dem*
-ηις	78	38	10	13	5	3	3
-αις	1	2	4	0	3	4	5

DAp	*PAp*	*Herm*	*Aphr*	*Hy* 19	*Cypria*	*Batr*
2	0	2	2	0	0	0
0	0	2	1	2	4	6

197 *ἐκγεγάονται* has parallels in some West Greek dialects, as we have seen: but it is better explained as an internal development of the epic diction.[149]
262 Σειληνός is first here before the fifth century, but its etymology is obscure and not necessarily Asiatic.[150]
267 *τεμένη* is an Atticism, but exactly paralleled in Homer (*τεμένη* λ 185).[151]
280 *νιν*. See above on ἕκᾱτι (147).

This exhaustive survey has produced almost nothing that can certainly be ascribed to any particular dialectal source: just as in the other Hymns, the Atticisms it reveals are only superficial and attributable to copyists. There are some possible Aeolisms, but none are in themselves compelling. As in the cases of *PAp* and *Herm*,[152] the Hymn's provenience must be determined on other grounds. The reference to a distinction between Phrygian and Trojan speech (113–16) and to the Aeneadae (196f.) suggests knowledge of the Troad, but whether the author was himself from that area is another question. Dialectal glosses and content having failed to give a conclusive answer, wider linguistic considerations remain. We have already seen that the poet's use of n-mobile probably can be cited as excluding all of the mainland but

Attica,[153] and that Ζηνός is more prevalent than we expect (5/12 cases). This at least is no random variation – statistical tests show that the odds on getting five cases if the true level were a Homeric 10% are small.[154] This suggests that either this feature somehow evaded archaising tendencies that were prevalent in most other criteria, or else the poet is hyper-ionising in this respect. Thus we return to the basic dilemma posed above – does the massive bulk of archaic diction represent a deliberate choice on the poet's part to counterfeit an archaic poem, or at least to imitate closely the effect of an archaic fixed text such as Homer's? Or instead do these features reflect an underlying tradition different from that seen in Homer and Hesiod?

If deliberate archaism is involved, it is readily distinguishable from the scattered phenomena observed in the later Boeotian tradition, which is in any case ruled out by n-mobile and Ζηνός. In Boeotia, it is apparent that false archaism in *Aspis* and *PAp* may partly derive from the influence of the text of Homer, fixed at an earlier time and presumably disseminated in this state: in *Aphr* many have discerned similar Homeric influence, both in language and themes. For imitation of Homer, then, a good *prima facie* case exists. But there are some features of the poem's diction which it cannot explain.

The alternative, if archaism and not the effects of a different tradition is in question, is archaism more thoroughgoing and consistent than even in *PAp* and *Herm*, where such criteria as *-ου* and *-οις* fall back in the direction of Homeric practice, but not as far as the criteria in which archaism is obvious like *-οιο* or the 'long' dative plurals.[155] It is difficult to believe that a poet of the archaic period, with no lexica or concordances, could or would achieve such consistent archaism, especially as our poet does not avoid post-Homeric usages, as we have seen at some length, and has numerous phrases in common with the other Hymns: he was certainly not out of touch with contemporary developments, either in diction or sophisticated narrative. Archaism in the 'short' dative plurals seems very improbable, since they contain no awkward extra syllables to impede the flow of oral composition, and are also unobtrusive: the fact of neologism, in using these endings before consonants rather than before vowels, would not have been noticed, either by the bards or by any audience whom they might try to impress with heroic diction evocative of the glorious days of their mighty forefathers. False archaism therefore seems most unlikely in this criterion, just as in the contracted o-stem genitive singulars, where there is only one suspicious result, and that is the result in *DAp* where the sample is smallest. Thus we expect these two criteria to behave in the same way, and elsewhere they do: but not here. Moreover, statistical methods prove that the results for *-ου*, and their twin, the results for *-οιο*, do not part company with the other criteria by some quirk of chance.[156]

This leads to a further point about consistency. Suppose (as is eminently probable) that the poet of *Aphr* did compose his piece either with various episodes of Homer in a text in front of him or with a rendering of them running through his mind: without some extraneous factor interfering, why should he adopt formulae for the genitive singular of o-stems that are consistently more advanced than those in the other criteria? One could understand if he borrowed a disproportionate number of formulae containing *-οιο*, an embellishment beloved by the post-Hesiodic bards of mainland Greece: but he does the exact opposite. If on the other hand fashion at some point dictated that *-οιο* was too old-hat for inclusion in up-to-the-minute epic verse, an idea that at once seems ludicrous when one thinks of the artificiality of Greek poetic diction in general and especially of the epic diction in its entirety, there is no apparent reason why the extra genitives should be placed more often in arsis before consonants or at line-end than in other positions. Witte[157] has demonstrated that there is a strong correlation between the shapes of nominal and adjectival stems and their propensity towards case-endings with or without an extra syllable, namely *-οιο* and *-ου*, *-οισι* and *-οις*, *-ῃσι* and *-ῃς*; but how can this make any difference? Reference to Witte's discoveries will not explain the divergent treatments of the genitive singulars and of the dative plurals here and in the *Erga*, and one expects the distribution of a relatively limited number of word-patterns to be a relatively stable feature of Greek hexameter poetry. Such stability has in fact been demonstrated by O'Neill's studies in Homer, Hesiod and Alexandrian hexameter verse.[158]

Neither the hypothesis of a shift of fashion nor the theory of imitation of Homer can explain the divergence between the o-stem genitive singular results and the remaining criteria. Another solution is required. One has already been adumbrated: the results are just what we would expect of a tradition that possessed the principles of formular modification from an early stage, but, until a recent period of Ionic influence, lacked most of the innovations we have been discussing. The exceptions would be the developments in the o-stem genitive singulars, which did undergo frequent modifications and consequently exhibit advanced usage. If the other features were for a considerable length of time absent from the spoken and poetic dialects available to the singers, then obviously they could not be introduced in the course of formular modification. It is remarkable that the two innovations in the genitive singulars of o-stems, namely the introduction of *-*οο* and its contraction to -*ου*, were found, when the vanishing-points of the various innovations were calculated by projecting back into prehistory, to be the two earliest innovations.[159]

Acceptance of this hypothesis does not of course exclude the possibility that *Aphr* has been influenced by Homer: the diction itself displays clear signs of Ionian influence, especially in the excessive use of East Ionic Ζηνός: why be influenced by Ionia, unless because a prodigious florescence of heroic epic, such as Homer represents, had occurred there? What the hypothesis does account for is the nexus of problems entailing the advanced frequency of modification in the Hymn, the advanced genitive singular results, and the retardation in the other criteria. Homeric influence there may well have been: but it does not suffice.

So the language of *Aphr* may best be explained by supposing that it derives from a non-Ionic tradition ultimately. Moreover, there are good reasons for associating the *Cypria* also with this tradition. Several pieces of evidence suggest this: the *Cypria* has a retarded level of neglects of digamma (2/8 cases; 25%): it has both results in the o-stem genitive singulars at advanced levels - only 2/10 cases are of -*οιο*, and of the remaining eight in -*ου* all but one are irresolvable. Further, just as in *Aphr*, preference is shown for Ionic Ζηνός (2/4 cases). Even the frequency of n-mobile is similar (2x in 50 lines, or $40^{0}/_{00}$). When this is added to similarities of content, it is clear that the diction of *Aphr* does not stand alone.[160]

Where then was the abode of this tradition? Unless we count the Attic formula in Hesiod, the only non-Ionic heritage of poetry for which there is firm evidence is the tradition of Asiatic Aeolis. Although, as so often, solid indications of geographical origin are in short supply in *Aphr*, we have received a number of hints: I am thinking of *σατίναι* (13), *τιμάοχος* (31), the Aeolisms in the parallel passage at *Erga* 504–35,[161] and the knowledge of the Troad revealed by the poet.[162] The similarity to the *Cypria* is ambivalent: Stasinus, one alleged author, was a Cypriot, but influences from Cypriot vernacular appear to be absent. Since we have seen that the influence of spoken vernacular dialects on the epic diction was minimal, at least after Homer, what matters is where the poets learnt their diction, not where they were born. The more fluid models of epic diction and its evolution developed subsequent to Parry's over-rigid system by such scholars as Hoekstra and Hainsworth permit us to exclude Cyprus in this respect, that we would expect an epic tradition isolated for several centuries to differ more profoundly than it does. The title *Cypria* may refer to the place of performance; Karageorghis' excavations at the royal necropolis of Salamis have proved that epic funeral customs appeared suddenly c. 750, which suggests that the epic was not known there before, but became very popular subsequently. For these reasons Cyprus seems unlikely as the area in which this tradition grew to maturity.[163]

The hypothesis implies that not only the Ionic changes like the introduction of Ζηνός and quantitative metathesis were delayed, but also the loss of initial digamma and the elision of 'long' dative plurals. The latter morphs were retained in the inscriptional dialects only in Attica, Ionia, Lesbos, Pamphylia, the Argolid and Crete.[164] However, this signifies little, as they were inherited from Indo-European and probably more widely distributed in the non-literate centuries; we can watch their disappearance in the inscriptions. The early loss of digamma, on the other hand, can be precisely delimited to Ionia and two adjacent areas, Attica and Lesbos, where it had certainly been lost by Sappho's time. We can link this with a curious fact: the Aeolic preposition ποτί was in the epic replaced by Ionic πρός, as is witnessed by the high frequency of *Silbenwägung* (i.e. 'lengthening' in thesis: πρὸ̄ς δῶμα for ποτὶ δῶμα) and 'Attic' correption before πρός (far more common than before e.g. πρό).[165] The form of the preposition is a further proof of the hypothesis of the Aeolic phase: in a continuous Mycenaean–Ionic tradition we would expect to find the East Greek assibilated form *ποσί (cf. Myc. /*posi*/), just as we would expect to find -ηο and not -ᾱο.[166] Now ποτί was replaced by πρός *after* the tradition began to neglect digamma, since ποτί is retained before once-digammated words as before those beginning with inherited vowels, while (e.g.) πρὸ̄ς οἶκον is scarcely attested. This means that the Ionic πρός only reached the tradition *after* digamma began to be lost.[167] Outside Ionia, Asiatic Aeolis is the only area that could combine ποτί (still found in East Thessalian, but evidently replaced on Lesbos by Ionic πρός before Sappho's time) with the early loss of digamma in initial position.[168] This is all very well as far as the tradition underlying Homer is concerned; but are we not trying to explain the diction of *Aphr* by postulating a tradition in which digamma was *not* lost until later? There is a discrepancy between the two traditions; how can that in which digamma was not lost until later possibly be Aeolic, as the other evidence seems to suggest?

There is certainly a discrepancy, but it need not alarm us.

The early history of Smyrna, and also dialectal and onomastic evidence from Chios, Erythrae and Phocaea, provide evidence for a northward expansion of Ionian population and speech at the expense of Aeolians;[169] the persistence of vestiges of Aeolic speech and institutions proves that the process was not always violent, and did not involve a total replacement of the population. Further north, recent reappraisal of the Lesbian dialect has revealed very extensive Ionic influence by Sappho's time.[170] Where Lesbian differs from East Thessalian it usually agrees with Ionic. From these facts we may conclude that Ionic speech spread northwards along the coast of Asia Minor, and a wave of Ionic influence extended even further. The two epic traditions, presumably of common origin and certainly very similar, can therefore be distinguished as follows: one would be in southern Aeolis and northern Ionia, i.e. the coastal region from Aeolian Cyme and Smyrna round to Chios, in which area the introduction of developed Ionic diction (with the loss of initial digamma and quantitative metathesis) led to the assimilation of the epic *Kunstsprache* to the vernacular as far as metre permitted; the other would persist further north, in Lesbos and the Troad perhaps, and only admit Ionic traits much later, partly indirectly through the impact of Ionian dialect on the Lesbian vernacular, and partly directly through the prestige of such brilliant Ionic poetry as Homer's. Thus the Ionic influence at this stage would differ from the shift to Ionic diction in the pre-Homeric tradition, since the introduction of features which never prevailed in local dialect (such as η for $\bar{a}$) would be motivated by literary considerations, and not by a shift in the vernacular at a time when there was no poetry sufficiently prestigious that it dictated the details of the dialect (in the time of Homer's predecessors the only constraint on adaptation of poetic forms to the vernacular was metrical, as the replacements of Aeolic forms indicate[171]). The growth and change of the Aeolic branch of the tradition must also be distinguished from that of the mainland branch, in which Homeric diction was adopted, dialect and all; if there was an earlier mainland branch, it had no impact on Hesiod, whose diction is thoroughly Ionic.

The hypothesis of a tradition in the border-lands between Aeolis and Ionia which was given an Ionic colouring by a natural shift in the local vernacular dialect will answer one prime objection to the theory of the Aeolic phase, that Greek literary genres do not normally change dialect: surely the epic dialect was not fixed until the prestigious flowering of Ionic epic represented by Homer. It is noteworthy that these border-lands are precisely the areas in which Homer is most insistently located by the ancient traditions.[172] But the hypothesis of the tradition underlying *Aphr* is less neat: would it not be simpler to suppose that it originated not in Aeolis but elsewhere, where digamma was retained?

Neither dialectal glosses nor knowledge of Aeolis nor the link with the *Cypria* nor the coincidence with a passage under Aeolic influence in Hesiod can in themselves prove that *Aphr*, or at least its type of diction, came from Aeolis – although I hope I may be permitted to remark that an alternative explanation for these items is by no means immediately apparent. However, my conclusion concerning this hymn rests, in the last analysis, upon a matter of belief, and seems likely to continue to do so, unless there is some unforeseen accession of new material: the belief is that an epic tradition developed in any more distance part of Greece would have looked very different. Even in a century the post-Hesiodic Boeotian tradition evolved distinctively.

As for the Hymn's date, this may certainly be fixed between Hesiod's *Theogony* and *Dem*; I have argued that greater precision is obtainable, if the poem's influence is to be discerned in several thematic and linguistic developments in Hesiod's *Erga*. If its underlying tradition is Aeolic, then this dating in literary terms can be checked in terms of relative linguistic chronology. In the north Aeolic tradition, the two criteria where innovation had occurred, before the sourthern branch diverged and admitted distinctive Ionic features, might be expected to approximate in their stage of development to the rate of development in Ionia. It is interesting to find that both o-stem genitive singular results are at a similar stage to *Th*, which is exactly right in terms of the hypothesis.

As for the problem of whether the Hymn was orally composed, it is certainly true that the structure and ideas it contains are more sophisticated than in the other extant Hymns, and we have seen that it is metrically more polished than most.[173] But I see no means, unless new technical criteria are discovered, of deciding whether an oral poet could have created such a masterpiece or not. Certainly the arguments of Hoekstra[174] and Podbielski[175] that the poet borrowed from Homer on the formular and thematic levels respectively cannot settle the question; they prove neither servile copying, nor deliberate literary imitation, where the parallels and differences were meant to be noticed by the audience, but rather adaptation on a par with that observed in *PAp*, where we saw no compelling reason to accept that writing, even if employed in the composition of the poem, made any difference at all to its style or content.

The origins of *Aphr* are lost in an obscurity that its poetic excellence little deserves; yet it is certainly later than Homer, and the hypothesis that it was composed in Aeolis, during Hesiod's lifetime (i.e., for me, in the decades before the middle of the seventh century), fits the known facts more closely than any other formulation proposed at present.

CHAPTER 9

OTHER HYMNS

(*a*) *The Hymn to Demeter*

Despite the length of this Hymn, I intend to restrict the discussion to a narrow compass, in view of Richardson's recent and thorough account of its diction, especially of the alleged Atticisms.[1] He concludes that, given the clear evidence for Attic transmission, the only Attic form which certainly cannot be assigned to this stage is Persephone's title Κόρη (439), the presence of which can be otherwise explained, since 'a non-Attic poet might as easily have paid her this compliment as an Attic one'.[2]

In these uncertainties, statistical results may assist. The frequency of n-mobile before consonants (46 cases per thousand verses) is greater than in Homer (35–37‰ verses), and of course much greater than in Hesiod, but less than in *DAp* (60‰); in the light of the advanced stage of the rest of the poem's diction, we would expect it to use n-mobile either very rarely, in line with the practice of the Boeotian and mainland tradition after Hesiod, or on the other hand more than in *DAp*, which represents the post-Homeric tradition of Ionia.[3] The Hymn's diction has in fact a markedly Hesiodic look, and its intermediate position in this criterion between the Homeric and Hesiodic traditions might be thought a strong argument for an Attic poet. However, the language of the ostensibly 'Hesiodic' *Megalai Ehoiai* is similar, with three cases of n-mobile in about twenty-six lines of fragments; if extrapolated, this would yield 115 cases per thousand verses, again far too high for Hesiod. Now this result could be due to a remotely conceivable freak of chance; or again, it could be a sign of Attic authorship; but some extant fragments concern Boeotia,[4] and thus the possibility that eventually part of the post-Hesiodic tradition in Boeotia underwent Attic or Ionic influence in this respect cannot be excluded. Thus we cannot prove Attic origins on these grounds. Two cases of hiatus preceding ἀγλαο- (54, 492) were discussed above;[5] both can be attributed to formular modification,[6] yet would be explicable if the poet's vernacular had lost initial digamma, and induced him to misapply the norms permitting hiatus before once-digammated words. But this is no more than a hint of Attic provenance, and coincidence cannot be excluded.

That the Hymn belongs to the Boeotian tradition proper (of *Aspis*, *PAp* and *Herm*) seems likely because of the rest of its diction. It shares with *PAp* and *Herm* the overuse of *-οιο* which is probably incipient in *Aspis*, and it avoids Ζηνός along with *Aspis*, *PAp* and *Herm*.

Dem also has a high proportion of the archaic morph *-άων* rather than contracted forms, and this is without doubt significant statistically:[7] if it is a deliberate feature, it might be a mark of Boeotian dialect, just as the archaism displayed by *Cat* in *-αο* may be. These phenomena serve to set *Dem* close to the followers of Hesiod. The position of the cluster, false archaism in *-οιο* and disuse of Ζηνός suggest that the Hymn falls between *Erga* and *Aspis* with *PAp*, where false archaism is dominant. Attempts have been made to date the Hymn more precisely by the detection of *imitatio*; in particular, Russo[8] tried to prove borrowing from the *Aspis* on the basis of parallels between the two: but all the scraps he cited are isolated forms or usages of little evidential value. Indeed Wyatt[9] reverses his diagnosis regarding the parallel seen as most significant: *Aspis* 269 is 'a clear imitation' of *Dem* 279. Nor can any more precise chronology be determined by historical means, apart from the *terminus ante quem* provided by the lack of reference to Athens, whose interest in the Mysteries began with Pisistratus at the latest.[10] *Aphr* provides a *terminus post quem*, but this is using the obscure to illumine the opaque: at least both the detection of imitation and the statistical method tell the same story, that the Hymn is substantially later than Hesiod's *Theogony*.[11] *Dem* has been considered the source of some parallels in *Hymn* 30 to Ge, but this is doubtful.[12]

Despite these close links with the later Boeotian tradition, there are some incompatibilities. False archaism in *-οιο* is not matched in other criteria where it would be anticipated, for example in the dative plurals in *-οισι* and *-ηισι*. Instead of false archaism in these features, we see results that are, in the main, very advanced, and consistently so. The sheer quantity of innovation is impressive, and it would be superfluous to illustrate it here, especially after Hoekstra's excellent discussion.[13] Thus the Hymn displays the final result of the uncontrolled development of tendencies prevalent in the epic diction even before Homer, which was halted by the beginning of the sixth century due to the more extensive use of false archaism, as exemplified in *Aspis* and especially in *PAp*.[14] *Dem* seems to represent a transition between Hesiod's natural use of the tradition, with a coherent cluster of results, and the later poetry reliant on fixed texts for much of its diction. In some respects, however, *Dem* differs from the Hesiodic tradition: Attica (not necessarily including Athens) seems likely enough as the home of such a marginal tradition, and in fact fits the facts rather well, in particular the use of n-mobile, which would be more problematic in other areas such as the north-east Peloponnese.[15] The poet's knowledge of some Aeolic poetry is no obstacle.[16] The date for the Hymn must be in the latter half of the seventh or the early sixth century: I consider that the linguistic evidence strongly favours a date earlier rather than later within this range.

(*b*) *Hymn 7 to Dionysus*

Attempts to place this 59-line poem have hitherto rested on dubious stylistic criteria, and the reference to the Tyrsenians (8). In fact its diction indicates a post-Homeric date, on the following grounds:

Digamma: observances 10, neglects 4, total 14, 28.6% neglects. This is closer to *Th* than to *Od*.

O-stem genitive singulars: *-οιο* 2, doubtful 1, *-ου* 2, total 5. Useless.

Dative plurals (o-stem only attested): 'long' 5, doubtful 4, 'short' 1, total 10. Only 50% 'long' is more advanced even than in *Dem*.

O-stem accusative plurals: before vowels 3, before consonants 5, total 8. 37.5% +V is slightly more advanced than in *Od*.

N-mobile before consonants: two cases, or 33.9 per thousand lines, slightly fewer than in *Il*; but this is very unreliable, as one more case would yield 50.8‰, closer to *DAp*, while one less would produce a Hesiodic level. Of all these, only the dative plural result is statistically significant.[17] Other post-Homeric features are scarce:

14 *ἐκάθητο* is found in Attic from the fifth century (and in Ionic? cf. v. 1. ap. Hdt. III 144, al.).

30 *ἔκ ποτ' ἐρεῖ αὐτοῦ τε* is an unparalleled phrase with a neglect of digamma and two definite contractions.

34 *θαύματα ἔργα* is shared with *Cat*, *Aspis* and *Herm*. I have suggested above that this may be a post-Homeric phrase rather than an archaism.[18] Even if mainland in origin, it could have wandered to Ionia, where the nautical content has induced many to place the Hymn. There is nothing to establish the Hymn's geographical origins, but it may tentatively be dated within the seventh century.[19]

(*c*) *Hymn 19 to Pan*

Although ten lines shorter than *Hy* 7, this poem offers more scope. The cult of Pan seems to have spread outside Arcadia by the early fifth century; despite the tale of his arrival in Athens after the battle of Marathon (Hdt. VI 105f.), his worship may have begun earlier elsewhere, for example in Thebes.[20] Note the following linguistic evidence:

Digamma: observance 1, neglects 5, total 6, 83.3% neglects. This would still be more advanced than even *Herm* if one instance had gone the other way; the sample, though small, is statistically significant when compared even with Hesiod's *Erga*.[21] This is consequently a very important result.

O-stem genitive singulars: *-οιο* 1, doubtful 1, *-ου* 1. This is useless.

A- and o-stem dative plurals: long 10, doubtful 1, short 3. The proportion of 'long' forms is identical to that in *Th*.

N-mobile before consonants: five times in 49 lines, or 102 per thousand. This is very often indeed; it is double the frequency in *DAp*, and similar to that in the *Megalai Ehoiai* (where the sample is smaller and less trustworthy).
There is one lone case of Ζηνί.

The Hymn has some features in common with *Herm*: the declension *δικέρωτα* (2, 37) and *ἡδυγέλωτα* (37) recalls *ἔρωτα* (*Herm* 449);[22] with *μοῦσα* 'song' (15), cf. *Herm* 447;[23] the participle *ὤν* (32) is also found in *Od*, *Cat*, *PAp*, *Herm* and *Hy* 29;[24] and new words, especially compound adjectives, are prominent.[25]

Moreover, the opening of *Herm* provides a literary *terminus ante quem*, as it has influenced 28ff.:

28 Ἑρμείην ἐριούνιον . . . /
. . . θεοῖς θόος ἄγγελος . . .
cf. *Herm* 3 ἄγγελον ἀθανάτων ἐριούνιον . . . ;
30 Ἀρκαδίην πολυπίδακα, μητέρα μήλων /
cf. *Herm* 2 Ἀρκαδίης πολυμήλου /;
31 Κυλληνίου cf. *Herm* 2;
34 *νύμφηι ἐυπλοκάμωι Δρύοπος φιλότητι μιγῆναι*,
cf. *Herm* 4 *νύμφη ἐυπλόκαμος Διὸς ἐν φιλότητι μιγεῖσα*.

Note here that *Hy* 18.4 with / Ἄτλαντος *θυγάτηρ* ~ is less close; *Herm*'s version is certainly the model for *Hy* 19, as *Herm* anticipates the proper use of the phrase in line 7.[26]

If *Herm* dates from the later sixth century, then Hymn 19 probably was composed at the end of the sixth century at the earliest; I would be surprised if it turned out to be later than the mid-fifth century.[27]

The use of n-mobile might suggest an Attic poet, but inconclusively: compare my remarks above on *Dem* and the *Megalai Ehoiai*. The alleged Atticisms are also inconclusive:
2 *πίση* / cf. sup. pp. 144 on *Herm* 76.
20 *πῠκνὰ ποσσίν*, cf. 23 / *πυκνὰ ποσίν*, from which 20 may be adapted. The 'Attic' correption before mute and nasal has parallels even as early as Hesiod,[28] and in any case Barnes emended to *πύκα*.
32 *ὤν*: v. n. 24.
There is one possible archaism – *σφιν* singular (19), also at *Hy* 30.9.[29]

(*d*) *Shorter pieces over 15 lines*

Occasionally one of the other poems or fragments in the corpus contains some interesting data. For convenience I set out in table 32 the dictional features of all other pieces over 15 lines long. Results from sample-sizes of under four cases are not tabulated. From left to right the columns give the number of lines, number of cases of n-mobile before consonant (results indicating high frequency are underlined), cases of initial digamma (percentage of neglects, sample-size in brackets, and an indication of the stage of diction in terms of the common units on figures 1 and 2), percentage of genitives in *-οιο* similarly expressed (results suggesting false archaism are underlined), percentage of 'long' o- and a-stem dative plurals (as previous), results in other criteria if available, and comment ('at Delphi' means that the poem explicitly refers to the cult at Delphi and was surely intended for performance there; 'as *Aphr*' means that the diction is thought to resemble that of *Aphr*; page references denote pages in this treatise).

Table 32. *The criteria in shorter pieces over 15 lines*

Work	*Lines*	*n-mob.*	ϝ	-οιο	-οιαι	*Other comment*
Hy 1	21	0				*POxy* 670 not included
Hy 6	21	1	17%(6) 0	33%(6)+4	100(6)−3	as *Aphr*? p. 273 n. 160
Hy 27	22	0		60%(5)−2		at Delphi: as *PAp*? pp. 111f.
Hy 28	18	2				
Hy 30	19	0				as *Dem*? p. 275 n. 12
Hy 31	19	0		71%(7)+3		
Hy 32	20	0	60%(5)+7			
Hy 33	19	0		57%(7)−1		
Thebais	16	1			80%(5)+1	
Cypria	50	2	25%(8)+2	20%(10)+7	54(11)+6	-*ου* 87%(8)+8, Z 50%(4)+8 as *Aphr*?: p. 176 n. 163
Il. Parva	34	3		33%(6)+4	80(5)+1	p. 176 n. 163
Il. Persis	17	1				
Epigr. 4	17	1				at Smyrna
Epigr. 14	23	0				-*ου* 75%(4)+6 =Hes. fr.303
Meg. Eboiai	26	3	25%(4)+1	50%(6) 0	75%(8)+3	p. 181
Melampodia	24	1	80%(5)+7	50%(6) 0	50%(4)+7	
Pir. Catab.	25	0		50%(4) 0		
Hes. fr.343	19	1		50%(4) 0	60%(5)+6	Ζηνός 1/1

CHAPTER 10

CONCLUSIONS

In a heterogeneous corpus such as that of the *Hymns*, it is not easy to sum up the answers (such as they are) to the questions about date, origins and diction formulated in Chapter 1, as these are sometimes tentative and dependent on complex arguments. The same applies to the problem of which, if any, of the *Hymns* are oral compositions: there may be intermediate stages on the journey to literate composition.[1] If we accept, as I believe we should, that writing played no part in the *composition* (as opposed to the recording) of the Homeric and Hesiodic poems, then it is at least clear that the two *Hymns to Apollo* do not differ from them, while, according to the tests applied in Chapter 2, the Hymns *to Aphrodite*, *to Demeter* and *to Hermes* (along with the *Shield of Heracles*) are increasingly suspect of being influenced by the use of writing in their composition.

Consequently, rather than restate the conclusions of Chapters 5–9 on the individual major Hymns, I shall recapitulate the method of linguistic dating, its difficulties and its implications, and then proceed to sketch an outline history of the tradition as a whole as it begins to emerge from the statistical studies of Chapter 3, and the analysis of the resultant data in Chapter 4.

The *a priori* reasoning behind the method is as follows. In an oral or mainly oral tradition, especially one with a metre as complex as the dactylic hexameter, formulae are preserved over long periods for reasons of convenience, or even necessity, as an aid to composition. Many formulae are handed down through the generations and preserve archaic forms, some extremely ancient indeed. On the other hand, it is clear that there was much scope for flexibility and originality in such traditions. Formulae are modified, where it is metrically possible, in accord with developments in the spoken vernacular, and such modification is an important part of bardic technique. Old formulae, rendered incomprehensible or grossly unmetrical by the passage of time, are replaced by more modern expressions. New formulae are constructed after the analogy of older models, and then there will be totally new elements in the poetry, as new themes are elaborated, and ancient formulae bedded in matrices of new words. Therefore one expects old formulae and archaisms to diminish in frequency through the generations, as innovative phraseology and language creeps in; and if this could be quantified, it might provide a yardstick useful for assigning approximate relative dates to the poems. It ought therefore to be possible to count archaisms and innovations in the poems and find out whether there is any consistent pattern of evolution in their diction.

To test this theory one needs features in which we know that an older form came to be replaced by a more recent one, preferably by the observation of formular modification as well as from philological evidence. The other condition to be satisfied is that the feature be of sufficiently frequent occurrence to offer some statistical reliability and avoid the vagaries of random chance. In Chapter 3 ten features, largely meeting these conditions, were studied, and when all the counting was done it became clear that, in Homer and Hesiod, there is a consistent pattern in all but one of them (in which Hesiod is inconsistent: but here the sample-sizes were smallest). Each time, the *Iliad* has the highest proportion of archaic forms, but the *Odyssey* is slightly more advanced. After this there is a very large shift in the same direction to the *Theogony*, and a smaller shift again to the *Works and Days*. Thus we obtain the sequence *Iliad*, *Odyssey*, *Theogony*, *Works and Days*, the last being the most advanced of the series.

This is all very well, but how reliable are the texts we are using anyway? The statistical method cannot be deployed to distinguish brief interpolations, and it can only test the text which we have. This is not quite true; we know quite a lot about the text preferred by the Alexandrian scholars, yet if one examines the readings of even Zenodotus, no consistent trends emerge and enable us to state that his text is older or younger than Aristarchus' or the vulgate. The readings they supported are not consistently more archaic or more innovatory; nor are those of the so-called *κοινή* or other manuscripts known to Hellenistic scholarship.[2] At any rate the problem of textual fluctuation applies throughout the corpus, and, given the very large numbers of phenomena used in this study, does not appear serious.

Another difficulty arises over what I have termed 'false archaism', namely the use of an archaic form or ending more often than it occurred in the 'natural' tradition at any given stage. Past mistrust of attempts to derive relative chronology from linguistic criteria was caused by the use of only one such criterion, namely the proportion of neglects of digamma, and by the failure to devise tests for abnormal behaviour, whether by random chance or for some other reason, in features of this kind. The solution is twofold: if more than one feature is studied, we can correlate different features together to see which behave inconsistently in particular poems; and then we can apply statistical tests to discover the probability that the divergence is merely a random event. We saw in Chapter 4 that, when this is done, some striking instances of false archaism appear among Hesiod's followers, in morphs with an extra syllable that are noticeable and easily manipulated: only in poems dated historically to the end of the seventh century and after do we find more extensive false archaism, where unobvious features too tend to fall back towards Homeric practice; this is certainly because these poets are learning much of their diction from texts fixed at a much earlier stage of the epic language, notably the *Iliad* and *Odyssey*. This is the situation envisaged by those who would reject the utility of the epic language as a chronometer: but it is in fact not difficult to discriminate between poems with false archaism of this sort and those without it. For in this situation, instead of clustering at approximately the same stage of diction, the various features are widely spread, and the consistent pattern of dictional evolution is broken. In human terms, these poets are learning to compose not by listening to their elders' poetry, so much as by hearing readings or recitations from memory, or by themselves reading, texts fixed at much earlier phases in the history of the bardic tradition.

However, where the results of the tests do indicate that several features are at a similar stage of linguistic evolution, I would argue that they do indicate that the poem concerned is at a particular stage of a coherent chronological development. In Hesiod's case, for example, his diction certainly participated in this development during his own lifetime; and a like evolution within the life-span of a single poet will account for the slight, but perceptible and consistent, dictional developments displayed by the *Odyssey* relative to the *Iliad*. Certainly the interval between the two great epics is no larger than that between Hesiod's two main works.

The argument that consistent treatment of several features is a chronological indicator has another implication which must be brought out. If I am right, it follows that the texts of the epics were fixed at different times. It is impossible that the Homeric epics were liable to *free* oral transmission until they were fixed in the time of Pisistratus, for instance; it is clear that the texts were fixed before the time of Hesiod, and it is difficult to refuse the conclusion that the texts were fixed at the time when each was composed, whether by rote memorisation or by oral dictated texts. The implication is not one I see any reason to avoid; it does not of course exclude the *a priori* likelihood of *popular* oral transmission, with varying degrees of freedom, during the archaic and classical periods, such as we know actually took place.[3]

The observation that Hesiod's diction (and Homer's too, if I may express a personal article of faith) evolved during his poetic career, brings us to a further possible objection to the method, that it is not independent of content. However, the features studied are at the phonetic and grammatical level, and not dependent on the lexicon; and owing to the employment of proportions and not absolute frequency of a given feature over a given number of lines it cannot be objected, for example, that the neglect of digamma in the *Works and Days* is distorted because Hesiod makes more frequent use of such words as οἶκος. At a more abstract level, however, the objection is harder to counter. It might be alleged, for example, that battle-poetry has more ancient antecedents than stories of nautical adventures, genealogies or gnomic and rustic verse. Such an approach is almost impossible to test on present evidence, at least within the early Greek tradition, with one important exception, and this is in Hesiod. It is sometimes assumed that *gnomai* and accounts of rural activities are likely to be the least traditional of all the types of hexameter poetry of the archaic period. Certainly it is true that the diction of the *Works and Days* is very advanced: but it is nonetheless not as advanced, by a good margin, as the narrative in the *Hymn to Demeter*, which is in terms of content reminiscent of scenes in Phaeacia and Ithaca in the *Odyssey*.[4] Moreover, *Works and Days* 1–200 consists largely of mythic narrative, and not of moral and agricultural precepts; Hesiod in fact retells the story of Prometheus and the creation of Woman, already given in the *Theogony*. And yet, when the language of these two hundred lines is studied scientifically, it is established that although it is somewhat less advanced in the linguistic criteria than the remainder of the poem, it is on the whole more advanced than the diction of the *Theogony*.[5] Hesiod's diction advanced, as we know; but it advanced despite the content.

On a smaller scale it is clear that innovation will tend to occur in specific types of passage, as witnessed by Shipp's discovery that similes and digressions are the fastest growth-points in Homer, and it is worth repeating the point made in Chapter 4, that we cannot expect a high degree of precision from a dating technique of this nature. At the level of individual poets, the rate of change may not have been steady, and individuals (and particular kinds of poem, e.g. genealogies) may have had their idiosyncrasies. However, I see no reason why the rate of development of the diction should not have been relatively constant when measured over a longer span, such as half a century; some evidence in favour of such an assumption was discussed in Chapter 4. Nor does there seem to be any evidence that the rate of change was altered when the epic tradition was transferred from Ionia to Boeotia; some of the innovations would be favoured by the mainland vernacular, others disfavoured, but on the whole the consistent evolution seems to have continued uninterrupted.

Although the detailed interpretation of the linguistic studies in Chapter 4 may never receive confirmation, I must nonetheless repeat that the consistent pattern I have detected seems impossible to explain unless the passage of time is to a considerable extent the cause. However, like all scientific theories, this one will only prevail if it can be corroborated by surviving all the tests which can be devised against it, and by accommodating any new facts that come to light: and it is liable to overthrow by any new theory with a greater power to account for all the facts yet established.

Tests may be devised against the theory from several quarters. The mass of linguistic evidence now accumulated is such that it would be very surprising if anyone were to find other criteria presenting a consistently different pattern from that which I have discerned. Another possible test would be to apply the same technique to other oral traditions with abundant *dated* poems covering at least two generations as a control case: in fact an elenchus of this kind is desirable as a goal of further research. But sceptics can always distrust such analogies.[6] Within the classical field, the crucial tests lie in two areas – the detection of *exemplum* and *imitatio*, and evidence of a historical nature. But before turning to these, two less productive areas must be dealt with; isolated linguistic forms, and the views of the ancients on the dates of Homer and Hesiod.

The use of isolated forms and usages for chronological purposes has repeatedly emerged during this study as unhelpful, given the limitations of our knowledge of early Greek. A passage need not be Hellenistic just because it exhibits some linguistic flotsam, washed ashore from the ocean of our ignorance, the like of which does not bob up again until the age of the Ptolemies and their learned poets. Nor is such beachcombing very productive of geographical conclusions, owing partly to lack of suitable comparative material, and partly to the tendency of some forms to float quite a distance from their place of origin. Were he not so garrulous about his homeland, Hesiod would leave us doubting whether his vernacular was Asiatic Aeolic, Attic, West Greek or of course Ionic; Boeotian would never have been surmised. Local idioms are remarkably scarce in the epos, and features with a statistical basis have produced more information, as we have seen in the paradigm of Zeus' name and the employment of ephelcystic nu.

Another test might be thought to be ancient opinions on the relation between Homer and Hesiod. Ephorus' claim[7] that Hesiod was the elder rests on the local patriotism of a Cymaean. The others were divided: Hellanicus, Pherecydes of Athens, Herodotus, Alcidamas and Archemachus believed them contemporaries, while Xenophanes, Chamaeleon, Heraclides Ponticus, Philochorus, Eratosthenes, Aristarchus, Apollodorus his pupil and others thought Homer earlier.[8] The controversy was continued by the Romans,[9] and was still lively in Pausanias' time.[10] On the whole the arguments used on both sides were very weak; a prime piece of 'evidence' will have been the contest between Hesiod and Homer, which goes back to the sixth century at least, as we have seen. However, we have also seen something of the dubious origins of this tale,[11] which seems likely to have no more solid a basis than the desire to synchronise two famous men, as in the case of Solon and Croesus. The later *Lives* of Homer ignore the Contest, and must derive ultimately from the Homeridae.[12] We have no external evidence to confirm either version: ulterior motives for inventing both can be imagined without difficulty. There was a decided shift in opinion towards Homer's anteriority by the Hellenistic period, and the adoption of a more systematic approach to chronological problems seems at least as likely a cause of this as the propaganda of the Homeridae.[13] In particular we know something of the approach of Aristarchus, consisting of the accumulation of isolated 'post-Homeric' features.[14] This shows that Hellenistic scholarship, with all the resources at its disposal, had no more solid evidence to work with than we possess, and that the greatest of these scholars judged that there was nothing in the whole of archaic or classical literature then extant which could prove Hesiod's anteriority. On the contrary, Aristarchus found many reasons to think Hesiod later.

Imitation is a more promising test. The theory would at once collapse if the *Odyssey*, for example, were found to copy Hesiod[15] (although there is also the problem of interpolations). However, Parry's work has greatly circumscribed the scope for the use of isolated phrases for this purpose, and we can only hope to detect *imitatio* and *exemplum* in certain strictly defined circumstances, of which an attempted codification is offered in Appendix D.[16] In fact none of the imitations of Hesiod by Homer as yet alleged meet these standards. Certainly we can establish the sequences *Theogony*, *Hymn to Aphrodite*, *Hymn to Demeter*, and also *Theogony*, *Works and Days* and *Shield of Heracles*; these are already orthodox. In addition, I have suggested that the *Delian Hymn to Apollo* influenced the *Pythian Hymn*; that the *Pythian Hymn* imitates the *Odyssey*;[17] that the *Hymn to Hermes* influenced the *Hymn to Pan*; and that the *Theogony* influenced both the *Hymn to Aphrodite* and the poetry of Semonides, which both in their turn influenced the *Works and Days*.

The final test is evidence of a historical nature, and this is intimately linked with the provision of absolute dates. Given a historical date, or preferably two, we can determine how accurate the theory is both in the order in which the poems are dated and in the relative distances between them. Unfortunately we have no agreed absolute dates: the consequences of adhering to particular dates for particular poems, and the stretching or compression of the relative framework when dates are supplied, are displayed in Appendix E. If, as argued above in the Excursus, the Lelantine war can indeed be dated to Archilochus' time, and if Hesiod was connected with it, and if Homer is not prior to the mid-eighth century and not later than its end, then the relative datings will be corroborated, but no universal agreement on these points exists at present.[18]

I shall now turn to sketch the development of the epic tradition as it begins to appear from these studies. My conclusions are depicted in figure 4 (p. 200). The history of the epic tradition begins long before Homer, and does not end with him. I have argued above that one further advantage of the linguistic technique is that it offers us an ability to project back and see in what sequence and at what intervals the various linguistic innovations studied began to appear in the poetic diction. As a result of this projection, along with other linguistic and also thematic and mythological arguments, I have pointed in Chapter 4 to Asiatic Aeolis as the area in which the epic evolved and matured during the Dark Ages, after it had been taken across the Aegean, presumably in the migrations of about 1000 B.C., from some area of Mycenaean culture (whether this was in East Thessaly and Boeotia or more to the south). In Chapter 8 reasons were given for supposing that this Aeolic tradition eventually divided; one segment remained in north Aeolis, and was at length, like the diction of Sappho and Alcaeus, exposed to the influence of both the Ionic vernacular and the diction of the developed Ionian tradition, after Homer or poets of equal greatness had conferred upon it overwhelming prestige. To this branch, it has been argued, belong at least the *Hymn to Aphrodite* (dating from Hesiod's time) and the *Cypria*.

Meanwhile, as Meister and others have argued, the tradition in southern Aeolis, in such places as Cyme, Smyrna and Chios, was in close touch with Ionic speech, and (whether through the historically attested northward spread of Ionians, or by the wanderings of poets) was taken over by speakers of the Ionic vernacular, not long before the time of the Homeric poems (see Chapter 4; the date of this event can be determined in relative terms, as shown in figure

4). This branch of the tradition had already admitted some Ionic features, notably the neglect of digamma, but at this point a whole series of such features is now attested, namely quantitative metathesis in -έω and -έων, and the eastern Ionic innovation Ζηνός for Διός; when projected back in figure 3 these all appear at the same stage of the development of the diction. It can also be established that during this phase the use of n-mobile to make position was increasingly frequent, and that the tendency to avoid putting o- and a-stem accusative plurals before words beginning with vowels began by Homer's time. It is curious (to speak with restraint) that the area, in which the evidence suggests that all this was taking place, is that most insistently identified by later Greek folk-traditions as the region where Homer was born and passed his life.

The *Delian Hymn to Apollo* shows that the tendencies operating within the poetic diction of Homer continued until substantially later within the Ionian tradition; but meanwhile, the Ionic epos was taken to Boeotia. Hesiod composes in the Ionian idiom, as a result, it seems, of the prestige of the Ionian poetry of Homer and poets like him. Moreover, the Ionian idiom adopted by Hesiod was at a much more advanced stage than Homer's; about this there can be no doubt. I have also argued that he was in touch, not only with some hexameter poetry in the Attic dialect (this depends on only one formula), but also with some poetry of the Aeolic tradition, notably the *Hymn to Aphrodite* (Chapter 8). Otherwise, some isolated forms excepted, there is little in his diction that is alien to the Ionic tradition, and this remains true of his successors; the light accusative plurals which he uses can now be seen to result from a tendency already present in Homer (although whether Ionian poets would have gone so far as to employ one of these forms where the short vowel is metrically guaranteed is another matter). Hesiod does, however, betray his mainland origins by neglecting to use n-mobile to make position as often as one would expect when the diction is otherwise so advanced; instead, he uses it less often than Homer had done.

After Hesiod, the mainland tradition develops noticeable idiosyncrasies. The diction of the *Hymn to Demeter* is generally more advanced than Hesiod's, but various characteristic developments begin to appear. Untypical is the more frequent occurrence of n-mobile (this might be a mark of an Attic poet): but the bard is beginning to introduce false archaism in the well-marked criteria *-άων* and *-οιο*. False archaism seems to be found in *-ᾱο* in the *Catalogue of Women*, a poem whose dating is rather problematic, as it cannot be prior to the *Theogony*, but is slightly less advanced in diction, and consistently so; this discrepancy is best explained by the inevitable bluntness of linguistic implements, which cannot be expected to be accurate within a decade. A similar feature typical of this later branch of the tradition is the neglect of the Ionic form Ζηνός, in which the *Hymn to Demeter* is followed by the *Shield of Heracles*, the *Pythian Hymn to Apollo* and the *Hymn to Hermes*. These three poems show an increasing amount of false archaism in several critieria, including both features well marked by an extra syllable such as dative plurals in *-οισι* and *-ησι*, and, to a lesser degree, others of which the poets could not possibly be aware, such as the proportion of o-stem genitive singulars in *-ου* which are definitely contracted. The archaism in digamma in the *Shield of Heracles* and the *Pythian Hymn to Apollo* accords with their very probably Boeotian origins. The date of these poems is known to be c. 600 B.C. and after, on historical grounds; such archaism as they display is caused by the use by these poets of much older texts, notably the Homeric epics. In the *Hymn to Hermes* we can trace this tradition, by this stage justly called debased or sub-literary dependent on our point of view, down to the later sixth century, and the *Hymn to Pan* is later still.

The present study owes a great debt to many predecessors, but especially to Hoekstra and Edwards; it confirms Hoekstra's views on how the epic developed, and concurs with both scholars in concluding that Hesiod and the *Homeric Hymns* represent relatively advanced stages in the extant development of the epic *Kunstsprache*. This makes the Homeric epics all the more remarkable, especially if Eumelus' hexameters cannot be dated back to the eighth century to relieve their isolation.[19] There are prospects that these linguistic tests can be used to examine the homogeneity of their diction. Preliminary work indicates that both poems emerge as substantial unities.[20] But the technique cannot prove more than unity of approximate date of composition for fairly large blocks of lines: unity of authorship is a separate issue. However, in the case of the *Hymn to Apollo*, yet more weight has been added to the overwhelming case for dividing the *Hymn* at around v. 181: but the internal unity of the two segments that result is upheld. It has also proved possible to make tentative advances towards understanding how, when and why the two *Hymns to Apollo* came to be associated together (see Chapter 5).

Thus it is claimed that some progress has been made towards solving some of the problems formulated at the outset, and even in illuminating part of the history and prehistory of the epic tradition as a whole; but there are still many gaps and uncertainties to remind us that ἡμεῖς δὴ κλέος οἶον ἀκούομεν, οὐδέ τι ἴδμεν.

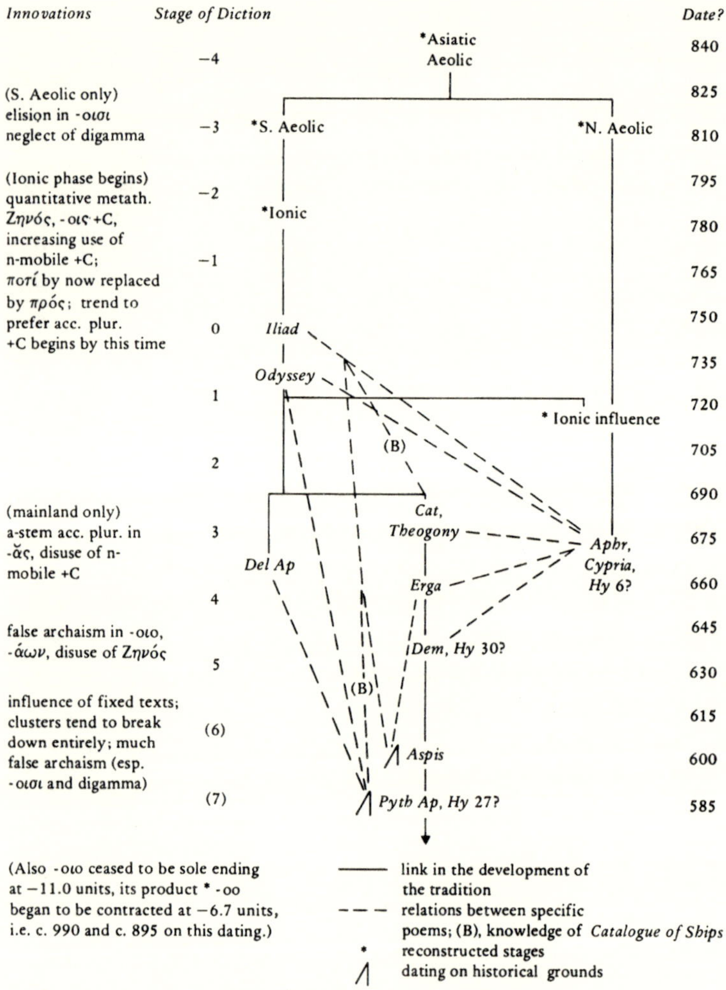

Figure 4: The history of the epic tradition.

The dates offered are obviously no more than approximate. They are midway within the range proposed at the end of Appendix E, and correspond to a table with *Erga* set at 660 and *x* multiplied by 3.4. Cf. pp. 228–31.

The position of *Herm* is not marked. It belongs in the line of descent from *PAp* towards the end of the sixth century, and *Hy* 19 to Pan takes the same line somewhat further on, but surely no later than the mid-fifth century.

APPENDICES

A. *Figures for the individual books of Homer, and Zenodotus' text*

Table for various criteria are here supplied for the individual books of Homer in the sequence and format used in Chapter 3.

Table 33. *Digamma in the individual books of Homer*

Il	Obs.	Negl.	Total	% Negl.	*Od*	Obs.	Negl.	Total	% Negl.
Α	68	14	82	17.1	α	46	6	52	11.5
Β	88	16	104	15.4	β	63	18	81	22.2
Γ	60	23	83	27.7	γ	58	12	70	17.1
Δ	69	12	81	14.8	δ	112	16	128	12.5
Ε	89	16	105	15.2	ε	49	17	66	25.7
Ζ	56	10	66	15.1	ζ	40	9	49	18.4
Η	52	12	64	18.7	η	36	13	49	26.5
Θ	54	9	63	14.3	θ	60	17	77	22.1
Ι	62	11	73	15.1	ι	54	25	79	31.6
Κ	33	7	40	17.5	κ	64	8	72	11.1
Λ	78	23	101	22.8	λ	79	18	97	18.5
Μ	43	8	51	15.7	μ	32	3	35	8.6
Ν	59	18	77	23.4	ν	38	11	49	22.4
Ξ	51	6	57	10.5	ξ	72	15	87	17.2
Ο	68	22	90	24.4	ο	52	14	66	21.2
Π	94	13	107	12.1	π	69	9	78	11.5
Ρ	70	11	81	13.6	ρ	81	17	98	17.3
Σ	61	16	77	20.8	σ	47	16	63	25.4
Τ	26	7	33	21.2	τ	74	9	83	10.7
Υ	45	8	53	15.1	υ	50	3	53	5.7
Φ	59	14	73	19.2	φ	48	11	59	18.6
Χ	53	4	57	7.0	χ	50	11	61	18.0
Ψ	79	19	98	19.4	ψ	47	7	54	13.0
Ω	81	13	94	13.8	ω	70	18	88	20.4
Total	1498	312	1810	17.2		1391	303	1694	17.9
Range: 7.0–27.7					Range: 5.7–31.6				

Table 34. *The genitive singular of masculine a-stems in Homer*

Il	*-αο*	% *-αο*	-εω̆/-ω+V	~+C	Total	Grand total
Α	2	50.0	2	0	2	4
Β	18	85.7	1	2	3	21
Γ	4	100.0	0	0	0	4
Δ	1	25.0	0	3	3	4
Ε	15	78.9	3	1	4	19
Ζ	1	50.0	0	1	1	2
Η	4	100.0	0	0	0	4
Θ	8	88.9	1	0	1	9
Ι	7	70.0	1	2	3	10
Κ	3	75.0	0	1	1	4
Λ	8	72.7	3	0	3	11
Μ	3	75.0	0	1	1	4
Ν	8	88.9	0	1	1	9
Ξ	3	60.0	1	1	2	5
Ο	10	76.9	2	1	3	13
Π	14	70.0	3	3	6	20
Ρ	14	93.3	1	0	1	15
Σ	3	50.0	2	1	3	6
Τ	4	100.0	0	0	0	4
Υ	10	76.9	2	1	3	13
Φ	10	90.9	1	0	1	11
Χ	5	100.0	0	0	0	5
Ψ	17	89.5	2	0	2	19
Ω	1	16.7	3	2	5	6
Total	173	77.9	28	21	49	222

Range: 100.0%–16.7%.

Table 34. (*Continued*)

Od	*-αο*	% *-αο*	-ε͜ω/-ω+V	~ +C	Total	Grand total
α	5	100.0	0	0	0	5
β	1	100.0	0	0	0	1
γ	1	50.0	1	0	1	2
δ	2	50.0	2	0	2	4
ε	0	-	0	0	0	0
ζ	0	-	0	0	0	0
η	0	-	0	0	0	0
θ	2	66.7	1	0	1	3
ι	0	0	3	0	3	3
κ	11	91.7	1	0	1	12
λ	21	95.4	1	0	1	22
μ	7	70.0	2	1	3	10
ν	3	100.0	0	0	0	3
ξ	5	71.4	1	1	2	7
ο	2	66.7	0	1	1	3
π	1	50.0	1	0	1	2
ρ	0	0	1	0	1	1
σ	2	50.0	2	0	2	4
τ	1	20.0	4	0	4	5
υ	2	66.7	1	0	1	3
φ	0	0	1	1	2	2
χ	1	33.3	2	0	2	3
ψ	2	66.7	0	1	1	3
ω	11	91.7	1	0	1	12
Total	80	72.7	25	5	30	110

Range: 100.0%–0%.

Table 35. *The genitive plural of a-stems in Homer*

Il	-άων	-έων	-έ͜ων	-ῶν	Total	%-άων
Α	2		2		4	50.0
Β	16		1		17	94.1
Γ	5		1	1	7	71.4
Δ	11		1		12	91.7
Ε	15		2	2	19	78.9
Ζ	5			1	6	83.3
Η	6	1			7	85.7
Θ	11				11	100.0
Ι	8		4		12	66.7
Κ	2			1	3	66.7
Λ	4		1	1	6	66.7
Μ	11	1	2	1	15	73.3
Ν	5				5	100.0
Ξ	10				10	100.0
Ο	12		1	1	14	85.7
Π	13		1		14	92.9
Ρ	5				5	100.0
Σ	12		3	1	16	75.0
Τ	4			1	5	80.0
Υ	6		1		7	85.7
Φ	2		2		4	50.0
Χ	11				11	100.0
Ψ	3			1	4	75.0
Ω	9			1	10	90.0
Total	188	2	22	12	224	83.9

Table 35. (*Continued*)

Od	-άων	-ἕων	-έ͜ων	-ῶν	Total	%-άων
α	4				4	100.0
β	5			1	6	83.3
γ	4		1		5	80.0
δ	8		4	2	14	57.1
ε	16				16	100.0
ζ	5				5	100.0
η	3		2		5	60.0
θ	3		1		4	75.0
ι	6		1		7	85.7
κ	10		1		11	90.9
λ	4			2	6	66.7
μ	8		1	2	11	72.7
ν	6		1		7	85.7
ξ	4				4	100.0
ο	1				1	100.0
π	6			1	7	85.7
ρ	5		2		7	71.4
σ	6				6	100.0
τ	6			2	8	75.0
υ	1		1		2	50.0
φ	2	1	3		6	33.3
χ	8		2		10	80.0
ψ	4				4	100.0
ω	5		1		6	83.3
Total	130	1	21	10	162	80.2

Table 36. *The genitive singular of o-stems in -οιο in Homer*

Il	-οιο	Other	Total	% -οιο	*Od*	-οιο	Other	Total	% -οιο
Α	40	25	65	61.5	α	33	32	65	50.8
Β	53	58	111	47.7	β	22	30	52	42.3
Γ	25	18	43	58.1	γ	34	38	72	47.2
Δ	43	31	74	58.1	δ	66	58	124	53.2
Ε	61	60	121	50.4	ε	28	25	53	52.8
Ζ	53	34	87	60.9	ζ	22	16	38	57.9
Η	33	32	65	50.8	η	18	23	41	43.9
Θ	40	38	78	51.3	θ	39	29	68	57.4
Ι	49	50	99	49.5	ι	22	33	55	40.0
Κ	29	33	62	46.8	κ	20	42	62	32.2
Λ	68	60	128	53.1	λ	37	48	85	43.5
Μ	22	24	46	47.8	μ	29	31	60	48.3
Ν	63	57	120	52.5	ν	23	14	37	62.2
Ξ	43	34	77	55.8	ξ	22	39	61	36.1
Ο	34	44	78	43.6	ο	38	36	74	51.3
Π	54	59	113	47.8	π	21	33	54	38.9
Ρ	59	49	108	54.6	ρ	30	33	63	47.6
Σ	45	44	89	50.6	σ	26	25	51	51.0
Τ	31	28	59	52.5	τ	39	42	81	48.1
Υ	30	25	55	54.5	υ	26	27	53	49.0
Φ	62	49	111	55.9	φ	37	59	96	38.5
Χ	29	24	53	54.7	χ	34	38	72	47.2
Ψ	72	71	143	50.3	ψ	13	24	37	35.1
Ω	56	65	121	46.3	ω	36	44	80	45.0
Total	1094	1012	2106	51.9		715	819	1534	46.6
Range: 43.6–61.5%					Range: 32.2–62.2%				

Table 37. *The genitive singular of o-stems in -ου in Homer*

Il	*-οι'	*-οο	*-ο'	+ϝ	Total	-ου	+ϝ	Grand total	% -ου
Α	3	8	5		16	9		25	36.0
Β	12	10	21		43	15		58	25.9
Γ	2	7	2		11	7	(1)	18	38.9
Δ	4	10	7	(1)	21	10	(1)	31	32.2
Ε	5	16	12		33	27	(1)	60	45.0
Ζ	4	9	10		23	11		34	32.3
Η	2	8	12		22	10		32	31.2
Θ	5	10	7		22	16	(1)	38	42.1
Ι	4	15	14		33	17	(1)	50	34.0
Κ	4	7	12		23	10		33	30.3
Λ	2	24	16		42	18	(1)	60	30.0
Μ	5	4	2		11	13		24	54.2
Ν	4	19	15		38	19	(1)	57	33.3
Ξ	1	10	9	(2)	20	14		34	41.2
Ο	5	11	6	(1)	22	22		44	50.0
Π	5	12	13	(1)	30	29	(2)	59	49.1
Ρ	6	20	8	(1)	34	15		49	30.6
Σ	4	15	12		31	13		44	29.5
Τ	-	7	11		18	10		28	35.7
Υ	5	8	5		18	7	(1)	25	28.0
Φ	5	13	11	(1)	29	20		49	40.8
Χ	5	7	3		15	9		24	37.5
Ψ	10	22	12		44	27	(1)	71	38.0
Ω	9	17	12		38	27	(2)	65	41.5
Total	111	289	237	(7)	637	375	(13)	1012	37.0

Range: 25.9–54.2%

Table 37. (*Continued*)

Od	*-οι'	*-οο	*-ο'	+ϝ	Total	-ου	+ϝ	Grand total	% -ου
α	5	9	7		21	11		32	34.4
β	3	6	13	(1)	22	8		30	26.7
γ	7	10	8	(1)	25	13		38	34.2
δ	6	20	11		37	21	(3)	58	36.2
ε	5	6	4		15	10		25	40.0
ζ	1	2	1		4	12	(1)	16	75.0
η	4	3	4		11	12		23	52.2
θ	2	8	8		18	11		29	37.9
ι	4	8	4		16	17	(1)	33	51.5
κ	3	11	9		23	19		42	45.2
λ	3	10	7		20	28	(1)	48	58.3
μ	4	9	9		22	9		31	29.0
ν	1	4	3		8	6		14	42.8
ξ	2	11	8		21	18	(2)	39	46.1
ο	5	9	9	(1)	23	13		36	36.1
π	-	12	6		18	15		33	45.4
ρ	6	6	8	(1)	20	13		33	39.4
σ	2	6	7		15	10		25	40.0
τ	4	8	8		20	22		42	52.4
υ	2	7	7		16	11		27	40.7
φ	7	21	12		40	19		59	32.2
χ	2	11	8		21	17		38	44.7
ψ	3	5	5		13	11		24	45.8
ω	6	9	7		22	22		44	50.0
Total	87	211	173	(4)	471	348	(8)	819	42.5

Range: 26.7–75.0%

Table 38. *The dative plurals of o- and a-stems in -οισι and -ηισι in Homer*

Il	-οισι	-ηισι	Long	% long	Total	*Od*	-οισι	-ηισι	Long	% long	Total
Α	51	7	58	77.6	75	α	54	11	65	91.5	71
Β	47	20	67	75.3	89	β	30	4	34	89.5	38
Γ	43	12	55	84.6	65	γ	54	6	60	80.0	75
Δ	32	15	47	85.4	55	δ	73	20	93	83.0	112
Ε	56	24	80	80.0	100	ϵ	28	19	47	90.4	52
Ζ	48	14	62	84.9	73	ζ	28	12	40	90.9	44
Η	50	8	58	87.9	66	η	27	9	36	87.8	41
Θ	33	20	53	88.3	60	θ	61	8	69	89.6	77
Ι	49	18	67	85.9	78	ι	37	15	52	74.3	70
Κ	45	14	59	84.5	70	κ	49	15	64	88.9	72
Λ	72	19	91	91.9	99	λ	51	11	62	89.8	69
Μ	31	18	49	86.2	57	μ	40	11	51	82.3	62
Ν	56	26	82	86.6	95	ν	33	7	40	86.9	46
Ξ	38	16	54	94.7	57	ξ	36	9	45	77.6	58
Ο	69	32	101	91.9	110	ο	39	12	51	78.5	65
Π	45	35	80	90.1	89	π	58	7	65	89.0	73
Ρ	48	18	66	84.6	78	ρ	50	13	63	88.7	71
Σ	38	25	63	81.8	77	σ	41	9	50	86.2	58
Τ	31	13	44	88.2	49	τ	57	8	65	83.3	78
Υ	28	11	39	83.3	47	υ	35	10	45	81.8	55
Φ	35	9	44	91.6	48	φ	36	7	43	84.3	51
Χ	32	9	41	86.3	48	χ	41	9	50	84.7	59
Ψ	81	8	89	84.1	106	ψ	32	5	37	94.9	39
Ω	60	19	79	81.6	97	ω	40	13	53	80.3	66
Total	1118	410	1528	85.4	1788		1030	250	1280	85.2	1502
Range: 75.3–94.7%						Range: 74.3–94.9%					

Table 39. *The dative plurals of o- and a-stems in -οις, -ηις and -αις in Homer*

Il	-οισ'	-ηισ' (+V)	Total	+ϝ	-οις,	-ηις,	-αις	(=+C)	% short (+C)	Total
Α	11	2	13	(1)	1	3		4	23.5	17
Β	9	6	15	(1)	7			7	31.8	22
Γ	3	5	8		2			2	20.0	10
Δ	4	1	5		3			3	37.5	8
Ε	11	5	16		3	1		4	20.0	20
Ζ	6	5	11					0	0	11
Η	3	4	7		1			1	12.5	8
Θ	4	2	6		1			1	14.3	7
Ι	9	2	11					0	0	11
Κ	7	2	9		2			2	18.9	11
Λ	6		6	(1)	2			2	25.0	8
Μ	2	3	5		1	1	1	3	37.5	8
Ν	8	4	12		1			1	7.7	13
Ξ	1	1	2			1		1	33.3	3
Ο	8	1	9					0	0	9
Π	5	3	8	(1)		1		1	11.1	9
Ρ	8	1	9	(1)	3			3	25.0	12
Σ	10	4	14					0	0	14
Τ	1	4	5					0	0	5
Υ	4	2	6		2			2	25.0	8
Φ	1	3	4					0	0	4
Χ	1	3	4		3			3	42.8	7
Ψ	12	3	15	(1)	2			2	11.8	17
Ω	9	3	12		4	2		6	33.3	18
Total	143	69	212	(6)	38	9	1	48	18.5	260

Range: 0–42.8%

Table 39.
(*Continued*)

Od	-οισ'	-ηισ'	-αισ'(+V)	Total	+ϝ	-οις,	-ηις,	-αις	(=+C)	% short (+C)	Total
α	4	2		6					0	0	6
β	1	3		4					0	0	4
γ	11	1		12		3			3	20.0	15
δ	7	4		11		5	3		8	42.1	19
ε	3	1	1	5					0	0	5
ζ	1	1		2		2			2	50.0	4
η	2	1		3		1	1		2	40.0	5
θ	6			6		2			2	25.0	8
ι	11	2		13		4	1		5	27.7	18
κ	5	2		7	(1)	1			1	12.5	8
λ	5			5			2		2	28.6	7
μ	7	1		8	(1)	3			3	27.3	11
ν	2	2		4	(1)	2			2	33.3	6
ξ	8			8	(1)	5			5	38.5	13
ο	5			5		9			9	62.3	14
π	6			6		2			2	25.0	8
ρ	4	1		5		2	1		3	37.5	8
σ	5	1		6		2			2	25.0	8
τ	10			10		3			3	23.1	13
υ	6	1		7	(1)	2	1		3	30.0	10
φ	4			4		2	2		4	50.0	8
χ	2			2		5	1	1	7	77.7	9
ψ	1			1		1			1	50.0	2
ω	9	3		12	(1)	1			1	7.7	13
Total	125	26	1	152	(6)	57	12	1	70	31.5	222
Range: 0-77.7%											

Table 40. *O-stem accusative plurals in Homer*

Il	-ους +V	-ους +C	+ϝ	% +V	Total
Α	2	8	(1)	20.0	10
Β	10	11		47.6	21
Γ	5	19	(3)	20.8	24
Δ	6	24		20.0	30
Ε	18	22	(1)	45.0	40
Ζ	3	6		33.3	9
Η	8	10	(1)	44.4	18
Θ	9	18		33.3	27
Ι	16	14	(1)	53.3	30
Κ	7	18	(2)	28.0	25
Λ	20	23		46.5	43
Μ	13	20	(1)	39.4	33
Ν	13	17		43.3	30
Ξ	16	14		53.3	30
Ο	10	18		35.7	28
Π	11	16		40.7	27
Ρ	9	5		64.3	14
Σ	5	7		41.7	12
Τ	7	11	(1)	38.9	18
Υ	9	6	(1)	60.0	15
Φ	18	14		56.3	32
Χ	9	5	(1)	64.3	14
Ψ	14	24		36.8	38
Ω	22	36	(1)	37.9	58
Total	260	367	(13)	41.5	627

Range: 20.0–64.3%

Table 40. (*Continued*)

Od	-ους +V	-ους +C	+ϝ	% +V	Total
α	6	7		46.2	13
β	4	6		40.0	10
γ	8	9	(2)	47.1	17
δ	8	23		25.8	31
ε	4	7		36.4	11
ζ	3	11		21.4	14
η	7	4	(1)	63.6	11
θ	6	8		42.9	14
ι	15	23		39.5	38
κ	12	18		40.0	30
λ	7	10	(2)	41.2	17
μ	6	10		37.5	16
ν	5	1	(1)	83.3	6
ξ	7	13		35.0	20
ο	6	14		30.0	20
π	5	8		38.5	13
ρ	12	18		40.0	30
σ	3	4		42.9	7
τ	8	9	(1)	47.5	17
υ	9	16		36.0	25
φ	4	6		40.0	10
χ	3	11	(1)	21.4	14
ψ	5	4		55.6	9
ω	8	21		27.6	29
Total	161	261	(8)	38.1	422

Range: 21.4–83.3%

Table 41. *A-stem accusative plurals in Homer*

Il	-ᾱς +V	-ας +C	+ϝ	% +V	Total	*Od*	-ᾱς +V	-ας +C	+ϝ	% +V	Total
Α	11	9		55.0	20	α	1	6		14.3	7
Β	22	14		61.1	36	β	9	4		69.2	13
Γ	3	3		50.0	6	γ	4	10		29.6	14
Δ	1	4		20.0	5	δ	8	11		42.1	19
Ε	7	7		50.0	14	ε	4	2		66.7	6
Ζ	10	6		62.5	16	ζ	3	3		50.0	6
Η	7	6		53.8	13	η	2	6		25.0	8
Θ	5	8		38.5	13	θ	1	4		20.0	5
Ι	10	21		32.2	31	ι	3	7		30.0	10
Κ	9	7		56.3	16	κ	7	5		58.3	12
Λ	9	21		30.0	30	λ	10	9	(1)	52.6	19
Μ	11	14		44.0	25	μ	2	11		15.4	13
Ν	5	9		35.7	14	ν	4	6		40.0	10
Ξ	4	10	(1)	28.6	14	ξ	2	6	(1)	25.0	8
Ο	6	3		66.7	9	ο	4	2		66.7	6
Π	10	8		55.5	18	π	4	3		57.1	7
Ρ	4	2		66.7	6	ρ	6	6		50.0	12
Σ	10	12		45.5	22	σ	3	5		37.5	8
Τ	6	1		85.7	7	τ	3	10		23.1	13
Υ	4	8	(1)	33.3	12	υ	5	7		41.7	12
Φ	5	6		45.4	11	φ	5	5	(1)	50.0	10
Χ	4	7		36.4	11	χ	10	9		52.6	19
Ψ	10	7		58.8	17	ψ	6	7		46.1	13
Ω	7	10		41.2	17	ω	6	10		37.5	16
Total	180	203	(2)	47.0	383		112	154	(3)	42.1	266
Range: 20.0–85.7%						Range: 14.3–69.2%					

Table 42. *Alternations in the paradigm of* Ζεύς *in Homer*

Il	Ζῆνα	Ζηνός	Ζηνί	Διός	Διί	Total Δ-	Total Ζ-	% Ζ-	Grand total
Α	0	0	0	11	4	15	0	0	15
Β	0	0	1	15	8	23	1	4.2	24
Γ	0	0	0	5	2	7	0	0	7
Δ	0	1	1	2	1	3	2	40.0	5
Ε	0	0	0	23	5	28	0	0	28
Ζ	0	0	0	3	5	8	0	0	8
Η	0	0	1	5	3	8	1	11.1	9
Θ	0	0	1	13	5	18	1	5.2	19
Ι	0	0	0	5	4	9	0	0	9
Κ	0	0	0	6	4	10	0	0	10
Λ	0	1	0	2	8	10	1	9.1	11
Μ	0	1	0	5	0	5	1	16.7	6
Ν	0	2	0	6	4	10	2	16.7	12
Ξ	1	3	0	10	1	11	4	26.7	15
Ο	0	2	1	13	3	16	3	15.8	19
Π	0	3	0	6	3	9	3	25.0	12
Ρ	0	0	0	5	3	8	0	0	8
Σ	0	0	0	3	2	5	0	0	5
Τ	0	0	0	2	2	4	0	0	4
Υ	0	0	0	8	3	11	0	0	11
Φ	0	1	1	13	2	15	2	11.8	17
Χ	0	0	1	3	1	4	1	20.0	5
Ψ	0	0	0	1	1	2	0	0	2
Ω	0	0	0	6	4	10	0	0	10
Total	1	14	7	171	78	249	22	8.1	271

Range: 0%–40.0%

Table 42. (*Continued*)

Od	Ζῆνα	Ζηνός	Ζηνί	Διός	Διί	Total Δ-	Total Ζ-	% Ζ-	Grand total
α	0	1	0	3	0	3	1	25.0	4
β	0	1	0	3	0	3	1	25.0	4
γ	0	0	0	4	0	4	0	0	4
δ	0	1	1	7	1	8	2	20.0	10
ε	0	1	0	5	0	5	1	16.7	6
ζ	0	0	0	6	0	6	0	0	6
η	0	1	0	0	3	3	1	25.0	4
θ	0	0	0	5	1	6	0	0	6
ι	0	0	1	7	1	8	1	11.1	9
κ	0	0	0	0	0	0	0	0	0
λ	0	2	0	9	0	9	2	18.2	11
μ	0	0	0	1	1	2	0	0	2
ν	0	0	1	8	1	9	1	10.0	10
ξ	0	0	0	5	1	6	0	0	6
ο	0	0	0	1	2	3	0	0	3
π	0	0	0	2	1	3	0	0	3
ρ	0	0	0	1	0	1	0	0	1
σ	0	0	0	0	0	0	0		0
τ	0	0	0	2	1	3	0	0	3
υ	0	1	0	3	1	4	1	20.0	5
φ	0	0	0	2	0	2	0	0	2
χ	0	0	0	3	0	3	0	0	3
ψ	0	0	0	1	0	1	0	0	1
ω	1	0	0	6	2	8	1	11.1	9
Total	1	8	3	84	16	100	12	10.7	112

Range: 0%–25%.

In table 43 I give a more detailed analysis of n-mobile before consonants in Homer. The instances are broken down into two main categories, those after epsilon and those after iota. Within the former I list adverbs in -θεν, κεν and verbal endings in -εν; in the latter nouns in -σιν and -φιν, then pronouns, and then verbs in -σιν.

Table 43. *N-mobile before consonants in Homer*

Il	-θεν	κεν	Vbs.	Total -εν	Nouns	Pron.	Verbs	Total -ιν	Grand total	‰ vv.
Α		9	7	17	9	2		11	28	45.8
Β	2	3	12	17	9	3		12	29	33.1
Γ		3	10	13	5	1		6	19	41.2
Δ	1	6	10	17	5	1	1	7	24	44.1
Ε		1	14	15	10		2	12	27	29.7
Ζ	2	7	5	14	3			3	17	32.1
Η	2	3	5	10	6		2	8	18	37.3
Θ		9	9	18	9	1		10	28	49.9
Ι	1	3	5	9	5	1		6	15	21.0
Κ		3	15	18	8	4	2	14	32	55.2
Λ	1	3	8	12	9	3		12	24	28.3
Μ	3	1	6	10	11	2	3	16	26	55.2
Ν	5		12	17	10	3	3	16	33	39.4
Ξ		1	7	8	6	1	3	10	18	34.5
Ο	3	1	9	13	10		1	11	24	32.2
Π	2	2	20	24	8	1	2	11	35	40.4
Ρ	3	1	15	19	12	3	1	16	35	46.0
Σ		2	3	5	3			3	8	13.0
Τ	1	3	6	10	2		1	3	13	30.7
Υ	1	2	5	8	2		1	3	11	21.9
Φ	2	2	9	13	4		1	5	18	29.4
Χ	1	2	11	14	8		2	10	24	46.6
Ψ	3		16	19	3	2	1	6	25	27.9
Ω	1	3	17	21	7		1	8	29	36.1
Total	34	70	236	340	164	28	27	219	559	35.6

Range: 13.0–55.2‰ verses.

Table 43. (*Continued*)

Od	-θεν	κεν	Vbs.	Total -εν	Nouns	Pron.	Verbs	Total ιν	Grand total	‰ vv.
α	1	3	3	7	4		1	5	12	27.0
β	2	5	8	15	7		2	9	24	55.3
γ		2	12	14	10	1		11	25	50.3
δ		7	7	14	9	3	2	14	28	33.0
ε		2	8	10	5		2	7	17	34.5
ζ		2	6	8	2		1	3	11	33.2
η	1	2	6	9	8			8	17	49.0
θ	1	4	12	17	8	2		10	27	46.1
ι	2	5	5	12	6	4	2	12	24	42.4
κ		3	11	14	6	2	1	9	23	40.0
λ	3	3	9	15	2	1	2	5	20	31.2
μ		2		2	6		1	7	9	19.9
ν	2	4	8	14	2		1	3	17	38.6
ξ		4	5	9	5	2	2	9	18	33.8
ο		7	4	11	5	1		6	17	30.5
π		6	4	10	9	2	3	14	24	49.9
ρ	2	2	4	8	4	1	1	6	14	23.1
σ		1	8	9	7			7	16	37.4
τ		2	8	10	7			7	17	28.1
υ	1	6	5	12	9		1	10	22	55.8
φ		1	8	9	10	1		11	20	46.1
χ		4	9	13	5	1		6	19	37.9
ψ		3	6	9	3			3	12	32.2
ω		3	8	11	7			7	18	32.8
Total	15	83	164	262	146	21	22	189	451	37.2

Range: 19.9–55.8‰

I append in table 44 the detailed analysis of the incidence of n-mobile in the other works in the epic corpus.

Table 44. *N-mobile before consonants in other works*

Work	-θεν	κεν	Vbs.	Total -εν	Nouns	Pron.	Verbs	Total -ιν	Grand total	‰ vv.
Th	3	3	9	15	5	1	1	7	22	21.6
Erga	1	4	2	7	4		7	11	18	21.7
Aspis	2		4	6	4	1		5	11	22.9
Cat			12	12	6	3	1	10	22	31.4
Dem		5	12	17	4	1		5	22	44.4
DAp		2	3	5	1	2	3	6	11	60.8
PAp			1	1	2	1	1	4	5	13.7
Herm	1	1	2	4	4		1	5	9	15.5
Aphr		1	7	8	5		1	6	14	47.8

I have during the course of this study employed totals for each of the Homeric epics as wholes. There is an assumption here, namely that each epic is as a whole homogeneous, although I would not wish to deny the possibility that some passages in each poem may be earlier or later than the main bulk by the monumental poet or poets. This is the position taken by several recent authorities, e.g. by Kirk in *The Songs of Homer*; the figures for individual books supplied here should help to resolve this question. The statistical work needed to evaluate them is complex and laborious, as what we are likely to find if the diction is not homogeneous are small but consistent differences and not necessarily results for individual criteria that are statistically significant. Preliminary study of these figures has tended to support the hypothesis that each epic is in general internally homogeneous, but this topic is too large to be dealt with here.

I have stated above that the variant readings propounded by Alexandrian scholars seem to be random in their effect rather than the reflection of texts set down in fixed form at earlier or later stages of the dictional development. The best test of this would be to measure one of the long texts with additional lines against the standard text in terms of the criteria. However, the incompleteness and poor preservation of such texts forbids this, and instead I shall examine the readings of Zenodotus, whose text was shorter than ours. In the figures for the whole of the *Iliad* which follow I have used all the variant lines, readings, omissions and additions known to have been favoured by Zenodotus (but not atheteses). (The figures were compiled from the apparatus criticus of Allen's Oxford Classical Text of the *Iliad*, third edition (1920).)

Digamma: observances +6 −18, neglects +4 −6: 17.2% (no % change).

-αο +1 −9, *-εω* +V +1 −2, *-εω* +C −1: 22.2% *-αο* (no change).

-άων −6, *-ῶν* −1: 83.9% *-άων* (no change).

-οιο +5 −18, others +5 −17: 51.9% *-οιο* (no change).

-ου: *-οι'* −1, *-οο* −8, *-ο'* +1 −3 (total −11), *-ου* +4 −5: 37.4% *-ου* (change of +0.4%).

-οισι +6 −9, *-ηισι* −8 (total −9), others +1: 85.3% 'long' datives (change of −0.1%).

-οις +V −1, *-ηις* +V −1, *-οις* +C +3: 19.5% +C (change of +1.0%).

-ους +V +1 −5, +C +2 −8: 41.5% +V (no change).

-ας +V −1, *-ας* +C +2 (*-ᾰς* +1): 46.6% +V (change of −0.4%).

Διί −1: 8.1% Z (no change).

N-mobile +C −2 +2: 559 cases in 15559 lines = 35.9‰, an increase of 0.3‰.

These figures are of course incomplete, owing to the limits of our knowledge of Zenodotus' scholarship. Zenodotus' text is slightly more advanced in some criteria, but the differences are negligible.

B. The diction of Erga 1–200

The diction of *Erga* 1–200 is here compared with that of the rest of the *Erga* and with that of the *Theogony*, to show how Hesiod's diction did tend to advance despite similar subject-matter.

Digamma: observances 18, neglects 11, total 29: 37.9% neglects. This is the same proportion of neglects as in the rest of the poem (44/116, 37.9%); *Th* has 33.7%.

-αο: 2/3 masculine a-stem genitive singulars are in *-αο*, but this is too small a sample for any conclusions.

-άων: there is one contracted a-stem genitive plural, and that is all.

-οιο: of o-stem genitive singulars, 8 end in *-οιο*, 17 otherwise, total 25: 32.0% *-οιο*. The rest of the poem has 28/100 cases in *-οιο*, or 28.0%; *Th* has 38.8%.

-ου: of o-stem genitive singulars in *-ου*, 2 may stand for *-οι'*, 1 for *-οο* and one for *-ο'* (total 6), while 11 are guaranteed as *-ου*, total 17: 64.7% *-ου*. The rest of *Erga* has 48/72 cases, 66.7%; *Th* has 53.6%.

-οισι: there are 26 cases of dative plurals in *-οισι*, 11 of *-ηισι* (total 37) versus 13 others, total 50: 74.0% 'long'. The rest of the poem has

63.0%, and *Th* has 71.8%. This criterion, and the next, contradict the general trend.

-οις: datives in -οις and -ῃς before vowels, 3 of each (total 6), before consonants or at line-end 6 and 1 respectively (total 7), total 13: 7/13 before consonants, or 53.8%. The rest of the poem has 22/34=64.7%, while *Th* has 53.6%.

-ους: of o-stem accusative plurals, 3 precede vowels and 12 consonants, total 15: 20.0% before vowels. The rest of *Erga* has 3/14 or 17.6%, while *Th* has 23.5%.

-ας: none of the 3 a-stem accusative plurals precede vowels.

Z: of the oblique cases of Zeus' name, 1/7 is in Ζην- (14.3%), compared with 5/14 (35.7%) in the rest of the poem, and 9/40 (22.5%) in *Th*. This goes against the trend.

N-mobile: there are four cases guaranteed before consonants, or 20 per thousand lines. The rest of the poem has 22.3‰: *Th* has 21.5‰.

These figures have two implications: as one would expect, on a small scale content does affect the diction, which is here slightly less advanced than that of the rest of the *Erga*; however, the diction is undoubtedly more advanced than that of the *Theogony*, despite the likeness in subject-matter. This is what one anticipated: where a strong tradition of past treatment of a particular topic exists, we can easily imagine how a poet would tend to borrow more preexisting phrases than in other circumstances.

C. The language of Th 901–1022 and Cat

It was remarked above (Chapter 4) that the last hundred lines or so of *Th* have often been suspected: West, for example, would end the work of the genuine Hesiod abruptly at line 900. Edwards (198f.) has shown that West's arguments from phraseology shared between this passage and *Cat* are not strong: but it is quite clear that the quantitative linguistic criteria indicate that at least the bulk of these lines do belong with *Cat* rather than with *Th* (although exactly where the passage begins is impossible to determine with certainty). Below I give the results for the features, and indicate how the percentages for *Th* and *Cat* are affected when the passage *Th* 901–1022 is subtracted from and added to their respective totals.

Digamma: observances 6, neglects 2, total 8: 25% neglects; *Th* 33.7%, 34.6% when revised; *Cat* 31.2%, 30.8% when revised.

αο: -αο 3, -εω 1, total 4: 75% -αο; *Th* 41.7%, revised to 25.0%; *Cat* 90.0%, when revised 88.6%.

-αων: -άων 7, other 1, total 8: 87.5% -άων; *Th* 61.5%, amended to 54.8%; *Cat* 66.7%, revised to 71.9%.
-οιο: -οιο 9, other 13, total 22: 40.9% -οιο; *Th* 38.8%, revised to 38.5%; *Cat* 39.3%, revised to 39.4%.

In these four criteria *Th* is each time more advanced if 901–1022 are transferred.

-ου: doubtful 6, -ου 7, total 13: 53.8% -ου; *Th* 53.6%, revised to 53.6%; *Cat* 51.5%, revised to 51.8%. No real change here.
-οισι: -οισι 8, -ῃσι 5 (total 13), others 7, total 20: 65.0% 'long' endings; *Th* 71.8%, revised to 72.6%; *Cat* 78.1%, revised to 76.4%.
-οις: -οις +V 5, -οις +C 1, -ῃς +C 1, total 7: 28.6% +C; *Th* 53.6%, revised to 57.1%; *Cat* 70.0%, revised to 62.2%; *Th* becomes more advanced again.
-ους: -ους +V 2, +C 2, total 4: 50.0% +V; *Th* 23.5%, revised to 21.3%; *Cat* 16.1%, revised to 20.0%. As previous.
-ας: -ας +V 0, +C 2, total 2: 0% +V; *Th* 16.6%, revised to 17.5%; *Cat* 31.6%, revised to 28.6%. *Th* becomes less advanced this time.
Z: Διός etc. 4, Ζηνί 1, total 5: 20.0% Z; *Th* 22.5%, revised to 22.8%; *Cat* 20.8%, revised to 20.7%.
N-mobile: 1 case +C in 121 lines, or 8.2 per thousand; *Th* 21.5‰, revised to 23.3‰; *Cat* 30.7‰ (based on a conservative estimate of 750 complete lines) revised to 27.6‰ (based on an estimate of c. 870 lines). A more liberal estimate of c. 1000 lines yields 24‰, the same as *Th*.

Thus if we transfer *Th* 901–1022 from *Th* to *Cat*, *Th* advances in seven of the criteria (but remains more archaic than *Erga*). The effect on *Cat* is interesting, as its results tend to cluster more closely than previously; outlying results tend to gravitate towards those in the middle. If these revised figures are used to recalculate figures 1–3, we obtain the results shown on table 45, which may be compared with that on page 81 above, in which the point on the common scale at which the average or mean of the cluster lies is followed by the number of criteria included in the cluster, and the spread of the cluster about the mean. This revision makes little difference to the overall picture. The most striking divergence between *Cat* and the works acknowledged as Hesiod's is the use of genitive singulars in -αο, less advanced than Homer. Random variation is not to blame, despite the fact that this is the least reliable criterion, as far as Hesiod is concerned: *Th* and *Erga* have populations of 12 (revised to 8) and 9 respectively, and it is possible that the result for *Th* is out of place, not that for *Erga*: even so, *Cat* can be shown to differ significantly from a postulated level of,

Table 45. *Clusters of criteria and errant results, from amended figures*

Work	Cluster at	Criteria	Spread	Errant results
Il	(0)	(10)	(0)	nil
Od	0.6	10	1.1	nil
Th	(3)	(10)	(0)	*αο* untrustworthy
Erga	3.5/3.9/3.6	7/9/10	1.3/2.3/4.0	*οιο*, *ου* +??; *αο* −??
Cat	2.6/2.5	8/9	1.5/2.1	*αων*??, *αο*
Aspis		no cluster defined		
Dem	4.6	5	1.1	*οιο*, *αων*, Z
DAp	3.4	4	0.9	*ου*
PAp		no cluster defined		
Herm		no cluster defined		
Aphr	0.1	6	2.4	*οιο*+, *ου*+, Z+

say, 65% *-αο* (z=2.83 for π_0=0.65). But we cannot be sure that this is false archaism: I suspect that the very high proportion of cases accounted for by patronymics is responsible, as these are basic to genealogical poetry and less readily modified than other formulae; but this is no more than a suspicion (note that 21/22 cases in λ are in *-αο*, again in genealogical contexts). Even if false archaism is involved, other characteristics of post-Hesiodic mainland poetry are absent, such as the disuse of *Ζηνός* and of n-mobile. The poem still has a coherent cluster of results, and these should be taken at face value.

It may be of interest to summarise the dialectal forms in the poem, to show that the differences from Hesiod are minimal:

25.28, 229.8 *ἄγηρος* appears to be a modification designed to admit the formula in which it occurs to the first half of the line. The peculiar alteration of an adjective in *-αος* > *-ως* has an exact parallel in Hesiod, *κεραοὶ καὶ νήκεροι* (*Erga* 529).[1]

26.8 Παρθᾶνος, cf. Π]ορθᾴων 11.2, Πορθάονος 26.5. If correctly transmitted, the *αρ* is presumably the West Greek and Attic–Ionic reflex of syllabic *r*, instead of Aeolic and Arcado-Cypriot *ορ*.[2] The form *Parthaon* is known from Ovid (*Met* VIII 542) onwards.[3] There is a by-form Πορθεύς at Ξ 115 and Antoninus Liberalis 2; cf. Mycenaean *Po-te-u*.[4] But its etymology is unclear. The contraction of *ᾱο* > *ᾱ* (typical of Thessalian, Phocian, Peloponnesian dialects, but not Boeotian except in the definite article)[5] in fact rests on an emendation: the papyrus reads *παρθαόνο̣ς*, and one could equally well restore Παρθέ͜ωνο̣ς, comparing variants at *Th* 94 and *Erga* 553.

43.63 *εὐθύ*[ς]: v. sup. p. 147.
45.4 *ἑωυτῆς* is the expected Ionic contraction of *ἕο αὐτῆς* (uncontracted at Τ 384, *θ* 211: accusative *ἑ αὐτόν* 2x *Il*, 2x *Od*, *Herm* 239). Dative *ἑωυτῆι* is well attested at *Th* 126. These are not hyperionisms,[6] but Ionic forms only to be expected in post-Homeric Ionic diction; the Atticism *ἑαυτῆς* would have been more surprising. Note however *Cat* 245 *ἵν δ' αὐτωῖ* where *οἷ* ~ could stand (this form of the reflexive is found at *Erga* 265 and often in Homer). *ἵν* has West Greek affinities.[7]
Ἑρμάωνι 64.17 (restored), 150.31; *Ἑρμάων ἀκάκητα* / 137.1, metrically equivalent to *Ἑρμείας* ~ (Π 185, *ω* 10). The datives have no metrical equivalent. In extant inscriptions *Ἑρμᾶν* < *-άων* is Laconian, and in Arcadian at Tegea and Pheneos;[8] also in Dorian bucolic (Bion X 8). A Peloponnesian origin for this form is thus likely.
66.4 *Ἑρμείης* is a post-Homeric form current in Ionia, already at *Erga* 68.[9]
69 *Ἀθάμα*,[10] 236 *Θόαν* display a curious treatment of stems in *-αντ-* also found in Alcaeus 387 L–P and *IG* 4.245 (Corinth, early sixth century) as well as in Hesiod's *Ἀτλᾱγενέων* (*Erga* 383).[11]
70.10, 169.2 *δίη* by analogy instead of inherited *δῖα* < **diw-yă* is again Hesiodic (*Th* 260); West[12] dubs it hyperionic, but analogy from the oblique cases could have operated even in Ionic, and this and similar cases given by West are better seen as signs of lateness relative to Homer than as definite proof of non-Ionian composition.
70.23 *Ἐρχομενοῦ* is the local Boeotian form, an archaism also persistent in Arcadia.[13] *Ὀρχομενός* occurs in Homer and at *Megalai Ehoiai* 257.4, and is restored (by mistake, surely, for *Ἐρχομενός*) at *Cat* 70.30, 70.35.
76.4(?), 145.16(?) *ἶσος* (cf. 276.2, *Erga* 752). Cf. sup. pp. 153f., 169.
135.6 *Ἀνδρομέδᾱς* is *prima facie* a genitive singular with long alpha retained contrary to the norms of the poetic diction. The dialects except Ionic (and this includes Attic) retain *ᾱ*, as also in *Λήδᾱ*. Contrast Ionic *Ἀνδρομέδη* (Hdt. VII 61, 150) and epic *Λήδη* (λ 298, *Cat* 23.5, 23.8, *Hy* 17.3, 33.2) with Attic *Λήδα* (Aesch. *Ag* 914 etc.).[14] But this possible Atticism or mainland feature is not metrically guaranteed, and might be only graphic.
195=[*Aspis*] 33 *Φίκιον* was apparently not limited to Boeotian, as Edwards has shown.[15]
204.91. *παρθένον οὖσαν*. For this apparent Atticism found in *Od*, *PAp*, *Herm* and elsewhere see pp. 117, 144f., and 185.
204.97f. *μεῖξαι κατ' ἀπείρονα γαῖαν* / *τυρβάξας*. Here either *τυρβάξας* is corrupt for an internal accusative (e.g. *τυρβασίας* Rzach, **τυρβάζας*

M–W), or *μεῖξαι* is a gloss that has ousted an object such as *πόλεμον* or *γενεάς*. If the latter, then *τυρβάξας* is an aorist participle of *τυρβάζω* formed as from a guttural stem, as regularly in West Greek, Thessalian, Arcado-Cypriot, and Thespiae and Coroneia in Boeotia.[16] Elsewhere in the corpus the phenomenon is limited to a few verbs in -*ίζω*.[17]

204.124 *γλωθρῶν* (for *βλωθρῶν*) in the papyrus, v.l. *χλωρῶν* in a citation. Frisk[18] seems over-cautious in denying that this word is related to Skt. *mūrdhā́*, OE *molda* 'head'; if so, it should be from **mlə₃dhrós*, and West therefore argues that this must be an Attic hyperionism, by analogy of Attic *βληχών* for Ionic *γληχών*, Doric and Boeotian *γλᾱχών*.[19] This is certainly possible, although it is surely equally possible that in this rare word the poet was influenced unconsciously by a vernacular with *γλέπω* and *γλέφαρον* (as in Alcman and Pindar) for the Attic–Ionic forms in *βλ*-.[20] If West is right, the poet was not necessarily Attic; he could have learnt the form second-hand from an Attic poet. We have seen in Hesiod's case that such borrowing did happen (*λαμπράν τε σελήνην*).[21]

To summarise, *Cat* is seen to be a mainland product due to not only isolated forms like *εὐθύς*, Peloponnesian Ἑ*ρμάων* and perhaps Ἀ*νδρομέδας* and *τυρβάξας*, but also the rarity of n-mobile; there are only three possible Atticisms, Ἀ*νδρομέδας*, *οὖσαν* and *γλωθρῶν*; the poet is close to Hesiod in some details; and neither Atticisms nor West Greek features are alien to his diction. Nor does the content indicate an Attic (or Chalcidian)[22] poet.

D. Exemplum and imitatio in the oral epic

In this treatise the reader will have observed a rather ambivalent attitude on my part towards the detection of literary models and copies in the poetic corpus with which we have been concerned. Milman Parry rendered the approach of many of his predecessors nugatory, and anyone who still claims to detect *exemplum* and *imitatio* in poetry of the oral formular style on the basis of isolated phrases only is now open to the attack that these may be no more than poetic formulae with a wider distribution in verse that has not survived. Such scholarship has largely ceased, but not altogether, as we have seen (v. sup. pp. 107f.). But it does not follow from recognising the possibility that most of these poems are oral compositions that imitative relationships cannot be detected, provided that they depend on something more substantial than shared formulae; even since Parry nobody has hesitated to admit that there are relationships of some kind between for example *DAp* and *PAp* or *Aphr* and *Dem*, where the parallels are so extensive and striking that coincidence can reasonably be excluded. Obviously the point at which different scholars exclude coincidence varies, but sometimes there are no dissenters.

The problems start when we consider the choice between direct borrowing and derivation from a common source. The temptation to deploy Occam's razor and excise the latter possibility because it involves an 'unnecessary' entity must be resisted. I have already issued a reminder that at least twice as much epos as we possess was still known to Hellenistic scholars (v. sup. p. 9). For instance, suppose that *Erga* 582ff. (the famous description of high summer) were lost; would many scholars prefer to postulate a hypothetical common source rather than derive *Aspis* 393ff. from Alcaeus 347 L–P, or vice versa? The reluctance to postulate lost sources arises from the all-too-human wish to extract too much from small amounts of evidence, and must be guarded against with vigilance.

Even if we are sure that coincidence can be excluded, and we are prepared to discount the possibility of a shared source, priority is very hard to determine on the basis of *exemplum* and *imitatio* alone; the use of these methods unsupported by historical or linguistic considerations (or preferably both) is to be avoided. Nonetheless, sometimes reliable conclusions can be reached, in favourable circumstances, which I shall now try to define; the discussion will mention all relevant cases I have noted in the corpus. In what follows I shall for convenience designate the presumed imitator simply as the imitator. Imitation may be presumed, if:

1. The imitator, but not his model, violates the 'law' of formular economy, i.e. if, in an imitative passage, he employs a phrase taken from the *exemplum* that differs from his own metrically equivalent phrase for the same essential idea. Examples: a) *Aphr* 258 uses ὄρος μέγα τε ζάθεόν τε instead of the normal ~ καταειμένον ὕληι (*Aphr* 285), when the poet is affected by the proem to Hesiod's *Theogony* (sup. p. 25). b) *Dem* 268f., in imitating *Aphr* 31f., borrows the adjective τιμάοχος, hereby breaching economy; cf. ὠρηφόρος *Dem* 192 etc. (sup. p. 163). c) *PAp* 525, in adopting ἀνειρόμενος from *DAp* 51, breaches economy with φωνήσας at *PAp* 425 (sup. p. 110).

2. The imitator introduces more advanced diction and/or modified formulae into his version. Examples: (a) formular separation, with a contracted genitive singular in *-ου*, occurs at *Dem* 355 θυώδεος ἔνδοθι νηοῦ /, 385 νηοῖο προπάροιθε θυώδεος, from *Aphr* 58 θυώδεα νηόν (sup. p. 164); (b) a 'short' dative plural is introduced at *Dem* 5

κούρῃσι. . . βαθυκόλποις / beside *Aphr* 257 *νύμφαι . . . βαθύκολποι* / (sup. p. 165), cf. *PAp* 259 and *DAp* 81 (sup. p. 111); c) *Dem* introduces necessary or indeed violent enjambement (i.e. a noun with which an adjective is in concord follows in the next line) at 268f. and 83f., and the latter is certainly a case of formular modification over line-end from *Aphr* 136. Note also *Aphr* 82 split between two lines at *Dem* 145f. (sup. pp. 163f.). These are less decisive than the first type of proof, but still valuable.

3. The imitator uses unglossed a form glossed in his model. Example: *Dem* 285 *εὐστρώτων λεχέων* beside *Aphr* 157f. *λέχος εὔστρωτον. . . χλαίνῃσιν ἐστρωμένον* (sup. p. 164).

4. The imitator uses an epithet merely for decoration that is functional in his exemplar. Example: *τιμάοχος* at *Aphr* 31 and *Dem* 268 (sup. p. 163). The observation of Podbielski's is nicely confirmed by the violation of economy at *Dem* 268.

5. The imitator uses dialectal elements that seem more appropriate to his model. Examples: *τιμάοχος* is more at home in *Aphr* than in *Dem* (sup. p. 163). More circumstantially, Hesiod, in the description of winter at *Erga* 504ff., uses some Aeolisms, which, I have argued, support my theory that he was influenced in this passage by the proem of *Aphr* (sup. pp. 165–9, especially 168).

6. The model is at the beginning and the copy in the body of the poems. In a wholly or predominantly oral culture the opening is likely to be the most familiar part of a poem, as it will be most often performed and most easily learned. Lord (*ST* 119) has remarked that the ends of oral songs are much more fluid than their beginnings. But this is a double-edged argument, as similarities might be due to the use of earlier versions here, and we need to be sure on other grounds that this is improbable; see for example p. 185, where it is shown that *Hy* 19.28ff. derives from *Herm* and not from *Hy* 18. Thus the opening is likely to be the most influential part of a poem. Examples: the proem of *Th* (2, 8) is certainly imitated by *Aphr* 285ff. (sup. p. 25); the opening of *Herm* is imitated by *Hy* 19.28ff. (sup. p. 185.); the opening of *Aphr* is probably imitated by Sappho 44 L–P (sup. p. 169) and by Hesiod at *Erga* 63ff., 519ff. (sup. pp. 165–9). One contrary example shows that this method is not foolproof: the parallels between the opening of *Dem* and *Aphr* 257, 259 and 284 (sup. p. 165).

7. When two versions of the same topic are extant from the lips of the same poet (i.e. for us, by Hesiod), it may be possible to suggest that specific divergences between them have arisen from the influence of another poem. Thus phraseological variation in the second of Hesiod's

two accounts of the creation of Woman (especially *Erga* 63f. beside *Aphr* 14f.), and his introduction of Aphrodite and others to adorn Pandora, suggest the influence of the opening of *Aphr* (sup. p. 167), while changes between his two appraisals of womankind and the transferred application of the drone simile to lazy men in the *Erga* may result from contact with Semonides (sup. pp. 96ff.). However, as Semonides did not compose in dactylic metre, corroboration from the diction is here unobtainable, and certainty therefore out of reach.

Regarding most passages estimates of probability will vary, and a strong case needs more than one type of support. Most confidence can be placed in the purely verbal considerations, headings 1–5; traditional ideas of appropriateness are more hazardous than any of these techniques. Diametrically opposed views have been taken of whether, for example, the motif of offerings as recompense for infertility is more apposite in *DAp* or *PAp* (sup. p. 109f.), although most people come down on the same side. The same is true of the vignette of the tender maiden sitting at home at *Erga* 519ff., and *Aphr* 14f. Arguments of this type are untrustworthy, and require confirmation by other means.

E. Possible absolute chronologies

It may be of assistance to indicate the range of possible chronologies for early Greek epic that remains if the relative linguistic placings of the poems are straightforwardly converted to absolute dates. This depends of course on the assumption that the rate of change was steady, an assumption which is bound to be in question, although I can see no *a priori* reason why, within a certain unquantifiable latitude of individual variation, it should be wrong; for an important argument in favour, v. sup. p. 93. In this framework a date of as early as c. 700 for Hesiod's *Theogony* is still defensible, if one is prepared to put the *Iliad* back to the middle of the eighth century.

To calculate tables 46 and 47, I have extracted from the table on page 81 the lowest common denominator, x, of the intervals between the most important poems, there expressed in terms of n, the units of the development of diction employed in Chapter 4. $x = 0.15n$. The use of x enables us to obtain whole numbers in the tables. In table 46, the vertical columns headed x, $2x$ etc. give the intervals between the poems in terms of x, $2x$ etc. The ratios obtained can then be converted to absolute dates if but one date is supplied, e.g. *Th* at c. 700. One can then read off the dates with various fixed points and various values of x in table 47: and with the aid of table 46, the reader

Table 46. *Intervals in the dictional development expressed in terms of their lowest common denominator*

Intervals (in terms of *n*)	*x*	2*x*	3*x*	4*x*	5*x*	6*x*	7*x*
Ionic phase (−1.8)–*Il* (0)	12	24	36	48	60	72	84
Il (0)–*Od* (0.6)	4	8	12	16	20	24	28
Od (0.6)–*Th* (3)	16	32	48	64	80	96	112
Th (3)–*Erga* (3.75)	5	10	15	20	25	30	35
Erga (3.75)–*Dem* (4.68)	6	12	18	24	30	36	42
Total	44	88	132	176	220	264	308
(*Th* (3)–*DAp* (3.5)	3	6	9	12	15	18	21)

may readily test other dates, e.g. *Th* at c. 720, which will be found to yield dates for *Il* of 740 at 1*x*, 780 at 2*x* etc., and for *Erga* of 715 at 1*x*, 710 at 2*x*.

Table 47. *Possible absolute chronologies*

	x	2*x*	3*x*	4*x*	5*x*
(a) If *Th* is set at c. 730, we obtain					
Ionic	762	794	826	858	890
Il	750	770	790	810	830
Od	746	762	778	794	810
Th	730	730	730	730	730
Erga	725	720	715	710	705
Dem	719	708	697	686	675
(b) If *Th* is set at c. 700, we obtain:					
Ionic	732	764	796	828	860
Il	720	740	760	780	800
Od	716	732	748	764	780
Th	700	700	700	700	700
Erga	695	690	685	680	675
Dem	689	678	667	656	645
(c) If *Th* is set at c. 685, we obtain:					
Ionic	717	749	781	813	845
Il	705	725	745	765	785
Od	701	717	733	749	765
Th	685	685	685	685	685
Erga	680	675	670	665	660
Dem	674	663	652	641	630

Table 47. (*Continued*)

	x	2*x*	3*x*	4*x*	5*x*
(d) If *Th* is set at c. 670, we obtain:					
Ionic	702	734	766	798	830
Il	690	710	730	750	770
Od	686	702	718	734	750
Th	670	670	670	670	670
Erga	665	660	655	650	645
Dem	659	648	637	626	615
(e) If *Erga* is set at c. 680, we obtain:					
Ionic	717	754	791	828	865
Il	705	730	755	780	805
Od	701	722	743	764	785
Th	685	690	695	700	705
Erga	680	680	680	680	680
Dem	674	668	662	656	650
(f) If *Erga* is set at c. 650, we obtain:					
Ionic	688	724	761	798	835
Il	675	700	725	750	775
Od	671	692	713	734	755
Th	655	660	665	670	675
Erga	650	650	650	650	650
Dem	644	638	632	626	620
(g) If *Erga* is set at c. 630, we obtain:					
Ionic	677	704	741	778	815
Il	655	680	705	730	755
Od	651	672	693	714	735
Th	635	640	645	650	655
Erga	630	630	630	630	630
Dem	624	618	612	606	600

Fortunately most of these possibilities can be excluded for various reasons:

1. The *Odyssey* surely falls between the start of colonisation in the West (c. 750) and the Argive and Attic vase-paintings (c. 670). We can therefore exclude as too low table (g) *x* and 2*x*, as too high table (a) 2*x*–5*x*, (b) 4*x* and 5*x*, (c) 5*x*, (d) 5*x*, (e) 4*x* and 5*x*, (f) 5*x*.
2. In order for *Th* to be imitated by Semonides, a date above 650 is preferable: thus we exclude table (g) *x*–4*x*.
3. Five years seems too small an amount of time to elapse between *Th*

Table 48. *Ranges of absolute dates*

The Ionic phase:	815–751
The *Iliad*:	755–725
The *Odyssey*:	743–713
The *Theogony*:	700–655
The *Erga*:	690–630
Dem:	678–600

and *Erga* – at least ten years ought to be allowed. We may therefore exclude all *x* columns.

In table 47, this leaves table (b) 2*x*, (c) 2*x*–3*x*, (d) 3*x*–4*x*, (e) 2*x*–3*x*, (f) 3*x*–4*x*, (g) 5*x*; any intermediate permutations are of course possible. In these tables, this yields the ranges of date shown in table 48.

Thus considerable latitude for scholarly argument persists: but it is clear that all the acceptable tables seem to favour a relatively high date for *Il* (c. 755–725), and that a date above c. 700 for *Th* is beset with difficulties. I am also doubtful that table (g) is acceptable, in view of the very low dating of *Th* it offers; if we avoid dating *Th* below c. 665, we obtain the range of dates shown in table 49.

I have adopted dates in the middle of these ranges in figure 4, which sketches the development of the epic tradition (p. 200).

Table 49. *Ranges of absolute dates*

The Ionic phase:	800–765
The *Iliad*:	750–725
The *Odyssey*:	743–713
The *Theogony*:	700–665
The *Erga*:	690–650
Dem:	678–625
DAp:	690–660

F. Eumelus and the Black Sea colonies

The sole poet with verses extant that might predate Homer is Eumelus of Corinth, who is usually assigned to the first Messenian War, in the latter part of the eighth century. Pausanias (IV 4.1) makes him contemporary with Phintas, during whose reign the trouble started. The two verses quoted, also by Pausanias (IV 33.2), from the *prosodion* he wrote for performance to Apollo on Delos by a chorus of men, clearly presuppose that Messenian liberty is threatened (cf. Bowra, *CQ* N.S. 13 (1963) 145–53):

τωῖ γὰρ Ἰθωμάται καταθύμιος ἔπλετο Μοῖσα
ἁ καθαρὰ⟨ν κίθαριν?⟩ καὶ ἐλεύθερα σάμβαλ' ἔχοισα

Bergk restored the anapaest, making the piece hexametric; whether rightly cannot be known. If the lines are hexameters, the Aeolisms in the text constitute clear evidence for the Aeolic tradition of hexameter poetry achieving a wider literary currency before the Ionian epic had attained sufficient prestige to affect the dialect, as it did for example in Hesiod's case. This would imply that Homer was not known on the mainland by Eumelus' time; but of course none of the Aeolisms here is metrically substantiated; if the lines are not hexameters they demonstrate instead an early Lesbian ascendancy in lyric more than a century before Sappho and Alcaeus: interesting, but not to the point here.

Further dates for Eumelus are 760 or 744 (Eusebius), and a synchronism with the Archias who founded Syracuse (Clem. Alex. *Strom* I 131.8). Now in addition to the *prosodion* we possess some 'Eumelian' fragments (to be found in Kinkel) of mythological and genealogical hexameter poems, in the Ionic dialect (including Ζηνός), to the greater glory of Corinth, which display considerable interest in and knowledge of the Black Sea: fr. 17 names Borysthenis as one of the three Muses, daughters of Apollo, implying acquaintance with the Dnieper, whereas Hesiod's knowledge does not extend beyond the Danube (*Th* 339, cf. West *Th* pp. 41f.). This knowledge of the remotest nook of the Euxine has usually been seen as corroboration of the high foundation dates of the Milesian colonies at Cyzicus and Trapezus (756 in Eusebius), even though similar dates are there assigned for Naucratis, Cyrene and the *floruit* of Thales (A. R. Burn, *LAG* 107f.)! Excavations at Sinope have produced nothing older than c. 625 (cf. R. Drews, *JHS* 96 (1976) 18–31), and these fragments remain the sole authority for the eighth-century foundation-dates. Indeed better evidence is the name Istrocles on a vase at Smyrna of c. 650, which implies that expeditions had sailed to the Danube by c. 670 at the latest, when Istrocles' proud father named his son after what must have been a pioneering voyage (had it been commonplace, it would hardly have been thus commemorated: so Burn, loc. cit.). The *terminus post quem* for this voyage must be towards the end of the eighth century, permitting Istrocles a long career as a potter. This man's signature thus leads to two conclusions: Hesiod's *Theogony* cannot date from much before the end of the eighth century, and the same is true of these fragments of 'Eumelus' *a fortiori*.

'Eumelus' knew more of the Euxine than did Homer: it is difficult to credit that he is earlier or even contemporaneous. Another obstacle is Hesiod's apparent ignorance of his work (cf. Jacoby, p. 299 of commentary on *FGH* 451).

Two solutions present themselves. Firstly, the date for Eumelus could be lowered to the Second Messenian War; but the notice that he was alive in Archias' time is firmly against this. Secondly, we may adopt an ancient view: Pausanias (IV 4.1) states that the *prosodion* was supposed to be Eumelus' only authentic poem. The other works are presumably later impostures. Although the linguistic evidence is sadly lacking from fragments so few and so brief, it seems probable that they date from the seventh century.

G. Thucydides' version of the Hymn to Delian Apollo

The text of *DAp* 140–6 has long been recognised as problematic. 143–5 have been suspected as adaptations, with minimal alterations, of 76 and 23f. respectively, and are thought to have replaced other verses, which are often identified as 179–81. The latter three priamel lines are now in a most anomalous position between *DAp* and *PAp*, but undoubtedly belong to the Ionian sphere, as they accord special prominence to Miletus. Humbert (p. 85 n. 1) considers that they must have been excised after the Persian conquest of Asia Minor rendered them inept; the Mermnad kings of Lydia had maintained good relations with Apollo. If so, this is proof of early editorial activity on the Hymn: it seems reasonable to blame Cynaethus, when he was trying to build a bridge between the Delian and Pythian sections. Although van Groningen is right to suggest that 140–2 and 146 were originally a doublet of 179–81, his contention (p. 315) that the doublet would be placed at the end of the poem in any case is inconsistent with the possible doublets at 135–8/139, and his own interesting suggestion of doublets at 6/7–9 (ibid., p. 305).

Wilamowitz (*IuH* 442) suggested that a version of the Hymn distinct from our hybrid explains Thucydides' variants here (cf. sup. pp. 2f.), especially 146:

ἀλλ' ὅτε (or ἄλλοτε) Δήλωι Φοῖβε μάλιστά γε θυμὸν ἐτέρφθης

Förstel (129ff. with nn.) suggests that ὅτε might mean 'since' here (cf. LSJ s.v. B), and refers the words to Thucydides himself. This seems no more acceptable than Burkert's rendering 'but when you took most pleasure in Delos – well, here we are. . .', which he considers appropriate for a newly inaugurated festival (*Arktouros* 60 n. 35). Neither of these account for the past tense in ἐτέρφθης, and van Groningen (p. 310) has shown that ἀλλ' ὅτε is very difficult if not impossible, and suggests that Thucydides had a version in which 143–5 were absent, and ἄλλοτε continued the priamel with past tenses at 141–2, which will best accomodate ἐτέρφθης. West (ap. *CQ* 25 (1975) 169) accepts ἄλλοτε, but wishes to avoid van Groningen's conclusion, which is awkward for any who believe that the Delian section is Cynaethus' work, and consequently suggests that Thucydides began to quote at 141, but a scribe omitted the intervening lines by mistake. But it is difficult to see why the lines should be omitted, unless 146 too began with ἄλλοτε: and the quotation of 141–5 would in any case be quite irrelevant to Thucydides' declared purpose. Thus it does appear that Thucydides had a text divergent from ours in this respect, as in several others (cf. sup. pp. 2f.), and the intervention of a Cynaethean recension is a convenient explanation of them.

The interrelation between these versions is surely as follows: the Thucydidean and 'Milesian' versions were originally doublets (i.e. 140–2, 146 = 179–81), incorporated in some texts in the order 140–2, 179–81, 146. After the fall of Croesus, and probably in 523/2 B.C., 179–81 were replaced by 143–5 (crude borrowings from elsewhere in the poem), and put after 178, presumably to smoothe the transition to *PAp*. Thucydides used a text without 143–5, not one derived via this late sixth-century editorial activity.

Observe that this conclusion is in harmony with the most natural interpretation of Thucydides' introduction of 165–72 with the remark that the poet ἐτελεύτα τοῦ ἐπαίνου: surely this is to be taken as a reference to the end of the Hymn, and not merely to the end of the maidens' praises. For ancient use of ἔπαινος to mean ὕμνος see Pfister, *Phil Woch* 1934, 146f. This is certainly how Aristides interpreted Thucydides' words, which he paraphrases with καταλύων τὸ προοίμιον (*Or* 34.35). Förstel (67) succeeds in showing that Aristides could be careless, but the fact that he quotes *DAp* 132 elsewhere is no disproof of his dependence on Thucydides here.

Thus, for several reasons, Wilamowitz seems to have been right.

H. γαῖα/γῆ, ξύν/σύν, κεῖνος/ἐκεῖνος

γαῖα and *γῆ*

At first sight γαῖα and γῆ appear to be unrelated synonyms, of different metrical shapes. One would therefore expect their distribution to be consistent, with one used in place of the other whenever this is

Table 50. *The incidence of γῆ and γαῖα in the epos*

Work	γῆ	γαῖα	Total	% γῆ
Il	4	124	128	3.1
Od	7	167	174	4.0
Th	11	50	61	18.0
Erga	3	18	21	14.3
Aspis	0	3	3	0
Cat	3	19	22	13.6
Dem	2	12	14	14.3
DAp	0	3	3	0
PAp	0	8	8	0
Herm	0	3	3	0
Aphr	0	1	1	0

metrically advantageous. But the reality is otherwise: γῆ is rare in Homer but more frequent in Hesiod. The occurrences of both forms, in all cases of the singular, in our corpus are shown in table 50: the number of instances of γῆ and γαῖα are in the first and second columns respectively, the total in the third, followed by the percentage accounted for by γῆ.

The increase is in line with the pattern seen in the criteria in Chapter 3, and suggests that γῆ is a more recent form. Twice it appears to be introduced by modification. At Φ 63 / γῆ φυσίζοος is modified from φυσίζοος αἶα / (Γ 234, λ 301, *Aphr* 125 in genitive singular: this is proved not so much by frequency as by the maladroit word-ending at the end of the second foot (cf. sup. pp. 36ff.)). Secondly, in / τίς γῆ τίς δῆμος (ν 233) and / τίς δῆμος τίς γαῖα (*PAp* 468) we see the alternation of P_1 and T_1 formulae.

The rarity of γῆ in Homer demands an explanation: we must reexamine its etymology. Frisk (s.v.) and Chantraine (s.v.) have nothing to offer on γῆ, but suggest that γαῖα might be a contamination of γῆ and αἶα, which is also unexplained. We can improve on this.

The Ionic plural form γέαι (found in Herodotus and inscriptions; the singular γέᾱ is found solely in glossaries) shows that the word is contracted. Like γῆ, it is readily derived from **gāi̯ă* < **géə₂-i̯ə₂*. With loss of intervocalic yod we obtain *γᾱᾰ, which in dialects outside Attica and Ionia would lead to γᾶ directly: in Ionic the fronting of *ā* yields *γηᾰ and then γέᾱ by quantitative metathesis, whence the contracted form. γαῖα can be derived from ablauting oblique cases, i.e.

i.e. $*g\partial_2\text{-}\underset{\frown}{i}\acute{e}\partial_2 s$. The Attic form γῆ has the right vocalism, cf. *ῆα > ῆ 'I was' (Lejeune, *Phonétique historique* 262: θέᾱ is from *θά̄ϝᾱ and so not comparable[1] – ibid. p. 281). I find that derivation from *gāia was first proposed by J. Schmidt (ap. *KZ* 26 354, 1) and accepted by Bechtel (*Vocalcontraction* 206f.) and H. W. Smyth (*Ionic* 340f.).

This etymology does not reveal any Indo-European cognates, but it does explain the rarity of γῆ in Homer, for the form depends on quantitative metathesis and subsequent contraction: cases of *γῆα would obviously be replaced by γαῖα when the form *γῆα disappeared from the spoken vernacular. Whether Hesiod used γῆ so much more because he had γᾶ in his own dialect, or because he was at a more advanced stage of the tradition than Homer, is a moot point, although I imagine that both reasons played their part.

When the 'vanishing point' for γῆ is extrapolated back (cf. sup. p. 87 with figure 3), it is found at −0.8, after quantitative metathesis at −1.8 as the sequence demands. This is a further confirmation of the method and the results it produces.

ξύν and σύν

P. Wathelet[2] has recently demonstrated that ξύν, already attested in Mycenaean, was in the process of being replaced by σύν in early Greek epic, showing that in most instances σύν may have replaced ξύν (although I am far from convinced that this could happen at the trochaic caesura, as before words shaped ⏑–⏑ beginning with σκ-, where this was metrically necessary).[3] His case may be supported by the increase in σύν from *Iliad* to *Odyssey*.

In table 51, the number of metrically guaranteed cases of ξύν is followed by those where σύν might be substituted, then by the far larger number where ξύν may be substituted for the σύν of our text (I have used the OCT), then the number of cases of σύν that are metrically guaranteed, the percentage they comprise, and the grand total.

I have amalgamated Hesiod, and omitted the other poems because

Table 51. *The incidence of ξύν and σύν in the epos*

	ξύν	ξύν(?)	σύν(?)	σύν	% σύν	Total
Iliad	30	7	155	44	18.6	236
Odyssey	13	15	65	54	36.7	147
Hesiod (*Theogony* and *Erga*)	3	2	15	10	33.3	30

the samples were very small, under ten. These figures support Wathelet's theory, not only because of the great number of cases of *σύν* where *ξύν* may have stood, in contrast to the small number of times the reverse is true, but also because of the increase between *Iliad* and *Odyssey*.

κεῖνος and *ἐκεῖνος*

I have examined the alternatives *γαῖα/γῆ* and *ξύν/σύν* offered by the epic tradition, and shown that consideration of their distribution in the *Iliad* and *Odyssey* may shed light on their phonological development. A similar case is *κεῖνος/ἐκεῖνος*. *ἐκεῖνος* appears to be limited to Attic in early inscriptions, and is only found in Ionia in inscriptions where Attic influence is suspected.[4] Lesbian too has only *κῆνος*. Yet *ἐκεῖνος* is well established in Ionic poetry and prose,[5] and cannot be eradicated from Homer as a superficial Atticism, however desirable this may seem to be.[6] It must therefore be accounted a feature of Ionian poetic diction, whence I suspect that it made its way into prose. But there is a new fact to be considered: statistical analysis suggests that it is a recent arrival in Homer.

Table 52 shows the frequencies of the two forms, followed by the percentage represented by *ἐκεῖνος*, and the total. Not all cases of these forms are of equal value: *ἐμ' ἐκεῖνος* could stand for *ἐμὲ κεῖνος*, while it is hard to remove *ἐστιν ἐκεῖνος* (I 63 etc.), as Chantraine remarks. Hence I have counted as doubtful all cases of *ἐκεῖνος* where *ᾰ*, *ε* or *ο* are elided, and vice versa regarding *κεῖνος* (the count was based on the OCT).

Results for poems other than the *Theogony* are even smaller: elsewhere in early epic *ἐκεῖνος* is certain once in the *Aspis* and once in the *Ilias Mikra* (fr. 4 Allen). At *ρ* 410 *ὄφρ' ἂν ἐκεῖθι* could be replaced by *ὄφρα κε κεῖθι*. *ἐκεῖσε* is doubtfully attested twice in the *Odyssey*, but *ἐκεῖ* or *κεῖ* (Lesbian *κῆ*) is never found.

The increase from *Iliad* to *Odyssey* suggests that *ἐκεῖνος* is a very recent arrival in the epic diction; it is a pity that there is not more evidence from Hesiod to bear this out. Nonetheless we should take

Table 52. *The incidence of κεῖνος and ἐκεῖνος in the epos*

	ἐκεῖνος	ἐκεῖνος(?)	κεῖνος(?)	κεῖνος	% ἐκ-	Total
Iliad	2	0	7	47	3.6	56
Odyssey	19	2	19	107	14.3	147
Theogony	0	1	0	4	20.0	5

another look at the etymology in the light of this distribution. The ἐ- of ἐκεῖνος is usually connected with the prefix seen in Oscan *etanto* etc.,[7] but if the form is recent in the epic then we are left with two possible explanations for its presence in Ionia: either it is borrowed from Attic (which is not impossible even at such an early date, cf. the Attic formula *λαμπράν τε σελήνην*, which appears in the *Theogony*, *Ilias Mikra* and *Homeric Epigram* 1[8]), or it has arisen independently, presumably by misdivision of words. Which is the truth I cannot tell.

NOTES

1. Introduction and methodology

1. V. e.g. Càssola IX–XXII; and my 'The structure of the *Homeric Hymns*'. Also now A. Lenz, *Das Proöm des fruhen griechischen Epos.*
2. Cf. M. L. West, *CQ* N.S. 20 (1970) 300–4. Contra: M. van der Valk, *AC* 45 (1976) 438ff. (but I am not convinced).
3. p. liv, n. 1.
4. Cf. Richardson 66–7; Merkelbach ap. *ZPE* 12 (1973) 212ff. (*Hy* 1).
5. Cf. Richardson 67ff., A&S xliii–lv, who list the citations. *POxy* 2737 fr. 1. 19. quotes *Hy* 21. 1.
6. A&S liiif.; Lesky, *GGL* 104 = *HGL* 85.
7. V. S. West, *The Ptolemaic Papyri of Homer,* 32–5; cf. *PAp* 425, 504ff. (Strabo's reading was already in Apollodorus, Aristarchus' contemporary; Förstel 44n. 573a.).
8. Cf. A&S xliii; M. L. West ad *Th* 590–1 and ap. *CQ* N.S. 25 (1975) 168n.3, Förstel 114–28.
9. Cf. now Förstel 128ff.
10. Other variants also suggest oral transmission, e.g. ἄντρον ἔσω ναίουσα and ἄντρωι ναιετάουσα (line 6; cf. the variation of single words in lines 5, 8 and 9). A third case is the *poemation* independently preserved after *Hy* 33 and in the 'Herodotean' *Life of Homer* (Allen V 197), where there are variants in lines 2, 4 and 5 of this type.
11. The manuscripts of *DAp* are wholly ignorant of Thucydides' version, and for *PAp* there is only M's reading at 352; for *Dem* M is almost sole witness, but compare *P. Berol* 13044 and *Dem* 256ff., 268.
12. Cf. Finnegan, *Oral Poetry* 160–8.
13. For further examples see R. Herzog's thorough discussion; also West, *Erga* pp. 61f.
14. Cf. Chantraine, GH^2 i 6.
15. Certain due to the rare use of dual for plural. V. inf. p. 122.
16. We would have to assume that aspiration was added later, through the influence of Homeric texts.
17. Cf. e.g. Càssola 616–22.
18. The texts of Homer etc. were obtained from Dr Michaelson of

Edinburgh: they lack accents or breathings, and are in Packard's transcription. These drawbacks are rarely serious. The programming was carried out by Dr J. L. Dawson under the auspices of the Literary and Linguistic Computing Centre, Cambridge, where a copy is kept. The new concordances to Hesiod and the *Hymns* (separately) by Tebben are similar.

19. Cf. A&S xliii–liii.
20. Cf. Richardson 67–70.
21. Cf. Fr. Solmsen, *Hermes* 88 (1960) 1–13; Lenz 97ff.; Förstel 475n. 697.
22. Discussion of these types of evidence will be resumed in the chapters on individual poems below.
23. Allen V 110–44, esp. 112. Cf. G. F. Else, *Aristotle's Poetics: the Argument* 604f.
24. Cf. Pavese *Stud* 125n.
25. See further Appendix D.
26. *SES* 39f.
27. Cf. West ad *Th* 910; Heubeck, *Die homerische Frage* 38f.; Förstel ap. *Glotta* 48 (1970) 163–80.
28. *Homère* II 46–61, 84–90.
29. 'Formulaic composition in the Homeric Hymns'; see also *Phoenix* 33 (1979) 1–18.
30. Cf. Hainsworth ap. *CQ* N.S. 14 (1964) 155–64.
31. *Homère* II 84–90.
32. Cf. *Mnemosyne* 7 (1954) 297ff.; id. 10 (1957) 193–225; Edwards 21.
33. *HMFP* passim.
34. V. inf. p. 16.
35. V. e.g. *Stud* 124ff.
36. *Trad* 111–65.
37. *Trad* 187–96; *Stud* 93–107.
38. *Stud* 63–84.
39. lxiv–lxxii.
40. *Th* p. 99.
41. *Die Vocalcontraction bei Homer*, passim.
42. *The Lay of Dolon* passim; *Homeric Essays* 296–311, 341ff., 351ff.
43. *The Unity of Homer*, passim. But see also his 'The comparative ages of Homer and Hesiod'.
44. ap. *Eranos* 54 (1956) 34–48, especially 34–9; and *Glotta* 38 (1960) 251–63: the figures are from p. 252. Ch. *MH* 209–11.
45. *Stud* 119–24.
46. *SES* 31–3. Cf. now those of Förstel, 55ff.
47. p. 208. Förstel, loc. cit. and 273f., is too pessimistic.
48. *SLH*^{2} passim.
49. V. inf. p. 52.

2. *The problem of oral composition*

1. *L'Épithète traditionnelle dans Homère* 4 (= *MHV* 4).
2. *The Epic Technique of Oral Verse-Making* 90 (= *MHV* 280).
3. *Oral Poetry* 16-24, 126-33.
4. Cf. Bowra, *Heroic Poetry* 354f. Pavese (*Stud* 52) accepts the argument that there is thus no need to admit the use of writing in the composition of the Homeric epics.
5. Cf. R. S. Spraycar, '*La Chanson de Roland*: an oral poem?'.
6. ap. *AJPh* 83 (1962) 337-68; *Hesperia* 29 (1960) 177-97.
7. *Trad* 199-230.
8. pp. 190-3.
9. V. nn.6-7.
10. *Stud* 117-18n. 6.
11. Cf. Hoekstra, *HMFP* 15.
12. Cf. inf. p. 140.
13. pp. 46-51; but contrast J. H. Gaisser, *TAPA* 104 (1974) 113-27.
14. p. 51.
15. pp. 72-3.
16. Chapter V, esp. 71ff.; v. also B. Alexanderson, 'Homeric Formulae for ships'.
17. Cf. my 'Equivalent formulae in the Greek epos', *Mnemosyne* forthcoming (1981).
18. *ST* 49f., 53.
19. ad *Dem* 113.
20. *Trad* 111-65.
21. V. sup. p. 20 on epithets of Apollo; cf. the obscure νυκτὸς ἀμολγῷ, retained in *Herm* in the more stereotyped proem (7), but elsewhere replaced by the comprehensible νυκτὸς ἐν ὥρῃ (67, 155, 400).
22. V. inf. pp. 38-9.
23. Cf. Edwards 53.
24. *Trad* 111-65.
25. Ch. VI, pp. 74-84.
26. We saw above (p. 25) that *Aphr* imitates *Th* elsewhere, and on pp. 153-4 below we shall see evidence that *Aphr* 29 imitates *Th* 585 and 602f. Thus *Aphr* 5 probably imitates *Th* 582, and is therefore a decisive early witness for the reading πολλά of the codices, not δεινά as in the papyrus: v. West ad loc.
27. ad loc.
28. V. sup. p. 25.
29. ap. *TAPA* 60 (1929) 200-20, = *MHV* 251-65.
30. ap. *YCS* 20 (1966) 105-52.
31. pp. 93-9. Cf. also Peabody, *The Winged Word* 125-43.
32. pp. 331-3.

33. ap. *TAPA* 107 (1977) 85–92.
34. ap. *TAPA* 109 (1979) 1–10. See now M. Cantilena, *Quaderni del Giornale Filologico Ferrarese* 1 (1980) 1–94, who, in examining the *Hymns* and *Batrachomyomachia*, comes to similar conclusions.
35. The OCT of Wilamowitz was used, and the stichomythia (53–74) omitted.
36. art. cit. 4, using Gow's OCT.
37. art. cit. 5.
38. 'Homeric enjambement', Appendix.
39. ap. *Hermes* 102 (1974) 200–6.
40. art. cit. 91.
41. p. 333. Note also Lord's demonstration that Međedović has more necessary enjambement than Ugljanin, a lesser poet (*TAPA* 79 (1948) 118).
42. *Les Formules et la métrique d'Homère*, = *MHV* 191–239.
43. *Metrische Beobachtungen* 10–12, 27f.
44. ad loc.
45. Cf. Hoekstra, *SES* 29f.
46. I 27ff., 42ff., III 351.
47. *SbOAW* 68 (1864) 465–6; I exclude *Th* 91, 862, *Erga* 477 as due to digamma.
48. OCT, minus the verses ejected by Allen.
49. *YCS* 20 (1966) 76ff.
50. *Glotta* 50 (1972) 1–10; cf. W. B. Ingalls, *Phoenix* 24 (1970) 1–12.
51. Cf. Richardson 63.
52. By this are meant μέν, δέ etc., and prepositives like καί, οὐ: I have hesitantly excluded the definite article, and δή, αὖτις, on the grounds that they may stand first (and therefore αὖτε is also excluded). Cf. W. Meyer, *SBA* 1884, 979ff.
53. *Pace* West, *Th* p. 95.
54. *Kunstspr.* 22; cf. Meyer l.c. 992ff.
55. *Griechische Laut- und Vers-Lehre* 64–5.
56. Cf. sup. n.52.
57. *Th* 30ff.
58. ap. *A Companion to Homer* 194.
59. *WSt* 20 (1898) 70–90 for the *Hymns*.
60. Richardson 61–2.
61. *Aristarchs homerische Textkritik* II 302ff.
62. Cf. Edwards 86–7nn.7–13. In *Cat* fragments 1 to 30 I counted 252 spondees to 633 dactyls, or 28.5% spondees.
63. Note the conclusions of T. van Nortwick (Stanford diss. 1975), that the frequency of metrically equivalent epithets and rarity of filler adjectives militate against oral composition in this poem.
64. Dihle's attempt (*Homer-Probleme*, passim) to show that the Iliadic *Aeneis* and *Dios Apate* (along with Hesiod's poems) are

literary in origin, on the grounds that they have a greater frequency of neologisms, *hapax legomena* and formula modifications, is unsuccessful for two reasons. He does not prove that other parts of the *Iliad*, which he deems largely of oral origin, have fewer of these features (Lenz has made the same point against Heitsch's views of the *Aeneis*): nor that these innovations are not caused by the further operation of tendencies already present in Homer, as will be demonstrated below.

3. Digamma, alternative morphs and other criteria

1. Cf. Parry, *Language* 10 (1934) 132 (= *MHV* 393).
2. pp. 137–9. Cf. West *Erga* p. 62.
3. pp. 133–5.
4. pp. 33–7.
5. Cf. Athanassakis *Hermes* 98 (1970) 130.
6. Cf. Hainsworth, *Flexibility* ch. III; Lord, *HSCP* 72 (1968) 15–34.
7. *GH* I ch. IX.
8. Cf. however J. Chadwick, *Mélanges Chantraine* 27–30. But v. Wyatt, 'Initial /wo/ in Greek'.
9. Despite Athanassakis' derivation (*Glotta* 49 (1971) 1–21) from *ϝιφίτιμος. V. *Archaeological Reports* 1975/6 p. 14; 1976/7 p. 36, for ϝελένᾱ.
10. Despite Myc. /*Iphemedeia*/, popular etymology may have operated.
11. *Glotta* 44 (1966) 145–6.
12. *GH* I 147.
13. Hamm, 23, 107.
14. Evidence against this reconstruction will be given below (pp. 87ff.).
15. Listed by Chantraine, *GH* I 146ff.; but 3% is hardly 'un assez grand nombre' out of 780 cases.
16. V. sup. pp. 14f.
17. pp. 123–6; cf. Pavese, *Stud* 117–18.
18. Cf. Pavese, *Stud* 66–7.
19. *GH* I 65, 70.
20. pp. 123–6.
21. pp. 126–30.
22. p. 43.
23. *SWH* 58–9; cf. Pavese *Stud* 117–18.
24. Cf. Chantraine, *GH* I 45. Wyatt (*ML* 171n.4, 176f.) is misled by focussing solely on cases where *i* precedes into attempting to deny this.
25. pp. 43f.

26. *Mnemosyne* 11 (1958) 97–116.
27. *SLH*[2] 50–5. His figures for the Hymns are rather incomplete.
28. Cf. Ventris and Chadwick *Docs*[2] 401.
29. Bechtel, *GD* III 136ff.; Smyth, *Ionic* 364–70, 379–82; West, *Studies* 93–4; Buck *GD*[2] 88.
30. *SWH* 62–8.
31. pp. 334–5.
32. pp. 43f.
33. This does not exclude the possibility that some go back a long way, cf. Hainsworth, *BICS* 14 (1967) 17–21.
34. pp. 23, 55f.
35. pp. 141–65.
36. Cf. Edwards 165. On *Herm* 106 and *Cat* 150.15, v. inf. pp. 144f.
37. V. Buck, *GD*[2] 68.
38. p. 141. But v. Giangrande, *Hermes* 98 (1970) 257ff.
39. pp. 142–6.
40. The testing of the two endings against one another is vitiated by the empirical fact that in Homer the o-stems tend to be ahead of the a-stems by approximately 5% each time, while in Hesiod this is reversed. The solution is to test for the result expected at the level of the cluster, as will be explained in Chapter 4, but this can apply only to *Cat* and *Dem*. According to the cluster, *Dem*'s o-stem result ought to be 12.7% +V: by the binomial theorem, the odds on obtaining 2/5 +V are then 0.106, i.e. just over 10%, so this result is not significant. By the same method, the expected o-stem result in *Cat* is 24.7% +V, and the observed 16.1 yields a value for z of 1.3, which is not significant. Likewise the a-stems' hypothetical value is 18.9% +V, which yields $z = 1.4$ when matched against the observed 6/19 +V. Again the odds hover around one in ten. But the o-stem result is no random fluctuation from a Homeric level of, say, 40% +V: this yields $z = 3.6$, highly significant. In *Herm*, assuming that the larger population (the o-stems) is closer to the true level, we expect the a-stems to be 4% above, on the analogy of the *Odyssey*, to whose level the o-stem result approximates: thus the expected result for the a-stems is 40% +V against the observed 5/21 or 23.8%, yielding $z = 1.5$, significant at 10% but not 5%. On *PAp*, v. inf. p. 125.
41. This will be confirmed in Appendix C, when the transfer of the disputed passage *Th* 901–1022 to *Cat* causes both of these results to converge towards such an intermediate level. V. inf. pp. 221ff.
42. *Trad* 190–2; *Stud* 93–4.
43. But there is little sign of oral epic in Thessaly: Pavese, *Trad* 219–22.
44. Cf. Bechtel, *GD* III 240; Buck, *GD*[2] 69; Thumb–Scherer 283; Schwyzer, *GG* I 337.

45. Cf. A. M. Davies, *Glotta* 42 (1964) 163.
46. Cf. the stereotyped *ἐνῶπα, ἐνδέξια* in Homer.
47. p. 152, and n.28.
48. Cf. Lejeune 131f.
49. The probability of two successes in eight trials is 0.156 by the binomial distribution, assuming an Iliadic level of 45% +V. The usage of elegiac and iambic poets, which I have compiled by hand from West (of Theognis I count only verses considered genuine by him), is as shown below.

Poet	+V a-stem	+C		+V o-stem	+C	
Archilochus	1	1		1	2	(elegiacs)
	2	5		3	5	(other metres)
Mimnermus	0	2		0	2	
Solon	1	2		6	3	(elegiacs)
	0	1		3	5	(other metres)
Theognis	3	7		12	10	
Tyrtaeus	1	3	(-ᾰς 3)	4	8	
Xenophanes	0	3		0	2	
Hipponax	3	6		5	5	
Semonides	0	3		0	4	

These results are very small, and show that Archilochus and Hipponax used long endings; unfortunately there is insufficient evidence to say the converse of Mimnermus, Xenophanes or Semonides. The mainlanders all use long endings, as one would expect given their vernaculars, but Tyrtaeus also knows those in -ᾰς (cf. inf. p. 144).
50. For a recent thorough survey see Wathelet ap. *Minos* N.S. 15 (1974) 195–225, who deduces from this dialectal distribution and lack of formular development that the inflection in *Ζηνός* is a late Ionic addition to the tradition.
51. Note also *Ζανός* on Chios and Delos.
52. Evidence from other poets is limited: Eumelus has *Ζηνός* (fr. 16K), Alcman only *Διός* (10x); likewise Alcaeus (10x, *Δία* 1x) and Sappho (4x, *Δία* 1x); Solon has *Ζηνός* twice, beside *Διός*, *Διί* (once each), and these latter are the only forms found in other early iambic, elegiac and lyric poets, and then rarely.
53. *HMFP* 78ff. Pavese (*Stud* 133–45) argues that n-mobile is not particularly Ionic, but includes no figures for Hesiod's use of it, so that his picture is gravely incomplete, and his attempt to deny Ionian influence on mainland poets in this matter unconvincing.
54. 12x *Il*, 2x *Od*.

55. GD^2 84, cf. Thumb–Scherer 267; H. W. Smyth, *Ionic* 287–9.
56. Hamm 40.
57. Thumb–Scherer 97.
58. pp. 43f.
59. Cf. Thumb–Kieckers 291f. V. inf. pp. 217–19 for detailed figures on the different types of ephelcystic nu before consonant in the epos.

4. Diachronic and regional developments

1. Cf. the pair γαῖα / γῆ, from the same root; the latter form is more frequent in *Od* than *Il*, and more frequent still in Hesiod, *Cat* and *Dem*, but as it throws no light on other hymns it is not dealt with here (v. Appendix H).
2. The chance that the true level is 0.33 is between 10% and 5% ($z = 1.43$ for $\pi_0 = 0.33$).
3. The expected incidence at the level of the cluster is 31.8% -οιο, or 23.8/75 cases. When compared with the observed 49.3% (37/75) both chi-squared and z-tests give results below the 1% probability level.
4. V. inf. pp. 181ff.
5. 63.6% of o-stem genitive singulars in *Argonautica* I: cf. sup. p. 52.
6. 77.3% neglects in *Argonautica* I (75/97 neglects).
7. V. sup. p. 55 with n.29.
8. V. inf. pp. 127, 143ff.
9. Cf. inf. pp. 119f., 128.
10. V. inf. pp. 140ff.
11. V. inf. pp. 129–31.
12. E.g. R. M. Cook, *CQ* 31 (1937) 204–14; Russo, *Hesiodi Scutum* pp. 29ff., and Guillon, *Études béotiennes* passim.
13. But this result may be a factor of genre: v. inf. pp. 222f.
14. If $\pi_0 = 0.496$, $z = 2.53$.
15. If $\pi_0 = 0.563$, $z = 2.56$.
16. Cf. sup. pp. 59f., inf. p. 144.
17. If $\pi_0 = 0.274$, $z = 0.94$.
18. p. 63.
19. V. inf. p. 174.
20. $z = 1.52$ for π_0(οιο)0.353: $z = 1.58$ for π_0(ου)0.58, both significant at 10% but not at 5% levels of probability.
21. V. sup. pp. 63, inf. 173.
22. V. sup. pp. 12f., 15f.
23. V. inf. p. 93.
24. Cf. Lord, *ST* 102–9; note also *ST* 44, on the introduction of neologisms by creative poets in poems telling of the remote past.

25. Cf. Appendix B.
26. Cf. Huxley's Irish analogies, *GEP* 192f., where strict discipline excluded local idioms.
27. Cf. Webster, *MH* 268f.
28. V. Appendix H.
29. Cf. inf. pp. 106f.
30. Cf. West *Th* p. 44.
31. Cf. Edwards 102f.
32. Note also *POxy* 2510 (Odysseus carries the corpse of Achilles), also from the *Ilias Parva* if we reject the view of Schol. Ar. *Hipp* 1056 in favour of Proclus on the *Aethiopis*. Note μάχᾱς for -ης, but also Ionic κα]τύπερθεν, αἴροντας, προσέφη.
33. *PMG* 77, 80, 81: but as transmitted, these are in the Homeric dialect!
34. V. sup. pp. 12f.
35. p. 203.
36. So already J. A. Scott, *TAPA* 61 (1930) xxvi; cf. G. S. Kirk ap. *Hésiode et son influence* 63f.
37. The conclusion of the *Theogony*, which leads into *Cat*, has been assigned to the sixth century by West, on account of its references to Medeius the eponymous hero of the Medes (*Th* 1001) and Latinus king of the Etruscans (1013ff.).

    Taking the Medes first, they are not actually mentioned in the text; to quote West (ad loc.), 'as Medeios has no other known *raison d'être*, there is a presumption that here too he is the archetypal Mede'. His *raison d'être*, in both senses, is that he is Medea's son: less than half of the male offspring in this section are rulers of barbarous nations (beside Memnon and Emathion, Phocus, and the sons of Odysseus and Circe, set Plutus, Geryon, and Phaethon). In the *Odyssey* (κ 136–9) Circe is daughter of Perse, as N. J. Richardson reminds me; this shows a nexus of Mede (through her sister Medea) and Persian already in the *Odyssey*, if indeed the names are related to the nations; is the *Odyssey* as a whole, or this part of it, to be redated to the sixth century on this account? In fact Perse may already appear in Mycenaean as *Pe-re-swa* (J. Chadwick, *Minos* 9 (1968) 65), and Medeios occurs as *Me-de-i-jo* at KN B 800. The presence of Medeios, a remote affine of Perse if we extrapolate from other sources (she is not to be found here, even behind a chadoor), has no sixth-century implications.

    Etruscans were trading with Greeks as far back as the eighth century; mainland Greeks could have heard of these important commercial contacts via Italian Cyme very early. Moreover, as West remarks (ad loc.), the poet 'has no conception of Italy as a continental land-mass at a much greater distance than the western isles of Greece'. This is surely some indication of an earlier date.

38. There is no solid evidence exactly which of the incidents Pindar narrates in *Pythian* IX he derived from *Cat*: the struggle with the lion has been questioned by Drexler (*Hermes* 66 (1931) 455–64). If Cyrene was carried off to Libya by Apollo in *Cat*, it is still not clear that this story was an *aition* for the Dorian settlement in north Africa. Malten (*Kyrene* 58ff.) argues that the name Κυράνα is formed from the spring Κύρα attested at the site.

However, as Drexler (art. cit.) showed, the story of the nymph Cyrene is certainly older than this and of Thessalian origin; Servius (ad *Aen* IV 337) records that Apollo 'transfiguratus in lupum cum Cyrena concubuit', a tradition of immemorial age, while Cyrene's genealogy is variously given, but always links her with Thessaly; her sister Alcaea was a city heroine of Larisa. There is no evidence at all for any Thessalian participation in the foundation of Cyrene (or in the population of Thera indeed), so why invent a foundation-legend involving *Thessaly* after a colonisation by men of *Thera*? Better surely to suppose that the settlers relied on an already existent legend when they named the site; perhaps they were prompted by a spring called in Libyan something like Κύρα. If in our *Catalogue* Apollo did carry his nymph across to Africa, we know not why, although legends of such transfers are common enough (e.g. Zeus and Europa, *Cat* 140); but there is no proof that it was because a city of that name existed there yet. Cf. Williams Callim. *h. Ap.* 88, 89 and 95.

For a *terminus post quem* for *Cat* of c. 720, see Schol. ad Ψ 683 (= *Cat* 74 M-W), referring to Orsippus: *νεώτερος οὖν* 'Ησίοδος ('Ομήρου) *γυμνὸν εἰσάγων* 'Ιππομένη *ἀγωνιζόμενον* 'Αταλάντηι (schol T).

39. Meier (pp. 184ff.) gives good reason to think that *Cat* 204.44f. is based on something very like B 557ff. The variations at 46 ~ B 561 and 48 ~ B 560 suggest *oral* knowledge and recomposition. But it is agreed that Hesiod himself knew poetry concerning the Trojan War, cf. West ad *Th* 337–70, so knowledge of such poetry is no bar to a Hesiodic data. Meier's other parallels with Homer (listed on his p. 206) are possible in some cases, but no compelling, being restricted in the main to unusual formulae.

40. Statistical stylometry might help here. The method is much developed since the study of sentence-length in Hesiod by Morton, Michaelson and Hainsworth, *Trans. Roy. Philos. Soc. Glasgow* 9 (1972) 61ff.: see for example the work of Geir Kjetsaa on Dostoyevsky.

41. This implies that *-*oo* was not inherited from *-*oso*. Certainly forms in *-*oo* must appear before they can be contracted! Πηνελέωο (Ξ 489) seemingly contradicts the sequence of

contraction before quantitative metathesis, but in fact this cannot go back to **Πηνελήϝοο, as the latter is unmetrical (Hoekstra, *HMFP* 32n.4).

42. The surprisingly recent dative plural results are discussed below p. 92.
43. This depends on the 'natural' rate of occurrence of heavy closed syllables before word-initial vowels and consonants. Edwards (p. 157) from a study of Hesiod's use of words in -ην, -ης and -ων (total size of target populations 679) found 43.4% +V. In a count of my own, 785/1475 genitive plurals in -ων preceded vowels (53.2% +V); this is from a count of all cases in *Iliad* A–Z, N–Π, *Odyssey* α–μ. The details are A–Z 261/502 (52.0% +V), N–Π 199/396 (50.2%), *Od* 325/577 (56.3%), an increase. These figures conflict with Edwards', and the difference will be found to be statistically significant. If Edwards' figures are followed, the shift began in Homer's own time; if, following mine, we allow a natural rate of 50% +V, the o- and a-stems begin to bias towards prevocalic position at −1.4 and −0.4 units respectively. Now the 'natural' proportion of word-initial vowels to consonants can be calculated from my concordance as 41.9% (of 2990 pages of entries, 1253 are of words beginning in vowels): this is based on the epic corpus as a whole (cf. sup. p. 7). Hesiod's practice seems to reflect a random distribution of this kind: but Homer's does not, at least in the genitive plurals. As this is no random feature, an explanation is needed, and the only one that occurs to me is that Homer (and presumably the early tradition, at least to some extent) tended to avoid overlengthening, i.e. placing heavy closed syllables before consonants. The result from the *Odyssey* even suggests that he improved at this – one of the factors contributing to the greater smoothness of the Odyssean verse. Yet in the accusative plurals we see both types falling back towards the random average for words beginning in vowels, and eventually below it; the light accusative plurals began by Homer's time, if not before.
44. Cf. e.g. Parry, *HSCP* 43 (1932) 22–47, = *MHV* 342–61, esp. 358ff.; Palmer ap. *Companion to Homer* 97–103; Hoekstra, *HMFP* 146–53.
45. *GH* I 509ff.
46. Cf. Webster, *MH* 160–2. As Webster says, the Aeolic epic cannot have been borrowed by the Ionians on their arrival, as this would not allow enough time for the Lesbian forms to arise; but the impossibility of this scenario is no disproof of the Aeolic phase, as Bethe and other exponents conceive it.
47. *Die homerische Kunstsprache* 146–71; he is followed by Wathelet, *Traits* 180–2, 376. Ruijgh (*Lingua* 21 (1968) 393–7) seems to

have had the same idea independently. There is no room here to rebut Wyatt's proposal (*ML* 100) of a phonetic rule applicable to Ionic *epic* only, and his other attempts to deny or minimise Aeolic elements (v. *GRBS* 16 (1975) 251–62). See next note.

48. *Traits* 215. The development is supported by the case of γῆ: v. inf. p. 236. Note δ]εσπόπεω ap. *POxy* 2509.18 (surely a fragment of *Cat*). Wyatt (*ML* 124n.2) tries to get rid of πυλέων etc. (which do not suit his phonetic law) by alleging that the analogy of s-stems influenced these forms, which is unparalleled and incredible. The date for this metathesis might instead represent the date of the Lesbian contraction of -ᾱο to -ᾱ, but the dating of Ζηνός shows that the Ionic phase began soon after this anyway.
49. *HMFP* 70.
50. Buck, *GD*[2] 46ff. Sappho and Alcaeus have lost the sound everywhere in initial prevocalic position, excepting only in the enclitic pronoun ϝε and its adjective, an environment which, as we saw in Homer's case (sup. pp. 44ff.), is not properly word-initial (cf. Hamm 23; Hooker, *The Language and Text of the Lesbian Poets* 23–7; R. Hiersche, *Glotta* 44 (1966) 1–5).
51. I refer to the Attic formula λαμπράν τε σελήνην in Hesiod and elsewhere, and also the epichoric verse-inscriptions in hexameters and other evidence (mentioned above, p. 84).
52. V. inf. pp. 177f.
53. *Odyssee und Argonautica* (1921).
54. Bethe, *Die Sage vom Troischen Kriege* III 81ff.; Murray, *The Rise of the Greek Epic*[4] 219–27; cf. Hoekstra, *HMFP* 150n.1 (but we cannot prove that this material was incorporated by mainland singers, and Bethe's view that the colonists were responsible is at least as likely to be right).
55. So Wathelet, *Traits* 246. A. M. Davies has attributed the spread of -εσσι in Aeolic to an early prevalence of -οισι (*Studies Palmer* 181–97).
56. *HSCP* 43 (1932) 12 = *MHV* 333. His whole section on the traditional poetic language (ibid. 6–23) is highly important for this study in general.
57. So too γῆ: v. inf. p. 234f.
58. This is still true if *Th* 901–1022 are transferred to *Cat.* Cf. inf. p. 221. The -αο figure is certainly unreliable, and the other three are (hardly coincidentally) those based on the smallest populations.
59. pp. 94–8.
60. This correlates with the false archaism in the true sense beginning during the latter half of the seventh century in epichoric verse-inscriptions from Corinth and Corcyra, with the false restoration of intervocalic digamma (cf. Buck, *GD*[2] 87). Cf. sup. p. 76.
61. *Erga* 654–9.

62. *Mor* 153F, cf. Schol. *Erga* p. 206 2–3 Pertusi.
63. *Th* p. 43.
64. Walcot, *Hesiod and the Near East* 118f., thought the tradition invented, because only if the corpse had been lost at sea could Hesiod have been summoned in time for the games. Surely he overestimates the distance between Ascra and Chalcis.
65. *Th* pp. 44f.
66. p. 448.
67. Jeffery, *Archaic Greece* 70n.4.
68. Will, *Korinthiaka* 391ff., dates the war's crisis to the early sixth century, on *a priori* grounds.
69. For bibliography here see Jeffery, loc. cit.
70. Jeffery, op. cit. 64.
71. *Geometric Greece* 200.
72. Thuc. I 13.3 (the date, either c. 721 or c. 704, depends on whether Thucydides refers to the end of the Archidamian or Decelean portions of the Peloponnesian War: the latter seems more likely).
73. *Historia* 6 (1957) 160ff., followed by W. Donlan, *TAPA* 101 (1970) 131ff.
74. p. 448.
75. Cf. Polybius XIII 3.4 with Walbank's note ad loc. I owe this reference to the kindness of D. Braund.
76. loc. cit.
77. *Early Greek Warfare* 90ff. West (*Th* p. 43) argues that as the Lelantine War was a cavalry war, 'it presumably took place before the encounter in Euboea recalled (by implication) by Archilochus, in which slings and bows are no longer used', but this does not follow.
78. Review of West, *Hesiod, Works and Days*, *JHS* 99 (1979) 170.
79. Note that a later date for the Lelantine War is more congruent with the reconstructions of Guillon (Forrest, *JHS* 86 (1966) 173).

    Two ditties that have been related to the date of the war need mention here. First, Theognidea: at 891–4 a voice deplores the ruin of Cerinthus and of the Lelantine Plain, and hurls curses at the Cypselids who are we presume responsible. This episode must date from mid-century or later: it is either irrelevant, or proof that the war flared up at that time (cf. Jeffery, *Archaic Greece* 66). Secondly, *Anth. Pal.* XIV 73, an early hexameter poem often called an oracle, which lists the excellences of each country, where are found the best land, horses, girls (Lacedaemon) and men (Chalcis): but better still are the Argives in linen breastplates, the goads of war: but you, the Megarians (or whomever one wishes to insult) are not in the running at all! It is usual to dismember this poem, and assign the lines on Chalcis to the time after the Lelantine War, and the addition about Argos to the aftermath of the battle of Hysiae in 669/8 (Andrewes, *The Greek Tyrants* 39f., Parke, *Delphic Oracle* I 424f.). The men of Chalcis could be being honoured for a relatively recent victory, and the following lines need not be later: after a list of the best, it is amusing to find something better still, and yet more so to find the political sting in the tail. This poem deserves to be treated more justly in future.

Walcot's arguments for an eighth-century dating of Hesiod require discussion here (*Hesiod and the Near East* 104–30). Whatever the cause of the migration of Hesiod's father from Cyme in Aeolis to Ascra, he must have gone to Boeotia, reasons Walcot, because there were as yet no colonies to go to: perhaps he went to the mainland along with other Cymaeans on their way to founding Italian Cyme, i.e. in the mid-eighth century. There is no *a priori* reason to exclude this hypothesis, but others are equally possible, and Walcot's supporting arguments are unconvincing. The Corinthian and Attic representations in the first third of the seventh century of the birth of Aphrodite and Perseus respectively do not necessarily evince Hesiod's influence: the artists may well have found these ideas elsewhere. Neither Archilochus' inauguration as a poet nor his use of animal fable necessarily parody or exploit Hesiod: both patterns may be traditional. Another study which assumes rather than proves the dependence of Archilochus on Hesiod is T. Breitenstein, 'Hésiode et Archiloque'.

80. *Th* p. 40n.4.
81. Cf. pp. 8f.
82. ad *Erga* 291.
83. Cf. *Orph.* 234 Kern, Soph. fr. 682, Eur. fr. 494N^2. The lines are thought to echo Hesiod by Lloyd-Jones, *Females of the Species* 18–21, and West ad *Erga* 702f.
84. Cf. West, loc. cit. But he is still suspicious: cf. *Erga* 373ff.
85. Note too the reference to Λιμός nearby (*Erga* 302): cf. Sem. 7.101. Parallels between Sem. fr. 1.6f. and *Erga* 96, 102, 1.13f. and *Erga* 152f., 1.19 and *Erga* 155, 1.20 and *Erga* 100, show the same pessimistic mood, whichever was the direction of borrowing. There is no problem in assuming contact between these poets: for Hesiod's possible travels on the mainland, cf. West *Erga* p. 31 (but it is now clear that the short accusative plurals were a feature of the *Ionic* poetic language as Hesiod learned it, and he need not have wandered to acquire them).
86. Cyril *adv. Iul.* 1.12: the *Suda* puts him 490 years after the Trojan war.
87. *Strom.* 1.21.

88. Cf. Appendix E. If the 'eared tripod' Hesiod won at Chalcis and subsequently dedicated was indeed a tripod-cauldron, we have a *terminus ante quem* for this event of c. 675, when such dedications ceased rather abruptly (Snodgrass, *Archaic Greece* 105f.).

5. *The Hymn to Delian Apollo*

1. E.g. most recently W. Unte, A. M. Miller; contra, M. L. West ap. *CQ* N.S. 25 (1975) 161ff. For an excellent survey of views, see Förstel 20–62, and now M. Baltes 'Die Kataloge im homerischen Apollonhymnus', *Philologus* 12 (1981) 24–43; Miller's important article (ap. *TAPA* 109 (1979) 173–86) merits special mention here. Although he does not deal with the vital arguments from diction and style against unity, he rightly points out that the form of 177–8 is not a standard type of hymnic *envoi*, but interprets the phrase *οὐ λήξω ἑκηβόλον Ἀπόλλωνα / ὑμνέων* quite literally as meaning 'I shall (now) continue with my song about Apollo' rather than 'I shall (in future) continue to sing of Apollo'. Jacoby (*Der homerische Apollonhymnus* 719) correctly stated that the choice here cannot be settled on linguistic grounds alone. The analogy of the standard hymnic ending *αὐτὰρ ἐγὼ καὶ σεῖο καὶ ἄλλης μνήσομ' ἀοιδῆς* predisposes one to Ruhnken's view; the shift to third person address is desirable after the second person address to the maidens, and rounds off the epilogue nicely by reversing the shift in manner of address at its opening, 165f.; the promise to celebrate the maidens' fame is a secular *quid pro quo* belonging closely to the *sphragis*, and does not correspond to the normal promise to the deity. Therefore 177f. fill a real gap, and the unusual features are due more to what has preceded than to any alleged sequel; the poet needed to demonstrate his respect for the god in concluding his hymn. He will no more fail to sing of Apollo than to spread the fame of the Delian girls in his future peregrinations.

   Thus in the hymnic tradition one expects not to take *οὐ λήξω* literally; and in this particular context the expression is amenable to a straightforward explanation. However, Miller's view has the strong justification, if the arguments below are correct, that the two Hymns were presented together in antiquity, indeed within the archaic period. That they form a sorry unity I have no doubt; but the unitarian view shows how unity might have been sought by an ancient audience faced with the hybrid version. In fact it was surely the potential ambiguity of *οὐ λήξω* that encouraged the juxtaposition of the two Hymns, whether this took place at Delphi or two generations later at Polycrates' Delian festival (or indeed at first one and then the other). V. inf. pp. 112ff.

2. See my 'The Structure of the Homeric Hymns: A Study in Genre', *Hermes* 109 (1981).
3. Cf. S. Abramowicz, *Études sur les Hymnes homériques* ch. IV.
4. Diss. Leiden 1940.
5. A. Frolíková, 'Some remarks on the problem of the division of the Homeric Hymn to Apollo'.
6. art. cit.
7. Cf. p. 65.
8. pp. 108ff.
9. *YCS* 20 (1966) 167f.
10. V. pp. 2f., also 149f., 241n.21.
11. See my 'Structure of the Homeric Hymns', *Hermes* 109 (1981) 16–8.
12. *Th* p. 79. This case is not in *SES* 21–6, where Hoekstra discusses other cases of modification in this poem. Cf. Richardson p. 37 (on *Dem* 203).
13. These are not in Hoekstra, loc. cit. Another case of violent enjambement is 87f. θυώδης . . . / βωμὸς καὶ τέμενος, modified from τέμενος βωμός τε θυώδης / (*Aphr* 59), itself modernised from Θ 48, Ψ 148 and θ 363 by the replacement of θυήεις with the more modern θυώδης (on adjectives in -ώδης v. inf. p. 135).
14. ad loc.
15. p. 27. The only forms in *DAp* that might be Attic are πόλεις (175, same phrase at B 648, *Cat* 141.17, merely graphic for -ῑς), and Ἀθηνῶν (30, cf. γ 278, *Cat* 43.67, also probably graphic).
16. Art. cit. 169. On the problems here, cf. now Förstel 101–9.
17. Cf. West, art. cit. 169f.; Càssola on 136–9; inf. pp. 233f.
18. art. cit. 165ff.
19. *SES* 21–5. He is wrong on *DAp* 181, cf. K 32f., *Th* 403.
20. For a refutation of his eccentric conclusions, v. inf. pp. 107f.
21. pp. 43–6.
22. But the text is probably corrupt: cf. West, *Textual Criticism and Editorial Technique* 19, and van Eck, Appendix III, who charges that ms. M contains numerous emendations. His charges are important and damaging, and the nature of M will need reassessment by future editors of the Hymns.
23. Cf. inf. p. 159.
24. These inscriptions, from Perachora, are dated by L. H. Jeffery to 625–575(?) (*LSAG* 131).
25. V. sup. pp. 100f.
26. Regarding direct and indirect speech, Homeric and traditional usage may not be identical: long and dramatic speeches were certainly one of Homer's peculiar glories (Aristotle, *Poetics* 1448b35f.), but alien to Hesiod (West *Th* p. 74); some of the *Hymns* have different conventions (Richardson, p. 41), and there

is no speech in the epos so bizarre as *Herm* 525ff., where Apollo's words slide into direct speech and out again without the expected formulae (Allen prints lacunae at 527 and 568, but this is to beg the question).

27. pp. 21f.
28. ibid. p. 24.
29. V. sup. pp. 38–9.
30. For more detail see my 'ΑΘΑΝΑΤΟΣ ΚΑΙ ΑΓΗΡΩΣ: the genealogy of a formula', *Mnemosyne* forthcoming.
31. *SES* 26.
32. ad loc.
33. Cf. Schröder 18. H. Koller, *Glotta* 46 (1968) 18–26, puts the process into reverse for a derivation of *μερόπων*, implausibly. Cf. Chantraine, *AIPhO* 4 (1936) 121–8.
34. LSJ s.v.
35. V. sup. pp. 9f.
36. LSJ s.v.
37. *SES* 25. But his identification of 4 as model of *ν* 56 is wrong: Τ 77 is better.
38. *Stud* 75. The evidence for Myc. / *espargmẹ[na]* / is strengthened by the presence of]*nu-ka* on the same fragment (KN X 7375), part of a compound in *-o-nu-ka*, typical of the cloth tablets. This makes Risch's interpretation *ἐσφαγμένα* most improbable (*Wortbildung*² 343n.86).
39. Cf. p. 83.
40. V. sup. figure 2, p. 74.
41. V. sup. pp. 27f.
42. Cf. sup. pp. 27f.
43. Similar views are entertained, for quite different reasons, by Schefold, *Wort und Bild* 43–52. Following Heitsch and P. von der Mühll, he argues that the Hymn predates certain scenes involving deities in the *Iliad*, as the gods were not distinguished individually until c. 600. He is obliged hereby to accept a drastic Pisistratean recension, but is arguing from false premises anyway. Heitsch (*Kyklos* 20–37) is convinced by Schröder, but see now Förstel 57f. with nn.79–82 for a thorough elenchus.
44. p. 17.
45. pp. 20f.
46. Cf. Richardson's review of Schröder, ap. *CR* 28 (1978) 145f.
47. ibid.
48. ibid.
49. V. sup. p.34 on *DAp* 30, 37, Ω 544, and *DAp* 36, cf. Ω 753.
50. The phrase recurs at Orac. 220.3 and 374.14 Parke–Wormell.
51. ad loc.
52. Allen and Sikes ad loc. Emendation to *μεγάλου* is unnecessary,

and to be eschewed.

53. Cf. Chantraine, *GH* 1 168; West *Studies* 79; Wyatt, *ML* 171f., 179f.
54. V. n.52.
55. p. 6, cf. Hoekstra, *SES* 25.
56. Cf. *Glotta* 56 (1978) 192–5: Edwards (p. 83) is wrong here.
57. pp. 27f.
58. V. inf. pp. 119ff., 127.
59. ap. *CQ* N.S. 25 (1975) 161–70. Cf. Förstel's critique of his ideas (p. 27 with n.14).
60. V. sup. pp. 100f.
61. Cf. now Förstel 294n.14.3.
62. Förstel (212–9, 234–7, 283) suggests that Apollo's peregrinations are a novelty in the myth, and modelled on those of Leto, and therefore secondary. The hypothesis is unverifiable. But see 294n.14.4 for a refutation of West's charge that the catalogue in *DAp* is rather inconsequential.
63. V. inf. pp. 119ff., 127f. For details see L. H. Jeffery, *Archaic Greece* 71ff.
64. Cf. now Förstel, p. 295n.14.5, for a more favourable appraisal of this passage.
65. V. sup. p. 109.
66. The parallel with *τρυγηφόρος* defends *οἴσεις* against *y*'s *πολλήν* (caused by the eye slipping to Ἀπόλλωνος in the next line). For similar cases where a parallel assists textual criticism, v. inf. p. 123f. on *βώμεσθα*, p. 271n.120 on *Erga* 64, and sup. p. 28 on *Th* 582.
67. Note also the topicality for the Pythian Hymn of δ 602 (*οὐ γὰρ πεδίοιο ἀνάσσεις*): the First Sacred War, with which this Hymn is intimately connected, was fought over the possession of the plain of Crisa, which had rendered the Crisaeans independent of the Amphictyons: its confiscation for the sacred flocks obliged them to rely on the cult for a livelihood. Cf. inf. p. 120.
68. A similar problem arises over the temple promised to Delos by Leto. There is no agreement that an early temple of Apollo has yet been found on Delos, despite the extensive excavations; but I shall show below that this is not in the least disturbing. H. Gallet de Santerre (*Délos primitive et archaïque* 91ff., 138ff.) argues that the so-called Building Γ is of Mycenaean date, and was in continuous use through the Dark Ages as a temple of Apollo, but no finds support either assumption at all conclusively (Coldstream, *Geometric Greece* 215): the plan is analogous to that of some Geometric temples (Drerup, *Griechische Baukunst in Geometrischer Zeit* O 5ff.), but it is of small and unimpressive, not to say miserable, dimensions. Burkert (*Arktouros* 62) argues

from this muddy situation that there was no temple until the *porinos naos* was erected in c. 540, and that the mentions of a temple show that the Delian Hymn post-dates this event: 'Artemis is hardly mentioned and definitely has to stand back . . . But archaeological exploration leaves no doubt that the sacred precinct was really Artemis'; it was her temple that was built first, about 700 B.C., and that remained the basic sanctuary . . . Archaeologists have been trying hard to find an 8th century temple suiting the accepted date of the hymn; they looked in vain.' As usual, Burkert has hit upon an important truth: that Apollo had no temple in early times can be corroborated by the story in the *Certamen* (315ff.), that the Delians dedicated the λεύκωμα or whitened board bearing the text of Homer's *Hymn to Apollo* in the Artemisium, and not, be it noted, in the temple of Apollo. This suggests that no roofed temple of his existed.

In this case, Apollo would meanwhile have shared his sister's abode, just as Zeus long had no separate bachelor residence at Olympia, only an altar and a place in the Heraeum. The analogies with Olympia are increased if we consider the position of the altar in each case - to the south or south-east of an eastward-facing temple in honour of a goddess. The temenos with altar and sacred palm-tree was the centre of the cult (cf. ζ 162f.), and the location of these has recently been established by G. Roux (*BCH* 103 (1979) 109–35). The altar of horns was housed in the large almost square building adjacent to and south of the Artemisium. This many-doored temple (actually called νεώς in an inscription during its construction) was erected by the Athenians in the fourth century (as Roux points out (112ff.), the *porinos naos* was only a small temple-treasury unaccompanied by an altar, and neither it nor its successors were ever centres of Apolline worship). Among parallels to this building, Roux cites the Pythion at Gortyn, unroofed and of the archaic period; at Delos it is uncertain whether there was any earlier roofed building, apart from the wooden baldachino (κερατών) protecting the god-built altar itself, since the area is badly denuded, usually to bedrock. Nor is it known when it was named the Pythion (Roux 109ff., 123ff.), although he suspects Athenian influence as the cause, and Pisistratus is an obvious agent (we shall see below that Polycrates provides a *terminus ante quem* for Pythian Apollo on Delos: but the title might be immensely older).

If a predecessor existed, it must have stood on the site of the Pythion; if there was none, the Hymn may be referring to the Artemisium, which Apollo seems to have shared with Artemis at some stage - I suspect that this is the true explanation (we do not expect too much reference to Artemis in a Hymn to Apollo, and the poet gives Leto and her daughter quite enough reverence at 14–18, 159ff., 165). Alternatively, we can account for both temple and oracle by surmising that the poet is giving expression to Delian aspirations as yet unfulfilled, and simultaneously prompting the Ionians to contribute more to the embellishment of Apollo's cult.

69. ap. *Philologus* 1937, 104ff.
70. *Phil Woch* 1934, 56. The observation is Gemoll's, p. 116 and ad *Hy* 27.15: cf. Förstel 84f.
71. On *ὄρη* (4, **Herm* 95) v. inf. p. 144: note also false archaism in -*οιο* (3/5 o-stem genitive singulars), no certain cases of n-mobile – both features of the diction of *PAp* – and a late stylistic feature, the accumulation of numerous introductory epithets at the start of the hymn before the first relative pronoun (cf. *Hy* 28; v. my 'The structure of the Homeric Hymns', *Hermes* 109 (1981) 10. *Hy* 27 and *PAp* might even be by the same poet. For a similar relation between *Aphr, Dem* and *Hy* 30, v. p. 275n.12.
72. *Aspis* argum. 10 = Stes. fr. 92; but cf. J. A. Davison, *Eranos* 53 (1955) 132ff.
73. Burkert, *Arktouros* 59, argues for 522. For 523 cf. H. W. Parke, *CQ* 40 (1946) 105ff.
74. S.v. *ταῦτά σοι* . . . For further sources, going back to Epicurus, and a defence of their value, cf. Burkert, art. cit. n.31.
75. As it stands, the reply looks innocent enough; but an insult can easily be found by reading TAYTA as *ταὐτά*, as Polycrates must surely have seen!
76. The same connection has been made independently by Burkert, art. cit. n.29. But he follows West in thinking *DAp* largely composed at this time (and detaches it from Cynaethus, unnecessarily). I am grateful to Professor Burkert for lengthy discussion and a preview of his paper.
77. E.g. by E. Vogt, 'Die Schrift vom Wettkampf Homers und Hesiods' (1959) 193ff., with bibliography. But Wilamowitz (*IuH* 404n.3) remarked on it 'seltsam, daß dies Selbstzeugnis nicht mehr angenutzt ist. Seltsam auch, daß es Philochorus unbeanstandet anzuführen scheint der nach Gellius III 11,2 Homer für älter als Hesiod hielt.' Philochorus must have deemed the fragment spurious; this would not prevent him from quoting it in a discussion of the etymology of *ῥαψῳδός*. Note a close anticipation of my argument below in some respects by Pfister ap. *Phil Woch* 1934, 149, but he puts events in the wrong order.
78. Förstel (81–4) leaves these verses unexplained. *τότε πρῶτον* may mean merely 'just then, at exactly that time' (cf. M. Chambers on Androtion F6, with parallels, ap. *JHS* 99 (1979) 151f.), but it is possible nonetheless that it means 'then for the first time', imply-

ing that there was a subsequent occasion, either when the poets met, or when hymns to Apollo were performed on Delos. The latter is accorded slight support by the word-order *ἐν Δήλωι τότε πρῶτον*, and I shall argue below that in fact these lines relate to the establishment of a Delian festival at which such hymns were presented. It is a curious and noteworthy parallel that Thucydides, in the celebrated account of the purification of Delos by the Athenians, where he quotes the Delian hymn and its sphragis as Homer's, records the institution of the Delia in 426/5 in the following words (III 104): *τὴν πεντετηρίδα τότε πρῶτον μετὰ τὴν κάθαρσιν ἐποίησαν οἱ Ἀθηναῖοι τὰ Δήλια.*

79. *Certamen* 62ff., 210ff. (Allen V p. 228, 233).

80. West notes that fr. 357 cannot derive from a poem generally attributed to Hesiod, or there could never have been a debate about which poet was earlier, and the Delian contest would have been famous ('The Contest of Homer and Hesiod' p. 440). However, his conclusion that Alcidamas cannot have known it, otherwise he would have set his contest at Delos instead of at Chalcis, does not follow. The contest by the Euripus is based on *Erga* 650ff., precisely the passage where Hesiod reveals his refusal to cross waters any wider than those. The Delian contest could have been refuted at any time, and no doubt was, by reference to these verses of the *Erga*. The passage was already celebrated enough to be echoed by Ibycus in his encomium of Polycrates. *Erga* 649 and 660 are echoed by Ibycus S 151.18, 23 Page, cf. Barron ap. *BICS* 16 (1969) 119ff., ad loc.: he also evokes Homer's *Catalogue of Ships*. We shall meet Polycrates, and Homer and Hesiod, below in indirect association, and Ibycus' echo gains point if he is undercutting the ideas of a rival at court about Homer and Hesiod meeting on Delos; my meaning will become clear from what follows.

I shall suggest below that there was a political motive for inventing a Delian contest; otherwise the choice is quite extraordinary. Delphi is far more obvious as a locale: both poets allegedly consulted the Pythia, and received the oracles foretelling their respective deaths (*Certamen* 56ff., 215ff.; cf. Pausanias X 7.2); why not arrange that they meet at this rival shrine of Apollo, rather than ferry the determined landlubber Hesiod across to windy Delos? The shaper of the tale must have had a powerful motive, and I hope to indicate it below.

Alcidamas is unlikely to have invented the idea of a contest between the two master-poets. West's difficulties (art. cit. 441) in imagining a likelier inventor than a sophist are resolved by parallels in 'Hesiod's' *Melampodia*, where Mopsus and Tiresias compete in prophecy (cf. especially frr. 273–4 M–W beside

Certamen 75ff., and fr. 278 beside *Certamen* 140ff.): such exchanges could, and did, occur in archaic poetry. Further, the eventual judgement on the bards as poets of peace and war may also be old. I see no good reason (despite West, art. cit. 443) to deprive Cleomenes son of Anaxandridas of the remark ascribed to him by Plutarch (*Apophth Lac* 223A, cf. Aelian *VH* XIII 9): *τὸν μὲν Ὅμηρον Λακεδαιμονίων εἶναι ποιητὴν ἔφη, τὸν δὲ Ἡσίοδον τῶν εἱλωτῶν· τὸν μὲν γὰρ ὡς πολεμεῖν, τὸν δὲ ὡς χρὴ γεωργεῖν παρηγγελκέναι.* There is no proof at all that this anecdote was fabricated in the fourth century, as a counterblast to Alcidamas' espousal of the Messenian cause. It may equally well be early evidence for invidious comparisons between the two poets, such as we would expect *a priori* anyway. Surely it replies to the notorious judgement of Panedes in Hesiod's favour (*Certamen* 207–10). If Alcidamas did not invent the idea of a contest, then his contribution to it is reduced to similar proportions as in his retelling of the poets' deaths (for which v. West, art. cit. 438), and in his reuse of preexisting puzzles (ibid. 440f.). I find myself in agreement on this point with N. J. Richardson (*CQ* 31 (1981) 1ff.), who has additional arguments.

West must be right to reject Bergk's and Allen's theory of a biographical poem on the contest by Lesches the cyclic poet (ibid. 438ff.). The tale of a poetic contest on Lesbos between Lesches and Arctinus (Phaenias ap. Clement *Strom* I 131.6) may have augmented the confusion at Plut. *Sept Sap Conv* 153F (Allen V p. 136), or Plutarch may simply be citing the source of Homer's opening gambit, namely Lesches' *Ilias Parva*. For valid defences of the authenticity of the Michigan papyrus of Alcidamas see West, art. cit. 434–8, and R. Renehan, *Studies in Greek Texts* 144–59.

81. So already A&S lix.
82. This is amply clear from their diction. The hybrid poem is cited as Homeric by such writers as Pausanias, Athenaeus and Stephanus of Byzantium, but we lack evidence from before the date of the constitution of the corpus of 'Homeric Hymns'. Strabo's citation of Hesiod for a line very like *PAp* 241 in fact refers to *Cat* 70.18; but this serves as a reminder of the Hymn's close relationship to Hesiodic diction.
83. I refer to W. F. J. Knight ap. *AJP* 62 (1941) 312f. Naive frauds, like the crude insertion of *Aspis* into *Cat*, then won ready acceptance, as witness the former's ancient ascription to Hesiod, even, it seems, by Stesichorus (*Aspis*, Hypothesis 10).
84. Förstel (98f.) suggests that the accusation arose from a desire to discredit the Homeridae in general, but this accords ill with the scholiast to Pindar, who is careful to distinguish Cynaethus and

company from the remaining Homeridae. It was the former who *ἐλυμήναντο* (Homeric poetry) *πάνυ*. Burkert (art. cit. 56f.) is right to say that 'this is a series of insinuations emanating, as it seems, from self-declared "genuine" Homerids or those who later took up their claims'. But I cannot agree when he suggests that the reason why the *Hymn to Apollo* alone became entangled in these polemics is that it terms its author 'the blind man of Chios'. This must, as he so cogently argues, refer to the divine Homer: but why should the Chian Homeridae reject the *Hymn* because it states that their founder lived on Chios? The *Lives* probably originate in Homerid tradition, and these, while ignoring any encounter with Hesiod, affirm that he *lived* on Chios (note that neither the *Lives* nor the *Hymn* yield any indication that he was *born* there: Burkert, art. cit. 57, neglects this distinction by talking of Homer's 'homeland', to the detriment of his argument).

Thus there is no reason on internal grounds why the Delian part of the *Hymn to Apollo* should have been rejected by the Homeridae, and there must have been an external reason. Rejection of the composite whole is readily comprehensible if Cynaethus welded extraneous matter, the *Pythian Hymn*, onto the Chian poem, and invented or popularised the romantic tale of a meeting between Homer and Hesiod on Delos at which they both sang a hymn or hymns to Apollo – and all this (in defiance of the traditions of the Homerids, which probably contain more truth than is nowadays recognised) as propaganda for a showpiece festival to celebrate an aggressive (and, in the event, short-lived) Samian tyrant.

85. There is no doubt that the festival was not only planned but also staged: Rheneia was joined to Delos by a chain (Thuc. III 104), and this was the natural occasion for the festivities; see Zenobius Athous 1.62, p. 356 Miller; Burkert, art. cit. 59f.
86. Whether fr. 357 M–W implies two independent hymns, or one composite one (with a poetic plural for singular, cf. Chantraine, *GH* II 30–3, Bacchylides XIII 223 Sn.), is obscure, but it is hard to see how two lines or more at the start of *PAp* could by accident have been replaced by the apostrophe to Apollo, lord of Delos and of Miletus, with which city Polycrates was at war (Hdt. III 39). V. inf. pp. 233f.
87. Thucydides may have had a text where *DAp* stood alone: inf. pp. 233f.
88. As Burkert says (art. cit. 54ff.), it surely marks the inauguration of a series of Syracusan rhapsodic contests: the report that Cynaethus' associates *τὴν Ὁμήρου ποίησιν σκεδασθεῖσαν ἐμνημόνευον καὶ ἀπήγγελλον* (schol. Pind. loc. cit.) recalls the Pisistratid reforms of the Panathenaea (for the evidence, v.

Allen, *Origins and Transmission* 226–38, especially 228, 229f., on first introducing Homer to Attica and on assembling his scattered works). The two traditions support one another: so now Förstel 94ff. Burkert (art. cit. 60) suggests that Polycrates was aping Pisistratus in this, as in the exploitation of Delos for hegemonic ends: 'at Athens, the Peisistratids had recently adorned the Panathenaia with rhapsodic contests, with recitals of "Homer". It was just natural for Polycrates to follow suit.' Burkert's conjecture can be confirmed from Athenaeus I 3, where both Pisistratus and Polycrates are reported to have kept collections of texts. This may be linked to the tradition (first in Aristotle fr. 611.10 Rose) that Lycurgus obtained texts of Homer *from Samos* and was first to introduce his poems to the Peloponnese (although Ephorus naturally outdid this by making Lycurgus meet him on Chios – Strabo X 480–2).

The late sixth-century date for Cynaethus is tenuously supported by the discovery at Gela in Sicily of an inscription commemorating a Cynaethus son of Epochus: its letter-forms may indicate a sixth-century date (Burkert, art. cit. 54ff.).

89. Art. cit. 57.
90. Again, I am independently in agreement with Burkert: art. cit. 60f.
91. On the attitudes of *guslari* to their predecessors' songs, v. Lord, *ST* 26–9.

6. The Hymn to Pythian Apollo

1. *La Composition littéraire archaïque grecque* 317f.
2. Cf. N. Austin ap. *GRBS* 7 (1966) 295–312, especially 310ff. Note also A. M. Miller's defence of this section (*Form and Generic Intention in the Homeric Hymn to Apollo*) and Förstel's defence in literary and mythological terms (257–63).
3. *οἱ* predominates over *τοί* wherever possible, indeed seems to have replaced it. This remarkable formula normally preserves *τοί*: similar cases are found 3x *Il*, 1x *Od*. There are not above twenty cases in the epos where *τοί* and *ταί* follow heavy closed syllables, and only seven where they begin the line, except in *Aspis* throughout the poem (176, 239, 278, 282, 283, 298, 345). Contrariwise *οἱ* is limited to 280–310 (7x), a vexed passage. Here line-initial *οἱ* may indicate another poet at work.
4. V. sup. p. 52. Cf. Edwards 65.
5. V. sup. pp. 64–9, esp. 67.
6. Cf. West ad *Th* 270–336, 306; and C. H. Whitman, 'Hera's anvils', *HSCP* 74 (1970) 37–42, who thinks Hera syncretised with Gaea here.
7. Cf. West ad *Th* 820–80.

8. Cf. A&S ad loc.
9. Statistical stylometry might profitably be applied to this question of authorship.
10. Rev. Càssola, *JHS* 97 (1977) 174f. *Hymns* 1 and 7 also end with direct speech from a god.
11. Cf. Xen *Anab* I 5.
12. Very easy paleographically: from ΙΘΥΝΤΕΘΕΜΙCΤΑ by haplographic omission of θε to ΙΘΥΝΤΕΜΙCΤΑ, μάλιστα being an attempt to restore sense. On the form ἴθυντε, v. inf. p. 124.
13. So Reiz: Càssola's εἴ κε is also possible.
14. Förstel's argument (200–2) that the frequent mention of Crisa in the Hymn proves that it *antedates* the city's destruction is wholly unacceptable, although the city's subsequent oblivion might support a date not too far removed from the destruction. But his *terminus post quem* of the mid-seventh century, on account of the first stone-built temple, seems to be correct.

    N. Robertson's suggestion that the First Sacred War is a creation of fourth-century propaganda (*CQ* 28 (1978) 38ff.) is cogently refuted by G. A. Lehmann (*Historia* 29 (1980) 242ff.).
15. *SES* 28–31, 33–4.
16. Ibid. 29, 31, 34.
17. A&S ad loc.
18. But contrast Pavese, *Stud* 148–51. I see no reason to think (as does Casadio, *Gnomon* 45 (1973) 644) these duals borrowed from Θ 447ff. No deductions as to the presence or absence of the dual from the poet's vernacular may be made from them. For parallels see West ad *Erga* 186.
19. *SES* 31.
20. *Stud* 142f.
21. ad 231–9.
22. *Stud* 83f.
23. p. 154.
24. *SES* 11ff.
25. Cf. Ventris and Chadwick, *Docs*^{2} 454.
26. Cf. C. J. Ruijgh, *Minos* 9 (1968) 122.
27. Schulze, *QE* 246n.2, Zumbach 30f.
28. *ML* 139ff.
29. Cf. M. Campbell ap. *CQ* N.S. 27 (1977) 467.
30. Cf. my remarks in *CQ* N.S. 29 (1979) 215f.
31. *SES* 31, 33.
32. Examples in Chantraine, *GH* I 424f.; cf. Schwyzer, *GG* I 767 (n.b. δέδοιγμεν for δεδοίκαμεν, Hdn. II 262).
33. Despite Hoekstra, *SES* 29, 34.
34. *Stud* 151f.
35. V. sup. pp. 77f.

36. By the binomial distribution, the chance that the theoretical mean is 3/9 in each case is 0.102 and 0.078 respectively.
37. By the binomial distribution, the chances of this are 0.0013 and 0.036 respectively.
38. Cf. sup. pp. 61f.
39. $z = 1.89$ for $\pi_0 = 0.23$. The odds are therefore 0.03.
40. $z = 3.40$ for $\pi_0 = 0.3$. The odds are therefore 0.0003.
41. p. 7.
42. εὐ- is unaugmented in Ionic: Smyth, *Ionic* 407, 466, 469; Chantraine, *GH* I 225.
43. pp. 133f.
44. *Le Bouclier d'Heraclès* passim. F. Jacoby (*Kleine Schriften* I 196) and J. Defradas (*Les Thèmes de la propagande Delphique* 55f.) had already suggested that the author might actually be a member of the Delphian priesthood, an early precursor of Plutarch.
45. 'Mitologia e propaganda nella Beozia arcaica', *Atene e Roma* XI (1966) 15–24, esp. 17.
46. Sordi, art. cit.
47. *BCH* 97 (1973) 59ff. He had previously thought *PAp* anti-Theban (*RÉG* 77 (1964) 283 ff.).
48. art. cit.
49. Pindar *Ol* IV 19 and schol. ad loc., Callim. fr. 668 Pf.
50. Strabo 422.
51. pp. 135f.
52. p. 140.
53. Cf. K. Förstel ap. *Glotta* 48 (1970) 169n.6, and now *Untersuchungen* 210f.
54. V. sup. p. 29. A. Giovannini, *Étude historique sur les origines du Catalogue des Vaisseaux* 64ff., supports his suggestion of a Delphian origin for the *Catalogue of Ships* with these parallels in an undoubtedly Delphian Hymn; but our poet's knowledge of *Od* and *DAp* as well undermines this part of his argument.
55. AHS ad loc. Perhaps the location of one of the gates of Hades there combined with Odysseus' *Nekyia* to generate the idea.
56. Strabo 350, 477 (v. sup. p. 2). Förstel 210f. suggests knowledge of *Od* here.
57. Cf. too Hes. fr. 266.8, *αὐτὰρ ἐπεὶ δαιτὸς μὲν ἐίσης* ~. This results from contamination with the standard preceding line in Homer, *οὐδέ τι θυμὸς ἐδεύετο δαιτὸς ἐίσης* (e.g. *π* 479): note the maladroit spondaic fourth foot.
58. Càssola ad 505 rightly rejects Debrunner's idea that *βαῖνον* proves imitation of A 437: cf. *ο* 499, and anyway M reads *βῆσαν*.
59. This is not a simile (cf. Förstel 473 n.686): could it be inspired by a 'long-haired' comet (cf. 450 on Apollo's coiffure)?
60. Hesiod's bones were venerated at Orchomenus (Paus. IX 38.4) by

Aristotle's time (ap. App. *Prov.* IV 92 = fr. 565, quoting an epigram attributed to Pindar by Tzetzes (*Vit. Hes.* 49) and others). Wilamowitz (*IuH* 411) had no good reason for ascribing their transfer from Naupactus to the fourth century rather than before, and one would not be surprised to find a link between the cult and this poetic tradition deriving from Hesiod. Cf. now R. Scodel, 'Hesiod redivivus', *GRBS* 21 (1980) 301–20.

7. *The Hymn to Hermes*

1. Cf. Càssola 171; Gräfe *Gymn* 70 (1963) 515ff. (defending 513ff.).
2. Eg. S. Eitrem, 'Der homerische Hymnus an Hermes', *Philologus* LXV (1906) 282; Gräfe art. cit. 524ff.
3. *SES* 10.
4. This is surely a later assimilation of the Homeric form to the vernacular. Cf. West *Th* p. 80 with n.3.
5. p. 224.
6. They are another indication of how recent quantitative metathesis is in Homer: cf. sup. pp. 87ff.
7. For the lost formular prototype here, v. sup. pp. 122–3 on *PAp* 540.
8. Chantraine, *GH* I 147f.; West ad *Erga* 526; cf. *Aphr* 9, sup. p. 44, inf. p. 166.
9. V. sup. p. 76.
10. p. 33; cf. Schwyzer, *GG* I 720f., 754. Another case in the Hymns is *PAp* 376 ἐξαπάφησε, cf. sup. p. 123; another is ἰάχησεν *Dem* 20, *Hy* 28.11, and ἰαχεῖ *Hy* 27.7, instead of ἴαχον as normal in Homer, cf. Richardson ad *Dem* 20.
11. Myc. *ka-ro-qo* (KN Sc 257 etc.) is unhelpful, due to the orthography; cf. *Glotta* 56 (1978) 193f.
12. p. 15; cf. p. 254n.13.
13. Cf. LSJ s.vv.
14. Cf. the useful lists of Huibregste, pp. 44–7, with statistics; and the results of T. van Nortwick, chapters 1–3 and Conclusions.
15. Especially p. 41.
16. V. pp. 183f.
17. *Arch Pap* 7 (1907) 4.
18. Hes. fr. 330 M–W, cf. Orphica fr. 261 Kern.
19. Pace Wyatt, *ML* 61f., there is no reason to reject derivation from **swādu-*.
20. Cf. Buck, GD^2 113; Chantraine, *GH* I 474f.; Pavese *Stud* 68.
21. pp. 29f.
22. The tradition about Cyllene was too strong to be ignored, despite the Boeotian tale of Hermes' birth at Tanagra (cf. Herter, *RhM* cxix (1976) 236n.147): contrast our Boeotian poet's attitude to

Onchestus (inf. pp. 148f.).

23. p. 44.
24. Pavese *Stud* 75.
25. *Stud* 76.
26. ad. loc.
27. *SES* 56.
28. *Stud* 76.
29. pp. 26f.
30. pp. 38ff.
31. p. 135.
32. ad loc., cf. Radermacher ad loc.; Richardson ad *Dem* 371f.
33. Cf. Gemoll 193; Càssola 170.
34. Càssola 173f.
35. Schmid-Stählin, *Geschichte des griechischen Literatur* i 238.
36. pp. 114f. But Dr Richardson reminds me of Achilles' words at I 404f.!
37. Cf. Parke, *Greek Oracles* 65f.
38. On the fall of Croesus and Delphi's 'wonderful apologia' cf. Parke, op. cit., 66–70; Parke and Wormell, *The Delphic Oracle* 129ff. Cf. also M. Dobson ap. *AJP* 100 (1979) 349ff., relating *Herm* to Croesus' oracles.
39. Cf. Càssola 94f.
40. *Gymn* 70 (1963) 524ff.
41. *Philologus* 56 (1906) 282.
42. *Antike Epostheorien* (1970) 20f.
43. *Studien zum Antiken Epos* (1976) 113–28.
44. *Hermes the Thief* (1947).
45. ad 128ff.
46. V. sup. pp. 125.
47. V. sup. pp. 125f.
48. V. sup. pp. 128ff.
49. p. 60. Alcaeus has of course (ἐκ-)γεγόνων.
50. For similar scribal Atticisms in *DAp* cf. p. 254n.15.
51. Cf. Richardson ad *Dem* 15.
52. pp. 58f.
53. p. 58.
54. Cf. Chantraine, *GH* I 56, Buck *GD*[2] 39: these are not limited to Attic.
55. p. 60.
56. *Hermes* 77 (1942) 103f.; cf. Edwards 147f.
57. A. M. Davis, *Glotta* 42 (1964) 162, cf. Edwards 150n.22: note Emped. 115.6 D–K μῡρίᾰς.
58. V. sup. p. 117.
59. Cf. Chantraine, *Morphologie historique du grec*, 335f.
60. Cf. Edwards 142, 144, 150n.22, 152.

61. p. 92n.1.
62. p. 113.
63. cf. Richardson rev. Càssola, *JHS* 97 (1977) 174f.; and Càssola ad loc.
64. p. 58.
65. ad *Erga* 427.
66. ad loc.
67. Buck, *GD*² 70; Bechtel, *GD* II 694; Lejeune, *Traité* 100ff.
68. s.v.
69. Zumbach 56; Pavese *Stud* 92; Chantraine, *GH* I 17.
70. For elision of *περί*, cf. Buck *GD*² 79; Edwards 108.
71. *KZ* 7 (1965) 28ff., followed by Càssola and Pavese, *Stud* 107.
72. AHS ad loc.
73. But also Alc. 67.3 L–P, Pindar, Bacch. etc. (LSJ s.v.).
74. pp. 59f: but only at *κ* 415, *υ* 93.
75. LSJ s.v.
76. p. 60.
77. e.g. Zumbach 58, 62.
78. *Stud* 93.
79. Càssola 174.
80. H. W. Smyth, *Ionic* 187 (Styra, Teos); LSJ s.v. *εὐθυωρία* (Heraclea, Arcadia).
81. p. 174.
82. *BB* XXII 272, cf. Allen and Sikes lxxiii, 133.
83. p. 57.
84. Exploded by Richardson p. 55.
85. Cf. Chantraine, *GH* I 52f. for similar contractions in Homer.
86. Cf. Chantraine, *GH* 469.
87. *Stud* 93. West's *παραὶ δαφνέων* (*Philologus* CX (1966) 150) demands an originally dendromantic oracle, which is possible.
88. Buck, *GD*² 107; in Mycenaean, KN V 114.
89. V. sup. p. 66.
90. V. sup. pp. 127f.
91. III 10.2.
92. 23; cf. Humbert 112f., Càssola 174.
93. Strabo p. 412.
94. Wilamowitz, *Glaube der Hellenen* I 212.
95. The bee-maidens are called *σεμναί* by M, *μοῖραι* by the other mss., which is surely a gloss, as Allen and Sikes remark ad 552. They point out that an Attic poet might well have refrained from giving them this title, in view of the Erinyes. See now S. Scheinberg, 'The Bee Maidens of the Homeric Hymn to Hermes', *HSCP* 83 (1979) 1–28.
96. V. sup. Chapter 2, esp. pp. 40–1.
97. Cf. sup. p. 3. *Hy* 18 is very close to *η* 245–7 (cf. lines 4, 6, 9).

98. Cf. p. 241n.21.
99. V. sup. p. 25.
100. V. inf. p. 185.
101. V. sup. p. 134.

8. The Hymn to Aphrodite

1. Note the imitation in Vergil, *Aeneid* I 314–35, 402ff. (B. Otis, *Virgil, a Study in Civilised Poetry* 235f.); also Propertius II 32.33–40, cf. *Aphr* 247–8, 256–66 (I owe this reference to the kindness of S. J. Heyworth); Moschus *Europa* 76ff., cf. *Aphr* 32ff.; 154f., cf. *Aphr* 193; 160, cf. *Aphr* 196f.; and also Musaeus, *Hero and Leander* 79, cf. *Aphr* 154; 160, cf. *Aphr* 155ff.; 264f., cf. *Aphr* 62ff. (cf. K. Kost *Commentary on Musaeus* 43ff.).
2. *Epistula ad Ilgen* lxxxix–xcv.
3. *Festschrift Snell* (1956) 1–14; *Die Ilias und ihr Dichter* (1961) 507–21.
4. *YCS* 12 (1951) 1–63, esp. 34.
5. *Aphroditehymnos, Aeneas und Homer* (1965) especially 13–40.
6. *HMFP* 75–83; *SES* 15f., 39–48.
7. *Mnemosyne* 20 (1967) 385–95.
8. *CJ* 50 (1955) 153–9.
9. *De hymno quarto in Venerem*, Stolpae 1878.
10. AHS before c. 700, Humbert c. 630, Càssola seventh century; so now van Eck 3ff., and P. Smith (see addenda to Bibliography).
11. op. cit. (n.5).
12. *Der homerische Aphroditehymnus und die Aristie des Aineias in der Ilias* (1975), 153–268.
13. Cf. sup. Figure 2 and p. 79.
14. Cf. sup. p. 63.
15. Cf. sup. p. 79.
16. Cf. sup. p. 65.
17. Cf. sup. pp. 77ff.
18. Especially *SES* 39–48.
19. Cf. sup. p. 11.
20. It is to be hoped that Postlethwaite will apply his technique to Hesiod, whom I expect to be closer to the Hymns than to Homer in this.
21. V. sup. pp. 12, 43, 45f., 52, 55.
22. Computed by E. Windisch, *De hymnis homericis majoribus* 67, as *Dem* 8 (1.6%), *DAp* 7 (3.9%), *PAp* 29 (7.9%), *Herm* 4 (0.7%), *Aphr* 20 (6.8%).
23. Hoekstra (*HMFP* 62) shows that 85 and 132 defend τε here.
24. *SES* 42f.
25. Also *Hy* 29.3f. ἔλαχες πρεσβηΐδα τιμὴν / καλὸν ἔχουσα γέρας καὶ

τιμήν (also of Hestia) beside *Aphr* 31 τιμάοχος, 32 πρέσβειρα. The two passages are related; how is unclear (in *Hy* 29 note only the 'Atticisms' σοῦ 4, ὤν 10). Cf. Solmsen, *Hermes* 88 (1960) 8n.2, 9n.5. Read τίμιον for τιμήν at *Hy* 29.4 (Franke).

26. V. n.25.
27. pp. 19–22.
28. V. sup. p. 28.
29. V. sup. p. 25.
30. Hoekstra, *SES* 43.
31. pp. 396f.
32. *GH* I 161f.
33. (δ)δεῖσα, δειμαίνω, Δεῖμος, Δεισήνωρ, δειλός, δεινός.
34. The parallel case of δήν and δηρόν has obs. 8x *Il*, 8x *Od*; negl. 5x *Il*, 2x *Od*, 1x *Herm*. Neither is of course included in the statistics for initial prevocalic digamma, sup. pp. 42ff.
35. I have nothing to add tc Hoekstra's discussion of Ἑρμέω 148 (*SES* 42, cf. Pavese *Stud* 146), a post-Homeric case of violent separation over a line-end.
36. It is discussed sup. p. 52.
37. Hoekstra, *SES* 44.
38. *SES* 42. Pavese (*Stud* 142) deems it a traditional genealogical formula, but n-mobile disproves this.
39. *HMFP* 79–82.
40. Cf. Frisk s.v., Càssola ad loc.; Humbach *ZVS* 81 (1967) 276–83; Szemerényi *JHS* 94 (1974) 144f.; Hooker *IF* 84 (1979) 115–17; van Eck ad loc.
41. p. 386.
42. Cf. West *Th* p. 79.
43. πότνια used incorrectly as a vocative is also mainly post-Homeric – apart from Z 305 / πότνι' Ἀθηναίη (for πότνα ~?): v. *Dem* 54, 492, *Hy* 30.6, Hom. *Epigr.* 7.1.
44. Zumbach 8.
45. Hoekstra *SES* 45.
46. Podbielski 86.
47. Cf. Heitsch 26.
48. Despite Leumann 75.
49. p. 28.
50. Cf. Casadio ap. *Gnomon* 45 (1973) 643.
51. pp. 387f.
52. *SES* 16.
53. Suhle, *De hymno quarto in Venerem* 18.
54. Heitsch 29.
55. Pace Hoekstra, *SES* 48n.20; cf. J. A. Davison, *Gnomon* 33 (1966) 646; M. I. Finley, *The World of Odysseus* 71, 96ff.
56. p. 30.

57. That Homer glosses this word is no reason to reject the etymology, despite Wyatt *ML* 71f.
58. Kamerbeek 388.
59. *BSL* 36 (1935) 131f.
60. *Stud* 152ff.
61. Casadio, *Gnomon* 49 (1977) 650; cf. Buck, *GD*² 118.
62. *SES* 39f.
63. pp. 607f., following Demetrius of Scepsis. P. M. Smith, 'Aineiadai as patrons of *Iliad* XX and of the Homeric *Hymn to Aphrodite*', *HSCP* 85 (1981) forthcoming, would have us disbelieve in historical Aeneadae, with insufficient reason I suspect.
64. As Hoekstra admits, *SES* 47n.14.
65. For other arguments against Hoekstra, cf. Lenz, *Aphroditehymnus* 28ff., 83.
66. AHS p. 351.
67. *De hymno quarto in Venerem* 17.
68. Pfeiffer ad Call. *Aetia* 1.3, anticipated by J. M. Edmonds, *CQ* 31 (1937) 51, Cf. also *Cat* 180.10, and *POxy* 2503.10.
69. p. 388.
70. It also occurs at 12, 71, 153, 173, 176, 273; Càssola ad loc.
71. *SES* 46, 47n.10.
72. Wyatt, *ML* 172.
73. p. 31.
74. Cf. Zumbach 15; Hoekstra, *SES* 10f., 19n.39.
75. p. 388; LSJ s.v. *ἕπω B II 4.
76. So too Podbielski, p. 87. But van Eck, pp. 5–6, agrees.
77. V. sup. p. 103.
78. p. 31.
79. *SES* 40f., after Gemoll ad loc.
80. *Homeric Grammar*² 221.
81. *Stud* 68.
82. *SES* 40f. But the owners are the ἀθάνατοι.
83. Kamerbeek, p. 393, cf. van Eck, p. 6.
84. Hoekstra, *SES* 41. On the problem of doublets see now P. M. Smith, *HSCP* 83 (1979) 29ff.
85. Hoekstra, *SES* 13.
86. Cf. my 'Equivalent formulae in the Greek Epos'.
87. Despite Lenz, *Aphroditehymnus* 87f., with a useful list of cases, and now van Eck.
88. 'L'huile d'Aphrodite', *Živa Antika* 26 (1976) 23–5.
89. Cf. Pavese *Stud* 76.
90. V. sup. p. 153.
91. Cf. sup. pp. 25, 154.
92. pp. 19–22.
93. Given these facts, Fr. Solmsen's suggestion that the description of

Hestia is influenced by *Th* 453ff. and 495ff. acquires plausibility (*Hermes* 68 (1960) 1–13). Cf. sup. p. 8; Lenz 97f.

94. *De hymno quarto in Venerem* (1878).
95. V. sup. pp. 10, 104f.
96. ap. *CJ* 50 (1955) 153–9.
97. V. sup. p. 2.
98. Cf. sup. pp. 129ff., on *PAp*; p. 268n.22.
99. For further criticism of this article cf. Lenz, *Aphroditehymnus* 51n.1.
100. Gemoll 259f.; Heitsch 38ff.; Podbielski 91f.; Richardson p. 40f.; Lenz 51n.1.
101. p. 91n.16: but Richardson (p. 248) argues that the epithet is functional in *Dem*. Van Eck (ad loc.) thinks it is borrowed from *Dem*.
102. p. 387; cf. Hoekstra, *SES* 56.
103. pp. 32f.
104. p. 91n.16.
105. Pace AHS pp. 336f.
106. But for an apparent link between *Dem* and Aeolic poetry, v. inf. p. 275n.16.
107. *Aphroditehymnus* 56.
108. Heitsch, pp. 38ff., argues that the phrase is more appropriate to a young girl than an old woman, and that *Dem* is therefore secondary. Note the imitation in Vergil, *Aen* XI 480.
109. p. 146.
110. Lenz, *Aphroditehymnus* 141–8 shows that the attempts that have been made to date *Aphr* relative to the *Cypria* are unsuccessful.
111. V. sup. p. 26.
112. Cf. sup. p. 134.
113. ad *Aphr* 14.
114. On n-mobile at the trochaic caesura cf. Hoekstra, *HMFP* 79f.; *SES* 23f.
115. ad *Erga* 519.
116. ad *Erga* 524.
117. 'Hesiod's Description of Winter', *CR* 30 (1916) 209–13. Cf. Steitz, *Werke und Tage des Hesiodos* 137, Goettling ad *Erga* 519–21, rejecting these lines. Sinclair ad 519 seems to ascribe the similarities to coincidence.
118. He thought *Aphr* 'a distinctly Ionian work'. There *is* surely a punning reference to the Boeotian month Boukatios in βουδόρα πάντα (504 – despite West ad loc.).
119. Cf. sup. p. 165.
120. Ξ 178f. is much more remote, and the parallel does not justify Neitzel's preference for D's reading διασκῆσαι at *Erga* 64 (*Homer-Rezeption bei Hesiod* 30f.): the parallel with *Aphr* defends the

vulgate here.

121. Cf. sup. pp. 25, 154.
122. O. Lendle, *Die 'Pandorasage' bei Hesiod* 21–60, is misguided in his attempts to expunge the alterations as interpolated.
123. Cf. Edwards 110; the parallel with 534 supports the explanation that this and 526 are Lesbian Aeolisms.
124. *Glotta* 44 (1966) 1–5, approved by Edwards 113.
125. I restrict myself to those accepted by West (*Th* 82ff.) and Edwards (ch. 8). The genitive plurals in -*ᾱν*, neglect of post-vocalic digamma in *κᾰλός*, *Th* 678 *περίαχε* and *Erga* 22 *ἀρώμεναι* are all open to satisfactory alternative explanations.
126. Cf. West ad loc.
127. Possibly the Description of High Summer (*Erga* 582–96) is influenced by the same source, since Hooker has argued (*The Language and Text of the Lesbian Poets* 80ff.) that 582ff. is not necessarily imitated by Alcaeus 347 L–P, but that both poets may be using a lost common source in Aeolic traditional poetry. I am not at all convinced, however.
128. Alternatively, 'Hesiod' may be a title, just as Stesichorus' original name is said by the *Suda* (s.v. *Στησίχορος*) to have been Tisias. This still does not exclude the possibility that Hesiod acquired his poetic skill from his father.
129. Cf. sup. p. 79.
130. For a suggestion of similar borrowing from Semonides by Hesiod cf. sup. pp. 97f.: on detecting *imitatio* cf. Appendix C.
131. This restoration fits the traces better than any other, but is said to exceed the space (Page, *Sappho and Alcaeus* 64f.).
132. Frisk, s.v., Pokorny, *Indogermanisches Wörterbuch* 534; cf. the Thracian tribes *Σάτραι*, *Σατροκένται* (A&S ad loc.). R. Schmitt (*Glotta* 44 (1966) 148ff.) shows that Phrygian, as a centum-language, is impossible as a direct source.
133. Cf. sup. pp. 153f.
134. Cf. West *Th* p. 82.
135. Cf. Edwards 107; sup. p. 154.
136. Cf. sup. p. 163.
137. p. 602; cf. A&S ad loc.
138. Cf. *Glotta* 56 (1978) 192ff.
139. *SLH*^{2} 146.
140. Cf. sup. p. 49.
141. Cf. sup. p. 147 on *Herm* 208.
142. Hoekstra (*SES* 16) remarks that *πεσέεσθαι* is never contracted in Homer, but cf. *μαχεῖται* Υ 26. These futures are probably extended by analogy from those of stems in liquids and nasals (note *καλέεσθαι* in the line before *Aphr* 127), and are not to be confused with the West Greek futures in -*σέω*, which are absent

from Homer (ἐσσεῖται B 393 etc. are surely cases of metrical lengthening to avoid a cretic, *pace* West ad *Erga* 503).

143. *Stud* 93f.
144. p. 388.
145. V. Allen V ix–xi.
146. *Sprachliche Untersuchungen* 53f.
147. Cf. Richardson pp. 53f.
148. -αις also at *Hy* 33.16, *Il Persis* 3.1, Hom. *Epigr* 4.15 (bis), 6.4, Hes. frr. 305.3, 343.16; in none of these is -ηις found. Cf. Hes. fr. 302.5 (-ηις).
149. V. sup. p. 157.
150. Cf. Frisk s.v.
151. Cf. sup. p. 144 on *Herm* 76.
152. Cf. sup. pp. 127, 132, 148.
153. Cf. sup. pp. 151–2.
154. By the binomial distribution, the odds are 0.0038, or 3.8%.
155. For false archaism in 'unobvious' features cf. sup. pp. 76f. and 125.
156. For -ου, z = 1.97 for the Iliadic level of $\pi_0 = 0.37$, which is significant at the 2.5% level of probability: for -οιο, z = 1.65 for the Iliadic level of $\pi_0 = 0.519$, significant at the 5% level of probability. The same pairing of phenomena in *Erga* looks less like chance in these circumstances (cf. sup. p. 79).
157. *Glotta* 5 (1914) 8–47.
158. *YCS* 8 (1942) 105–78.
159. V. sup. pp. 87ff. with Figure 3.
160. Cf. too *Hy* 6 to Aphrodite (21 lines): Zeus' name does not appear, but in six cases of digamma there is only one neglect, and there are six 'long' dative plurals and no others: moreover the o-stem genitive singulars are advanced – 2x -οιο, 4x -ου, doubtful never. N-mobile +C occurs once.
161. V. sup. pp. 173f.
162. V. inf. p. 177; but the same might be said of the *Iliad.*
163. The references to Aphrodite as queen of Cyprus in *Aphr* 293, *Hy* 6.2f., *Hy* 10, and her visit to Cyprus (*Aphr* 58ff.), do not of course prove Cypriot authorship, cf. θ 362f.! Charon of Lampsacus (ap. Paus. X 38.11) considered the title τὰ Ναυπάκτια to derive from the poet's nationality and not the place of performance, although most Greeks ascribed it to a Milesian. The same might be true of τὰ Κύπρια (or Κυπριακά). But the argument Pausanias uses to support this case is *a priori*, and indicates that he is as much in the dark as we. The diction of the *Ilias Parva* (34 lines) is similar to the *Cypria* in most respects where it can be checked, but the statistics are unreliable as the sample is so small, and the ascription to Lesches of Lesbos was not uncontested in antiquity any-

way (cf. Allen, *Origins and Transmission* 61ff.).

164. Cf. p. 244n.29.

165. V. *Glotta* 57 (1979) 24–9.

166. art. cit.

167. art. cit.

168. Cf. sup. p. 90.

169. Cf. Huxley, *The Early Ionians* 34: Ionian influence affects the pottery at Smyrna from c. 800 BC (Coldstream *Geometric Greece* 262), and the city was Ionic by 688 (Paus. V 8.7; J. M. Cook ap. *BSA* 53–4 (1958–9) 11ff.).

170. V. E. Risch, 'Die Gliederung der griechischen Dialekte in neuer Sicht' *Mus Helv* 12 (1955) 61–76; W. Porzig, 'Sprachgeographische Untersuchungen zu den altgriechischen Dialekten', *IF* 61 (1954) 147–69. A. Lopez Eire (Proc. 5th Spanish Congress of Classical Studies, 457–79) argues for a mixed dialect.

171. This vital point is sometimes missed: it was however crucial to Milman Parry, who puts it as follows: 'The conclusions of those who have demonstrated that the variety of forms observed in epic language could be explained by necessities of versification have already given rise to the objection that this would deprive the poet of all power of choice. A complicating factor is that words and forms borrowed from alien dialects are among the principal means of ennobling the style of Greek poetry. Thus E. Drerup protests that to make the exigency of verse alone responsible for the non-Ionic elements in Homeric language is to exclude from the problem "that subjective element which in all poetry, without exception, determines the formation of language and verse: I mean, the art of the poet . . ." He goes on to add that if the poet uses such forms as τάων, πάντεσσι, ἄμμες, it is not because he had to: he could perfectly well have used the Ionic forms of these words, if in a different part of the line . . . But here Drerup is wrong and K. Witte is right: the former's reasoning is based on a fundamental error: one cannot speak of the poet's freedom to choose his words and forms, if the desire to make this choice does not exist. Homer had inherited from his predecessors a language whose several elements were used solely in accordance with the needs of composition in hexameters. If it had been otherwise, if this or that archaic or Aeolic word or form had survived chiefly because it was able to give the style the nobility of a λέξις ξενική, then the system of epic language would have included a multitude of metrically equivalent elements. But this is not the case . . . Homer's use of this or that archaic or dialectal form is a matter of habit and convenience, not of poetic sentiment' (*L'Épithète traditionnelle* 26f., = *MHV* 21f.).

172. As early as Pindar at least (fr. 279 Bowra: Chios and Smyrna).

173. V. sup. pp. 35ff.
174. *SES* 39ff., 46, 47n.10.
175. p. 81.

9. *Other Hymns*

1. pp. 52–6.
2. p. 55; cf. sup. p. 170.
3. V. sup. p. 66.
4. frr. 246–62 M–W, especially 257, with the Attic or Boeotian form Ὕηττος. Its diction reveals little, but 1/4 neglects of digamma, 3/6 o-stem genitives in -οιο, and 6/8 long dative plurals suggest false archaism in these criteria, rather as in the Boeotian *PAp*.
5. pp. 33f.
6. Cf. Richardson ad locc.
7. If π_0 of getting the contracted form = 0.5, z = 2.5, so the odds on obtaining only 3/16 (as in *Dem*) are very low indeed, about 1 in 180.
8. ad *Aspis* 341.
9. *ML* 116.
10. Cf. Richardson pp. 5–11. Burkert (review of Richardson, *Gnomon* 49 (1977) 440–6) has argued for a sixth-century date, detecting a *terminus post quem* in the reference to the temple (270ff.), which he identifies with the 'Solonian' building: but the Mycenaean edifice may have continued in use until then (Coldstream, *Geometric Greece* 332).
11. V. sup. pp. 163ff.
12. The opening recalls *Aphr* (*Hy* 30.3, cf. *Aphr* 5 – cf. sup. p. 28): note πότνια vocative (sup. p. 269n.43): 7f., cf. *Dem* 486f.; 9, cf. *Dem* 450; 16, cf. *Dem* 1 (modified with synizesis in θε͜άν); 18f., cf. *Dem* 494f. A&S think *Hy* 30 the borrower, but the modification in *Dem* (1, θε͜άν where *Hy* 30 has θεά in the same phrase) could be used to argue the reverse; there are certainly no grounds for accepting the *a priori* view that short Hymns are necessarily prior to the long ones in our collection. But I think both of these theories are wrong. We have seen that *Dem* borrowed from *Aphr*: *Hy* 30 appears to do the same, and is similar in other respects to *Dem*: surely this indicates that the two have a similar genesis, if not on the lips of the same poet? Unfortunately *Hy* 30 holds no clues as to its origin. *Hy* 27 is a similar case (cf. sup. p. 111 on parallels with *DAp* and *PAp*).
13. *SES* 39–46.
14. Cf. sup. pp. 76f., 124f.
15. But note Theognis' usage (sup. p. 67).
16. He knew at least *Aphr*; in addition, the phrase φαινόλις Ἠώς

(51) shared with Sappho 104a1 L–P (modified by separation to φαίνολις ἐσκέδασ' Αὔως; cf. Moschus 4.121) indicates direct or indirect knowledge of other Aeolic poetry besides. *Aphr* has πότνια ἠώς equivalent to this (223, 230, cf. Sappho 157 L–P), presumably by analogy with πότνια Ἥρη etc.; there are no other equivalents in the epos. I have argued that *Aphr* and other Aeolic poetry was known to Hesiod, and 51 may be no more than a borrowing from a lost work of his or a follower's.

17. $z = 2.23$ if π_0 is set at the Odyssean level of 0.852, significant at the 2.5% level.
18. V. sup. p. 137.
19. T. B. L. Webster (ap. *Le Monde grec: Hommages à Claire Préaux* 91) argued that *Hy* 7 was written c. 530, relating it to the famous cup by Exekias depicting Dionysus ship-borne. This is hardly cogent proof. (I owe this reference to the kindness of Professor M. C. Stokes.) See A&S 227ff.
20. V. Càssola pp. 361f.
21. $z = 1.94$ for $\pi_0 = 0.379$, almost significant at the 2.5% level.
22. V. sup. p. 135.
23. V. sup. p. 136.
24. V. sup. pp. 117, 145.
25. Cf. Càssola p. 364.
26. V. sup. p. 3.
27. There seems to be no valid reason to date this, or any of the poems in the corpus, except *Hy* 8 to Ares, much later, however short they are: cf. A&S p. 230; Càssola p. 364; Förstel 88 with nn. Bossi's dating of *Hy* 19 to the fifth or fourth century (*Museum Criticum* 13–4 (1978–9) 7–22) became known to me too late to be taken into account, but is not persuasive.
28. Cf. West *Th* p. 98.
29. As this occurs in Attic poetry, it has inevitably been labelled Attic: but see Càssola ad loc., and cf. sup. p. 159 on ἑ plural. Buck (*GD*[2] 98) thinks it Doric; it also occurs in Herodotus, but not in Attic prose (LSJ s.v. σφεῖς).

10. Conclusions

1. See now the excellent account of writing and oral tradition in Beaton, *Folk Poetry of Modern Greece* 179ff. I would not wish to exclude absolutely the possibility that these poets themselves learnt to write and, as it were, dictated their texts to themselves; I am however opposed completely to the notion that writing has had any influence on the style or content of their poems.
2. See Allen, *Origins and Transmission* 279ff., and Appendix A.

3. In the light of the nature of the earliest inscriptions, the suggestion that the alphabet developed specifically or largely in order to record hexameter poetry is gaining in plausibility (cf. Snodgrass, *Archaic Greece* 82f.). Note the important arguments of Pucci (*Hesiod and the Language of Poetry* 140f.) that Hesiod in the *Erga* presupposes that the *Theogony* is a fixed text.
4. V. Richardson 32f., 339–43.
5. V. Appendix B.
6. Finding a suitable tradition is difficult and perhaps impossible, not because of insufficient documentation, but because of the uniquely complex metre of the epos. The hexameter's complexity compared with the simplicity of the stichic metres of other traditions seems to have dictated a higher level of formula rigidity (and also of economy) than is found elsewhere. It was this formular rigidity which brought about a considerably greater retention of linguistic archaisms than in other oral poetries of which I have knowledge. This recognition of formular rigidity does not of course contradict the work of recent years on how the tradition developed and can be seen to develop; nor does it oblige one to embrace any kind of artistic determinism – for a talented singer, the medium offered great creative potential, as is evident from the poems which are extant. But without it, we cannot resolve the paradox that the highly sophisticated Homeric tradition seems stylistically *more oral* than the rest – more formular, more thrifty, and more archaic, at least in diction. This is the work of the hexameter; and until a tradition that possesses not only extensive poems covering a considerable period of time, but also a metre as demanding as the hexameter, can be found, the orality of the Homeric tradition will never be approached, though the scop or guslar stand before us and sing. Other epics, be they South Slavic or Saxon, are less formulaic, less thrifty, and less retentive of archaism, and it is the hexameter that makes the difference.
7. *FGH* I 277, cf. F. Jacoby, *Das Marmor Parium* 152f.
8. Cf. Rzach ap. P–W VIII s.v. 'Hesiodos', 1173ff.; Jacoby, comm. on *FGH* 328F210.
9. Cf. Aulus Gellius *NA* III 11.
10. IX 30.3. His words are still worth quoting: *περὶ δὲ Ἡσιόδου τε ἡλικίας καὶ Ὁμήρου πολυπραγμονήσαντι ἐς τὸ ἀκριβέστατον οὔ μοι γράφειν ἡδὺ ἦν, ἐπισταμένωι τὸ φιλαίτιον ἄλλων τε καὶ οὐχ ἥκιστα ὅσοι κατ' ἐμὲ ἐπὶ ποιήσει τῶν ἐπῶν καθεστήκεσαν*. Cf. the Tzetzean *Life of Hesiod* (Allen V p. 223, 27–32), which rejects the *Certamen* as a later invention *τῶν νεωτέρων* (an Aristarchan turn), and thinks Homer anterior; the phrasing, curiously like Pausanias', may derive ultimately from Aristarchus via Proclus

(Ὅμηρος γὰρ ὁ χρυσοῦς, ὡς ἐγῷμαι, μᾶλλον δ' ἀκριβεστάτως ἐπίσταμαι, πολὺ . . . παλαιότερος Ἡσιόδου ὑπῆρχε). For Aristarchus and Aristonicus designated as the ἀκριβέστεροι, cf. schol. *τ* 203, *χ* 31 with Eustathius 1861.52.

11. sup. pp. 112ff.; Walcot, *Greek Peasants* 1ff., with whom I very much agree.
12. Cf. West *Th* p. 47n.3.
13. Despite West, loc. cit. His argument that the order Orpheus, Musaeus, Hesiod and Homer, in which the poets are named in early writers, proves Hesiod's priority is not cogent. As he says, Orpheus and Musaeus owed their alleged priority, not to the genuine antiquity of their poems, so much as to the propaganda of their devotees (surely too to the obviously mythical character of Orpheus); but we know of a guild devoted to Hesiod's interests, and he certainly had followers: and there were others who clashed with the Homeridae. The judgement of Panedes in Hesiod's favour (*Certamen* 207ff.) derived from early sources of this kind.
14. See West *Erga* p. 65ff., and on *Th* 223, 338 and 947–55; also Severyns, *Le Cycle épique dans l'école d'Aristarque* passim, whom he does not cite.
15. As alleged by Sellschopp, *Stilistische Untersuchungen zu Hesiod.* For a refutation see Edwards, ch. 10, and see now H. Neitzel, *Homer-Rezeption bei Hesiod* (1975), arguing strongly that Hesiod imitated Homer.
16. V. inf. pp. 225–8: this appendix treats all the major cases proposed in this study.
17. Both this poem (sup. pp. 2, 239n.7) and the *Aspis*, both acquainted with Homer, are sources for interpolations into the Homeric epics (on *Aspis* 156–60 and Σ 535–40 see Lynn-George, *Hermes* 106 (1978) 396ff.). Have these poets had some hand in the transmission?
18. For a useful survey see Edwards 203–6 with notes. The picture does not seem to have altered since he wrote. See Appendix E.
19. V. Appendix F.
20. V. Appendix A.

Appendix C. The language of Th *901–1022 and* Cat

1. See my 'ΑΘΑΝΑΤΟΣ ΚΑΙ ΑΓΗΡΩΣ: the genealogy of a formula', *Mnemosyne* forthcoming.
2. Buck, *GD*^{2} 20.
3. Cf. Paus. VIII 24.1, P–W *RE* XXII^1 335.
4. PY An 519.7, al. I find this better than / *Phoiteus* / or / *Ponteus* /, which are proposed in Ventris and Chadwick *Docs*^{2} s.v.
5. Buck, *GD*^{2} 37f.

6. Cf. West *Th* p. 81.
7. Buck, *GD*² 98f.; Schwyzer, *GG* I 604ff.
8. Bechtel, *GD* I 350; Thumb–Kieckers 87.
9. Cf. sup. p. 265n.4.
10. Ap. Galen, *de plac Hipp et Plat* I 266.7 Müller: two other lines quoted there (with one case of Διός) are surely from *Cat* also (Allen V p. 149).
11. Cf. West ad loc.; Pavese (*Stud* 90) is overbold to call it an Aeolism.
12. *Th* p. 80.
13. Buck, *GD*² 43f.; cf. Myc. / *Erkhomenos, Erkhomenātāo* /.
14. Cf. Björk, *Das Alpha Impurum* 50, 352; and sup. p. 247n.32 on *POxy* 2510.
15. p. 106; cf. *Th* 326, and West *Th* p. 88.
16. Bechtel, *GD* I 284; Buck, *GD*² 115f.
17. Chantraine, *GH* I 340f.; cf. *Erga* 764.
18. s.v.
19. *Glotta* 41 (1963) 282–5.
20. On these, v. J. Chadwick, *Trans. Phil. Soc.* 1969, 95f.
21. Edwards 102f.
22. So Schwartz, *Pseudo-Hesiodea* 487ff. His reasoning is highly speculative.

Appendix H. γαῖα / γῆ, ξύν / σύν, κεῖνος / ἐκεῖνος

1. The same is true of βασιλῆα > βασιλέᾱ, where again intervocalic digamma is involved and its recent loss explains the absence of contraction: Lejeune, op. cit., 259.
2. '*Études de linguistique homérique 2: les formes* ΞΥΝ *et* ΣΥΝ'.
3. The frequency at trochaic caesura may be due to the alternation of P_2 and T_2 formulae.
4. Bechtel, *GD* III 168–9; Smyth, *Ionic*, 207–8.
5. Smyth, op. cit., 448–9.
6. Cf. Chantraine, *GH*² I 276–7.
7. Cf. Chantraine, *Dict. ét.* s.v.; Frisk, s.v.
8. Cf. Edwards 102f.

BIBLIOGRAPHY

This bibliography is not intended to be exhaustive. It does include all the works referred to in the text, and also some others in two categories: the more significant works on epic diction which have appeared since Edwards' book; and recent items, and some earlier ones of importance, concerning the *Hymns*. Works cited in the text by author's name only are prefixed with an asterisk; abbreviations for titles are given after the entry. See also Addenda at end.

Abramowicz, S. *Etudes sur les Hymnes homériques*. Wilno 1937.

Agostino, B. D'. 'Osservazioni a proposito della guerra lelantina', *Dialoghi di Archeologia* 1 (1967) 20–37.

Alexanderson, B. 'Homeric formulae for ships', *Eranos* 68 (1970) 1–46.

Allen, T. W. *Homeri Opera, Tomus V, Hymnos Cyclum Fragmenta Margiten Batrachomyomachiam Vitas continens*, Oxford 1912. (Allen, V)

id., *Tomi III–IV, Odysseae libros continentes*, 2nd edn. Oxford 1917–19.

with D. B. Monro. id., *Tomi I–II, Iliadis libros continentes*, 3rd edn. Oxford 1920.

with E. E. Sikes. *The Homeric Hymns*. London and New York 1904. (A&S)

with W. R. Halliday and E. E. Sikes. *The Homeric Hymns*, 2nd revised edn. Oxford 1936. (AHS)

Homer: the Origins and the Transmission. Oxford 1924.

Altheim, F. 'Die Entstehungsgeschichte des homerischen Apollonhymnus', *Hermes* 59 (1924) 430–50.

Andrewes, A. *The Greek Tyrants*. London 1956.

Appel, W. 'Sur l'hymne homérique à Dionysos', *Meander* 23 (1978) 541–50.

Athanassakis, A. 'Hiatus, word-end and correption in Hesiod', *Hermes* 98 (1970) 129–45.

'An enquiry into the etymology and meaning of ἴφθιμος in early epic', *Glotta* 49 (1971) 1–21.

Review of Càssola, *AJP* 59 (1976) 297–9.

'Homeric KANKANOS', *TAPA* 106 (1976) 1–9.

Austin, N. 'The function of digressions in the *Iliad*', *GRBS* 7 (1966) 295–312.

Barnes, H. R. 'Enjambement and oral composition', *TAPA* 109 (1979) 1–10.

Beaton, R. *Folk Poetry of Modern Greece*. Cambridge 1980.
Bechtel, F. *Die Vocalcontraction bei Homer*. Halle 1908.
Die griechischen Dialekte. Berlin 1921–4. (Bechtel, *GD*)
Beekes, R. S. P. 'The structure of the Greek hexameter', *Glotta* 50 (1972) 1–10.
Bethe, E. *Homer: Dichtung und Sage. I Ilias, II, Odysee; Kyklos; Zeitbestimmung, III Die Sage vom troischen Kriege*, Leipzig 1914–27.
Bickerman, E. Review of Càssola, *Athenaeum* 54 (1976) 518–22.
Bingen, J. (ed.) *Le Monde grec; Hommages à Claire Préaux*. Brussels 1975.
Björk, D. J. *Das Alpha Impurum und die tragische Kunstsprache*. Uppsala 1950.
Blumenthal, A. von, 'Prosodisches bei Hesiod und Tyrtaios', *Hermes* 77 (1942) 193–4.
Boedeker, D. D. 'Aphrodite's entry into Greek Epic', *Mnemosyne* Suppl. 32. Leiden 1974.
Boettcher, R. *De Hymno in Mercurium Homerico*. Halle 1906.
Boisacq, E. *Dictionnaire étymologique de la langue grecque*, 3rd edn. Paris 1938.
Bolling, G. M. 'The dative plural of the o- and a-stems in Homer', *Language* 21 (1945) 261–4.
Bona, G. 'Inni omerici e poesia greca arcaica', *RFIC* 106 (1978) 224–48.
Bowra, C. M. *Heroic Poetry*. London 1952.
'Two lines of Eumelus', *CQ* N.S. 13 (1963) 145–53.
Homer. London 1972.
Bradeen, D. W. 'The Lelantine War and Pheidon of Argos', *TAPA* 68 (1947) 223–41.
Breitenstein, T. 'Hésiode et Archiloque', *Odense University Classical Studies* I. Odense 1971.
Brown, N. O. *Hermes the Thief*. Wisconsin 1947.
Buck, C. D. *The Greek Dialects*, 2nd edn. Chicago 1955. (Buck, GD^2)
Buck, R. G. *History of Boeotia*. University of Alberta 1979.
Bulmer, M. G. *Principles of Statistics*, 2nd edn. Edinburgh and London 1967.
Burkert, W. Review of Richardson, *Gnomon* 49 (1977) 440–6.
'Kynaithos, Polycrates and the Homeric Hymn to Apollo', ap. *Arktouros: Hellenic Studies presented to Bernard M. W. Knox*, pp. 53–62. Berlin 1979.
Burn, A. R. *The Lyric Age of Greece*. London 1960. (Burn, *LAG*)
Campbell, M. 'BΩΣΕΣΘΕ again', *CQ* N.S. 27 (1977) 467.
Carey, C. 'Homeric Hymn to Apollo, 171', *CQ* N.S. 30 (1980) 288–90.
Casadio, V. Review of Hoekstra, *SES*, *Gnomon* 45 (1973) 641–5.
Review of Pavese *Trad*, *Gnomon* 49 (1977) 446–54.

Review of Pavese *Stud*, *Gnomon* 49 (1977) 645–52.
*Càssola, F. *Inni omerici*. Milan 1975.
Chadwick, J. 'The Group *sw* in Mycenaean', *Minos* 9 (1968) 62–5.
'Greek and Pre-Greek', *Trans Phil Soc* 1969, 80–98.
Chambers, M. 'Androtion F6: τότε πρῶτον', *JHS* 99 (1979) 151f.
Chantraine, P. 'Grec ἐκγεγάονται (Hymne homérique à Aphrodite 197)' *BSL* 107 (1935) 131–2.
Morphologie historique du grec. Paris 1945.
Grammaire homérique: Tome I: Phonétique et morphologie, 2nd edn. Paris 1973; id. *Tome II: Syntaxe*. Paris 1963. (Chantraine, *GH*).
Dictionnaire étymologique de la langue grecque. Paris 1968–81.
Charalampos, Ph. ''Ο Ὁμηρικὸς ὕμνος εἰς Ἀπόλλωνα', *Athena* 56 (1952) 286–309.
Christensen, H. *De Hymno in Apollinem Homerico*. Kiel 1876.
Clayman, D. L., and van Northwick, T. 'Enjambement in Greek hexameter poetry,' *TAPA* 107 (1977) 85–92.
Coldstream, J. N. *Geometric Greece*. London 1977.
Cook, R. M. 'The date of the Hesiodic *Shield*', *CQ* 31 (1937) 204–14.
Crespo, E. 'La cronología relativa de la metátesis de cantidad en jónico-atico', *Cuadernos de Filología Clásica* 12 (1977) 185ff.
Elementos antiguos y modernos en la prosodia homérica, *Minos* Suppl. 7, Salamanca 1977.
Danielewicz, G. 'Hymni homerici minores quanam arte conscripti sint', *Symbolae Philologorum Posnaniensium* 1 (1973) 7–21.
Davis, A. Morpurgo, '"Doric" features in the language of Hesiod', *Glotta* 42 (1964) 138–65.
and Meid, W. (edd.) *Studies in Greek, Italic and Indo-European Linguistics presented to L. R. Palmer*. Innsbruck 1976.
Davison, J. A. 'Quotations and allusions in early Greek Literature', *Eranos* 53 (1955) 125–40.
Review of Heitsch *Aphroditehymnos*, *Gnomon* 33 (1966) 645ff.
From Archilochus to Pindar. London and New York 1968.
Defradas, J. *Les Thèmes de la propagande delphique*. Paris 1954.
Deubner, L. *Der homerische Apollonhymnus*. *SBAW* 1938 248–77.
Devantier, F. *Die Spuren des anlautenden digamma bei Hesiod*. I, Jever 1878; II–III, Eutin 1894–7.
Diels, H. and Kranz, W. *Die Fragmente der Vorsokratiker*, 6th edn. Berlin–Grunewald 1951–2. (D–K)
Dihle, A. *Homer-Probleme*. Opladen 1970.
Dittmar, F. *Prolegomenon ad Hymnum in Cererem specimen*. Halle 1882.
Dobson, M. 'Herodotus I 47.1 and the *Hymn to Hermes*', *AJP* 100 (1979) 349–59.

Donlan, W. 'Archilochus, Strabo and the Lelantine War', *TAPA* 101 (1970) 131–42.

Dornseiff, F. *Die archaische Mythenerzählung. Folgerungen aus den homerischen Apollonhymnus*. Berlin 1933.

'Zum homerischen Hermeshymnus', *RhM* 87 (1938) 80–4.

Drerup, E. 'Der homerische Apollonhymnus', *Forschungen und Fortschritte* 12 (1936) 31–3.

'Der homerische Apollonhymnus. Eine methodologische Studie', *Mnemosyne* III 5 (1937) 81–134.

Drerup, H. *Griechische Baukunst in Geometrischer Zeit* (*Archaeologia Homerica* II, O). Göttingen 1969.

Drews, R. 'The earliest Greek settlements in the Black Sea', *JHS* 96 (1976) 18–31.

Drexler, H. 'Nachträge zur Kyrenesage', *Hermes* 66 (1931) 455–64.

Ducat, R. 'Le Ptoion et l'histoire de la Béotie a l'époque archaïque. À propos d'un livre récent', *REG* 77 (1964) 283–90.

'La Confédération béotienne et l'expansion thebaine à l'époque archaïque', *BCH* 77 (1973) 59–73.

Dunbar, H. *A Complete Concordance to the Odyssey of Homer.* Oxford 1880. Revised B. Marzullo, Hildesheim 1960.

Durante, M. *Sulla Preistoria della Tradizione poetica greca* I, II (Incunabula Graeca 50, 64). Rome 1971–.

Ebeling, H. *Lexicon Homericum*. Leipzig 1880–5.

Eberhard, E. *Die Sprache der ersten homerischen Hymnen verglichen mit derjenigen der Ilias und Odyssee*. Progr. Husum 1874.

Metrische Beobachtungen zu den homerischen Hymnen. Magdeburg 1886.

Eck, J. van. *The Homeric Hymn to Aphrodite. Introduction, Commentary and Appendices*. Diss. Utrecht 1978.

Review of Lenz, *Mnemosyne* 33 (1980) 180–2.

Edmonds, J. M. 'Some notes on the Homeric Hymns', *CQ* 31 (1937) 49–52.

*Edwards, G. P. *The Language of Hesiod in its Traditional Context*. Oxford 1971.

Edwards, M. W. 'Some features of Homeric craftsmanship', *TAPA* 97 (1966) 115–79.

'Homeric speech introductions', *HSCP* 74 (1970) 1–36.

Eitrem, S. 'Der homerische Hymnus an Hermes', *Philologus* LXV (1906) 248–82.

Else, G. F. *Aristotle's Poetics: the Argument*, Harvard 1957.

Evelyn-White, H. G. *Hesiod, the Homeric Hymns and Homerica* (Loeb Classical Library). London 1914.

'Hesiod's Description of Winter', *CR* 30 (1916) 209–13.

Fernández Delgado, J. A. 'Poesía oral gnomica en los Trabajos y los Días; una muestra de su dicción formular', *Emerita* 46 (1978) 141–71.

Review of Peabody, ibid. 466–8.

Fick, A. 'Die ursprüngliche Sprache der homerischen Hymnen', *Beiträge zur Kunde der indogermanischen Sprachen* 9 (1885) 195–246.

Fietkau, H. *De carminum hesiodeorum atque hymnorum quattuor magnorum vocabulis non homericis*. Königsberg 1866.

Finley, M. I. *The World of Odysseus*. London 1956.

Finnegan, R. *Oral Poetry*. Cambridge 1977.

Förstel, K. 'Sprachliche Kriterien für eine innerhomerische Chronologie?', *Glotta* 48 (1970) 163–80.

* *Untersuchungen zum homerischen Apollonhymnos*. Bochum 1979.

Foundation Hardt. *Hésiode et son influence*. Entretiens sur l'antiquité classique, VII, Geneva 1962.

Fontenrose, J. Review of N. O. Brown, *Hermes the Thief*, *Classical Philology* 44 (1949) 203ff.

Forderer, M. Review of Zumbach, *Gnomon* 30 (1958) 94–100.

Anfang und Ende der abendländischen Lyrik. Amsterdam 1971.

Forrest, W. G. 'Colonisation and the rise of Delphi', *Historia* 6 (1957) 160–75.

Review of Guillon, *JHS* 86 (1966) 173.

Forssmann, B. 'περ' ἰγνύσι *h. Merc.* 152', *ZVS* 69 (1964) 28–31.

Fraenkel, H. *Wege und Formen frühgriechischen Denkens*, 2nd edn. Munich 1960.

Francke, K. *De hymni in Cererem homerici compositione dictione aetate*. Progr. Gelehrtenschule, Kiel 1881.

Freed, G. and Bentman, H. 'The Homeric Hymn to Aphrodite', *CJ* 50 (1955) 153–9.

*Friedlander, P. (with H. B. Hoffleit). *Epigrammata*. Berkeley 1948.

*Frisk, H. *Griechisches etymologisches Wörterbuch*. Heidelberg 1960–70.

Frolíková, A. 'Some remarks on the problem of the division of the Homeric Hymn to Apollo', *Acta Universitatis Carolinae Philologica et Historica* I 99–109. Prague 1963.

Gaisser, J. H. 'Noun–epithet combinations in the Homeric Hymn to Demeter', *TAPA* 104 (1974) 113–27.

Garbrah, K. A. 'A linguistic analysis of selected portions of the Homeric *Odyssey*', *Glotta* 47 (1969) 144–69.

García Ramón, J. L. *Les origines postmycéniennes du groupe éolien*. *Minos* Suppl. 6, Salamanca 1975.

'En torno a los elementos dialectales en Hesíodo. I el elemento occidental', *Cuadernos de Filología Clásica* 11 (1976) 523–43.

Gehring, A. *Index Homericus*. Leipzig 1895.

*Gemoll, A. *Die homerischen Hymnen*. Leipzig 1886.

Giangrande, G. 'Der stilistische Gebrauch der Dorismen im Epos', *Hermes* 98 (1970) 257–77.

Review of G. P. Edwards, *JHS* 92 (1972) 188–92.

Giovannini, A. *Étude historique sur les origines du Catalogue des Vaisseaux*. Bern 1969.

Glavičić, B. 'La struttura del verso e della proposizione in Esiodo' (Serbo-Croat, with a résumé in Italian), *ŽA* 21 (1971) 65–102.

Görgemanns, H. 'Rhetorik und Poetik im homerischen Hermeshymnus', *Studien zum antiken Epos* 113–28, Beitr. zur klass. Philol. 72, Meisenheim am Glan 1976.

Göttling, C. *Hesiodi Carmina*. Leipzig 1831. 3rd edn revised by J. Flach, 1878.

Gräfe, G. 'Der homerische Hymnus auf Hermes', *Gymnasium* 70 (1963) 515–26 (written in 1953).

Graf, F. *Eleusis und die orphische Dichtung Athens in vorhellenistischer Zeit*. Berlin 1974.

Greenhalgh, P. A. L. *Early Greek Warfare*. Cambridge 1973.

*Groningen, B. A. van. *La Composition littéraire archaïque grecque*. Amsterdam 1958.

Guillon, P. *Le Bouclier d'Héraclès et l'histoire de la Grèce centrale dans la période de la première guerre sacrée*. Aix en Provence 1963.

Hainsworth, J. B. 'The Homeric formula and the problem of the transmission', *BICS* 9 (1962) 57ff.

'Structure and content in epic formulae: the question of the unique expression', *CQ* N.S. 19 (1964) 155–64.

'A note on elision in Homer', *BICS* 14 (1967) 17–21.

The Flexibility of the Homeric Formula. Oxford 1968.

Review of Pavese *Trad*, *CR* 26 (1976) 52–3.

Review of Richardson, *CR* 27 (1977) 3–4.

*Hamm, E.-M. *Grammatik zu Sappho und Alkaios*, 2nd edn. Berlin 1957.

Hansen, P. A. *A list of Greek Verse Inscriptions down to 400 B.C.* Copenhagen 1975.

*Hartel, W. von. *Homerische Studien* I, *SbOAW* 68 (1864); II, ibid. 76 (1872); III, ibid. 78 (1874).

Hayslett, H. T. *Statistics Made Simple*. London 1968.

*Heitsch, E. *Aphroditehymnos, Aeneas und Homer: sprachliche Untersuchungen zum Homerproblem. Hypomnemata*, Heft 15. Göttingen 1965.

Epische Kunstsprache und homerische Chronologie. Heidelberg 1969.

'Der delische Apollonhymnus und unsere Ilias', ap. *Kyklos: Festschrift R. Keydell*, Berlin 1977, pp. 20–37.

Hermann, G. and Creuzer, F. *Briefe über Homer und Hesiodus vorzüglich über die Theogonie*. Heidelberg 1818.

Herter, H. 'Hermes, Ursprung und Wesen eines griechischen Gottes', *RhM* 119 (1976) 193–241.

Herzog, R. *Die Umschrift der älteren griechischen Literatur in das ionische Alphabet*. Leipzig 1912.

Heubeck, A. 'Thukydides III 104', *WSt* 79 (1966) 148–57.

Die homerische Frage. Darmstadt 1974.

Hiersche, R. 'Zu Sappho 2, 9D: κὰμ μὲν γλῶσσα ἔᾱγε "die Zunge ist gebrochen"', *Glotta* 44 (1966) 1–5.

Grundzüge der griechischen Sprachgeschichte. Wiesbaden 1970.

Die Sprache Homers im Lichte neuerer Forschungen. Innsbruck 1972.

Hilberg, I. *Das Prinzip der Silbenwägung*. Vienna 1879.

Hoekstra, A. 'Une formule para-homérique', *Mnemosyne* 7 (1954) 297–9.

'Hésiode et la tradition orale', *Mnemosyne* 10 (1957) 193–225.

Homeric Modifications of Formulaic Prototypes. Amsterdam 1965. (Hoekstra, *HMFP*)

The Sub-Epic Stage of the Formulaic Tradition. Amsterdam 1969. (Hoekstra, *SES*)

Hofinger, M. *Lexicon to Hesiod, with inverse index*. Leiden 1973–8.

Hooker, J. T. *The Language and Text of the Lesbian Poets*. Innsbruck 1977.

Hoz, J. De. 'Poesía oral independiente de Homero en Hesíodo y los himnos homéricos', *Emerita* 32 (1964) 283–98.

*Huibregste, P. K., 'De homerische Apollohymnus'. Diss. Groningen 1940.

Humbach, H. 'διιπετής und διοπετής', *ZVS* 81 (1967) 276–83.

*Humbert, J. *Homère, Hymnes*. Éd. Budé, Paris 1936.

Hurst, A. 'L'huile d'Aphrodite', *ŽA* 26 (1976) 23–5.

Huxley, G. L. *The Early Ionians*. London 1966.

Greek Epic Poetry. London 1969. (Huxley, *GEP*)

Ingalls, W. B. 'The structure of the Homeric hexameter. A review', *Phoenix* 24 (1970) 1–12.

*Isler, F. 'Quaestiones metricae'. Diss. Greifswald, 1908.

Jacoby, F. *Die Fragmente der griechischen Historiker*. I–II, Berlin 1923–30; III, Leyden 1940–58. (Jacoby, *FGH*)

Der homerische Apollonhymnus. Sitzungsber. Preuss. Ak. Wiss. 15 (1933) 682–751.

Kleine Schriften I. Berlin 1960.

Janko, R. 'A note on the etymologies of διάκτορος and χρυσάορος', *Glotta* 56 (1978) 192–5.

'The use of πρός, προτί and ποτί in Homer', *Glotta* 57 (1979) 24–9.

'ΒΩΣΕΣΘΕ revisited', *CQ* N.S. 29 (1979) 215f.

'The structure of the Homeric Hymns: a study in genre', *Hermes* 109 (1981) 9–24.

'ΑΘΑΝΑΤΟΣ ΚΑΙ ΑΓΗΡΩΣ: the genealogy of a formula', *Mnemosyne* forthcoming.

'Equivalent formulae in the Greek epos', *Mnemosyne* forthcoming.

Jeffery, L. H. *The Local Scripts of Archaic Greece*. Oxford 1961. (Jeffery, *LSAG*)

Archaic Greece. London 1976.

Jones, F. P. and Gray, F. E. 'Hexameter patterns, statistical inference and the Homeric Question: an analysis of the La Roche data', *TAPA* 103 (1973) 187–210.

Kakridis, I. T. 'Zum homerischen Apollonhymnos', *Philologus* 92 (1937) 104–8.

'Ἡ *παράταξη τῶν οὐσιαστικῶν στὸν Ὅμηρο καὶ στοὺς Ὁμηρικοὺς Ὕμνους*', Ἐπιστημονικὴ Ἐπετηρὶς Φιλοσ. Σχολῆς τοῦ Πανεπιστ. Θεσσαλονίκης, Παραρτ. IV, 1960.

Kamerbeek, J. C. 'Remarques sur l'Hymne à Aphrodite', *Mnemosyne* 20 (1967) 385–95.

Karageorghis, V. *Salamis in Cyprus: Homeric, Hellenistic and Roman*. London 1969.

Kern, O. *Orphicorum Fragmenta*. Berlin 1922.

Kinkel, G. *Epicorum Graecorum Fragmenta*. Leipzig 1887.

Kirk, G. S. 'Objective dating criteria in Homer', *MH* 17 (1960) 189–205.

The Songs of Homer. Cambridge 1962.

'The structure and aim of the Theogony', ap. *Hésiode et son influence*, Fondation Hardt, Entretiens sur l'antiquité classique, VII, 1962, pp. 63–95.

(ed.) *The Language and Background of Homer*. Cambridge 1964.

Review of Hoekstra, *HMFP*, *Gnomon* 38 (1966) 737–40.

'The structure of the Homeric hexameter', *YCS* 20 (1966) 76–104.

'Verse-structure and sentence-structure in Homer', ibid. 105–52.

'Formular language and oral quality', ibid. 153–74.

Homer and the Oral Tradition. Cambridge 1976.

Knight, W. F. J. 'Integration and the Hymn to Apollo', *AJP* 62 (1941) 302–13.

Knøs, O. V. *De digammo homerico Quaestiones* I–III, in *Upsala Univ. Årsskrift* 1872, 1873, 1879.

Köhn, A. 'Quaestiones metricae et grammaticae de hymnis homericis'. Diss. Halle 1865.

Kolk, D. 'Der pythische Apollonhymnus als aitiologische Dichtung'. Diss. Meisenheim am Glan 1963.

Koller, H. 'Πόλις Μερόπων Ἀνθρώπων', *Glotta* 46 (1968) 18–26.

Kost, K. *Commentary on Musaeus*. Bonn 1971.

Koster, S. *Antike Epostheorien*. Wiesbaden 1970.

Krafft, F. *Vergleichende Untersuchungen zu Homer und Hesiod*. Göttingen 1963.

La Roche, J. 'Untersuchungen über den Vers bei Hesiod und in den homerischen Hymnen', *WSt* 20 (1898) 70–90.

Laidlaw, W. A. *A History of Delos*. Oxford 1933.

Leeuwen, J. van. *Enchiridium Dictionis Epicae,* 2nd edn. Leiden 1918.
Lehmann, G. A. 'Der "Erste Heilige Krieg" - eine Fiktion?', *Historia* 29 (1980) 242–6.
*Lejeune, M. *Phonétique historique du mycenien et du grec ancien.* Paris 1972.
Lendle, O. *Die 'Pandorassage' bei Hesiod.* Würzburg 1957.
*Lenz, L. H. *Der homerische Aphroditehymnus und die Aristie des Aineias in der Ilias.* Bonn 1975.
Lesky, A. *Geschichte der griechischen Literatur,* 2nd edn. Bern 1963. (Lesky, *GGL*)
A History of Greek Literature (translated by C. de Heer and J. Willis). London 1966. (Lesky, *HGL*)
*Leumann, M. *Homerische Wörter.* Basel 1950.
Liddell, H. G. and Scott, R. *A Greek–English Lexicon,* 9th edn. revised by H. Stuart Jones and R. McKenzie, Oxford 1940, with a supplement 1968. (LSJ)
Lloyd-Jones, H. J. and others. *Females of the Species.* London 1975.
Lobel, E. and Page, D. L. *Poetarum Lesbiorum Fragmenta.* Oxford 1955. (L–P).
Lopez Eire, A. 'The present state of the problem of the Greek dialects', *Proceedings of the 5th Spanish Congress of Classical Studies* (1979) 457–79.
Lord, A. B. 'Homer and Huso III: Enjambement in Greek and South Slavic heroic song', *TAPA* 79 (1948) 113–24.
The Singer of Tales. Cambridge, Mass., 1960. (Lord, *ST*)
'Homer as oral poet', *HSCP* 72 (1968) 15–34.
Ludwich, A. *Aristarchs homerische Textkritik.* Leipzig 1884–5.
Lyding, E. 'Homeric enjambement'. Diss. Bryn Mawr College, 1949.
Lynn-George, J. M. 'The relationship of Σ 535–540 and Scutum 156–60 re-examined', *Hermes* 106 (1978) 396–405.
Magnien, V. 'Deux questions homériques. I. Genitifs en *-οιο* et *-ου*', *Mémoires de la Société linguistique de Paris* 22 (1922) 165–71.
Malten, L. *Kyrene. Sagengeschichtliche und historische Untersuchungen* (Philologische Untersuchungen 20). Berlin 1911.
Matthews, V. J. *Panyassis.* Leiden 1974.
McLennan, G. R. 'Enjambement in the Hymns of Callimachus', *Hermes* 102 (1974) 200–6.
*Meier, W. D. *Die epische Formel im pseudohesiodeischen Frauenkatalog.* Zürich 1976.
*Meister, K. *Die homerische Kunstsprache.* Leipzig 1921.
Merkelbach, R. 'Ein Fragment des homerischen Dionysos-Hymnus', *ZPE* 12 (1973) 212–15 (re *POxy* 670).
Merkelbach, R. and West, M. L. *Fragmenta Hesiodea.* Oxford 1967. (M–W)
Meuli, K. *Odyssee und Argonautika.* Berlin 1921.

Meyer, W. 'Zur Geschichte des griechischen und des lateinischen Hexameters', *SBA* 1884, 979–1089.

Miller, A. M. 'Form and generic intention in the *Homeric Hymn to Apollo*'. Diss. University of California at Berkeley, 1977.

'The "address to the Delian maidens" in the *Homeric Hymn to Apollo*: Epilogue or transition?', *TAPA* 109 (1979) 173–86.

Milne, H. J. M. 'Dionysiaca', *Arch Pap* 7 (1907) 3–10.

Minton, W. W. *A Concordance to the Hesiodic Corpus*. Leiden 1976.

Monro, D. B. *A Grammar of the Homeric Dialect*, 2nd edn. Oxford 1891.

with T. W. Allen: see the latter.

Morton, A. Q. and Winspear, A. D. *It's Greek to the Computer*. Montreal 1971.

with S. Michaelson and J. B. Hainsworth. 'The authorship and integrity of the poems of Hesiod', *Philosophical Journal* (*Transactions of the Royal Philosophical Society of Glasgow*) 9 (1972) 61–79.

Muñoz Valle, I. *Investigaciones sobre el estilo formular épico*. Valencia 1974.

Murray, G. *The Rise of the Greek Epic*, 4th edn. Oxford 1934.

Nagler, M. N. *Spontaneity and Tradition: a study of the oral art of Homer*. Berkeley 1975.

Nagy, G. *Greek Dialects and the Transformation of an Indo-European Process*. Cambridge, Mass. 1970.

Comparative Studies in Greek and Indic Meter. Cambridge, Mass. 1974.

The Best of the Achaeans. Baltimore 1979.

Neitzel, H. *Homer-Rezeption bei Hesiod*. Bonn 1975.

Niles, J. D. 'On the design of the Hymn to Delian Apollo', *CJ* 75 (1979) 136–9.

Northwick, T. van. 'The Homeric *Hymn to Hermes*: a study in early Greek hexameter style'. Diss. Stanford 1975.

'*Apollônos apatê*: associative imagery in the Homeric *Hymn to Hermes* 227–292', *CW* 74 (1980) 1–5.

Nöthiger, M. *Die Sprache des Stesichorus und des Ibycus*. Zürich 1971.

Notopoulos, J. A. 'Homer, Hesiod and the Achaean heritage of oral poetry', *Hesperia* 29 (1960) 177–97.

'The Homeric Hymns as oral poetry: a study of the post-Homeric oral tradition', *AJP* 83 (1962) 337–68.

'Studies in early Greek oral poetry', *HSCP* 63 (1964) 1–77.

*O'Neill, E. G., Jr. 'The localisation of metrical word-types in the Greek hexameter. Homer, Hesiod and the Alexandrians', *YCS* 8 (1942) 105–78.

Otis, B. *Virgil, a Study in Civilised Poetry*. Oxford 1963.

Packard, D. and Meyers, T. *Bibliography of Homeric Scholarship 1930–1970*. Malibu, California 1974.

Page, D. L. *Sappho and Alcaeus*. Oxford 1955. (Page, *S&A*).

The Homeric Odyssey. Oxford 1955.

History and the Homeric Iliad. Berkeley 1959.

Poetae Melici Graeci. Oxford 1962. (Page, *PMG*).

Palmer, L. R. 'The language of Homer', Chapter IV of *A Companion to Homer*, ed. A. J. B. Wace and F. H. Stubbings, 75–178. London 1962.

The Greek Language. London 1980.

Parke, H. W. 'Polycrates and Delos', *CQ* 40 (1946) 105–8.

Greek Oracles. London 1967.

and Wormell, D. E. *The Delphic Oracle*, 2nd edn. Oxford 1956.

and Boardman, J. 'The struggle for the tripod and the First Sacred War', *JHS* 77 (1957) 276–82.

Parry, M. *L'Épithète traditionnelle dans Homère*. Paris 1928.

Les Formules et la métrique d'Homère. Paris 1928.

'The distinctive character of enjambement in Homeric verse', *TAPA* 60 (1929) 200–20.

'Studies in the epic technique of oral verse-making. I. Homer and the Homeric style', *HSCP* 41 (1930) 73–147.

'Studies in the epic technique of oral verse-making. II. The Homeric language as the language of poetry', *HSCP* 43 (1932) 1–50.

'The traces of the digamma in Ionic and Lesbian Greek', *Language* 10 (1934) 130–44.

The Making of Homeric Verse: the Collected Papers of Milman Parry, edited, with an introduction, by A. Parry. Oxford 1971. (Parry, *MHV*)

Paulson, J. *Studia Hesiodea I. De re metrica*. Lunds Univ. Arsskrift 23, Lund 1887.

Index Hesiodeus. Lund 1890.

Pauly, A., Wissowa, G. et al. (edd.) *Real-Encyclopädie der klassischen Altertumswissenschaft*. Stuttgart, 1894–. (P–W, *RE*)

Pavese, C. O. *Tradizioni e generi poetici della Grecia arcaica*. Rome 1972. (Pavese *Trad*)

Studi sulla tradizione epica rapsodica. Rome 1974. (Pavese *Stud*)

Peabody, B. *The Winged Word*. Albany 1975.

Pellizer, E. 'Tecnica compositiva e struttura genealogica nell'Inno omerico ad Afrodite', *QUCC* 27 (1978) 115–44.

Pfeiffer, R. *Callimachus*. Oxford 1949–53. (Pf.)

History of Classical Scholarship, from the Beginnings to the End of the Hellenistic Age. Oxford 1968.

Pfister, R. 'Der homerische Apollonhymnos', *Phil Woch* 1934, 145–54.

Pickard-Cambridge, A. *Dithyramb, Tragedy and Comedy*, 2nd edn. by T. B. L. Webster. Oxford 1962.

Podbielski, H. 'Contributions aux recherches sur l'Hymne homérique à Aphrodite', *Roczniki Humanistyczne filologia klasyczna Warszawa* 18, 3 (1970) 5–34 (Polish, with French summary).
* *La structure de l'Hymne homérique à Aphrodite à la lumière de la tradition littéraire.* Series Komitet Nauk o Kulturze Antycznej Polskiej Akademii Nauk, Archiwum Filologiczne 27, Wrocław 1971.
*Pokorny, J. and Walde, H. *Vergleichendes Wörterbuch der indogermanischen Sprachen.* Berlin and Leipzig 1930.
Porter, H. N. 'Repetition in the Homeric Hymn to Aphrodite', *AJP* 70 (1949) 249–72.
'The early Greek hexameter', *YCS* 12 (1951) 3–63.
Porzig, W. 'Sprachgeographische Untersuchungen zu den altgriechischen Dialekten', *IF* 61 (1954) 147–69.
*Postlethwaite, N. 'Formulaic composition in the Homeric Hymns', Diss. Sheffield 1972.
'Formula and Formulaic: some evidence from the Homeric Hymns', *Phoenix* 33 (1979) 1–18.
Prendergast, G. L. *A Complete Concordance to the Iliad of Homer.* Revised by B. Marzullo, Hildesheim 1962.
Preziosi, P. G. 'The Homeric Hymn to Aphrodite. An oral analysis', *HSCP* 71 (1966) 171–204.
Priem, J. 'Der homerische Hymnus auf den delischen Apollon', Diss. Posen 1878.
Pucci, P. *Hesiod and the Language of Poetry.* Baltimore 1977.
*Radermacher, L. *Der homerische Hermeshymnus.* Sitzungsbericht der Akad. Wiss. Wien 113 (1931) 1–245.
Regenbogen, O. 'Gedanken zum homerischen Apollonhymnus', *Eranos* 54 (1956) 49–56.
Reichelt, C. *De dativis in -οις et -ηις (-αις) exeuntibus.* Progr. Breslau 1893.
Reinhardt, K. 'Zum homerischen Aphroditehymnus', ap. *Festschrift Bruno Snell* pp. 1–14, Munich 1956.
Die Ilias und ihr Dichter. Göttingen 1961.
Renehan, R. *Studies in Greek Texts. Hypomnemata* 43, 1976.
*Richardson, N. J. *The Homeric Hymn to Demeter.* Oxford 1974.
Review of Càssola, *JHS* 97 (1977) 174–5.
Review of Schröder, *CR* 28 (1978) 145–6.
Review of Lenz, ibid.
Review of West, *Hesiod, Works and Days, JHS* 99 (1979) 169–71.
Risch, E. 'Die Gliederung der griechischen Dialekte in neuer Sicht', *Mus Helv* 12 (1955) 61–76.
Wortbildung der homerischen Sprache, 2nd edn. Berlin 1974.
Robertson, N. 'The myth of the First Sacred War', *CQ* N.S. 28 (1978) 38–74.

Rose, H. J. Review of N. O. Brown, *CR* 62 (1948) 153–4.
Rossi, L. E. Review of Hoekstra, *SES: Göttl gel Anzeigen* 223 (1971) 170–1.
'I poemi omerici come testimonianza di poesia orale', ap. *Storia e Civiltà dei Greci*, dir. R. B. Bandinelli, vol. I, 1, pp. 73–147. Milan 1978.
Roux, G. 'Le vrai temple d'Apollon à Délos', *BCH* 103 (1979) 109–35.
Ruijgh, C. J. *L'Élément achéen dans la langue épique*. Amsterdam 1957.
'Les datifs pluriels dans les dialectes grecs', *Mnemosyne* 11 (1958) 97–116.
'Observations sur la "methathèse de quantité"', *Lingua* 21 (1968) 393–7.
'Les noms en -won (-āwon, -īwon), -uon- en grec alphabétique et mycénien', *Minos* 9 (1968) 109–55.
*Russo, C. F. *Hesiodi Scutum*. Florence 1950.
Santerre, H. G. de. *Délos primitive et archaïque*. Bibliothèque des Écoles françaises d'Athènes et de Rome, fasc. 192. Paris 1958.
Schefold, K. *Wort und Bild: Studien zur Gegenwart der Antike*. Basel 1975.
*Schmid, W. and Stählin, O. *Geschichte der griechischen Literatur*. Munich 1929–48.
Schmidt, J. *KZ* 26 345, 1.
Schmidt, K. H. 'Dativ und Instrumental im Plural', *Glotta* 41 (1963) 1–10.
Schmitt, R. 'Die Hesychglosse σάτιλλα. Eine Nachprüfung', *Glotta* 44 (1966) 148–51.
Schröder, J. *Ilias und Apollonhymnos*. Beiträge zur klass. Phil. 59. Meisenheim am Glan 1975.
Schürmann, J. *De generi dicendi atque aetate hymni in Apollinem homerici*. Gymn. Progr. Arnsberg 1859.
Schultze, W. *Quaestiones epicae*. Gütersloh 1892. (Schultze, *QE*)
Schwartz, J. *Pseudo-Hesiodea*. Leiden 1960.
Schwyzer, E. 'Die nominale Determination in den indogermanischen Sprachen (mit Exkursen über den "phrygischen" Artikel und über homerischen τοῖο, τάων, τοῖιν, τοῖσι(ν), τῃῖσι(ν))', *ZVS* 63 (1936) 145–67.
* *Griechische Grammatik* I–III. Munich 1953–60.
Scott, J. A. *The Unity of Homer*. Berkeley 1921.
'The comparative ages of Homer and Hesiod', *TAPA* 61 (1930) xxvi.
Sealey, R. 'From Phemios to Ion', *REG* 70 (1957) 312–51.
Segal, C. 'The Homeric Hymn to Aphrodite: a structuralist approach', *CW* 67 (1974) 205–12.
Sellschopp, I. *Stylistische Untersuchungen zu Hesiod*. Hamburg 1934.
Severyns, A. *La Cycle épique dans l'école d'Aristarque*, Liège 1928.
Homère II: le poète et son oeuvre. Brussels 1946.

Shewan, A. *The Lay of Dolon.* London 1911.
Homeric Essays. Oxford 1935.
Shipp, G. P. *Studies in the Language of Homer*, 2nd edn. Cambridge 1972. (Shipp, *SLH*²)
Sinclair, T. A. *Hesiod, Works and Days.* London 1932.
Smyth, H. W. *The Greek Dialects. I. Ionic.* Oxford 1894.
Snell, B. et al. *Lexikon des frühgriechischen Epos.* Göttingen 1959-.
Snodgrass, A. M. *Archaic Greece.* London 1980.
Solmsen, Felix. *Untersuchungen zur griechischen Laut- und Verslehre.* Strasburg 1901.
Solmsen, Friedrich. 'Zur Theologie im grossen Aphrodite-Hymnus', *Hermes* 88 (1960) 1–13.
Hesiodi Theogonia, Opera et Dies, Scutum. Fragmenta selecta, ed. R. Merkelbach and M. L. West. Oxford 1970.
Sordi, M. 'Mitologia e propaganda nella Beozia arcaica', *Atene e Roma* 11 (1966) 15–24.
Sowa, C. A. and Sowa, J. 'Thought clusters in early Greek oral poetry', *Computers and the Humanities* 8 (1974) 131–46.
Spraycar, R. S. '*La Chanson de Roland*: An Oral Poem?', *Olifant* 4 (1976) 62–74.
Steitz, A. *Die Werke und Tage des Hesiod.* Leipzig 1869.
Sterrett, J. R. S. *Qua in re hymni homerici quinque maiores inter se differant antiquitate vel homeritate.* Boston 1881.
Stiewe, K. 'Der Erzählungsstil der homerischen Demeterhymnus'. Diss. Göttingen 1954.
Suhle, *De hymno quarto in Venerem.* Stolpae 1878.
Tebben, J. R. 'A metrical and lexical analysis of the Homeric Hymns.' Diss. Ohio State University, Columbus 1971. Cf. *Dissertation Abstracts* 32 (1972) 6400A.
A Computer Concordance to Hesiod. Hildesheim 1977.
A Computer Concordance to the Homeric Hymns. Hildesheim 1977.
Teske, A. *Die Homer-Mimesis in den homerischen Hymnen.* Greifswalder Beiträge zur Literatur und Stilforschung 15, 1936.
Thiele, 'Prolegomena ad hymnum in Venerem homericum IV'. Diss. Halle 1872.
*Thumb, A. *Handbuch der griechischen Dialekte*, 2nd edn. Vol. I revised by E. Kieckers, Heidelberg 1932; vol. II by A. Scherer, 1959.
Troxler, H. *Sprache und Wortschatz Hesiods.* Zürich 1964. (Troxler, *SWH*)
Trüber, H. 'De hymno in Venerem homerico'. Diss. Halle 1903.
Unte, W. 'Studien zum homerischen Apollonhymnos'. Diss. Freie Univ. Berlin 1968.
Valk, M. van der. 'On the arrangement of the Homeric Hvmns', *AC* 45 (1976) 419–45.

'A few observations on the Homeric Hymn to Apollo', *AC* 46 (1977) 441–52.

Ventris, M. and Chadwick, J. *Documents in Mycenaean Greek*. 2nd edn. Cambridge 1973. (Ventris and Chadwick, *Docs*²)

Vogt, E. 'Die Schrift vom Wettkampf Homers und Hesiods', *RhM* 102 (1959) 193–221.

Wackernagel, J. *Sprachliche Untersuchungen zu Homer*. Göttingen 1916.

Wace, A. J. B. and Stubbings, F. H. (edd.). *A Companion to Homer*. London 1962.

Wade-Gery, H. T. 'Kynaithos', ap. *Studies in Greek Poetry and Life, Essays presented to Gilbert Murray* pp. 56–78, Oxford 1936.

Walbank, F. W. *A Historical Commentary on Polybius*. Oxford 1957–79.

Walcot, P. *Hesiod and the Near East*. Cardiff 1966.

Greek Peasants, Ancient and Modern. Manchester 1970.

Wathelet, P. *Les Traits éoliens dans la langue de l'épopée grecque*. Rome 1971.

'Le nom de Zeus chez Homère et dans les dialectes grecs', *Minos* 15 (1974) 195–225.

'Études de linguistique homérique 2: les formes ΞΥΝ et ΣΥΝ', *L'Antiquité Classique* 46 (1977) 158–64.

Webster, T. B. L. 'Early and late in Homeric diction', *Eranos* 54 (1956) 34–48.

From Mycenae to Homer. London 1958. (Webster, *MH*)

'Notes on the writing of early Greek poetry', *Glotta* 38 (1960) 251–63.

'Homeric Hymns and Society', in *Le Monde grec: Hommages à Claire Préaux*, ed. J. Bingen, pp. 86–93. Brussels 1975.

Weiss, R. *De digammo in Hymnis homericis quaestiones*. Budapest 1889.

West, M. L. 'Hesiodea', *CQ* N.S. 11 (1961) 130–45.

'γλωθρός', *Glotta* 41 (1963) 282–5.

'Epica', *Glotta* 44 (1966) 135–48.

* *Hesiod. Theogony*. Oxford 1966 (cited '*Th* p. 84' and 'ad *Th* 84').

'The contest of Homer and Hesiod', *CQ* N.S. 17 (1967) 433–50.

'The eighth Homeric Hymn and Proclus', *CQ* N.S. 20 (1970) 300–4.

'Stesichorus', *CQ* N.S. 21 (1971) 302–14.

Iambi et elegi graeci. Oxford 1971–2.

'Greek Poetry 2000–700 B.C.', *CQ* N.S. 23 (1973) 179–92.

Studies in Greek Elegy and Iambus. Berlin and New York 1974.

'Cynaethus' Hymn to Apollo', *CQ* N.S. 25 (1975) 161–70.

* *Hesiod. Works and Days*. Oxford 1978 (cited '*Erga* p. 84' and 'ad *Erga* 84').

West, S. *The Ptolemaic Papyri of Homer*. Cologne 1967.

Whitman, C. H. 'Hera's Anvils', *HSCP* 74 (1970) 37–42.

Wilamowitz-Möllendorff, U. von. *Der Ilias und Homer.* Berlin 1916. (Wilamowitz, *IuH*)

Die Glaube der Hellenen. Berlin 1931–2.

Will, E. *Korinthiaka.* Paris 1955.

Williams, F. *Callimachus: Hymn to Apollo, a Commentary.* Oxford 1978.

Willcock, M. Review of Càssola, *CR* 27 (1977) 266–7.

Windisch, E. *De hymnis homericis majoribus.* Leipzig 1867.

Witte, K. 'Zur homerischen Sprache', I–II *Glotta* 1 (1909) 132–45; III–IV *Glotta* 2 (1910) 8–22; V–XI *Glotta* 3 (1912) 105–53; XII ibid. 388–93; *Glotta* 4 (1913) 1–21, 209–42.

'Über die Kasusausgänge -*οιο* und -*ου*, -*οισι* und -*οις*, -*ῃσι* und -*ῃς* im griechischen Epos', *Glotta* 5 (1914) 8–57.

s.v. *Homeros, Sprache* in Pauly–Wissowa *Real-Encyclopädie* VIII (1913) 2213–47.

Wölke, H. *Untersuchungen zur Batrachomyomachie.* Beiträge für klass. Philol. 100, Meisenheim am Glan 1978.

Wyatt, W. F. 'Initial /wo/ in Greek', *Language* 39 (1963) 231–4.

Metrical Lengthening in Homer (Incunabula Graeca 35). Rome 1969. (Wyatt, *ML*)

'Aeolic reflexes of labiovelars in Homer', *GRBS* 16 (1975) 251–62.

'Homer's linguistic ancestors', *EEThess* 11 (1975) 133–47.

'Homeric *πρός ποτί προτί*', *Studi Micenei ed Egeo-Anatolici* 19 (1978) 89–123.

*Zumbach, O. *Neuerungen in der Sprache der homerischen Hymnen.* Zürich, Winterthur 1955.

Addenda

Austin, N. *Archery at the Dark of the Moon.* Berkeley 1975.

Baltes, M. 'Die kataloge im homerischen Apollonhymnus', *Philologus* 12 (1981) 24–43.

Bickerman, E. 'Love story in the Homeric Hymn to Aphrodite', *Athenaeum* 54 (1976) 229–54.

Bona, G. 'Inni omerici e poesia greca arcaica', *RFIC* 106 (1978) 224–48.

Bossi, F. 'La datazione di [Hom.] *Hymn. Pan*', *Museum Criticum* 13–14 (1978–9) 7–22.

'[Hom.] *Hymn. Ven.* 7', ibid. 23–4.

Brillante, C., Cantilena, M., and Pavese, C. O. (edd.). *I Poemi epici rapsodici non omerici e la tradizione orale* (Atti del Convegno di Venezia). Padua 1981.

Casadio, V.'[Hom.] *Hymn.* XXV (*Mus.*)', ibid. 25–7.

Cavallini, E. '[Hom.] *Hymn.* X (*Ven.*)', ibid. 29–34.

Danielewicz, J. 'Morfologia hymnu antycznego, na materiale grechich zbiorów hymniczych.' *Wyd. I. Univ. w Poznaniu, ser. Filol. klas.*, 8, Poznan 1976 (Polish, with an English summary).

Giangrande, G. 'Der stilistische Gebrauch der Dorismen im Epos', *Hermes* 98 (1970) 257–77.

Review of Edwards, *JHS* 92 (1972) 188–92.

Griffin, J. 'The Epic Cycle and the Uniqueness of Homer', *JHS* 97 (1977) 39–53.

Hoekstra, A. *Epic Verse before Homer. Three Studies.* Amsterdam 1980.

Janko, R. Review of P. Smith, *CR* 31 (1981) 285f.

Jensen, M. S. *The Homeric Question and the Oral-Formulaic Theory.* Copenhagen 1980.

Lenz, A. *Das Proöm des fruhen griechischen Epos.* Bonn 1980.

Martino, F. De. 'Un straniero navigato nell'inno omerico *ad Apollo*', *Belfagor: Rassegna di Varia Umanità* 35 (1980) 573–7.

'ΑΛΛΗ ΑΟΙΔΗ (in coda all'inno omerico *ad Apollo,* 545–546)' *AC* 49 (1980) 232–40.

Palmer, L. R. *The Greek Language*. London 1980.

Richardson, N. J. 'The Contest of Homer and Hesiod and Alcidamas' *Mouseion*', *CQ* N.S. 31 (1981) 1–10.

Scheinberg, S. 'The Bee Maidens in the Homeric Hymn to Hermes', *HSCP* 83 (1979) 1–28.

Scodel, R. 'Hesiod redivivus', *GRBS* 21 (1980) 301–20.

Smith, P. M. 'Notes on the text of the Fifth Homeric Hymn', *HSCP* 83 (1979) 29–50.

Nursling of Mortality: a Study of the Homeric Hymn to Aphrodite. Frankfurt, al., 1981.

'Aineiadai as Patrons of *Iliad* XX and of the Homeric *Hymn to Aphrodite*', *HSCP* 85 (1981) forthcoming.

West, M. L. 'Conjectures on 46 Greek Poets', *Philologus* CX (1966) 147–68.

INDEX OF PASSAGES CITED

INDEX OF GREEK

GENERAL INDEX

Printed in the United Kingdom
by Lightning Source UK Ltd.
121257UK00001B/148

9 780521 035651